NEGOTIATIONS AND CHANGE

NEGOTIATIONS AND CHANGE

From the Workplace to Society

Edited by
THOMAS A. KOCHAN
and DAVID B. LIPSKY

ILR PRESS

An imprint of

CORNELL UNIVERSITY PRESS

Ithaca and London

First published 2003 by Cornell University Press

Printed in the United States of America

Library of Congress Cataloging-in-Publication Data

Negotiations and change : from the workplace to society / edited by
Thomas A. Kochan and David B. Lipsky.
    p. cm.
Includes bibliographical references and index.
  ISBN 0-8014-4007-6 (cloth : alk. paper)
  1. Negotiation in business. I. Kochan, Thomas A. II. Lipsky, David
B., 1939–
  HD58.6 .N468 2003
  658.4'042—dc21
                        2002009833

Cornell University Press strives to use environmentally responsible suppliers and materials to the fullest extent possible in the publishing of its books. Such materials include vegetable-based, low-VOC inks and acid-free papers that are recycled, totally chlorine-free, or partly composed of nonwood fibers. For further information, visit our website at www.cornellpress.cornell.edu.

Cloth printing   10 9 8 7 6 5 4 3 2 1

Contents

PART V: THE FUTURE OF NEGOTIATIONS

Acknowledgments

The largest debt we owe is to Robert B. McKersie. This volume had its genesis in a conference in honor of McKersie, held at MIT on October 30–31, 1998, on the occasion of his forthcoming retirement from the faculty of MIT's Sloan School of Management. The organizers of the conference especially wanted to recognize the profound influence McKersie has had on the study of bargaining and negotiation. His landmark book, *A Behavioral Theory of Labor Negotiations,* co-authored with Richard E. Walton and published in 1965, laid the intellectual foundation for much of contemporary thinking about the theory and practice of negotiation. Walton and McKersie were initially motivated by a desire to enhance our understanding of labor-management relations, but since publication of the book, their behavioral theory has permeated the conceptual and practical underpinnings of negotiations in a wide variety of settings. The conference organizers chose participants who would do justice not only to the behavioral theory's influence in labor-management relations but also to its influence in environmental, community, and other types of negotiations.

Although the papers in this volume focus on McKersie's influence on the theory and practice of negotiations, the editors also want to underscore the breadth of his interests and achievements. He received a B.S. in electrical engineering from the University of Pennsylvania and, in 1959, a D.B.A. from the Harvard University School of Business. He then joined the faculty of the Graduate School of Business at the University of Chicago but left in 1971 to become dean of the School of Industrial and Labor Relations at Cornell University, serving with distinction until 1980. While at Cornell, he completed a major study of productivity, published with co-author Lawrence Hunter as *Pay, Productivity, and Collective Bargaining* (St. Martin's, 1973).

In 1980, McKersie joined the faculty at MIT where he launched a multiyear project that resulted in the publication of *The Transformation of American Industrial Relations* (Basic Books, 1986; reprinted by ILR Press, 1994), co-authored with Harry Katz and Thomas Kochan. The Academy of Management recognized *The Transformation of Industrial Relations* as the best book published on management in 1986. McKersie then returned to the subject of negotiations, joining forces with Richard Walton and Joel Cutcher-Gershenfeld to write *Strategic Negotiations: A Theory of Change in Labor-Management Relations* (Harvard Business School Press, 1994; reprinted by ILR Press, 2000), a book that comes close to matching the influence of Walton and McKersie's *A Behavioral Theory*. Cutcher-Gershenfeld, McKersie, and Walton also published a companion volume to *Strategic Negotiations* called *Pathways to Change: Case Studies of Strategic Negotiations* (W. E. Upjohn Institute, 1995). At the same time that McKersie was engaged in these various projects, he returned to academic administration, serving as the deputy dean of the Sloan School from 1991 to 1994.

It is fair to say that the force of McKersie's personality has bolstered the penetration of his scholarly work into diverse arenas. In McKersie we find a unique blend of intellectual brilliance, visionary leadership, and moral authority. He has been a role model for countless colleagues, scholars, and students over the course of his forty-year career, and he has had a transforming effect on every institution with which he has been affiliated. The behavioral theory was an idea whose time had come not only because of its inherent intellectual value but also because it was fortunate to have McKersie as its principal proponent. The editors, therefore, want to express our most profound thanks to Bob McKersie for inspiring this volume.

The editors also wish to acknowledge our gratitude to the members of the committee that planned and organized the 1998 conference: John F. Burton Jr., Paul S. Goodman, Edward J. Lawler, Richard M. Locke, Mary P. Rowe, and Susan Cass Wright. We are especially grateful for the financial support we received from Dean Lawler and the School of Industrial and Labor Relations, Cornell's Institute on Conflict Resolution, MIT's Institute for Work and Employment Research, the dean's office of MIT's Sloan School of Management, the Harvard Program on Negotiation, the Edna McConnell-Clark Foundation, Inland Steel, and last but certainly not least William Shea.

The editors want to thank the McKersie children—William, Elizabeth,

Robert, and Alison—for their assistance in organizing the 1998 event and Ronald Ehrenberg, David Knapp, Malcolm Lovell, Charles Vest, and especially Arnold Weber for the key roles they played at the conference.

We also want to thank most sincerely all those at Cornell and MIT who did the hard work and heavy lifting that made this volume possible: Karen Boyajian, Bob Julian, and especially Missy Harrington. The volume greatly benefited from the excellent editorial assistance of Fran Benson, Louise E. Robbins, and especially Elaine Goldberg. We are certain all the authors want to join us in acknowledging their indebtedness to Elaine, who shepherded them through the long process of preparing their papers for publication. Finally, the editors would certainly be remiss if we did not thank our wives and families for their love and patience.

NEGOTIATIONS AND CHANGE

Introduction

People have always tended to proclaim that their era is one of significant change, especially when their era is at the dawn of a new century. Our era is no exception. Indeed a good case can be made that major, perhaps historic, changes are occurring today in our workplaces and societies, driven by global market, technological, political, and demographic forces. But an even stronger case can be made that what distinguishes those past eras that are remembered as periods when change was translated into significant economic and social progress is that they were ones in which leaders of key institutions managed change effectively.

An important part of managing change involves negotiation. The essence of negotiation lies in identifying the interests of those involved and satisfying mutual interests while finding efficient and equitable trade-offs or compromises among interests that conflict. Negotiations entail crafting new agreements, sometimes explicitly and formally involving exchanges between parties, sometimes with the help of a neutral third party, and sometimes implicitly through the day-to-day informal interactions of people, groups, and organizations. So to understand how well decision makers are managing change, they—and citizens in general—need to assess how well both these tacit and formal negotiations are being carried out.

Recognition of the interdependence between negotiations and change has led to an explosion of research and teaching on these topics. Much of this activity can be traced back to a landmark study published in 1965, *A Behavioral Theory of Labor Negotiations* by Richard Walton and Robert McKersie. That book laid the analytical foundation for much of the innovation in applied practice that has occurred over the last thirty-five years in this area. Moreover, while the title and much of the content of that work focused on collective bargaining and labor relations, Walton and McKersie also discussed the application of these ideas to a key topic of negotiations in society of that era, civil rights. In our book we take stock of what has been learned since then and apply it to several key areas of change at work and in employment relations. We start at the workplace and examine the changing nature of the employment relationship itself, the growing role of groups and teams at work, the changes in relations between workers and supervisors, and the role of work systems in improving organizational performance. Then we return to the arena of labor negotiations, focusing on how the principles of negotiation are now being used and debated—not only in the formal collective bargaining process but also in the broadening arena in which labor negotiations occur—as unions and companies explore whether or not, and in some cases how, to create partnerships and whether or how to bring new groups, such as women's organizations, into the negotiation process. And, like the original book, we extend our analysis beyond the work and employment sphere to see how negotiation concepts are being used to manage change and controversy in several key areas of society. We also take a good look at how teachers and students are engaging in the study of negotiations and provide a quick historical picture of how this has evolved and where it might be going.

Our underlying goals here are both to look back at where we have come from—taking stock of how we are using negotiation theories and tools to study, teach, and manage change—and to look ahead and suggest ways we can use these concepts and tools to improve the management of change for all the stakeholders affected by these issues.

We divide the book into five sections. Part I contains an overview of the basic concepts developed by Walton and McKersie, now a fundamental part of teaching, practice, and research in negotiations, and a chapter by Greenhalgh and Lewicki that should help students and teachers put the materials they cover in their proper historical context. Part II takes up the changing world of work. Part III goes back to the roots of this field by exploring the changing role and scope of negotiations in labor-management relations, and Part IV samples social arenas in which negotiations are crucial to achieving constructive change. In the final section of the volume, McKersie and Walton consider how the principles of their behavioral theory can be adapted and used by practitioners and scholars in the future. In this introduction, we set the stage for the analysis that follows by examining the link between change and negotiations and exploring how this link has evolved over the years.

Workplace Change and Tacit Negotiations

Broad political, economic, social, and technological changes are reshaping how we organize work. These new forms of work in organizations have important implications for both the theories and the practice of negotiation. The basic questions are, How does the changing nature of work challenge our underlying ideas about theories and practice? And how do we redesign our theories and practice in light of new organizational forms?

The importance of tacit (unstated or informal) rather than conscious (or formal) negotiations is no better illustrated than in the changes taking place in the employment relationship itself. Denise Rousseau explores this issue by reviewing changes in the "psychological" contract at work and its implications for the human resources profession. Essentially, she makes the case for surfacing these psychological and less conscious changes—for putting them on the table, so to speak—so they can be dealt with more explicitly and effectively.

A long-standing area of tacit negotiations in organizations, and a key arena in which change is either promoted successfully or subtly undermined, is in the supervisory role and its relations with subordinates and superiors. Yet the role of supervisors is changing as authority is delegated further down the organizational hierarchy and the rhetoric of much of organizational change comes to involve terms like "self-managing" teams or "semi-autonomous" work groups. How are we preparing supervisors to renegotiate their roles in organizations today, both to support and to facilitate change in the teams and groups they are responsible for? These issues are taken up in the chapter by Janice Klein.

Perhaps the most visible examples of new forms of work and organizations are the expanded use of teams and various types of groups at work. Yet our theories for managing groups have yet to be updated to take account of the variety of group work taking place in organizations today. Paul Goodman and Jeanne Wilson explore one particular type of team—a type they call exocentric teams. These teams come and go quickly, or take on the features others have described as "virtual" in nature. That is, they may meet more by remote technology than face to face and their membership may change frequently. Making such teams work in the relevant time frame is indeed a challenge to all involved and requires skills in the negotiation and management of group dynamics that few researchers or practicing managers yet appreciate. Thus, this chapter amply illustrates the interdependence of negotiation and change in organizations.

The final two chapters in Part II demonstrate the links between and among negotiations, the role of systems in work organizations, and conflict resolution. One of the truly successful arenas of change in U.S. work organizations in the past decade has been the resurgence of the manufacturing sector. A major reason for the successful rebound of American manufacturing is found in the ability and willingness of workers, managers, and unions to increase flexibility in work systems and to support and successfully integrate new technologies into their work processes. John Paul MacDuffie illustrates how negotiations, both formal labor-management negotiations and informal day-to-day interactions on the shop floor, support or limit the development and full utilization of new work systems in manufacturing.

Nowhere has the theory and practice of negotiations had as big an effect as on the use of alternative dispute resolution systems in organizations. This effect started with the traditional grievance procedures developed in union-management relations. In the past several decades, however, new models have evolved that go far beyond formal grievance procedures. Furthermore, the goals of these systems have expanded, shifting from one of adjudicating disputes over individual employment contract issues to delivering and ensuring organizational justice and the prevention of formal disputes. Much of this expansion has been fueled by changing workplace demographics and an expansion in the scope and intensity of laws and regulations covering such areas as discrimination, safety and health, and the rights of disabled workers. Mary Rowe and Corinne Bendersky review these developments and suggest the need for a "systems" perspective if managers and policy makers are to move successfully from dispute resolution to the realm of ensuring organizational justice.

Together, these authors show that the basic concepts of negotiation in organizations are being used on a daily basis, whether recognized or not. The chapters in Part II illustrate precisely how these concepts play an important part in an organization's routine processes and activities. In doing so, they apply the first principle of effective negotiation—bringing to the surface the issues and interests of the parties involved and uncovering the root causes of potential tension, conflict, or problems.

Transformations in Labor-Management Relations

Fundamental changes in the nature of labor-management relations have occurred over the past several decades. As World War II ended, the predominant industrial relations problem of the day was how to make collective bargaining work effectively in the face of record levels of strike activity. Over the decades of the 1950s and 1960s, considerable progress was made in harnessing the collective bargaining process to one of rather orderly, periodic negotiations in which the threat of strikes motivated the parties in the vast majority of cases to reach agreements without an actual work stoppage. (Strikes occurred during less than 10 percent of all negotiations in the United States in the 1960s and 1970s and less than 5 percent in the 1990s.) Collective bargaining and unions became the social and economic engine for improving wages, expanding the array of fringe benefits available to workers, improving the quality of working conditions, and strengthening human resource management practices.

When Walton and McKersie wrote *A Behavioral Theory of Labor Negotiations,* the formal collective bargaining process was the centerpiece of labor-management relations. It was the key process in producing organizational change in unionized firms. More specifically, a caricature of collective bargaining and industrial relations circa 1965 would read something like the following:

> In the decades following World War II a general consensus among industrial relations professionals was that "free collective bargaining"—a process in which the parties were left to their own devices to negotiate and reach agreements and had the freedom to strike if a mutually acceptable agreement could not be achieved—was the optimal way of dealing with labor-management issues. The feeling was that government should stay out of the process, except to help the parties through mediation, but even mediation was an intervention controlled by the parties. Negotiations were highly ritualized with positional bargaining, strike threats, and contract deadlines serving as the motivating forces for reaching agreement. Bargaining achieved incremental improvements and adjustments in employment conditions and spurred on both union and nonunion competitors to match the settlements and spread a pattern, thereby taking wages and other employment standards out of competition.

But by the 1980s, conditions had changed. Private sector union growth had stopped as early as 1960, in the face of the gradual but steady emergence, and then expansion, of a new set of nonunion companies and industries. The entire high-technology sector grew up largely without union representation. So in the 1980s the confluence of a deep recession, a shift to a conservative Reagan presidency and political climate, and strong competitive pressures from Japan and other lower-cost countries produced unprecedented changes in labor-management relations. Unions and companies experimented with employee participation and teams; wage and benefit concessions dominated the collective bargaining agenda; and some firms developed new "partnership" arrangements in an effort to transform their bargaining relationships, shifting from the level of the workplace up to the strategic levels of decision making by bringing union representatives into various forms of consultation, information sharing, and joint governance.

As a consequence of these changes, the bargaining process has been under a great deal of pressure to modify and adapt. Some have argued that it has been too slow to adapt and has lost some, if not most, of its force as a change process. How much of that 1965 caricature is still accurate? What has shifted in bargaining specifically and labor-management relations more generally? How, if at all, have labor and management adapted to the changes in their environment, to those occurring at the workplace or higher levels of strategic decision making in the firm, and to the new issues of interest to workers and employers today? How should labor-management relations adapt in the future? These are the broad questions that are taken up in Part III.

The common point across all the chapters in this section is that today (indeed for the past twenty years or so) the key negotiations, and the key changes in labor-management relations, are as likely to involve the basic form and structure of the bargaining relationship as the specific items to be included in a bargaining agreement at the time of formal negotiations and contract renewal. Perhaps the strongest conflicts occur during union-organizing campaigns. These are often highly adversarial processes that involve workers risking, or in fact losing, their jobs. At the workplace, negotiations are over work restructuring along the lines discussed in the prior section—how to reduce job classifications, introduce more flexible work systems and teams, and so forth. And as we will see in this section of the book, efforts to introduce and sustain various forms of partnerships have also proved controversial and rather slow, in both the United States and Britain.

In the first chapter in this section, Joel Cutcher-Gershenfeld reports on efforts in the United States to introduce "interest-based bargaining" concepts and tools. Interest-based bargaining is the applied descendant of the concept of "integrative bargaining" introduced by Walton and McKersie in 1965. Indeed, as Greenhalgh and Lewicki suggest in their chapter, this concept may have had wider application outside labor negotiations than inside the field. That too may be changing, however, if the numbers in a recent national survey of labor and management negotiators reported by Cutcher-Gershenfeld are any indication. Cutcher-Gershenfeld starts his chapter by reviewing how the tools of interest-based bargaining that derive from the Walton and McKersie theory are being applied in the training for, and conduct of, collective bargaining negotiations. Exposure to these concepts is rather widespread, but Cutcher-Gershenfeld points out that actual use is more limited, sustained use is rare, and the challenges in using these tools successfully are great. But then so are the pressures and challenges facing collective bargaining as an institution in society. Clearly, the formal negotiation process has to do its part to step up to the different issues, pressures, and people coming to the bargaining table today.

The arena of labor-management relations has expanded well beyond the formal bargaining process, however, and the tools of negotiation are every bit as critical to these newer arenas as to the traditional negotiation forum. There are various ways to engage management at a strategic level, for example. One of the most frequently used terms for this level of engagement is the "labor-management partnership." This loose term usually is meant to connote processes in which management shares information, consults, and perhaps co-decides strategic business issues that are likely to affect the future of the firm with worker representatives. Phillip Beaumont and Laurence Hunter, focusing on the international arena, describe the gradual shift in the locus of labor relations from the formal negotiation table to efforts to create labor-management partnerships that extend from the workplace to strategic management processes and the corporate boardroom. While they examine experiences in Britain, they might just as well be describing labor-management partnerships in the United States, Canada, Australia, or any other country with an Anglo-Saxon heritage. Partnerships are difficult to form and sustain, yet they may be absolutely essential as part of a package of adaptations in labor-management relations today and in the future.

There is currently a lively debate, played out in the chapter by Saul Rubinstein and Charles Heckscher, over whether the current organizational interest in maintaining flexibility over what work to do in-house and what to outsource to specialized suppliers renders the partnership model obsolete. Rubinstein and Heckscher offer an engaging point-and-counterpoint analysis of where partnership models might succeed and where they might fail, given changes in enterprise and industrial structuring. Partnerships only make sense if the boundary of a firm is fairly stable so that managers and worker representatives have reasonably clear and stable constituencies. In a world of uncertain markets and technologies, where firms seek to focus on their "core competencies" and outsource all other parts of their value chain, partnerships are unlikely to be of interest to employers or sustainable for unions. Here new models that mirror the "network" features of emerging industrial and organizational structures may be needed. But the negotiation task here is Herculean, for it is not even clear who the parties are, much less how a representative structure and negotiation process might be created. But, then, such is the history of most negotiated structures. The first task is to figure out who the parties of interest are and how to build a structure and process for engaging them on matters of mutual concern or interest.

All these developments, at least in the United States, take place in the context of firms that focus largely on the traditional goal of maximizing shareholder wealth. If anything, the shareholder revolts of the past decade have increased the power and voice of shareholders in corporate governance and decision making. But the question of the basic goals of the firm and its governance structures and processes are also increasingly up for negotiations, as Lee Preston delineates in his chapter. While such "negotiations" currently take place more in academic journals and in politicians' rhetoric than in a large number of actual organizations, these issues may be the principal subject matter of the next phase of real-life negotiations. Clearly, if labor relations practitioners are to have a significant influence on key corporate strategic decisions, then they must have access to or join these governance processes in some way. One way is to have worker representatives appointed to the corporate board of directors or board of supervisors. There is no single model of corporate governance, however, or of how employees might fit into different governance models. Preston provides a useful survey of the most well-known governance models found in companies and countries around the world.

In the next chapter, Robert McKersie focuses directly on the role of union-nominated directors on boards of American companies. There has never been extensive union participation on American boards of directors, and McKersie estimates that currently there are no more than thirty to thirty-five companies where the union role on the board of directors is significant. In the past, union-nominated directors sat on the boards of various companies in the airline, trucking, and steel industries, but some of these companies no longer exist. Nevertheless, examining the role of union-nominated directors casts light not only on the issue of union participation on corporate boards but also on the larger implications of including multiple stakeholders in corporate governance. Drawing on discussions he has had with union-nominated directors, McKersie examines several dilemmas these individuals face in fulfilling their responsibilities. For example, all members of corporate boards, including union-nominated directors, have the duty of protecting stockholder interests. But union-nominated directors also have the responsibility of representing the union leadership and the rank-and-file membership. Serving these dual interests requires union-nominated directors to engage in a delicate balancing act, and, as McKersie notes, there are many examples of directors who have "fallen off this high wire." His examination of several critical issues, including executive compensation, collective bargaining, union organizing, and confidentiality, casts light on how union-nominated directors have attempted to deal with the dilemma inherent in their role. McKersie's study makes it apparent that union-nominated directors can play a very useful role in corporate governance, but he is not optimistic about the number of companies that have union representation on their boards expanding. He notes that the idea does not have many champions in either the management or the union community. Nevertheless, given the benefits of union representation on corporate boards, McKersie concludes by advocating the expansion of the concept.

Numerous observers have noted that there is often a mismatch between the racial and gender characteristics of the participants in labor-management relations and the demographics of the work force they represent. In the last chapter in this section, Kirsten Wever addresses this issue directly by posing the proposition that traditional union-management negotiations and political agendas have not adequately taken women's issues into account. They have not done so in part, she argues, because women are underrepresented in leadership positions of unions and companies and at the political and collective bargaining tables where labor and business sort out their priorities and issues. So she raises another structural challenge: how to bring women and the issues of greatest importance to them into the negotiation structures and processes within and across countries.

Wever focuses particularly on how the growing role of women in European countries is not yet reflected in an altered agenda for collective bargaining, or in political agendas at the national or supranational European level, but the same point could be made for American women and labor market institutions. Securing a strong voice for women is perhaps the biggest challenge facing traditional labor-management relations processes in the developed world, and perhaps even in the industrializing world. Negotiating a seat at the table for new voices is again a necessary precondition to the effective use of negotiations in labor-management relations today.

What all this suggests is that we are, and have been for some time, in an era in which the basic institutions of labor-management relations are themselves up for "negotiation" and change. The question is whether we are able to negotiate institutional change and innovation or whether we must first experience large-scale destruction of the existing system before a new set of structures and processes for resolving the legitimate interests of

workers and employers rises out of its ashes. That perhaps is the most profound question for the negotiators and change agents in labor-management relations today. The chapters in Part III provide a sample of the
stresses and problems experienced so far and the challenges that lie ahead.

Negotiations in Other Arenas

The basic theoretical concepts and generic techniques of negotiations have
been used to foster change in a wide variety of domains. We sample a few
of these in Part IV to illustrate the reach of these concepts and the potential value those skilled in the use of such tools can add to society. Extending negotiations into these diverse domains requires a degree of intellectual flexibility, practical agility, and knowledge of the "local" culture and
institutions. No two negotiating contexts are alike. Norms of behavior,
protocols, or tactics of negotiations that work in one setting may fail mis-
erably or be misinterpreted or unacceptable in another. Thus, we do not
propose that by learning the basics of negotiations, "you can negotiate
anything," as some books in airport bookstores would have you believe.
Instead, as these contributions suggest, an understanding of the basics,
and a deep understanding of and appreciation for the specific institutional
and cultural features of a setting, are powerful starting points for engaging
the issues and searching for constructive solutions to vexing problems.

Max Bazerman and Andrew Hoffman examine how the use of principles derived from the behavioral theory of negotiations can help resolve
disputes between parties with competing environmental and economic objectives. They contrast the two negotiation perspectives most frequently
applied to environmental disputes: On the one hand, there are those who
believe that the relationship between economic competitiveness and environmental protection is inherently a "win-lose" one. They believe protecting the environment invariably reduces economic competitiveness, and
vice versa. On the other hand, there are those who believe that environmental disputes, when viewed through the right frame of reference, can
usually be converted into a "win-win" scenario. They maintain that economic and environmental objectives can be made complementary. Bazerman and Hoffman argue that both views are overly simplistic, however.
Adopting Walton and McKersie's framework, they posit that environmental disputes are best viewed from a "mixed-motive perspective." That is,
these disputes simultaneously have both competitive and cooperative dimensions or, using Walton and McKersie's terminology, both distributive
and integrative aspects. Recognizing the mixed-motive nature of environ-

mental disputes, according to Bazerman and Hoffman, promotes the more effective search for optimal solutions.

The concepts developed by Walton and McKersie can also be fruitfully applied to community planning and public policy disputes, according to Lawrence Susskind. Although there are important similarities between collective bargaining disputes and public policy disputes, according to Susskind, there are also significant differences. For example, formally, collective bargaining involves two distinct entities (the union and the employer) whereas public policy disputes typically involve many parties. Susskind notes that long-time mediators are often astounded to find that a public policy dispute may have thirty or more participants—or even one hundred—at the bargaining table. Also, the system of selecting bargaining agents is well established in collective bargaining but much less developed in public policy disputes. Moreover, although the use of mediation has been systematized in collective bargaining disputes, Susskind notes that it has not been in public policy disputes and he doubts that it ever will be. In view of these and other differences between collective bargaining and public policy disputes, can a theory that has its roots in the former be relevant to the latter? Can the practices that have proved effective in the one area be transferred to the other? Susskind considers these questions in his chapter, concluding that some of the lessons that have been learned in labor relations can be applied in public policy disputes provided there is sufficient sensitivity to both the similarities and the differences in these two areas. At the end, he stresses the critical role experienced neutral parties need to play in this bridging effort.

In the final chapter of this section, Lavinia Hall and Charles Heckscher consider the issue of "identity" in negotiations. They note that most theories of negotiations assume that the parties have "secure and independent identities and identifiable interests." For many categories of real-life negotiations, however, this assumption is erroneous. Particularly in cases in which one side has a history of dominating or oppressing the other, Hall and Heckscher emphasize, the parties themselves may have very different conceptions of their own identities. These conceptions can become issues in the negotiation process, posing obstacles to the resolution of disputes. Hall and Heckscher explain how anthropology can make a useful contribution to understanding the role of identity in negotiations, applying concepts such as collective identity, shared memory, and group pride to the problem of negotiating identity. They cite several conflicts between a dominated group and an oppressor in which identity was a critical issue, and focus particularly on a bitter dispute involving a Mohawk Tribe in Canada, developers, and the government over whether a golf course should be built on a sacred Mohawk burial ground. One faction of the Mohawk Tribe, attaching primacy to the tribe's sense of historical identity and oppression, vigorously resisted the golf course project, while another faction, much less concerned with the tribe's identity, stressed the economic benefits of the project. Hall and Heckscher provide a prescription, based on their analytical framework, for handling intractable disputes of this type.

Conclusion: The Future of Negotiations

We close the book with a look to the future, appropriately drawing on the masters who started this process—Robert McKersie and Richard Walton. We give them the last word in this volume, where they not only take a glance backward but also look forward into the future of research on, as well as the teaching and practice of, negotiations. As they point out, no one could have predicted in 1965, when their *Behavioral Theory* first appeared, that the field of negotiations would become the "growth industry" it is today. In the 1960s, for example, very few business schools and law schools offered courses on negotiations, but today almost all do. (At Cornell, for example, negotiation courses are offered regularly in at least *five* different colleges.) As the chapters in this volume amply demonstrate, Walton and McKersie's theory has proved to be relevant in a wide variety of settings. Indeed, the robust nature of their theory is a phenomenon seldom encountered in the social sciences. Truly, Walton and McKersie's behavioral theory has stood the test of time, and every scholar and practitioner in the field of negotiation has been the beneficiary of their extraordinary contribution.

Part I

The Behavioral Theory of Negotiations

1

Conceptual Foundations

Walton and McKersie's Subprocesses of Negotiations

THOMAS A. KOCHAN

DAVID B. LIPSKY

Walton and McKersie's 1965 book, *A Behavioral Theory of Labor Negotiations*, provides much of the conceptual underpinnings of what grew into the modern-day teaching of negotiations in business, public policy, law, and other professional schools. We therefore believe that it is useful to outline the basic concepts and ideas introduced by these authors. We do so, however, with a word of caution. There is no substitute for the original. Every student should have the pleasure of struggling (as we did the first time it was assigned to us as students) with the tongue twisters like "attitudinal structuring" and the many other new terms and theoretical ideas introduced in the book!

The Four Subprocesses of Negotiations

The heart of the Walton and McKersie model are four subprocesses that together make up the negotiation process. The authors draw on a wide range of literature and theories from economics, psychology, group dynamics, and industrial relations to develop these subprocesses.

Distributive Bargaining

The *distributive bargaining* subprocess refers to how negotiators resolve differences when their interests or positions are in conflict. In game theory this is referred to as a zero-sum game; behavioral scientists sometimes call this a win-lose process. Negotiators are assumed to start bargaining with a gap between their positions. The bargaining task is to locate a compromise on a continuum somewhere in between. Bargainers are further assumed to have some *target* point and some *resistance* point in mind that influence their offers and counteroffers. The target point reflects the aspirations or most-favorable goals each party has for the outcome, while the resistance point captures the least-favorable outcome acceptable to each party. If there is a gap between resistance points, as in Figure 1.1a, there is said to be a negative contract zone, and an impasse (perhaps a strike in labor negotiations) is likely.

A positive contract zone (Figure 1.1b) indicates an overlap in bottom-line positions: potential for an agreement exists. What keeps the parties motivated to negotiate when their interests are in conflict? They are assumed to be tied together in an ongoing interdependent relationship. Each party needs the other to satisfy its interests. The employer needs the workers and is in an ongoing bargaining relationship with the union. The workers need the employer for their livelihood. So, in this model the alternative to an agreement is a temporary impasse or strike, not a permanent ending of the relationship as might be the case if a buyer and seller of a used car cannot agree on an acceptable price.

Walton and McKersie go on to use a variety of behavioral science concepts to illuminate how negotiators think about their interdependence, how they make decisions, how the concession-making process unfolds, and how parties use commitment tactics to enhance their individual gains. While for some, distributive bargaining is the full story of negotiations, it is only the starting point in the Walton and McKersie model.

Integrative Bargaining

Integrative bargaining refers to the process of seeking joint gains by either approaching or expanding the Pareto-optimal frontier. The parties see themselves as having a joint problem. Walton and McKersie present a problem-solving model to explain the dynamics of reaching an agreement. Integrative bargaining can take place over a single issue in which the parties identify a common objective or over multiple issues, some of which involve conflicting interests and some, shared interests. They refer to the latter situation as a *mixed-motive* situation and see this as the most common type of negotiation. When facing a mixed-motive negotiation, the task is to look for trade-offs across the issues that leave both parties better off than if they dealt with each separately. Later, other behavioral scientists

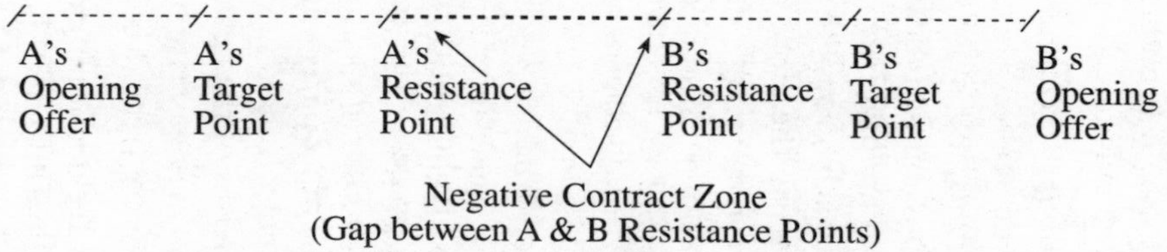

A's Opening Offer — A's Target Point — A's Resistance Point — B's Resistance Point — B's Target Point — B's Opening Offer

Negative Contract Zone
(Gap between A & B Resistance Points)

Figure 1.1a. Contract Zones in Distributive Bargaining: The Case of a Negative Contract Zone

A's Opening Offer — A's Target Point — B's Resistance Point — A's Resistance Point — B's Target Point — B's Opening Offer

Positive Contract Zone
(A & B Resistance Points Overlap)

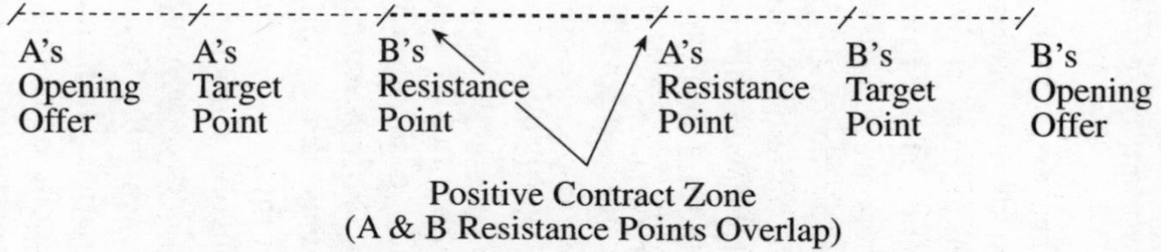

Figure 1.1b. Contract Zones in Distributive Bargaining: The Case of a Positive Contract Zone

would use the term *win-win bargaining* to describe integrative bargaining. Some would equate integrative or win-win bargaining with Fisher and Ury's concept of *interest-based or principled negotiations*, although Fisher and Ury distinguish their concept from both distributive and integrative bargaining (Fisher and Ury 1981).

Intra-organizational Bargaining

A third subprocess, *intra-organizational bargaining*, recognizes that negotiators often do not act as individual decision makers. Instead, they serve as representatives of *groups* or *organizations* and must answer to these constituents. This feature gives rise to the possibility, indeed the likelihood, that there are diverse views or interests within these organizations. Thus, negotiation needs to take place within each group to reconcile differences and unite negotiating efforts. Each party therefore has to engage in several levels of *intra-organizational bargaining*—negotiating within the team and with the constituency—in order to build consensus within the party.

Attitudinal Structuring

Finally, Walton and McKersie realized that it makes a difference how the parties view each other in the bargaining process. The fourth subprocess, *attitudinal structuring*, specifically addresses these perceptions and proposes ways that negotiators can shape the other party's attitudes to advance either their own or their mutual advantage. It makes explicit that negotiations involve more than the substantive terms of the deal. Negotiations also produce relationship outcomes. Parties may increase or decrease their trust in each other as a result of how they are treated by the other party in negotiations. In turn, these perceptions will shape the context for future interactions or rounds of negotiation the parties have with each other. An important part of negotiation, therefore, involves a judgment of how hard to push one's temporary bargaining advantage or power if doing so might produce a negative reaction from a party to an ongoing relationship like a marriage, a work group, a strategic business partnership, or a labor-management relationship.

While these subprocesses are introduced separately, much of the art and science of negotiations lies in how they interact. Low trust inhibits integrative bargaining. Failure to resolve intra-organizational conflicts prior to bargaining slows the concession and compromise processes in distributive bargaining. Negotiators who engage in integrative bargaining when constituents have low trust in them or their bargaining counterparts risk rejection of tentative agreements. Poor communications, perhaps because of low trust, may lead to impasses even when a positive contract zone exists. All the dynamics and the ultimate outcome of negotiations are influenced by the relative power of the parties.

This brief summary only introduces the broad features and central concepts in the Walton and McKersie model. We leave it to the authors of the other chapters in this volume to illustrate the many ways this theory has shaped the research, teaching, and practice of negotiations in the years since its publication.

2

New Directions in Teaching Negotiations

From Walton and McKersie
to the New Millennium

LEONARD GREENHALGH

ROY J. LEWICKI

It is always useful for students and teachers alike to understand the origins and evolution of concepts that undergird their field of study. It is equally important to understand the changing contexts in which these concepts are being applied. In this chapter we provide both perspectives by tracing the way the study, teaching, and practice of negotiations have evolved since the publication of the seminal study that has inspired many of the innovations in this field: Walton and McKersie's *A Behavioral Theory of Labor Negotiations* (1965).

Until the 1960s, the study of negotiation had been largely within the province of economics, collective bargaining, or international diplomacy. Economists—notably game theorists—had modeled negotiations primarily as transactions. A transaction, in this context, is an economic exchange that is conceptually isolated from the noneconomic bonds between the parties, their history, and their future relationship. Negotiation was characterized as "competitive decision making," or a process in which independent actors make decisions, as principals or agents, in situations where outcomes depend partly on the other party's decision. Note that the parties were *in*dependent (from the standpoint of the relationship) but the situation was *inter*dependent (in the sense that the decision could not be made without the other party's consent). The classic work of John Nash (1950) epitomizes this intellectual tradition. It models relationships in terms of the type and nature of the parties' interde-

The authors are indebted to Deborah Chapman for ideas and comments as this manuscript was evolving, and to the other contributors to this volume.

pendence—which could be zero-sum, positive-sum, or some mixture of the two.

Most scholars who did research on negotiation had applied the foundational economic models to real-world negotiations by adding in contextual factors, rather than looking at negotiation in situ, and developing theory and research that best explained what was being observed. In the case of collective bargaining, for example, much was known about how unions functioned as institutions and how industrial relations managers dealt with them (see, for example, Dunlop and Healy 1953). The teaching of negotiation in this context involved adapting and applying the economic theory of interdependent decision making to the peculiarities of the union-management context. This is not surprising since most of the research and teaching text on labor negotiations at that time was written by well-known labor economists such as Reynolds (1952–1978) or Chamberlain and Kuhn (1965). Works such as these focused heavily on showing how labor negotiations were different from other market transactions because they were embedded in ongoing relationships and reflected the particular needs and features of labor relations such as the use of collective power, the role of labor law, and the evolution of professional norms and traditions in this particular field.

Viewed from this perspective, the relationship between the negotiating parties was seen as fundamentally adversarial, because unions wanted to get more for their constituents and management wanted to give them less. Negotiating "skill" or expertise was often defined as maximizing utility on behalf of one's own constituents and taking advantage of whatever opportunities arose to achieve positive-sum outcomes. The motive for seeking positive-sum outcomes was hardly philanthropic, given the pervasive enmity in the relationship. Rather, it was easier to get the other party to *accept* outcomes that allowed a negotiator to improve utility that came at no cost—or, better still, with increased benefit—to the other party. Mutual gain, in short, was motivated by self-interest (see Greenhalgh 2001).

The Walton and McKersie treatise transformed our understanding of the negotiation processes by providing a richer view of negotiation phenomena. While their four subprocesses of distributive bargaining, integrative bargaining, attitudinal structuring, and intra-organizational bargaining described in the previous chapter maintained some intellectual roots in the transactional, game-theoretic approaches (such as the use of payoff matrices to describe choices and decisions facing negotiators), the book also documented an *inductive* approach to the study of collective bargaining. It showed that collective bargaining was not a single unitary process but rather a context in which four negotiation subprocesses played out. As the book's title suggests, a behavioral theory was formulated to explain the dynamics of each subprocess.

Scholars soon recognized that the enriched perspective provided by Walton and McKersie was highly generalizable to negotiations in other contexts, and the work spurred a wealth of research both within and outside the collective bargaining domain (see reviews by Greenhalgh 1987b; Lewicki, Weiss, and Lewin 1992; Pruitt and Carnevale 1993; and Rubin and Brown 1975). These efforts, in turn, broadened the scope of what could be taught. Knowledge dissemination (teaching) is always dependent on knowledge creation (research). Prior to 1965, research and teaching had concentrated almost exclusively on applying economic theories of rational decision making to the negotiation context. The book took its readers beyond this limited perspective in that it *integrated* economics with behavioral science using collective bargaining as a case in point.

Recognition of the value of this broader perspective stimulated a large number of laboratory studies during the decade 1965–1975. The body of knowledge grew quickly, and the knowledge base that could be used for pedagogy increased dramatically. Social psychologists, behavioral decision theorists, and personality theorists investigated the strategic and tactical nuances of integrative and distributive bargaining processes (Lewicki, Weiss, and Lewin 1992; Pruitt 1981; Rubin and Brown 1975). Similarly, group-dynamics researchers and coalition theorists explored what went on within constituencies, as did various researchers investigating "the agency problem"—the temptation of agents to pursue their own interests rather than their constituency's (Murnighan 1986, 1991).

The Boom in Negotiation Education

As the body of knowledge grew, it found broader application. Particularly noteworthy was its extension into the fields of law and business. Negotiation had always been taught in collective bargaining courses, but by the 1970s negotiation courses had sprung up in various institutions in which a faculty member had a particular expertise in negotiation and wanted to share that knowledge with students.

Students in these professional schools wanted to learn both theory and application. The theory was made available to them through various texts that emerged. Many texts were little more than a "popularized" presentation of the basic ideas introduced in the Walton and McKersie volume. Others greatly elaborated and extended the themes, showing the form they took in different contexts and adding in subsequent research findings (see, for example, Lewicki, Litterer, Minton, and Saunders 1994; Raiffa 1982; Thompson 1998). Still others were adjunct texts, showing how cognitive biases affected the way negotiators made decisions (see especially the work of Max Bazerman and his students). Finally, writings emerged on the broader systems in which dispute resolution occurred in organizational contexts (Ury, Brett, and Goldberg 1988; Rowe 1993a). All of the writings owed a considerable intellectual debt to Walton and McKersie.

The application of the theory was accomplished to some extent through cases and films that documented actual negotiations but, more significantly, through experiential exercises. An experiential exercise is another form of case study, one that is different from traditional case studies in that students become full participants in the case. They are given the basic scenario and asked to take the role of negotiator and do what they think best in that situation. The variety of experiences that arise from different interpretations of the role and the negotiating problem, negotiators' personalities and styles, and the tactics used by the parties allows the instructor to show how these various factors lead to different processes and outcomes. At the same time, students get an opportunity to practice negotiation skills and improve their individual effectiveness.

In business schools, there has been a tendency to concentrate on cases that teach both distributive and integrative bargaining but with an increasing emphasis on integrative processes. Distributive bargaining is often the way the untrained negotiator approaches all bargaining interactions (Bazerman and Neale 1992), and instructors therefore often start the course with distributive-bargaining problems as a way to explore its limited advantages and applications and its significant disadvantages and dilemmas. However, students do not find the haggling process particularly interesting once they have learned and practiced the basic techniques, so there is a tendency to move on quickly to more challenging problems.

Integrative (and mixed-motive) bargaining is more complex because it often requires great creativity and ingenuity—which can be stimulated by examples in texts but cannot be taught by simply reading about it. It *must* be practiced. Intra-group bargaining is receiving growing attention as a result of the increased emphasis on work groups and task forces in organizations. In most group settings in organizations, the multiple parties to a problem are expected to resolve their differences in a single meeting.

Attitudinal structuring has received the least attention. This may be due to the limitations of the Heider (1958) model on which Walton and Mc Kersie based their discussion, but a broader examination of current teaching practices reveals a more fundamental neglect. While there has been a strong and compelling literature on persuasion and attitude change in so-

cial psychology and on influence tactics in the field of organizational behavior (see Cialdini 1993), few instructors integrate that work into their
courses to show students how to recognize or construct a good persuasive
message or to counter the persuasive messages being posed by the other
party. (Management communication scholars who also teach negotiation
are an exception.)

Some Critiques of the Field

Even as teaching and research on negotiation were blossoming, some dissatisfaction was being expressed about the directions in which the body of
knowledge was evolving. The first critique concerns external validity.
Economists in the 1940s and 1950s had theorized about how decisions are
made in a simple two-party, equal-power transaction between strangers.
This scenario is a good one for investigating *basic* game-theoretical concepts. Perhaps the most widely used example from game theory is the classic prisoners' dilemma. This is an example of where both parties will be
better off if they cooperate by taking the others' interests into account and
trust each other, both will lose if neither trusts the other, and one will lose
and the other will win if only one party engages in cooperative trusting behavior. The example refers to a situation where two suspected partners to
a crime are interrogated separately and asked to testify against the other.
If neither agrees to do so, they will both go free. If one does implicate the
other, he or she will go free and the other will get convicted. If both report
on the other, they both get jail terms. Unfortunately, however, simple one-
time game-theoretic scenarios like this became the paradigm case when
others took up the study of negotiations in the 1960s and 1970s, with
little scholarly debate about whether it remained an appropriate tool,
given broader, practice-focused research objectives.

The scientific process used in this line of inquiry traditionally involved a
deductive elaboration of the existing theory, followed by a laboratory
study to investigate whether the hypothesized effects materialized. The
stimulus scenario was constrained to be simple enough (a matrix game or
a simple bargaining problem, for instance) that it would test the theory
without introducing competing explanations of the results. This led to
new knowledge, but generalizability of the findings was limited to what
would be predicted to happen in similarly constrained scenarios. The new
knowledge was transmitted to students by placing them in a scenario that
was a close analog of the laboratory simulation—one that was constrained in such a way that the students could see, experientially, that the

documented effects occurred. In other words, students participated in replications of research simulations and learned from direct experience how people respond in such scenarios.

The criticism of this approach to teaching is that the learning doesn't match students' everyday experiences. Critics didn't—and couldn't—argue that the teaching was scientifically unsound: the faculty member was, after all, teaching what was supported by published research evidence. The problem was that "it just wasn't real." In contrast, the strength of the Walton and McKersie subprocesses was that they arose, *inductively*, from observational studies of what negotiators actually did. Their findings led them to conclude that there was much to be explained beyond what economists had been seeking and finding in their laboratory studies. Teachers faced a similar issue in their classrooms. The economics-oriented paradigm led them to emphasize isolated two-party transactions, serial transactions within the prisoners' dilemma framework, and the formation of abstract coalitions. Students became expert at dealing with these contrived scenarios, but analogous scenarios rarely came up in their daily lives.

To grasp the external validity problem, consider this. A homework assignment to describe the last ten negotiations a student was personally involved in produces consistent results: On average, only one of these negotiations is with a stranger or involves an isolated transaction. The other nine involve a more complex negotiation with someone they know well. Most often, the respondents have been negotiating with a spouse or partner, a family member, a roommate, a coworker, or a boss—people with whom they have a past history and an anticipated future relationship. They can't treat these negotiations as context-free struggles to claim value in pursuit of self-interest or create value for joint gain; therefore, some of the advice given in popularized texts seemed—and was—too simplistic. For example, the respondents seldom had an alternative to a negotiated solution; they couldn't separate the person from the problem; and they didn't need to focus on interests rather than positions—instead, their commonwealth bond made interests inseparable within the dyad (Greenhalgh 2001). Indeed, in the context of the growing practice of family mediation, a key issue is deciding whether to work on identifying and addressing the underlying relationship issues producing conflicts or to end the relationship and help the parties negotiate an amicable and fair separation or divorce. In short, much of what was being advocated wasn't helping students be more effective in *everyday* negotiations, because the research on which the teaching was based had been conducted outside the relational frame in which the parties were operating.

Another source of discontent was the apparent gender and cultural biases in what was being presented as the normative approach to negotiating. The theoretical underpinnings of the body of knowledge we teach was developed in large part by relatively affluent Western white males culturally situated in a free-enterprise context. Their world view emphasized individualism, self-interest, economic rationality, dominance-submission, rights, and rules. As a result of this cognitive bias, negotiations came to be viewed as contests of sorts in which the objective is to win without violating explicit rules (Greenhalgh 1987a). The idealized models developed by economists emanated from this perspective and formed the foundation on which social psychologists, behavioral decision theorists, and personality psychologists built their own elaborated models of negotiation. A number of efforts to explain whether non-Westerners or women negotiated differently were inconclusive, largely because these studies continued to use transactional paradigms that elicited biased responses (see Rubin and Brown 1975; Lewicki, Litterer, Minton, and Saunders 1994).

If the research paradigm is biased, the knowledge it generates will be biased. Instructors will feel virtuous about teaching material that is based on empirical research, but what they teach may be bad advice in many real-world situations. For example, as a result of teaching a version of *game* theory, students will learn to view negotiation as a game[1] of sorts—a contest to be won, within the rules, using guile, power, and whatever other advantage can be mustered. This may ruin deals, destroy relationships, and cost them their jobs.

An alternative approach, arising from the study of gender and cultural differences, emphasizes relationships rather than games. From this perspective, a dispute is not an opportunity to win a contest but rather a strain in a relationship that must be addressed and, ideally, healed. The introduction of this perspective provided an enriched body of knowledge that could be taught, and teaching materials were developed to emphasize how different relationships led to different outcomes, how the relationship could be managed, and how the future relationship needed to be considered as an outcome of negotiations alongside economic benefit.[2]

Interestingly, this evolution of the field was foreshadowed by Walton

---

[1] The masculine emphasis on winning is so strongly infused in this paradigm that even integrative solutions are described as win-win, a clear oxymoron (see Greenhalgh 1987a, 2001).
[2] Note that some studies that purport to investigate the effects of relationships do not step far enough outside the old paradigm to provide adequate insight. For example, a game-theory simulation that simply includes future consequences (such as a two-trial game or an iterated prisoners' dilemma) remains rooted in individualism, self-interest, economic rationality, rules, and power differentials, not in the broader bonds between the parties.

and McKersie's concern with *attitudinal structuring*. In a sense, relationships between the parties—not simply attitudes—were what the authors had discovered as an important negotiation phenomenon. But in 1965 there wasn't much known or being studied in the area of relationships on which the authors could draw, nor was there a theory of relationships on which researchers reading their work could draw. But today the knowledge base has evolved to the point where teachers can be very sophisticated in diagnosing what is likely to increase or decrease negotiators' effectiveness in dealing with unions, individuals, groups, other businesses, or other nations. Construing disputes as relationship strains encourages a broader range of approaches that can be used to deal with them. Negotiation is the process of addressing disputes by generating agreement (in other words, commitment to a joint course of action). Alternatively, either party can use power (the ability to get the other party to do something he or she wouldn't do in the absence of influence), and a variety of power or leverage "tactics" are available. A third alternative is conflict resolution (the process of arresting and reversing the emotional escalation of disputes). A conceptualization of relationships between the parties that is more comprehensive than economic exchange thus encourages a broader repertoire of approaches to dealing with disputes. Teaching can then focus on the skills involved in using this spectrum of tactics effectively, as well as on selecting particular tactics based on the relational context. The use of power, for example, can enhance outcomes, but it also usually creates relationship strains of its own by adding dominance-submission to the relational dynamics.

Changes in the Business World

The theoretical perspective that undergirds knowledge of negotiation has advanced considerably in response to these critiques. But another factor is providing even greater impetus for evolution of the field: the organizational context in which negotiations take place has been changing very fast. The changes have wide-ranging consequences for what needs to be taught. Teaching has to focus on negotiation situations that are far more complex than has been the case in previous decades.

Much of the early theory viewed negotiating parties as unitary actors (or at least as groups with essentially a homogeneous membership), whether there was only one party or many. As a result, negotiations between businesses—or between unions and managements—could be taught as negotiations between agents representing those entities (subject, of course, to the successful completion of intra-organizational bargaining processes to resolve internal dissensus). This was a convenient simplification, because considering "the party" as a single generic actor allowed scholars to apply all of their individualistically oriented theory to the intra-group, inter-group, intra-organizational, and international levels.[3] But as we approached the new millennium, we saw the business world become much more complex: increasing dispersion and disaggregation were accompanied by greater centralization and integration. These apparent paradoxes are inherent in the new forms of organizations that have emerged. Thus, there were four key trends that needed to be accommodated in negotiation models.

Globalization

As we noted earlier, the paradigm case[4] that has fostered the development of negotiation theory has been an economic transaction between two actors of equal power. Each party struggled to control the situation in order to maximize its own utility in the context of markets, hierarchies, and contracts (Williamson 1975). This schema, however, was proving inadequate to portray the emerging global context of business negotiations.

Negotiations in the global arena are often between multiple actors with unequal power. Consider three examples: U.S. businesses often negotiate not only with their foreign business counterparts but also with an agency of the host country's government, such as Japan's Ministry of Economy, Trade and Industry (METI); a jet engine manufacturer negotiating with an airline may also have to negotiate with allied airlines functioning as a buyer's cooperative; and the Social Partnership in Scandinavia involves three parties in collective bargaining—the union, the management, and the government (Greenhalgh and Indridason 1998). Furthermore, traditional hierarchies have become rare: they have been supplanted by new business forms (as in the case of *keiretsu* and Western value-chain consortia); major markets are evolving into complex oligopolies (such as the European Community); and global contracts don't follow the Western legal form (consider Japanese one-page contracts, for example). The enormity of

---

[3] This was made easier by the tradition in law—which has also greatly influenced the development of negotiation theory—to deal with collective entities as if they were individuals. The corporation, for example, is treated in many legal formulations as a person.

[4] It is the basic case in the sense that once it is understood theoretically and empirically, everything else is viewed as a variant of this scenario. For example, unequal power is studied *in comparison with* equal power; a coalition in a triad reduces to the two-party case (two against one); intra-group negotiations are studied in terms of how they differ from dyadic negotiations; and so on.

these changes has overwhelmed the traditional negotiation paradigm. The law of requisite variety (Weick 1979) requires that the analytical tools be as complex as the organizational systems they are trying to model, and the traditional economic models of negotiation—laudable from the standpoint of scientific parsimony—are simply not comprehensive enough for the task (see, for example, Weiss 1993).

Extended Organizations

Even when the negotiation is between only two organizations, their form may be very different from the unified hierarchical structures of the past. In earlier decades, organizations were structured to encompass all of the functional areas needed for self-sufficiency. They competed in domestic markets against similar structures, bought from similar supplier organizations by means of arms-length contracting, and sold to similar organizations that functioned as an independent channel of distribution.

The new-generation organizations are different. Their boundaries are fluid, so that networked business entities function as extended organizations. That is, each organization is situated in a value chain and makes contributions according to its domain of distinctive competency. Thus, instead of negotiating in the context of competitor, buyer, and seller relationships, organizations are perpetually recruiting, coordinating, and improving value-chain partners.

The classic coordination and control mechanisms (hierarchy, market, and contract) are ill-suited to a world in which value chains compete with other value chains. The hierarchy keeps changing as the "organic" network molds itself to respond to new competitors, technological shifts, currency fluctuations, regulatory changes, political upheavals, and industry transformations. Market mechanisms become de-emphasized as value chains try to capture the loyalty of organizations that confer competitive advantages. And formal contracts are not helpful because their specificity requirements tend to lock the parties into arrangements that need to be constantly adapting to new developments. As a result, instead of a stable structure, there is *a negotiated order* that is in constant flux. Negotiating—and re-negotiating—that order involves managing strategic business relationships (Greenhalgh 2001).

Diversity

A body of theory developed to model the behavior of Anglo-Saxon males may not fully generalize to the new participants in the U.S. domestic work force, much less to peoples in foreign cultures. While it is important not to stereotype people by their gender or race, some evidence shows that compared to men, women tend to be less individualistic, less driven by rules, and less preoccupied with winning, for example; they tend to be more relationship-oriented (Greenhalgh and Gilkey 1993). African-Americans and His-panic-Americans tend to be more communal. Asian-Americans tend to be more concerned with preserving social face. A Western economist would say they simply have a different utility function, but people from these groups would retort that Western economists "don't get it"—that is, they don't see that others experience dispute resolution within a different cultural frame-work. They would point out that negotiators might *not* be concerned with utility gain at all but rather with loyalty and commitment to the relation-ship. Negotiation theory for the twenty-first century, and those who teach and use negotiation tools, have to accommodate such different perspectives.

Technology

Advances in technology have changed many things in the organizational world. The most significant, from a negotiation perspective, is the process of communication. The older, transactional view of negotiations envi-sioned a face-to-face meeting in which the parties would reach an agree-ment that would bind them to a course of action until the term of the agreement expired and they could meet again to renegotiate the arrange-ments. Negotiation was episodic. Today, an increasing amount of commu-nication is instant, virtual, and unconstrained in time and space. So it is feasible for a negotiation to be perpetual rather than episodic, as it is in many long-term relationships with spouses, coworkers, and bosses. And given the availability of new technologies, many negotiations, or new up-dates on them, are now broadcast broadly and quickly to constituents, po-tential allies, the media, and the public. In this way these "publics" are be-coming active parties to negotiations in fields as diverse as labor relations, international affairs, business transactions, and even congressional and court proceedings. Negotiation theory and training need to adapt to these features of the current reality.

Impact on New Approaches to Teaching Negotiation

This evolution in the organizational context calls for commensurate evolu-tion in the teaching of negotiation. This will not be easy to accomplish because there is considerable investment in the old paradigm (see Kuhn 1970); a defensive reaction fulminates among those who have the greatest stake in the old paradigm, particularly in the face of suggestions that it could be made more useful to practitioners. In fact, there is nothing *wrong* with the old paradigm. It is not being attacked. Rather, it is being lauded as a solid *starting point* for the field's evolution. From our perspective, there are four major directions in which the teaching of negotiation must advance.

Negotiation as the Management of Relationships

The traditional view of negotiation visualizes a process of managing transactions. An alternative view sees those transactions as events in an ongoing relationship (Greenhalgh 2001). From the latter perspective, what matters most is the nature of the relationship, or perhaps the type of relationship one is trying to develop with the other over time, rather than the details of the deal. The details of the deal are likely to matter more than relationships, however, when parties are engaged in truly "one-shot deals," such as the buying or selling of a house or a used car from a stranger.

Suppose, for example, you are negotiating a completion date. Traditional models have you focusing on price-delivery trade-offs, your ability to get a better completion date from someone else, your rights under contract law to enforce a commitment, your aspirations, expectations, opening bids, and the like. These factors may become less important in certain relationships. Imagine negotiating with your spouse or partner over when you must end your winter vacation; or with your boss over the due date for a work assignment; or with a strategic alliance partner over when a product or service can be brought to market.[5] In these completion-date negotiations, the traditional elements of a negotiation strategy take a back seat to relational considerations.[6]

The different perspectives of agents or representatives and their principals also need to be taken into account in teaching and practicing negotiation. Aspiring lawyers, for example, need to be taught that their overzealous advocacy for a particular client's cause may need to be tempered by the realization that the client will have to face and live with the other party long after the lawyer moves on to another assignment. Even the lawyer may need to worry about the reputation he or she develops—the profes-

[5] That is, hold the scenario constant, vary the relationship context, and imagine the differences.

[6] Note that the three examples are typical of everyday life, whereas the transactions modeled by the old paradigm are atypical.

sional world is much smaller than most people realize and reputations travel far and fast!

Students and practitioners, therefore, need to become sophisticated diagnosticians of relationships and relationship strains. The classic relationship categories—cooperation-competition, or market-hierarchy-contract—only scratch the surface of what scholars now know to be salient in relationships between negotiators. These antiquated notions assume a particular type of rationality is operating: the individualistic pursuit of self-interest. There are other types of rationality operating in the world, such as relational rationality (Greenhalgh 2001)—the pursuit of commonwealth interests (the notion of doing something *for the relationship*, a concept that is opaque to many Western white males, even though it determines many of their choices). Furthermore, the field has concentrated on two dimensions of relationships—exchange and trust—whereas there are fourteen measurable dimensions that negotiators take into account when dealing with another party (Greenhalgh and Chapman 1995).

The general point here is that teaching needs to prepare people for the real world, where they spend much of their time and energy managing relationships through negotiation processes.

Negotiation as the Management of Emotions

The emphasis on economic rationality that has pervaded the field of dispute resolution (see Raiffa 1982) has overshadowed a more basic phenomenon: people's emotional reactions in disputes. Disputes are, in their very essence, emotional experiences. In fact, without emotion, we wouldn't *have* a dispute—simply a different perspective. So the management of disputes needs to focus heavily on the management of emotion.

The biggest danger in negotiation is escalation of the conflict (Greenhalgh 1986). Escalation is a cycle of attaching meanings to issues, reacting emotionally to those meanings, ruminating, redefining the issues, attaching new meanings to the new issues, reacting emotionally to the new meanings, and so on (Davidson and Greenhalgh 1999). A student or practitioner who cannot diagnose and manage these emotions cannot negotiate effectively; therefore, the teaching of negotiations needs to include significant coverage of emotional dynamics.

Negotiation as the Management of Interdependent Personalities

The classic models of negotiation assumed negotiators to be idealized actors with uniform personalities—what used to be called the Economic

Man. Personality psychologists have conducted hundreds of studies that show, in essence, how deviations from the idealized model affect negotiated outcomes of simulated transactions (see Rubin and Brown 1975). The old approach has led to a skewed way of teaching people about personality and its effects.

Probably the most frequent means of covering the topic of negotiator personality has been to have students or practitioners fill out a self-assessment instrument such as the Thomas-Kilmann Conflict Mode Instrument (Kilmann and Thomas 1977).[7] This instrument identifies tendencies to serve the test taker's personal interests, the other party's interests, or some combination. But it is rooted in the classic paradigm: it considers tendencies *with respect to* the Economic Man assumption of pure self-interest.

An alternative perspective on negotiation is to construe the negotiation process as *the interaction of interdependent personalities*. This approach makes no normative assumptions about a particular kind of rationality but rather looks at negotiator effectiveness in terms of adaptation to individual differences. Such adaptation is immensely important in the real world because personality has a strong impact on relationships, processes, utility structures, style, and tactics. A good negotiation course or training program will provide negotiators with insights about themselves and others. Negotiators need to know, for example, about gender differences, cultural differences, passive-aggressiveness, conflict-avoidance, need for power, relationship-orientation, Machiavellianism, bullying tendencies, capacity for empathy, and many more dimensions that are likely to explain most of what is going on in the dispute and the negotiation (see Gilkey and Greenhalgh 1986). This material can be taught effectively, and students are very receptive to it.

Negotiation as the Management of Complexity

The business world has changed. Businesses need to be managed by people who are good negotiators. But in the context of the changing world of business, the definition of what constitutes a good negotiator has evolved. It is not someone who can wring every last ounce of utility from an isolated transaction. Nor is it someone who can discover the Pareto-optimal frontier and converge easily on the Nash equilibrium. These are certainly important skills, but they are not enough to equip twenty-first-century managers for the challenges they face. The greatest economic impact

---

[7] There are several instruments that accomplish almost the same assessment task, such as the Rahim Organizational Conflict Inventory (Rahim 1983).

in the new millennium will result from successful interactions of networks of boundaryless organizations, dispersed across the globe, seizing momentary competitive advantage and then adapting quickly to defend or regain it when it is challenged (D'Aveni 1994).

To prepare managers for this world, we need to understand negotiation in its broadest context, and we need to put people in simulations that provide complexity that mirrors their real-world challenges. The used-car dyadic exercises, triadic coalition games, and group dynamics exercises all provide useful building blocks, but much of the learning must come from simulations of what managers actually do in the businesses that are making a difference in the new economy.

Part II

Workplace Change and Tacit Negotiations

3

Changing Psychological Contracts

Implications for Human Resource
Management and Industrial Relations

DENISE M. ROUSSEAU

This chapter looks at the new meanings that changes in employment have brought to core concepts pertaining to the employment relationship and its supporting institutions. The starting points for any analysis of change and negotiations at work are the implicit and explicit terms of the employment contract. In previous work I have referred to how people interpret these terms as the "psychological contract" at work (Rousseau 1995). Both the implicit expectations and obligations employees and employers bring to the employment relationship and the explicit terms contained in written contracts or personnel policies affect the conduct of human resource management and industrial relations. Both cause changes in the issues that surface in negotiations at work, and in planned organizational change implementation. Here I examine changes at work from the perspective of their effects on the psychological contracts people have for employment, and discuss the implications of these changes for those responsible for setting or negotiating employment terms. To highlight these issues, I place more emphasis on the changes underway than the elements of stability and continuity, recognizing that both are part of the workplace realities today.

How would we characterize the traditional psychological contract governing standard employment relations over the past several decades? The simple notion that employees would get a fair day's pay for a fair day's work captures a good deal of what the parties expected to exchange. Beyond this general level, however, there was also an expectation that loyalty

I thank Richard Walton for his thoughtful comments regarding an earlier version of this paper. Thanks are also due to Elaine Goldberg and Tom Kochan for their helpful input.

and good performance would be rewarded with security. Lay-offs were certainly a potential for most workers and a likely reality for some, but they were normally expected to occur only when an organization was experiencing financial difficulties or as a temporary response to normal seasonal or cyclical fluctuations in product demand. Over time, tenure with an employer was expected to increase both economic security (lower probability of lay-off, higher wages, and more benefits) and psychological security in the form of greater commitment, loyalty, and sense of belonging.

Demands for employment flexibility have brought a new look to contemporary employment relations. For American businesses, these demands result from two fundamental, seemingly conflicting forces: (1) shifts toward contingent capitalism, which put short-term market factors and interests of owners ahead of workers, and (2) movements in the direction of cooperative capitalism, which builds a community of interests, blurring the boundaries between workers and owners (Derber 1994; Carnoy, Castells, and Benner 1996: 54). Lean production firms reflect the former and team production systems, the latter. This dichotomy may ring true but is not clear-cut in practice: even high-performance firms committed to teamwork and humanized labor-management relations (union or nonunion) subcontract business services and down-size their core labor force, and most lean production firms have fairly stable core labor forces and pay relatively high wages and benefits to their core workers. Both types of employment systems are associated with significant changes in the meaning of a number of traditional concepts in employment relations: security in income and employment is now described as "employability"; loyalty and attachment are giving way to "multiplex commitments"; and fixed work structures and rules are being replaced with "flexible alternatives." These new meanings strain established institutional arrangements concerned with solving problems related to security, attachment, and work structure, namely, the traditional functions of human resource (HR) management and industrial relations (IR), and set the context for both individual and collective negotiations of employment contracts today. Following discussion of these new meanings, I address critical HR and IR activities and the institutional challenges they reflect:

- Developing, accessing, and retaining human capital (knowledge, skills, and competencies) where attachment between worker and firms has been weakened—or "solving the 'commons' problem."
- Creating financial assets for workers that are portable and allow for more active management by the worker—or "blurring the boundary between workers and owners."

- Building relationships and developing skills fostered by ongoing interactions (a new focus for unions and professional associations)—or
  "networks of relational wealth."

New Meanings for Old Employment Concepts

I never wanted to be a dancer.
I wanted to be a short stop for the Pittsburgh Pirates.

Gene Kelly

As Gene Kelly's work history suggests, people can experience considerable change in the course of a career. Unlike the case of this famous
dancer, however, the most commonly experienced career changes for the
generations at work in the 1990s had little to do with the choices they personally made and everything to do with major upheavals in the settings in
which they worked: the nationwide demise of job security and concomi-
tant new forms of employment arrangements and work structures (trends
highlighted by Kochan, Katz, and McKersie 1986).

From Job Security to Employability

Employability is the term used in the new economy as the New Contract's
replacement for the wage and job security the Old Contract provided via
organizational membership and seniority. The decline of job security for
the traditional core work force has been fueled by global competition, the
decline of the manufacturing sector in the United States (and with it, traditional unionism), and a shifting view of labor as a variable rather than a
fixed cost. Employability, for most firms, implies that although the firms
can no longer guarantee their employees long-term jobs, they will do their
best to provide training and learning opportunities that will render them
highly valued, that is, "employable," when and if they look for jobs in the
external labor market.

Widespread skepticism from labor and dissembling by management regarding the real meaning of employability suggest to many commentators
that the promise of this New Contract term has not yet been realized. *Employability* can mean "you ain't got no job security." Or, it can mean a
more secure future based on greater and more flexible employment opportunity. Charles Handy (1989) and other management commentators have
argued that a flexible work force moving through a variety of firms offers

both workers and firms economic advantage. Making the promise of employability a reality, however, depends on how well firms and workers implement two features of the new economy.

The first is market discipline in job duties and assignments, which means creating and negotiating employment conditions that have value on the external market as well as within the firm's internal market. Since there is greater likelihood of employment entry and exit for any given worker in the new economy, HR practices must address the future opportunities to which current job requirements can be converted. Otherwise, employees risk investing time and energy in developing skills and knowledge that deprive them of future job security. True employability comes from job assignments and training activities that build the work force's market potential. Boeing, as a case in point, runs a nineteen-week small-business training program, in collaboration with the State of Washington and community leaders, to help turn skills acquired at Boeing into the basis for small-business development. Firms that promote employee contacts with others in their profession (as is common, for example, in engineering or computer programming) promote both internal and external visibility, thereby enhancing the market value (inside and outside the firm) of individual skill and knowledge. The ever greater emphasis on results in firms coincides with the increasing need for individuals to demonstrate their capabilities to their current as well as potential future employers. Job assignments that emphasize accountabilities (such as managing people, money, and measurable outcomes) are more likely to be credited by both the external market and the current employer than are poorly specified assignments.

Related to market discipline in job assignments is the leveraging of career competencies: applying existing skills, knowledge, and personal networks to new markets (as, for instance, in services and technology). It is critical that some proportion of the duties and responsibilities employees perform be in economic growth areas. This shifting in the mix of duties workers are accountable for is the responsibility of all parties who shape the employment relationship—management, union, and the worker. To structure tasks in another fashion mortgages the future to achieve today's short-term objectives. To be an employer of choice in a competitive labor market, firms must offer opportunities that develop future career options, inside and outside the firm. In the United States, a significant portion of the work force regularly reads Help Wanted ads, even when they are not actively looking for a new job (Rafaeli 1998). Keeping talented people requires assuaging their concerns that they will be less employable in the future by remaining with the firm today.

Consistent with the old notion of management by objectives, where some portion of the portfolio of goals was often developmental in nature, HR will increasingly need to include in the bundle of skill development and performance requirements tied to future growth opportunities. Building future competencies out of current assignments is critical to promoting the long-term career interests of employees. That is what 3M has traditionally done with its "15 percent rule" (expecting employees to bootleg 15 percent of their time to spend on new innovative endeavors) and "25 percent rule" (expecting to generate 25 percent of sales revenue each year from new rather than existing products).

The second feature of the new economy that is crucial to future employability is internalizing the external, or creating more opportunity for collaboration outside as well as inside the firm. Creating employee networks outside the firm (with others in the profession, clients, suppliers, and so forth) generates broader business knowledge among employees. Increasingly, "knowing who" (our relationships with others) is becoming as important as "knowing how" (our skills and knowledge). Moreover, it is "knowing who" that drives the new collaborative efforts increasingly sought from the contemporary work force. Such collaboration includes (1) cross-functional activities, whereby people with broad contacts throughout the firm become better informed and more credible; (2) boundary-spanning activities, whereby information and credibility flow between, say, a customer and a supplier; and (3) professional, occupational, and alumni networking, whereby people carry distinctive and specialized knowledge to and from the firm. At Cap Gemini, consultants working away from the office on client assignments for months at a time return periodically to the company offices to share learning and advice on technical problems and maintain personal ties to colleagues and Cap Gemini itself. Network ties are both private goods that people possess and public goods through which shared interests can be pursued.

In effect, people with "know how" and "know who" are much more likely to be truly employable by both their present and future employers.

Multiplex Commitments

Recent research on loyalty and attachment indicates two striking findings: (1) worker commitments to a variety of stakeholders are consistently positively intercorrelated, and (2) contingent workers (at least those who are in this job category voluntarily) typically manifest commitment levels at least as high as those of full-time employees. These findings affect how we conceptualize some traditional notions regarding worker attachments to firms. They suggest, first, that worker capacity to create and sustain commitments to stakeholders need not be fixed but can expand as work relationships increasingly involve multiple constituencies. They further suggest that full-time regular employment is not a necessary condition of high commitment to such organizational stakeholders as customers, clients, coworkers, or the firm itself.

Workers with Multiple Commitments

Loyalty and attachment traditionally have been examined as attributes of individual employees, particularly in terms of their willingness to remain with, and buy into the values of, the firm that employs them. A decade ago, the realization hit that such attachments were a two-way street, shaped by employer treatment of workers as well as by worker predispositions. This two-way street more recently has come to resemble a superhighway, with the influx of traffic on all sides creating networks of relations among workers, customers, employers, subcontractors, and labor intermediaries. Nonetheless, loyalty in terms of worker contributions toward high employer performance continues to be prized as a competitive advantage, even though there are a host of claimants on a worker's attachment.

One issue regarding attachment of workers to the organization relates to multiplex commitments for workers whose roles demand responsiveness to the needs and interests of multiple parties—the firm, clients and customers, work groups, and professional associations, for example. Not surprisingly, research indicates that high performers have strong commitments to multiple stakeholders. The knowledge economy, coupled with the value placed on responsiveness to internal and external customers, increases the contribution of worker attachments to a firm's success. Elsewhere in this book, Goodman and Wilson describe new forms of work groups, exogenous groups characterized as a function of their multiple external ties. Multiple commitments to a variety of constituents from external and internal customers to the team itself are endemic to effective exogenous work groups.

Multiplex commitments raise the question of how people manage potential conflicts among the demands of the firm, work group, clients, and their professions. Role conflict is an old concept in organizational research (Katz and Kahn 1965), but traditional organizational hierarchies were designed to minimize inherent contradictions and competing goals through functional or divisional forms. Even matrix organizations, structured to pit functional interests against the demands of specific projects or markets, tended to lean toward the priorities of one or the other (Galbraith 1977). Contemporary, highly interdependent work groups with both internal and external constituencies cannot rely on a chain of command, however, to buffer them from competing interests. How such groups will find synergies and manage conflicting interests among stakeholders depends to a great extent on common superordinate goals and the creation of relationships among constituencies. Recognition of the importance of these complex relationships and the potential for conflicts that arise as a natural part of interactions within and across them has led to the growth of new options and systems for dispute resolution in organizations, an issue Rowe and Bendersky explore in detail in this volume.

Research on dual as well as multiple commitments indicates a positive correlation among worker commitments to a variety of stakeholders. Thus, work-group commitment is positively related to organization-level commitment, as is profession and union commitment (Sturdevant Reed, Young, and McHugh 1994). Commitment as a form of emotional attachment and identification with the interests and values of various organizational constituents appears to be expansive, rather than constrained or limited. What limits there may be to this expansiveness are yet to be determined.

Firms with Different Attachments to Different Workers

The challenge for firms seeking high commitment from their core work force is to sustain it while hiring other workers with different employment agreements. The growth of contingent workers, contractors, and outsourcing creates challenges for internal equities in the firm. The U.S. labor market has always been marked by high turnover and many job changes for one large segment of workers (particularly women and minorities) and highly stable employment for another. This pattern has remained largely unchanged since the 1960s (Carnoy, Castells, and Benner 1996). What has changed is the face of the individuals in these differentiated roles. Where once white men had the stable jobs and women and minorities tended to occupy more transient positions, today's work force is more demographically diverse. With fewer obvious differences between the attributes of individuals in stable jobs and those in the more "flexible" ones, it is easier for people to compare themselves with each other and to identify inequities. Attachment to an employer by long-term employees appears to be eroded when they work alongside others whose status is avowedly contingent (Pearce 1993). Moving toward diversified employment arrangements under the same roof to promote flexibility appears to signal greater worker vulnerability to market pressures and increased managerial control over future employment (Carnoy, Castells, and Benner 1996: 57).

This tendency toward differentiation into flexible and stable employment arrangements is now replicating itself among employment agencies. The labor intermediaries to which firms outsource labor are party to a variety of different agreements with hiring firms. Many firms, in fact, are finding it advantageous to create long-term stable relations with the firms to which they outsource. In their research, Alison Davis-Blake and Joseph Broschak (2000) observe that many firms prefer temporary employment agencies that can provide them with the same temps over time, reflecting a preference for the greater familiarity and firm-specific knowledge that stability brings with the flexibility of only paying for the employee's time when needed.

Flexible Alternatives

Flexible work structuring, including new work-group arrangements and broader skill development, is a reaction to competitive pressures for both innovation and faster responsiveness to customer demands, as well as to demographic changes in the work force. Such changes alter the bases for employee relations with peers and supervisors. One major shift is in the basis of workplace trust—from familiarity and interpersonal relationships to reputation and established competencies. A consequence of the rising number of employees working part-time or on flexible and different schedules, including professionals and those with direct ties with customers, is the decline of interpersonal contact and informal relations at work. Part-timers often work through their lunch hours and breaks to get their tasks done while in the office, and many flex-timers do not come into the office at all (see Clark 1999).

There are four requirements to successful implementation of flexible structuring in the New Contract: (1) promoting widespread business knowledge among workers so that they can participate effectively in new forms of organizing, (2) creating social networks in which reputations for competence can be established, (3) broadening workers' skill base so that they can function effectively in flexible arrangements, and (4) encouraging the active involvement of workers in the design of such systems.

To actively participate in designing their own jobs, work structures, and career paths—a hallmark skill in more flexibly structured workplaces—individuals must be able to turn novel, ambiguous, challenging circumstances into a clear set of tasks and goals. Many of the traditional guides for action at work, such as job descriptions or direct supervisory contact, have broken down or been displaced by escalating and unpredictable job demands. The capacity to structure ambiguous situations to achieve what are likely to be multiple goals, from several stakeholders, is a critical requirement that traditional HR practices cannot address.

Active involvement requires a work force committed to the goals of the larger organization—a requirement difficult to achieve with a highly transient work force. Good indicators of active involvement are employment stability and continuity in client, customer, and supplier relations, allowing the firm to use this stability to create its own innovative and appropriate responses to market opportunities. A work force with a reservoir of knowledge about work systems, suppliers, and customers can deploy these to meet the firm's multiple and changing goals. In essence, a stability that can create flexible solutions is necessary to manage multiple, and potentially competing, goals successfully.

Flexible structuring between workers, particularly women, is also increasing because of worker demand. Other forms of flexible arrangements—including flexible scheduling or the use of part-timers, even in professional roles—are most evident in firms dependent on nontraditional work forces, particularly women with young children (Ingram and Simon 1995). Evidence to date suggests that such arrangements are provided by firms and, as Klein suggests in her chapter, by supervisors, idiosyncratically, when individual workers valued as high performers seek special arrangements (Clark 1999). It has long been true that the highest performers were best able to negotiate idiosyncratic deals, particularly with regard to flexibility in the time and place of work. Increasingly, this flexibility is being extended to a broader array of employees to help support family and life-style needs. Widespread adoption has been hampered by a variety of institutional factors, however, including HR policies regarding promotion and related career opportunities (consider, for example, constraints on the creation of part-time partners in law firms).

Flexibility as Instability

Charles Perrow (1996) has pointed out that the rise of corporations in the United States in the twentieth century and the mobility they spawned contributed to an erosion of civil society, the local community of family, and stable relations that provided child care, entertainment, and support in time of need. Many American firms took that support structure on as a means of ensuring a reliable committed work force, only to shed it at the end of the century. An America at Work Consulting survey indicates that commitment is highest to employers that recognize the importance of personal and family lives. Employer support for balancing work-related and non-work-related aspects of life predicts commitment better than the ability to buy stock, profit-sharing participation, or bonuses (see also Friedman, Christensen, and DeGroot 1998). An increasing proportion of the work force reports missing more work days due not to sickness but to stress or the need to provide for a child or an elderly parent. Firms once again are responding to this need for support as changes in the civil society, such as the decline in the number of nonworking mothers and in the availability of extended family-based child care, may to some extent be irreversible.

External Resources as a Condition of Flexibility

Just as employers now need greater flexibility to reallocate work and adjust their work force to rapidly changing or more uncertain conditions, employees need to have more resources available to support their more frequent moves across jobs and organizations (Leana and Rousseau 2000). Portable benefits (such as pensions, health insurance, and skill credentials) are important resources for this purpose. So are aspects of civil society that help build personal resources outside the firm to enhance both one's income security and the stability of the broader social and multi-firm community. These resources are not important just to the individuals involved. They also serve as critical contributions to the community and to employers toward rebuilding a strong civil society in a flexible work world. Building outside resources may directly assist the firm, as in the case of Bill Gates's stipulation to veteran Microsoft employees to take some of their money out of that company. By converting at least some of their Microsoft holdings into alternative investments or resources spent on the community, Microsoft employees can make decisions regarding Microsoft with less concern for risks to their personal wealth. More often, however, the returns to civil society accrue through the broader social infrastructure such an action creates, of closer ties between employees and their families, of stronger occupational and industry networks, and of cities and towns enriched by volunteer service. The interdependence among the needs of employees and their families, employers, and civil society is not well understood, however, and is not yet usually featured in the design of HR policies or the renegotiation of employment contracts. This too will need to change if the requirements of flexibility continue in the future.

Career development is increasingly cyclical rather than linear, as it was assumed to be in earlier models of the career-development process. More rapid career changes are related to new notions of what success is (what Phil Mirvis and Tim Hall [1996] refer to as "new forms of psychological success"). Family responsibilities and the desire for personal development are promoting labor-force participation patterns for both women and a small but growing number of men that correspond to the traditional pattern for women at work: entering, exiting, and re-entering (sometimes many times). This "feminization" of work, described by Nanette Fondas (1996), involves both down-shifting (temporarily exiting) and up-shifting (temporarily increasing) work commitments. Similarly, phased retirement, common in Europe, retains contributions of valuable employees and promotes social identity attached to both work and family. Firms that promote civility as a collective response to changing circumstances will foster a more committed work force and a healthier societal environment by strengthening the civil society. How this civility can be better managed is a major challenge for the HR function in the contemporary firm.

A Final Note on the Meaning of Flexibility

U.S. employment statistics suggest some surprising trends. Though many construe contingent employment to mean instability, if we focus on the amount of time workers spend in a particular job with an employer, evidence suggests that over half of all part-time workers age twenty-five and older had 3.9 or more years of tenure with their current firm (from 1987 data cited in Carnoy, Castells and Benner [1996]). Carnoy and his colleagues suggest that rather than use "full-time contract" as the main definition of a worker who is "attached" to an employer, the main criterion of attachment should perhaps be time spent working with the employer, no matter what the legal status of the relationship. Many American firms swayed by legal counsel and fearing litigation prefer to say that there is no commitment or regular contract, even while they act as if there is. Consider, for example, the case of moral tenure in universities for adjuncts and non-tenure-track faculty members. Adjunct faculty actually tend to have relatively stable, enduring arrangements with the universities that employ them. Levesque and Rousseau (1999) report high commitment among adjunct faculty, particularly those with regular contact with full-time members and those included in the university's social activities.

Institutional Challenges

> We live, then, in a period of rapid transition from one type or structure of society to another.
>
> James Burnham (1941:9)

Notice the year on the quote. If James Burnham, a critic of the "managerial revolution" in modern organizations, saw drastic societal changes in 1941, it is probably a fair statement that "drastic" change is getting to be commonplace. The changes in employment I describe in this chapter create serious strains for both HR and IR as the institutions traditionally focused on solving employment-related problems. We address three basic challenges these institutions face from shifts in the meaning of fundamental employment concepts.

Human Capital and the Commons Problem

Highly skilled workers are a key ingredient to the economic success of firms and society. Firms characterized by an active HR function have accessed and retained workers at higher levels of skill than those typically available on the external market. Moreover, unionism has historically been associated with higher skill levels when unionized firms are compared with nonunionized firms in the same industry (Kelley 1996). The most competitive firms typically have been those that provide their own training and development, thereby improving upon skill levels in the existing labor market. Rival firms can do considerable damage to an employer via poaching, however. This long-standing problem continues to act as a disincentive for individual firms to invest in training. When significant numbers of employees are hired away, cognitive and emotional ties linking members to the firm, its external stakeholders (customers and suppliers), and each other can be eroded (Coff and Rousseau 2000). Moreover, where external networks play a larger role in generating the firm's capability than do internal factors, a rival might gain access to the firm's external ties by luring key employees away. Unlike internal connections between people and the firm, the external contacts might yield valuable industry information that applies to the rival as well as the local firm. The employee might even be able to coax customers to follow him or her to the rival.

The irony is that the unfreezing of worker-firm attachments, through down-sizing and increased mobility, has altered the incentive structure for human capital investments. The ability of firms to access appropriately skilled workers is affected by both the extent of competition from other firms and societal supports for the education and training of the work force. In many respects, the United States is a leader in access to education, particularly for potential new entrants (sixteen to nineteen years old) into the work force. Serious shortages in appropriately trained workers from traditional educational institutions, however, have placed a premium on experience gained within firms. Labor mobility, combined with widespread poaching by firms that do not train, has created a perceived disincentive for training on the part of many firms. Harry Van Buren (2000) refers to this dilemma as a "commons" problem, in which employer self-interest brings about collective disaster in the labor market.

Overcoming the commons problem may require collaboration among employers to support educational institutions and training and development activities. One example of such a collaboration is an arrangement under which San Francisco hotels have contracted with the local union to form a training consortium to develop the skills of union members who work in any or all of the ten hotels participating. Since movement of the work force tends to be among these hotels, training investments are recaptured. Successful investments in training and development require employer involvement in both the development and the support of training activities to ensure that learning is targeted to the workplace. Institutionally, it is important that the HR function engage in community-building activities to promote a commons of available workers with appropriate skills from which employers can draw. Maintaining alumni relations with former employees can also address the commons problem by creating new ways to access resources. By creating goodwill and ongoing relations with former employees, firms expand their resource opportunities in the form of potential future clients, job referrals, and the potential for rehiring talented, well-trained people who know the organization. Alumni relations are indicative of richer ties between firms and the work force through relationship building (impacting both workers' decisions to leave and where they choose to go).

Blurring the Boundaries between Workers and Owners of Capital

Regardless of organizational rank (blue-collar worker, white-collar professional, executive, or independent contractor), workers are increasingly aware of the functioning of economic markets and their effects both on their firms and on them individually. The conflicts of interest characterizing owners and labor from the industrial revolution to the mid-twentieth century have been transformed to some extent in many American firms, both union and nonunion, by a shift toward employment relations based on trust and partnership. This partnership can entail greater sharing of financial information with workers ("open-book management"), which makes external market issues more salient to employees than was traditionally the case (Rousseau 2000). Partnership and shared information reinforce the individualistic value that persons are equal, as well as the community-oriented message that labor, management, and owners are in the same boat and have interests in common.

Concomitantly, greater risk sharing between workers and owners is evident in the shift of fixed wages (salary) to variable compensation (incentives tied to firm performance: Rynes and Gephart 2000). As a result, entrants to the U.S. labor market are more likely to expect an equity stake in the firm or profit sharing. This effect has also been observed in workers who have been laid off because of down-sizing and then hired by subsequent employers. Having paid the price for one firm's response to a competitive marketplace, re-hired workers report that more of their pay is contingent on the firm's performance, and they expect to be compensated if the firm does well, though not necessarily with job security (Fogarty and Rousseau 1999). These forces coupled with another feature of U.S. institutions, the relatively weak retirement support from the government-maintained Social Security system, have led increasingly to workers' participation in the stock market and familiarity with financial issues. The general public, and specifically workers, have become more aware of economic markets in the past decade. Declining voter perception since the 1980s regarding the government's power to influence markets in an increasingly global economy (Castells 1997), and the shift away from New Deal policies formulated under U.S. President Franklin Roosevelt and toward private markets during the Reagan era, have altered wage profiles and made the market a more salient force in wage determination than either collectively negotiated contracts or wage norms. Stock ownership by employees is another relevant trend (Parus 1998).

In the future, further fundamental shifts in U.S. employment may be fueled by a blurry boundary between owners and laborers created by access to capital markets. Despite an acrimonious labor history, particularly from the nineteenth century until just prior to World War II, the distinction between labor and management has been reduced by higher education among workers, the rise of white-collar professionals, the service economy, and demographic changes. The social gap between management and labor has also been reduced somewhat through more participative management based on trust and mutual self-interest (Miles and Creed

1995). (The social separation of owners and workers characteristic of France and Germany applies somewhat less in the United States where social boundaries are relatively loose to begin with.) Growth of both pension funds and the aging population means that more Americans identify with the value of their asset holdings, worry about inflationary consequences of higher wages, and side with the financial sector in its drive for higher profit margins. In addition, ease of access to capital markets afforded by public stock trading and customer service–oriented investment houses have helped make stock market participation more commonplace.

Labor-management relations for the last one hundred years display a trend toward increased trust and reduced social distance between workers and managers, which has contributed to economic growth both for U.S. firms and for the U.S. economy as a whole. Thus, although divergent terms in the employment agreement are expected for workers and managers, greater similarity in the psychological aspects of employment relationships (that is, greater convergence among individual psychological contracts) across (fewer) organizational levels are expected in those firms shifting toward cooperation and mutuality. Yet the psychological features of employment have outpaced changes in institutions governing work. The laws governing employment relations continue to try to draw a clear distinction between "exempt" and "nonexempt" employees, or between "workers" and "supervisors and managers." Unions continue to rely on distrust and deep dissatisfaction with employers as the basis for justifying their existence and organizing new members. Wage and benefit gaps between highly valued "knowledge" workers and others have increased rather than declined. All these features will require change if the institutions and the HR policies and practices governing employment are to adapt to the changing nature of work and the psychological contracts these changes are producing.

Unions, Professional Associations, and "Relational Wealth"

New models for unions and professional associations follow from the issues raised with the work-force changes discussed here. The traditional credentialling and bargaining roles unions play have weakened in the face of shifting work and labor-force demographics (Kochan, Katz, and McKersie 1986). The somewhat blurring boundary between labor and owners in terms of both social stratification and broader worker participation in capital markets further challenges the social assumptions on which trade unionism has been based. Nonetheless, there is a critical role unions and other professional associations may elect to play. Workers need ongoing skill development, networks for reputation, and professional contacts outside the firm, regardless of whether they are employed by "good" or "bad" employers. Relying on dissatisfaction or distrust at work is not, therefore, an adequate basis for unions' responding to the needs of contemporary workers in flexible work settings. For professionals, occupation-based associations have long played such roles (consider, for example, the American Accounting Association and American Psychological Association). For nonprofessionals, the importance of ongoing development and professional contacts suggests new functions for unions as occupation-based associations, a change that can be thought of in terms of "relational wealth." Both workers and firms in the new economy rely increasingly on mechanisms for creating and disseminating occupational skills and reputation ("knowing who knows how"). Where unions focus more on skill development in the solution to the commons problem, as in the case of the hotel unions described earlier, their role is transformed to being a labor intermediary leveraging both their ties to labor and their expertise in training and development.

Human Resource Management as a Positive Bureaucracy

Bureaucracy is a word with a bad rap. Colloquially, we use it to refer to "red tape" and senseless rules. In its original usage, however, it referred to consistent and fair management of organizational procedures, where *competence* (not favorites or politics) was the central theme. Just as the role of unions and IR must change in the new economy, so too must HR management. Historically, the role of HR has had to adapt as the nature of employment relationships changes. In the early years of the twentieth century, personnel departments were largely paperwork offices, handling payroll, recruitment, and record-keeping duties. Later, as unions grew, the IR functions of these departments rose in importance and power. In recent decades, as unions declined and line executives challenged HR professionals to add value to their operations, HR executives have sought to become "strategic partners" to management in running the business and matching employment practices to business needs. This evolution continues. HR has important roles to play in managing the multiplex of contemporary employment relations, setting norms for guest workers operating on site, and protecting the firm's reputation in a competitive labor market. It is also a potential investment center, where competitive advantage is built for the firm through training, retaining intact work groups whose special knowl-

edge provides the firm with distinctive competencies, and building relations with labor intermediaries to provide appropriately skilled contingent
workers to supplement the firm's core workers. In effect, HR will need to
shift from being an internally focused staff unit to being a key player in the
management of the firm's boundaries with its environment. Making this
shift will require, in turn, a major change in the rhetoric and the ideology
that have dominated the HR profession for the past two decades. Instead
of merely stressing the need to become strategic partners with top executives and line managers internally and to protect the firm from union organizing, government regulations, or industry and community responsibilities, HR professionals once again will need to take on a more external
alliance—bringing perspective to their jobs and their professional responsibilities (Rousseau and Arthur 1999).

Conclusion

The changes in the psychological and explicit terms of employment contracts described here provide a foundation for the discussions that follow
in this book. They create pressures for change in the roles and behaviors of
supervisors, HR and IR professionals, unions and associations, and community and other civil institutions, and ultimately in the public policies
that govern workplace relations. Managing these changes effectively will
tax all the skills and tools of negotiations available to the individuals,
groups, and organizations they affect.

Not surprisingly, there is little consensus on the future of HR management and IR. Yet, as the saying goes, we need solutions as complex as the
problems they would solve. The new meanings for old concepts and the
new roles for traditional institutions described here are intended to add to
the debate among workers, managers, and scholars who search for insights, practices, and theory to make this complexity both accessible and
friendly.

4

Changing Relations between Supervisors and Employees

From Deal Making to Strategic Negotiations

JANICE A. KLEIN

First-line supervisors live in a world of continuous negotiations. They have to make instantaneous choices that impact both short- and long-term performances of their work group and of the organization as a whole. Most scholars, even those who recognize situational leadership (see Yukl 1989 for a summary of the various leadership theories), have taken a relatively static view of the role. In reality, however, the supervisory role is a series of strategic negotiations. First-line supervisors are expected to manage the daily fire fighting associated with meeting production requirements while developing their team in line with long-term strategic change.[1] They are asked to play multiple roles in an ever changing environment and are faced with a series of tensions, such as empowering versus monitoring performance and coaching versus disciplining.

Many supervisors approach their job as a series of trade-offs rather than as an opportunity to build future capabilities. Under such an approach, they are pulled in multiple, competing directions and end up focusing on either the short or the long term without considering how each of their actions impacts the other. This pattern leads to dysfunctional behaviors that

I thank the participants of the 1998 Negotiated Change Institute Workshop for helping to test the concept of strategic negotiations as it applies to first-line supervisors; Todd Huston and Dan Klein for their comments and suggestions; and especially Joel Cutcher-Gershenfeld, for his encouragement, guidance, and input in the development of this paper.
[1] This chapter focuses primarily on the changing role of first-line supervisors in large organizations attempting to introduce some form of employee empowerment. The argument, however, also applies to traditional organizations that have chosen not to move toward greater involvement of the work force. Even in those cases, supervisors typically strive to build camaraderie within their work groups.

54

create strained workplace relations and disenchantment with the supervisory role. As a result, the first-line supervisor has come to be seen as the culprit of everything that goes wrong at the workplace, making it harder and harder to find people willing to fill supervisory openings. The personal toll for those currently holding the position has also been extremely high. Many supervisors either burn out and leave, abdicate their role, or merely put in their time hoping they can wait out the latest management fad.

The role of the supervisor has always been seen as problematic because it is in the middle between labor and management. Today, however, both the importance and the difficulty associated with the role have increased dramatically. Today's tension comes not only from being in the middle of the hierarchical structure but also from almost minute-by-minute role shifts. The first-line supervisor therefore must be viewed as having multiple, concurrent, interdependent roles, some aimed at nurturing team development while others require forcing organizational objectives on unwilling stakeholders.

To better explain this role, I utilize a strategic negotiations framework laid out by Walton, Cutcher-Gershenfeld, and McKersie (1994). In this framework, choices that supervisors make in how they enact their roles are seen as more than just tactical moves—they are seen as strategic choices with significant long-term implications. In many respects, this is similar to the challenges executives and union leaders face in managing changes in large systems. Thus, examining the challenges associated with strategic negotiations and assessing how they apply in the case of the first-line supervisor have broad implications.

I begin by looking historically at the first-line supervisory role. Then I discuss the challenges of leading strategic negotiations at the workplace level, to help supervisors, as well as their managers and team members, better understand the tensions they are facing. Too many supervisors and senior managers see their role in terms of either short-term control or long-term team building and fail to attend fully to the tensions and interdependencies between these two critical activities.

Historical Look

Over the years, there have been waves of research on the changing role of first-line supervisors. Frederick Taylor (1911) highlighted the role in his description of scientific management, which began the diminution of the traditional supervisory power base. Under his "functional foremanship," the supervisory role was divided into eight jobs, many resembling the functional staff groups that exist in today's organizations—manufacturing, engineering, maintenance, accounting, human resources, and so forth. The traditional supervisory duties were carved up and dispersed to various support groups, leaving supervisors with only the day-to-day administration of workplace activities. Each of the support groups then built up their own rules and regulations, further narrowing the discretion of first-line supervisors.

In the 1940s, the rise of the Foremen's Association of America (FAA) highlighted the difficulties facing supervisors and their concerns about their loss of stature and power. The Taft-Harley Act, which was passed in 1947, rubbed further salt into their wounds, excluding supervisors from the definition of "employee" for the purposes of collective bargaining.[2] In essence, this act left them in no-man's-land between management and labor and led to a series of articles referring to the supervisor as the man in the middle (see, for example, Gardner and Whyte 1945).[3] As Wray (1949: 301) stated,

> In short, the position of foreman has some of the characteristics of management positions but lacks other crucial ones. Such marginal positions are common in society, and there is reason to believe that they are especially difficult to occupy effectively and with peace of mind. With respect to management, the foreman's position is peripheral rather than in the middle. The poor fellow is in the middle, of course, in the sense that a person may be the middle one of three in a bed; he gets it from both sides!

Throughout the 1950s supervisory issues received a great deal of attention as organizations attempted to improve the role through better selection procedures and training programs. Academic interest in the role subsided over the next decade, however, as attention shifted to the emerging field of organizational development.

The next major attack on the role came in the 1970s with the introduction of self-directed work teams and the belief that the role could be eliminated. The decision to eliminate supervisors was both philosophic (employees are adults and can manage themselves) and economic (supervisors comprise a large percentage of costly overhead salaries). Even where supervisors were not totally eliminated, spans of control increased significantly, with many supervisors managing multiple teams, often across sev-

[2] This applies solely to the private sector within the United States. Throughout most of the world and within the U.S. public sector, supervisors have collective bargaining rights.
[3] At that point in time, gender-specific language was used although women occasionally held first-line supervisory roles.

eral shifts. Lawler (1986: 105) wrote, "As teams mature and develop, the leader's role changes. It becomes more that of facilitator and communication link. It is often apparent at this point that team leaders can work with multiple teams."

After companies attempted to eliminate or reduce the number of supervisors, it became apparent that a viable role for supervisors still existed but that it was evolving as organizations moved from a control to a commitment philosophy (Walton 1985). Articles and books in the 1980s and early 1990s emphasized that first-line supervisors needed to shift to being team coaches, advisors, and facilitators (see, for example, Schlesinger 1982; Manz and Sims 1993). The transition has been painful, however, and the struggle has continued through the 1990s. Although teams often perform well without supervisors for the first few months as team members become energized by their new-found freedom, issues soon arise that require the knowledge or authority of first-line supervisors or managers. Thus, supervisors must be able to gauge when their teams are capable of taking on greater responsibility and when they themselves must step in and perform traditional supervisory activities. As Hackman and Oldham (1980: 212) aptly noted in describing the supervisory challenge, "The process will have more in common with shooing chickens across the barnyard than with planting regular rows of corn in a freshly plowed, rectangular field."

Traditional Supervisory Power Bases

When one thinks of the supervisory role, two extremes typically come to mind: the authoritarian boss and the participative consensus builder. Although many scholars paint the role as if it were in transition from one extreme to the other on the road to empowerment, it really is a continuum that supervisors span on a daily basis. Empowerment requires leadership. Furthermore, a part of building trust is making hard decisions, such as administering discipline (Handy 1995: 46): "Trust is tough. The reality is, however, that even the best recruiter and the best judges of character will get it wrong sometimes. When trust proves to be misplaced—then those people have to go. Where you cannot trust, you have to become a checker once more, with all the systems of control that involves." In addition, current competitive pressures often require traditional control behaviors in forcing issues that are not palatable to all team members (reduced resources and lay-offs, for example). To understand the seesaw that supervisors face, it is instructive to look at each extreme.

The traditional control supervisor uses positional power to force employees into compliance through the use of threats of retaliation. In reality, though, many supervisors in traditional organizations often have limited authority to carry out those threats because the power base for disciplinary decisions ultimately rests outside their purview, in the labor relations office. As a result, the best they can do is make life either pleasant or miserable at the workplace. The primary vehicle for doing this has traditionally been deal making (Gardner and Whyte 1945; Schlesinger and Klein 1987). For example, supervisors might reward an employee who has put in extra effort to meet a production crunch with a plum job. Or, rather than going through all the bureaucratic paperwork of discipline procedures, a supervisor might assign a recalcitrant employee to a "bum" task.

The term *deal making* often brings to mind illicit behavior between bookies and horse traders. But in its purest form, it is merely an exchange made by two individuals who hold commodities (both tangible and intangible) that the other desires. Although we may not label it as such, deal making is part of our everyday life, beginning with interactions between parents and children ("Clean up your room and you can stay up and watch TV"). On a management level, deal making involves the exchange of a behavior by one individual for some sort of behavior or reward by another. The problem with many of the traditional supervisory deals is that they are often arranged under the table as a way to bypass bureaucratic policies and procedures. In addition, deal making can be perceived as favoritism toward one employee over another. Thus, it is officially discouraged, although it continues to be the prime source of traditional supervisory power.

The other extreme of the supervisory continuum is the team coach or advisor whose role is merely to facilitate team development and effective team-member interaction. In its purest form, this supervisor has minimal, if any, positional power. The assumption is that the work system can be designed in a manner that leads to employees' commitment to the work and self-management of their day-to-day activities (Hackman and Oldham 1980; Pasmore and Sherwood 1978). The role of the supervisor under this view is to motivate employees through fostering commitment to shared goals. Scholars promoting this end of the continuum typically recognize that work teams still need some leadership, but their general belief is that traditional supervisory tasks will be eliminated as teams become self-sufficient.

Experience has shown that few teams mature to the level of self-management, however, due to a myriad of factors, including individual team-member preferences and capabilities, technological constraints, and economic conditions that lead to changes in the composition of the team. In addition, many organizations that have moved toward empowerment are now reversing their course. Hence, since most teams are somewhere on the road to or from self-management, the role of the first-line supervisor must constantly adjust to the current organizational context (company values, management philosophy, and technology).

Despite these trends, many scholars continue to look at the role as in transition. Since the transition has been going on for decades, however, it seems more likely that supervisors may actually have to live along the entire continuum and to learn to apply traditional supervisory tactics when necessary in concert with their new team-leader responsibilities.

Viewing the Role through a Negotiations Lens

Viewing the first-line supervisory role through a negotiations lens reveals that supervisors are caught in a classic struggle between distributed and integrative bargaining (Walton and McKersie 1965). The empowerment movement has encouraged fostering team development as supervisors are taught to delegate their responsibilities and act solely as coaches or facilitators. At the same time, though, supervisors are expected to discipline employees using traditional industrial relations procedures, which often turn into hard forcing negotiations. Few supervisors are skilled at managing the tensions and challenges of moving between the two roles. Most view them as merely contradictory rather than as building any long-term capability. Without thinking about the long-term consequences, most supervisors typically deal with each situation on a tactical basis. Skillful supervisors, however, think two steps ahead and consider the interdependencies between the actions. They recognize that each action may solicit a counteraction by their employees, and they develop alternative or contingency plans to address various situations.

As entities strive to become high-performance work organizations, they are asking supervisors to act more like strategic thinkers and change agents. One of the main difficulties facing first-line supervisors, however, is their limited ability to control their own destiny. Since first-line supervisors are part of a larger system of embedded negotiations, that system directly impacts their ability to manage their environment. It is rare that all organizational policies and practices are totally aligned with company and senior leadership vision as organizations enter large-systems change processes. Furthermore, senior management may be well intentioned in driving strategic change, but middle management and all the supporting functional groups may lag behind in their thinking. If so, mixed messages are sent to the workplace, and first-line supervisors are left to make the final translation to the work force. Since many were mentored by previous generations of leadership, however, their skills and personal managerial philosophies may also run counter to their organization's current strategic direction. To aggravate the situation, many supervisors are the last to be trained and are often left out of the communications loop. All too often, they hear of changes from their employees, a situation that further undermines their authority.

In the past scholars have talked about supervisors being caught in the middle between managers and employees. That continues today, but the more problematic struggle is being caught between multiple roles and having limited control over managing the levers that smooth the transition between fostering team development and forcing hard decisions. For example, supervisors are often caught in short-term local conflicts that limit their ability to look strategically. Administrative processes and procedures at hand also drive them to force decisions that undermine team cohesion. Similarly, when developing their team, they are unable to deal with larger systemic issues, which forces them to focus solely on internal team dynamics. In the long run, this can lead to external system-wide problems undermining team-member attitudes.

As Cutcher-Gershenfeld, McKersie, and Walton (1996: 39–40) noted, managing the tension between fostering relationships and forcing initiatives can be quite difficult:

> The essence of strategy involves anticipating the future consequences of present actions. In the case of fundamental change, forcing strategies need to be sufficiently restrained to anticipate and support recovery after the forcing initiative. Similarly, fostering strategies need to be sufficiently robust to anticipate and address inevitable conflicts that follow and may even result from the fostering. The ideas seem simple, but the many challenges that arise in the contest of forcing and fostering make the effective implementation of either change strategy exceptionally difficult.

Although supervisors are in more of a tactical as opposed to a strategic role, the same tensions exist in their daily activities as they concurrently confront forcing and fostering issues. Unfortunately, most supervisory training focuses on either fostering or forcing but not the interdependencies between the two roles. Hence, one way to better understand the task facing first-line supervisors is through exploring how the key challenges in concurrently forcing and fostering issues apply to them. Table 4.1 pro-

Table 4.1. Strategic Negotiations Challenges

Fostering	*Forcing*
Building relationships	Picking battles
Constructing internal consensus	Maintaining resolve
Generating results	Underestimating counter-forcing
Maintaining continuity	Keeping the forcing under control
Anticipating conflicts	Recovery afterward

Source: Cutcher-Gershenfeld, McKersie, and Walton 1996.

vides a summary of these challenges. As will be seen, supervisors are in a pivotal position to possess critical knowledge to manage these challenges, but that knowledge is often not tapped. Furthermore, supervisors typically lack the authority or clout to utilize that knowledge outside their immediate work group.

Challenges in Fostering Team Development

The role of team leader or coach is primarily a fostering position of facilitating collaborative problem-solving processes. Many supervisors find the fine line between abdicating power and fostering team development to be extremely difficult to walk, however. They recognize that conflicts are bound to arise but often assume that their hands are tied because they were instructed to let the teams work out the problems. There are times when they are also tempted to let the conflicts fester so that management will finally recognize that supervisors are needed. As a result, they abdicate their authority. Unfortunately, even those supervisors who skillfully foster team development can look like "marshmallow managers." As Fisher (1993: 158–59, 161) notes,

> If we watch effective team leaders work, it is easy to come away with the misconception that this is a passive activity. Commitment-eliciting managers delegate a lot. They sometimes refuse to get involved in certain "management-type" decisions that they believe belong to the team. It may appear like gutless acquiescence or responsibility dodging to the casual observer. In fact to some observers these team leaders look like marshmallows—soft, squashy, and indecisive. . . . Effective team leaders are just as strong and passionate and bullheaded as traditional supervisors. But they demonstrate their strength in fundamentally different ways.

The concept of strategic negotiations provides supervisors with a framework for this new team-leader role, which recognizes the need to force some issues to achieve effective team-based operations. One of the key lessons is to establish an environment in which teams understand that supervisors will and should force some issues. As summarized in Table 4.1, there are five key challenges in doing this.

Building Relationships

Building relationships based on mutual trust and respect within the team is something that every good supervisor attempts to do. Included in the trust between supervisors and their team members is an expectation that supervisors will stand up for what is right for their team and not be walked over by any individual, whether a team member or an individual external to the team. This, in turn, typically requires some sort of forcing. The traditional control supervisor often did this through deal making, but the relationships were on a one-on-one versus a team basis and the commitment was typically toward the individual, not toward organizational goals. The role of the team leader or coach is focused more on building internal relationships between team members and between the team and support functions or other boundary roles (Ancona and Caldwell 1992). The challenge is to help team members learn to handle conflicts that will arise and develop a clear understanding as to why and where supervisors may have to step in and force a decision. They must also understand that when this occurs, it is not necessarily a breach of trust. Building and maintaining a long-term relationship in an environment focused on short-term economic pressures is often problematic, however. Since trust is based on reducing vulnerability, uncertainty, and risk (Meyerson, Weick, and Kramer 1996), every reorganization or reduction in the size of the work force undermines the relationships supervisors have built.

Constructing Internal Consensus

One of the primary roles for team development is creating a shared vision and building commitment to the team's goals and objectives. Good supervisors recognize the needs of individual team members and help their teams generate internal cohesion. They also help their team members understand the linkage between the team's goals and the larger organizational objectives through sharing information and educating team members as to business realities. Such an understanding helps to minimize the disruption caused by changing competitive priorities that lead to turnover within the team or in groups supporting the team, but each time this occurs, the task of building internal consensus must begin again. Many successful supervisors view change as an opportunity to realign their team members to the team's objectives. The degree to which they are able to sustain this internal consensus over the long haul, though, is dependent on the alignment of the team's internal consensus with the larger organizational culture and company vision (Schein 1992; Collins and Porras 1994).

Generating Results

Creating a high-commitment work environment takes time and rarely generates short-term results. In many cases, the training and team-building sessions add costs on a short-term basis, making it even more difficult to generate short-term performance gains. At the same time, employees are looking for "what's in it for me" and often demand additional compensation in exchange for additional team duties. Supervisors typically have limited ability, other than personal persuasion, to encourage their team members to generate enhanced performance. The deal-making opportunities supervisors often relied on as a means of rewarding employees in the past are evaporating, as teams take on greater and greater responsibility for daily tasks (Klein 1984). The task of job assignments, for example, is now typically delegated to teams, thus eliminating a powerful chit once held by supervisors. Even where innovative reward systems have been implemented to ensure that all parties are fairly recognized and compensated, many employees still see unfair distribution of gains, leaving supervisors to explain why market realities reward senior managers with executive bonuses and stock options.

Maintaining Continuity

A major challenge lies in managing leadership turnover and not reverting to old habits. Unfortunately, though, the human tendency is to revert to what is comfortable in the face of a crisis. As a result, supervisors schooled under traditional control mechanisms often find it difficult to stay the course and work at fostering relationships while solving periodic crises. The immediate pressures of daily fire fighting also often require supervisors to take swift actions, a move that can be interpreted as traditional supervisory control. Supervisors must be careful to minimize such occurrences and must find the time to explain their actions so that they are not viewed as reverting back to old behaviors. In addition, since supervisors have no control over turnover of middle or senior leadership, the supervisory challenge is in managing the transitions and buffering their work groups from changes in management philosophy or direction. Even maintaining continuity over their own actions can become difficult, though, with constantly changing signals and priorities from above.

Anticipating Conflicts

Even in the most progressive team-based operations, conflicts that require traditional supervisory control do occur. At a team level, personality conflicts between team members or poor performance may require supervisory intervention. At a larger system level, organizational initiatives often create conflict at the workplace. The introduction of lean manufacturing practices and standardized work methods, for example, restricts team-member behavior and can run counter to attempts to build autonomy within self-managing teams (Klein 1991). Supervisors are usually the first to recognize these unforeseen complications. They are in an ideal position to highlight hot spots for senior leadership before issues develop, but their input is seldom solicited in the design and implementation of new strategic initiatives. Furthermore, supervisors are closest to the work force and can recognize situations in which coalitions may be forming that might require a forcing response.

Considering these five challenges makes it clear that the task of fostering team development is complicated by (1) individual supervisory actions (such as avoiding the temptation to revert to traditional control behaviors), (2) team-member concerns (such as increased work-force diversity leading to a broader array of employee needs), and (3) organizational forces (such as management decisions and actions that influence team development). This begins to explain why the transition to the team coach or advisor role has been so problematic. We now turn to the challenges of forcing issues and will once again find that individual supervisory actions, team-member concerns, and organizational forces influence supervisory attempts to restrain forcing behaviors.

Challenges in Forcing Issues

Supervisors find themselves having to force issues on both a tactical and a strategic basis. Daily, supervisors must deal with disciplinary or performance issues that require traditional supervisory control tactics. At a strategic or system level, issues are often forced by senior leadership, and supervisors are left with no alternative other than to implement any changes that stem from those decisions. Supervisors have many choices, on the other hand, in how they deliver messages and force issues within the purview of their work group.

Forcing issues may appear to be relatively straightforward for traditional control supervisors, but few supervisors enjoy the role of forcing issues counter to the wishes of their employees. In addition, forcing is particularly problematic when it has detrimental ramifications on their efforts to build an effective team. In this regard, Cutcher-Gershenfeld, McKersie, and Walton (1996) identified five key challenges in taking a forcing stance on issues.

Picking Battles

One might argue that deal making is the ultimate example of picking battles. Supervisors have traditionally chosen when to cut a deal and when to use formal channels of discipline. The challenge is to make the choice in a manner that builds long-term capability and does not undermine team development. Another critical factor to consider is the perceived fairness of the battle. In other words, is it a battle the work force views as appropriate in handling the situation, whether it is a problem employee or a response to a competitive threat? In cases where the battles have already been picked by middle or senior management, supervisors have little choice as to whether they will wage the battle, but, as noted already, they typically have a fair amount of discretion in how they package or frame the message. As such, the perceived fairness is dependent on how well the supervisor has prepared the team for the forcing and the degree to which the supervisor has considered all its ramifications, including the impact on the well-being of individual team members and the relationships between team members.

Maintaining Resolve

When it comes to maintaining resolve (holding firm to core underlying interests) and speaking with one voice, individual supervisors can ensure that their own actions are consistent, but they are often left to explain mixed messages being sent throughout the organization. Good supervisors typically act as a buffer between multiple constituencies and are skilled at translating multiple initiatives into a common theme to minimize the disruption of program-of-the-month slogans. They have a long-term vision of how they want to develop their team, and they anticipate potential derangements so that they are not surprised by disruptions, either internal or external to their team. Thus, they avoid being whipsawed by continually changing priorities and ensure that their own commitments can be carried out despite those changes.

Underestimating Counter-forcing

Supervisors are in a pivotal position to predict and recognize the potential for bottom-up counter-forcing and can typically identify the source and degree of force that is likely to occur. Their key challenges on this front are twofold. First, they need to step back from the daily fire fighting to see where the counter-forcing may be developing. All too often, supervisors are caught up in reactive behaviors. They lose sight of the long-term objective and are interested only in solving immediate problems, regardless of how those fixes might impact the long-term development of their team. Second, they need to find an appropriate audience to hear their input on where the counter-forcing may occur outside the purview of their work group. Even if the counter-forcing is within their own team, the root cause for the behavior may lie in a larger system issue.

Keeping the Forcing under Control

Aside from coalition building, supervisors often have little influence over third parties or over when senior or middle management decides to escalate a crisis. Their primary task is to buffer any negative team effects from higher-level forcing. On a local basis, supervisors also need to avoid responding to counter-forcing in any way that might escalate the battle even further. This requires keeping their emotions intact and letting personal affronts roll off their backs. Once again, contingency planning helps. Successful supervisors have developed norms within their team so that team members do no overreact to situations and openly discuss concerns before they escalate to all-out battles.

Recovery Afterward

Supervisors see firsthand the cumulative effect of both local and system-wide forcing actions. They are typically left with the task of trying to re-establish constructive relations after forcing has occurred. Strategic-thinking supervisors provide as much advance warning as possible to their team members to cushion the forcing. In this regard, recovery is highly dependent on the extent to which there are clear and accepted expectations that forcing will occur at times. Hence, all ten challenges of fostering team development and forcing issues are tightly coupled. Successful recovery from forcing is a direct result of effective conflict anticipation, and vice versa.

Once supervisors understand that team development and forcing issues can coexist and can actually enhance the outcome of both, they can learn to predict the consequences of their own actions. The more problematic forcing is that which is forced on them and comes from outside the supervisory purview. For that, they can only restrain the delivery process in a way that facilitates recovery once the forcing has occurred.

Implications

Rather than looking for ways to eliminate a problematic role, organizations should be investigating ways to make the supervisory role more palatable and effective. It is time to be up-front with supervisors and admit that their role is multifaceted. Their primary role is to foster team development continually through leadership, training, and facilitation. At times, however, they are also expected to take hard actions to improve individual and team performance. When doing so, they need to think about how their actions impact overall team development. In both roles, their objective is to build mutual respect and trust between management and labor and among team members within their team.

Because the role of first-line supervisors is a continual give-and-take between forcing and fostering, supervisors need assistance in learning how to move between the two strategies. The competencies required to manage concurrent strategies are seldom part of the criteria for selecting supervisors. Depending on their organization's management philosophy, current supervisors are most likely selected to be either a traditional control boss or a team facilitator, not both. Similarly, most training programs focus on one end of the continuum or the other, not the interaction between the two. This analysis shows that organizations should incorporate negotiations training into their management and supervisory development programs.

One might argue that the ability to manage the forcing and fostering challenges requires a level of sophisticated abstract thinking only acquired through advanced education. Granted, undergraduate and graduate-level training no doubt helps individuals grasp the subtleties associated with switching back and forth between forcing and fostering. Unfortunately though, most college graduates will not stay in a supervisory role. They view it as a brief stepping stone in their career development. Furthermore, many successful supervisors and shop-floor union stewards who do not have advanced education engage in strategic negotiations on a regular basis. Union stewards, for example, are skilled at going with the ebb and flow to meet their constituency's needs. First-line supervisors, however, have dual constituencies to satisfy, both the work force and management, which often puts them in a tug-of-war between competing interests. In addition, practicing strategic negotiations requires time to think and time away from daily fire fighting, a rare commodity for most supervisors.

It is not possible to separate strategic change initiatives from daily tactical issues. They are highly interactive, and supervisors sit at a point of maximum leverage. Their actions influence the receptivity of the work force to new initiatives and set the stage for future rounds of negotiations. Supervisors are also in an ideal position to know the pulse of the work force; typically they also know which battles are likely to erupt and to have long-term consequences. Unfortunately, their input is not typically sought. Senior leadership needs to develop clear, direct, and unfiltered lines of communication with supervisors. It also needs to appreciate how its actions influence supervisors and their ability to implement strategic change. In many cases, management is forcing supervisors to foster good relations with teams but is doing little to foster good relations between supervisors and management.

Because of their marginal position in the hierarchy, many supervisors feel vulnerable and are unwilling to voice concern over new management initiatives. One vehicle to begin constructive dialogue is a supervisory network that allows supervisors a forum to share concerns among themselves, learn from one another, and discuss issues as a group with middle and senior management. Such a supervisory network lays the ground for enabling supervisors to manage the strategic negotiations challenges in two critical areas. It facilitates capability building through peer education, and it provides time away from the job to think and contemplate the implications of actions and behaviors on long-term goals and objectives.

There is no question that the positional power of the traditional supervisor has shifted as supervisors are asked to share responsibility in managing daily operations with empowered teams. But that does not require total abdication of power. In many cases, supervisory power will still be exercised through deal making. In fact, deal making will occur whether one wants it or not because reciprocity is an everyday process. Forcing through deal making may actually be an effective way to pick certain battles while keeping the forcing under control. The key for supervisors is to recognize that their role encompasses more than deal making. Today's supervisor is being asked constantly to manage the tension between team development and production output—in other words, to manage strategic negotiations at the workplace. Recognizing the interdependencies in concurrently managing forcing and fostering strategies should help supervisors deal with their role in today's changing industrial landscape.

5

New Forms of Work Groups

Exocentric Teams

PAUL S. GOODMAN
JEANNE M. WILSON

This chapter is about the changing nature of work groups and the implications of these changes for workplace practices, management of change, and future research about groups. Specifically, we examine the following questions: What are the basic changes in the structure and process of forms of work groups? What are the implications of these changes for practice and research on groups in organizations?

The theme of this chapter is that fundamental changes in the nature of work groups require new theoretical and methodological approaches to the study of groups and new ways of managing groups, both by group leaders and by those who design and oversee them. Since these new forms of groups span new boundaries (geographical, organizational, functional, and temporal), they present new challenges for negotiation and conflict resolution. We therefore highlight a number of these challenges that the changing nature of groups poses to their leaders and members.

Assumptions about Groups

Our theory and research about groups are based on the basic images of what a group looks like and what it does. We often think of a group as a set of people who come together to work in the same place and at the same time. We also think of a group as a set of people who work together over a period of time. These features—working in the same place, at the same time, and over a period of time—are what we call assumptions about groups. These assumptions have served as the basis of group research over

70

the last thirty years. Surfacing and delineating assumptions, particularly as new forms of groups emerge, are key to the development of theory, methods, and practice. Take a work group that exists over time, for example, and another that disbands after solving a problem in a short time span, say, one day. These two very different scenarios require a different focus and approach for both researchers and practitioners. Although the general definition of the group may be the same in the two cases, the role of leadership and the measures used to judge effectiveness will be different for a group with a very short time horizon, as opposed to one with a long time horizon. Greenhalgh and Lewicki note similar issues for negotiations in short- and long-term groups in chapter 2 of this volume. For example, members of long-term groups will need to worry more about the quality of their interpersonal relationships and the carryover effects of their day-to-day interactions.

There has been a substantial change in the nature of groups at work, and many of the assumptions we have about traditional work groups do not apply to these emerging forms. Before we delineate some of the key features and assumptions about this new form of work group, let us briefly present a historical perspective of our assumptions about groups and the roles they have traditionally played in organizations.

Historical Perspectives

Prior research in the social psychology of groups has had a major impact on how we think about groups today. Specifically, work by Steiner (1972) and McGrath (1984) and others has shaped both our approaches to the study of groups and organizations and our understanding of such concepts as size, composition, leadership, and cohesiveness of groups.

We have assumed that people come to the same place at the same time to work on a group task and that the processes among group members lead to certain levels of group output. The composition of the group (size and homogeneity) and the type of group task impact on the group processes. The fact that most of the early work on groups was done in a laboratory setting further sharpened these assumptions. The laboratory setting, probably as much as the theory, focused attention on the relationship among antecedents (such as size), internal processes, and outputs. There was little attention to the environment or external processes. Similarly, there was an underlying assumption in this research that we could specify clear performance requirements or the outputs or outcomes of a group and link a set of these internal processes to those outcomes.

In the 1980s, the growing use of teams in organizations posed challenges to the prevailing models of group behavior and spawned a major new interest in group research in organizational settings (Sanna and Parks 1997). One dominant stream of this research focused on changing levels of participation, autonomy, and control in groups. The assumptions were that these structural changes (self-designing teams) impacted processes such as problem solving and coordination, and in turn these processes contributed to enhancing group output. Although the themes of this research differed from those in the earlier social-psychology literature, many of the descriptive assumptions were the same. People still came together in the same space and at the same time to produce a product. The underlying assumptions concerning the ability to specify group output and to link antecedents and processes to that output remained the same.

There is also a growing body of research that has focused on topics such as group composition (size, tenure, and diversity), intra-organizational contextual variables (rewards and supervision), and internal group factors (cohesiveness, motivation, and cognition) (Cohen and Bailey 1997; Guzzo and Dickson 1996). These studies have emphasized the importance of objective measures of performance and have defined group effectiveness in terms of outputs, consequences for members (attitudinal and behavioral), and enhancement of team capabilities.

The vast majority of research that has been reported involved groups within a single organization, with stable full-time members. Although the researchers attempted to cover interesting and unique forms of groups, most of these groups still conformed to traditional assumptions. The research on flight crews, for instance, covered groups with changing membership but members who all worked for the same organization, interacting in the same time and place, with very clear and measurable outcomes. Even research on computer-assisted groups has involved groups that were co-located and simply used a group decision support system to augment their group decision-making process (Guzzo and Dickson 1996).

Recent literature reviews acknowledged that "external processes are all but ignored" in the bulk of group research (Cohen and Bailey 1997). There are a few examples of work that has explicitly tried to redirect our assumptions, however. Ancona's work (1990; Ancona and Caldwell 1992), for example, has focused our attention on communications processes external to the group, rather than the more typical emphasis on internal group processes. More recent models of group process have also tried to go beyond the traditional internal focus and highlight the embedding processes of groups. Argote and McGrath (1993), for instance, include external relations as one of four major processes involved in group work (along with construction, operations, and reconstruction).

Analysis

With this brief review as a context for our discussion, we now turn to the differences between traditional and emerging forms of teams. The basic focus of our analysis is on the different assumptions and their implications for theorizing about and managing groups.

Traditional Teams

Most theory and empirical research on groups in organizations has been focused on traditional teams. Table 5.1 lists some of the key assumptions inherent in traditional teams. The table is divided into three categories: effectiveness, membership, and structure. Traditional teams tend to have operational, internally defined measures of effectiveness (for example, revise the list of frequently asked questions for an updated version of a piece of software) and are made up of a stable set of co-located members of one or more work units. While there are other dimensions in the group literature, these categories seem to provide a reasonable way to describe groups and present our analysis. The following examples highlight how these dimensions play out in several different types of traditional teams.

Example 1a: Mining Crew 2-North
This underground coal-mining crew is composed of regular union miners and a supervisor; it has one of the best productivity and safety records in the mine. Together, mine and corporate managements define what acceptable performance is, with the output measured in terms of tons per hour. The crew works eight-hour shifts in the 2-North section of the mine. A high degree of internal interdependence exists among the crew members: failure of any one job sharply reduces the total output of the crew. The average length of service in this crew is approximately two and a half years.

Example 1b: Shared Service Center Team
This group of accountants and clerks handles all the expense reports for one segment of a large sales organization. The group has been so productive that the company has been able to sell its report-processing capabili-

Table 5.1. Contrasting Traditional and Exocentric Teams

	Traditional	*Exocentric*
Effectiveness	Internal	External
	Operational	Diffuse
Membership	Same organization	Different organizations
	100% in group	< 100% in group
	Stable	Dynamic
Structure	Co-located in space and time	Distributed in space and time
	Internally interdependent	Externally interdependent

Source: Reprinted from P. S. Goodman and J. M. Wilson, "Substitutes for Socialization and Exocentric Teams," in *Technology*, ed. T. L. Griffith, copyright 2000, p. 57, with permission from Elsevier Science.

ties to other parts of the organization. The group's effectiveness is measured in terms of errors (those reported by internal users, plus those detected during a semi-annual audit), costs per transaction, and customer satisfaction (as measured in an annual survey of a sample of users). The team is interdependent in two ways: multiple members are involved in the serial processing of tasks, and the team is responsible for scheduling its own work, planning its own training, and providing performance feedback to one another. By most measures—productivity, accuracy, and customer satisfaction—this is a very successful team.

What are the underlying assumptions of these two groups? The first is that they produce an identifiable output, which is certified by the organization. While the final product needs to meet the approval of the customer (sales representatives, for example), in both cases the definition of acceptable levels of output is determined internally. The second assumption is that one can specify the production function for these groups. Specifying the production function means you know how group inputs will affect outputs. For example, the quality of the mining equipment, the nature of the physical conditions, and the familiarity of team members with their jobs and with each other will affect the level of output for the group. In terms of membership, in each case team members were part of the same organizations, worked full-time in the team, and expected to work together over time. In terms of work, members of both groups operated in temporal and spatial proximity, and their work was defined primarily by its internal independence.

We have presented a unitary view of traditional teams in order to anchor the concept. Clearly, there may be variations along these dimensions. Members may not spend 100 percent of their time in the group, for example, and there may be forms of internal and external interdependencies. The dimensions presented in Table 5.1 provide a means for conceptualizing the distinctions between traditional and exocentric teams.

Exocentric Teams

A new form of group has emerged over the past five to ten years. We have labeled this form *exocentric*, referring to the group's focus on external activities and relationships. Key assumptions inherent in exocentric groups are listed in Table 5.1. They tend to be made up of individuals located in different places, representing different organizations, or not always available to participate in person in team meetings. Their effectiveness may often be harder to judge because their goals may be more diffuse or varied, depending on what each of the organizations supplying members wants to get out of the group interactions. Members are more likely to come and go as priorities and job assignments in their respective organizations change. The development of these exocentric groups has been driven by many forces. First, the globalization of work has placed people in distributed environments, while the development of information technology has created new opportunities for bridging space and time. In 2002 over 16.5 million teleworkers were active in the United States alone (www.gilgordon.com), and that number is expected to grow rapidly (Kraut 1994). Second, there is a greater priority for building effective customer-supplier relationships (Fichman and Goodman 1996), a fact that has led to new teams bridging space and time boundaries. Joint ventures and strategic alliances (with groups cutting across organizational boundaries) are increasing, in fact, by as much as 25 percent per year (Crandall and Wallace 1997). Third, the drive for improving performance in the light of growing global competitiveness has contributed to innovations in group structure and process, such as virtual arrangements. Collaborative work in virtual arrangements is predicted to be the number one trend in the workplace over the next ten years (Kemske 1998). It's not surprising, then, that recent surveys have shown that among companies currently using teams, 82 percent expect to expand their use of virtual teams (Development Dimensions International, 1997).

The concept of exocentric teams can be clarified by examining examples of different types of teams that fit under this heading. We examine three, each one selected to illustrate one of the three dimensions that characterize exocentric teams.

Example 2a: Computer Emergency Response (CER) Teams
These groups have only recently come into being, to match the explosive growth of the Internet. The goal of CER teams is to prevent or minimize attacks on the Internet, such as when someone illegally obtains or modifies

information from another user, either for economic gain (industrial espionage) or for other malevolent reasons. An intruder in one case switched names in medical records that were connected to diagnoses for cancer.

The major role of the CER team is to identify when an attack is occurring and to advise users what to do. A major product of the CER team is an advisory, which may be sent to hundreds of thousands of people, telling users how to prevent or minimize the effects of an attack. Each attack leads to the creation of a new team, since attacks are totally unpredictable.

Since issuing advisories is dependent on when an attack occurs, members may not always be on a CER team at any given time. Thus, at other times they perform other duties. While CER team members often work in the same physical setting, much of their work is externally focused. Working on an advisory may include members from other CER teams, vendors, and service providers, for example.

Example 2b: Customer-Supplier Team

This team's goal is to minimize stock shortages by coordinating activities in an important supplier and customer relationship. In this example, the supplier is a large consumer-products company (called G&P here) and the customer is a major retail organization (referred to here as Well-Mart). The constituencies for this team are both organizations.

Members work together in the same space and time, although they come from the two different organizations with different cultures, rewards, and procedures. Their challenge is to manage external relationships, including the factories, production scheduling, and distribution priorities of G&P, as well as the stores, warehouses, and distribution and purchasing priorities of WellMart. Membership in the team is a full-time responsibility for about half of its members. The peripheral members spend an average of 20 percent of their time on team activities. Internal relationships exist in this team, but they are not the primary focus of attention. The core members return to their parent organizations after a one-year assignment. Thus, their loyalties and home-organization peers and bosses are the primary constituents and concerns of these team members.

Example 2c: Software Development Teams

These teams build software systems for the customers of a large global software company. While the goals are to provide on-time delivery of a software system that provides value for the customer, the constituencies for this team are primarily internal to the company. In terms of membership, the team comes from the same organization, the work typically re-

quires 100 percent of the team members' time, and the team remains together until the product is completed. In most cases, this is around eighteen months.

The principal difference is that these team members are widely distributed geographically—in the United States, Southeast Asia, India, and the
United Kingdom. Hence, their work is in different locations in different
time zones. This is a twenty-four-hour-a-day operation in which the work
gets passed off to a different time zone as each segment of the team com-
pletes its shift.

What We Know about Exocentric Work Groups

There is not meant to be one stereotypic exocentric group, and the three
we have selected highlight different dimensions of exocentric groups. The
emerging literature on this topic has focused mainly on the dimension of
group work distributed in space and time. This literature has highlighted
some of the major differences in groups working in a distributed environment versus a proximate (or co-located) environment. One critical issue in
distributed groups is providing a sense of cohesion and shared identity.
Team members who are co-located can easily initiate spontaneous casual
interactions, but these are less probable in distributed groups (Tang,
Isaacs, and Rua 1994). Limited interaction leads to a lack of peripheral
awareness of fellow team members (Benford, Brown, Reynard, and Green-
laugh 1996), which in turn leads to conflicts and misunderstandings
(Cramton 1997).

There is also evidence that when some group members are co-located and
some are not, more coordination takes place among the co-located subgroup
(Bellotti and Bly 1996). Responsibility and commitment may decline among
members who do not meet face to face (Olson and Teasley 1996). These phenomena may contribute to in-group–out-group dynamics that make cohesion and trust more problematic in distributed groups (Kraut 1994).

The dimensions of space and time represent only one way to characterize exocentric groups. There are some others. In exocentric groups there
may not be a product as there is in traditional groups. In the
WellMart–G&P case, for example, the major goal is minimizing stock outages. This is a measure of coordinating activities, not a direct product. As
such it is hard to measure the contribution of doing the job well. Compare
this to the mining example, in which coal is sold to a power company to
create energy. The output here can be measured easily in both tons and
revenue generated. The criteria for the team's effectiveness in the other ex-

amples of exocentric groups are often very diffuse. It is very difficult to assess the value of an advisory in the CER team case, for several reasons. First, the advisory goes out to hundreds of thousands of people, most unknown to the team. Second, there is rarely any feedback. Third, it is hard to assess the impact of an advisory. Consider the following. You receive an advisory but do not implement the suggested activities, and you are not attacked. Was the advisory effective?

The role of constituencies may also differ. In the CER team, members are focused primarily on external constituencies. In the WellMart–G&P case, the primary constituencies for the team are the two organizations. In the shared service center team, the primary focus is on internal constituencies.

Membership in exocentric groups may be composed of people in different organizations, and members may not allocate 100 percent of their time to the team. In the WellMart–G&P and CER teams, members work on other activities as well as the group's. In all three cases, membership is reconstituted periodically. A CER team lasts as long as it takes to generate an advisory, perhaps two or three days. For the next incident, a new team is formed. On the other hand, the software development team disbands in twelve to eighteen months, when the software is completed.

Exocentric Groups and Models of Group Effectiveness

The basic thesis of this chapter is that current models of group effectiveness may not be applicable to new forms of work groups because the basic assumptions that are inherent in most current models of group effectiveness are violated in exocentric teams. Let us approach this argument by exploring some current or traditional models of group effectiveness, their assumptions, and their limitations with respect to exocentric teams.

Current Models of Group Effectiveness

Diagrams representing some models of group effectiveness are presented in Figure 5.1 (Hackman 1983; Ancona 1990; Cohen and Bailey 1997). Our focus is meant to be illustrative, not comprehensive or evaluative. A cursory examination indicates a common set of antecedent variables (group composition and organizational context), processes (such as task and maintenance), and criteria (like performance, satisfaction, and adaptation). All these models are presented at a very general heuristic level, without specification as to functional form or the manner in which

A.

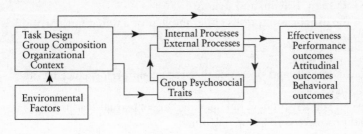

B.

INPUTS	TRANSFORMATION	OUTPUTS
Group Composition Group Structure Resources Organizational Context	Internal Processes Task Maintenance	Performance Satisfaction Adaptation

C.

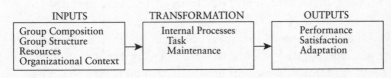

Figure 5.1. (A) Heuristic model of group effectiveness (simplified from Cohen and Bailey 1997). (B) Traditional model of group performance (from Ancona 1990). (C) Normative model of group effectiveness (from Hackman 1983).

context or tasks might change the relative importance of variables in the models (Goodman, Ravlin, and Argote 1986).

Some of the usual assumptions either implicit or explicit in these models are as follows:

- One can specify and operationalize the group performance or other outcomes.
- One can specify a model linking external contextual features and internal processes with group outcomes.
- Group members come from the same organization.
- The group exists over a period of time.
- The group exists in temporal and spatial proximity.
- The group is defined primarily by its internal interdependence.

Now it could be argued that these assumptions either are too restrictive or are not incorporated in these models. They are explicit or implicit in the current traditional models of group effectiveness, however, in six ways. First, most models specify outcomes, such as productivity, member satisfaction, and turnover, which have been measured in many studies (Guzzo and Dickson 1996) and used by managers in judging the success of teams or groups. While these traditional measures may still apply to some exocentric groups, their members' goals are more likely to vary given the different time horizons, motivations to participate, and organizational objectives involved. Second, although the models are somewhat general, they come with clear theoretical arguments and empirical evidence that antecedents, such as group composition, affect group performance, given certain task conditions. Implicit in this assumption is the notion that designers can change these features to change group outcomes.

Third, the assumption that members come from the same organization is derived from two sources. The use of organizational context in most models refers to the organization within which the group works, and most of the empirical research is on groups within the same organization. Fourth, in many of the models (see Hackman 1983, for example), the capability of a group to exist and adapt over time is another measure of effectiveness. This makes a good deal of sense if you are interested in stable groups, such as mining or service center teams. Adaptation over time is less relevant if the group goes out of business in two days. Fifth, from early work on the social psychology of groups to current-day group research, the focus has been on groups in which members are spatially and temporally proximate, in the same organization. Theoretical work on group composition or socialization, and on the group development or socialization processes these models encourage (Moreland and Levine 2000), implicitly focuses on face-to-face groups. Emphasis is given to communication, conflict resolution, and other internal processes that are critical to successful face-to-face interactions.

Last, in the current models, there is still a strong focus on internal processes as the drivers of group outcomes. Clearly, work by Ancona and Caldwell (1992) and others indicated that external processes are important. However, in traditional groups, internal processes have been *dominant* drivers of group outcomes, with some consideration given to external processes. In exocentric teams, though, internal processes are not the key drivers.

Are Current Models Applicable to Exocentric Groups?

These assumptions have guided our research on groups, explicitly or implicitly, over the years. As new forms of groups emerge, the question is whether these assumptions are still applicable in the models of effectiveness. We argue that for exocentric teams there may be different assumptions:

- It may not be possible to specify a clear measure of effectiveness.
- The links among external factors, internal group process characteristics, and effectiveness may be difficult to specify.
- Group members may come from multiple organizations, rather than a single organization.
- The group may be reconfigured continually over time.
- Group members may be separated in space and time.
- External interdependence is key for group survival and success.

The next question is, If the traditional assumptions are violated, what are the implications of that violation for understanding and assessing new forms of groups? We believe those implications are best examined by looking at the performance criterion problem and the selection of predictors.

The Performance Criterion Problem

The CER team example is a good case through which (1) to illustrate why specifying a performance outcome is difficult and (2) to explore some interesting implications for both research and practice. Remember, the main job of the CER team is to identify and warn people about attacks on the Internet. The advisories for minimizing attacks and their consequences are one of the major deliverables. The problem in identifying and measuring the effectiveness of the group, though, is inherent in its structure. The advisories can go to hundreds of thousands of people. Since there are no reciprocal interactions between the team and the people receiving an advisory, though, as there are between a supplier and a customer, there may be little or no feedback on the advisory.

Let's assume we can look in on a person receiving an advisory. The person implements the advisory and is not attacked. Or the person does not implement the advisory and is not attacked. Or the person does not implement the advisory immediately, subsequently introducing elements of several advisories and other expert opinions during a system reconfiguration. The question is whether the advisory was effective. The time between receiving the advisory, acting, and the consequences is unclear. It is difficult to causally link the advisory to reductions in negative consequences, and thus reductions in negative consequences cannot be used as a criterion for effectiveness.

The basic point is that in certain types of exocentric teams the performance assessment problem is intractable because of the structure of the group and its task. Some standard options are open to researchers and practitioners when the criterion is difficult to specify. First, one can go back to other criteria, such as group satisfaction or morale. The main problem with this approach is that it begs the question of whether satisfaction is conceptually different from performance. Another problem is that some exocentric teams have a very short life. While one clearly can measure satisfaction at any time interval, conceptualizing satisfaction in both permanent and nonpermanent groups seems a very different task. To sharpen this point about time intervals and criteria, consider the criterion of group turnover rates as a means of assessing satisfaction. This is a concept that clearly makes sense in permanent groups but is difficult to use as an indicator of effectiveness in a group that might exist for only a few days.

Another standard option when there is a performance criterion problem is to move back to interim criteria. For example, in the CER team case, we could look at how long it took to release an advisory. The challenge in using interim criteria is to be able to link these criteria, either theoretically or empirically, to the ultimate performance goals of the group. What is the work the group must get done for the organization to function well? This question is not easily answered here, however. It is not obvious that the time taken to release an advisory is positively or negatively related to the effectiveness of a CER team.

The Selection of Predictor Problem

Let's assume one can specify criteria for group effectiveness. Another question concerns how predictors from current group research help our understanding or management of exocentric teams.

The models in Figure 5.1 provide a set of predictors. Recent reviews (Cohen and Bailey 1997; Guzzo and Dickson 1996) present compilations of findings on factors that affect group effectiveness, including such factors as familiarity, group mood, and leadership. The question is whether these findings generalize to exocentric groups.

Familiarity

To sharpen this analysis, we start with our own work on familiarity and show that it is rooted in traditional group assumptions and does not easily generalize to exocentric teams.

Familiarity refers to the level of knowledge team members have about their own job, the team members they work with, and the environment or context in which the group works. The basic argument is that familiarity enhances group performance in interdependent groups. The knowledge coworkers have of each other's work styles and habits facilitates work when the conditions are characterized by interdependence and uncertainty. Decreases in familiarity via absenteeism or turnover have been seen to reduce performance (Goodman and Garber 1988; Goodman and Leyden 1991).

The issue is whether familiarity helps us understand exocentric teams, such as the WellMart–G&P team. We think not. Both the theoretical reasoning and empirical analysis for familiarity were done on traditional teams, which come to work for the same organization every day and produce a service or product over time. Within certain parameters (such as the quality of their machinery), the output of the group is largely determined by how well each member does his or her activities and how well they coordinate these activities. Familiarity assumes learning over time in recurrent activities.

The WellMart–G&P team does not work that way. They do not produce a regular product through regular activities. Much of their work is piecemeal and indirect. For example, assume the team identifies a way to improve the forecasting of the demand for a product in a region, with the expectation of reducing future outages. Their job is to convince the appropriate people in marketing for G&P and purchasing for WellMart, plus some other people in such areas as information systems, to implement the new forecasting system. This activity is likely to be nonrecurrent, but the familiarity concept assumes recurrent work activities, as are seen in the cases of the 2-North miners or shared service center team.

The familiarity concept also assumes high levels of internal interdependence, and while some coordination is needed in the WellMart–G&P team, it is a relatively loosely coupled system, compared with the two traditional work-group examples. The familiarity concept also assumes stability in membership to permit members to learn about each other and their work environment, but some exocentric teams are continually reconfiguring with new members.

Group Mood

Another example of the difficulty in generalizing predictors from traditional groups to new forms of groups can be found in the research on mood. Evidence has been accumulating that group mood affects the behavioral outcomes of group members (such as absenteeism), as well as group performance (George 1990). George argues that there is both theoretical and empirical support for the importance of group mood (when individual affect is consistent within work groups). One basis for this argument is that attraction, selection, and attrition forces operate to create and maintain a consistent level of affect in traditional work groups. It seems unlikely, however, that these influences would operate the same way in exocentric groups.

In the case of cross-organizational teams, for instance, it seems unlikely that the G&P members would have been selected or socialized in the same way as the WellMart members. In addition, in the CER teams, members may not work together long enough to develop the consistency of affective relations that would be required for a group mood.

For distributed groups, weakened social-influence processes would likely lead to less consistency in affect. In fact, George and Brief (1992) have acknowledged that group mood is less likely to develop when group members are physically separated from each other.

Leader Behavior—Monitoring and Feedback

A third example illustrating the difficulty of generalizing findings from traditional groups to exocentric groups comes from empirical research on leadership with groups. One of the emerging findings in traditional group literature is that monitoring by leaders is related to improved group performance. In a study of police sergeants, Brewer, Wilson, and Beck (1994) found that sergeants who spent more time monitoring performance had higher-performing teams. Sergeants who spent more time doing the technical work themselves (in this case, patrolling the streets) had less effective teams.

Komaki, Desselles, and Bowman (1989) obtained a similar result in their study of captains of sailing crews. In this study, the captains remained with the boat while crews rotated across boats for various races, and success was measured by the number of races each captain won. The researchers identified two leader behaviors associated with success: monitoring performance and providing feedback about consequences.

Although monitoring may be possible and effective with traditional groups, its effects are less predictable with exocentric groups. If, as noted, the performance criteria themselves are not clear in some exocentric groups, it would be difficult for their leaders to provide accurate or useful feedback about consequences. In such ambiguous circumstances, attempts to provide feedback might result in simply communicating or reinforcing leader biases and assumptions to the groups. CER team leaders, for example, might rely on their own idiosyncrasies or implicit theories about effective groups in the absence of any clear performance measures.

Monitoring and feedback may be even more complicated in geographically distributed teams. One of the difficulties with working in these settings is the lack of social and context information. Cramton (1997) noted the tendency of remote members to misattribute the causes of problems. As in many ambiguous situations, outcomes were often attributed to internal factors rather than to situational constraints. Remote members often interpreted lack of response, for example, as a lack of interest.

Misattribution is especially problematic for leaders, whose attributions would have much more serious consequences for group members but would be subject to the same biases due to the lack of contextual information. Leaders' attributional biases affect not only their level of disagreement and conflict with subordinates (Fadil 1995) but also their performance evaluations (Knowlton and Ilgen 1980). Clearly, leaders' monitoring of performance will not have the same effects in exocentric teams as in traditional teams.

New Approaches to Exocentric Teams

Thus, many of the predictors of group process and outcomes identified in the literature may not fit exocentric groups. This dilemma creates a benefit. It forces us to rethink how we have been doing research on teams and to develop new perspectives for shaping how exocentric teams are designed and managed in practice. Here we focus on two questions: How should we rethink the unit of analysis of groups, and What new concepts should we explore?

Events as Windows on Performance

In the past, both research and management attention have focused on the group itself and its ongoing or day-to-day antecedents, processes, and outcomes. In settings where group effectiveness is difficult to determine, group membership is constantly reconfiguring, and work is done in a distributed environment, it may be more sensible to focus on critical events as units for research and for interventions to change group behavior or performance.

Such a change would be fairly fundamental, representing a theoretical shift from looking at large systems and their outcomes to understanding events within systems. Weick and Roberts's (1993) description of landing planes on an aircraft carrier represents a critical event in the life of an organization. It captures many of the actors, structures, and processes of the organization, as well as its environment. It is only one of many events, however, and it is unlikely that the events combine neatly to provide a picture of the aircraft carrier as a whole. For a CER team, determining whether there is a crisis or getting information from a vendor or another CER team does represent a critical event in the life of this team.

To advocate studying events raises a series of questions. Should we adopt an effectiveness perspective and examine whether a particular landing or set of landings on an aircraft carrier is accident-free? Or should we focus on the processes of organizing and coordinating this complex event? Or should we examine the processes of coordination in light of some effectiveness criteria, such as accidents? While any of these event-based approaches can be a form of effectiveness study, the unit of analysis, time frame, and predictors will be different from those in traditional group-effectiveness studies.

Another problem is that we do not have a good way to identify events, to determine which should be selected and why. In the CER team example, we used two critical events in the work process—determining if there is a crisis and writing an advisory. We identified these two events because they are central to the functioning of this group. For the Well-Mart–G&P team, negotiating with suppliers whose primary task is minimizing outages seems to be a central event. Thus, if one has a rich understanding of the team, identifying some critical levers appears fairly straightforward. For other situations, however, we need other analytical ways to uncover less obvious central events. The ability to identify key events will be an important mechanism for intervening and improving the performance of exocentric groups.

New Concepts for Analysis

The features identified in Table 5.1 to show contrast between traditional and exocentric teams can be used to generate new conceptual issues in the study of groups. We specifically examine two group processes: reconfiguration and joint optimization.

Reconfiguration Processes

One feature of exocentric teams is that they are dynamic, or continually reconfiguring. The CER teams tend to reconfigure in days, while the software development teams tend to reconfigure after projects are done, typically in months. This is in sharp contrast to traditional teams, which are relatively stable.

The start-up processes involved in reconfiguring offer a new opportunity to examine another aspect of group functioning. How do these teams get started? Why do some start up faster than others? How are roles learned and coordination and communication activities enacted? Do norms develop for short-term exocentric teams?

While there is a socialization literature on groups (Moreland and Levine 2000), that literature is largely rooted in assumptions about longer-term traditional teams or groups, such as fire-fighting units or SWAT teams, that respond to unique events but remain intact over time. It is difficult to imagine how the socialization cycles advocated by Moreland and Levine (2000) can be compressed in a three-day CER team.

Reconfiguration means changing membership and changing discreet tasks. The basic idea in reconfiguration poses two interesting learning issues that have not yet been addressed in group research: short learning curves and transfer over time. These issues pose exciting opportunities for new research on groups and new challenges for group participants and managers.

Short Learning Curves

The start-up processes in exocentric groups are brief but critical. The question is why some teams move up this short-interval learning curve faster than others. A variety of interesting factors may play a role. First, members of CER teams are loosely coupled. A good deal of their work is divided among the members, although there is some common work to be done. If roles are well rehearsed, group learning rates should be faster in a loosely coupled system than a more interdependent system because there is less need to learn more complicated coordination and routines.

Second, the relationship between the group and the next level of analysis (the department, for instance) may shed light on the slope of the learning curve. The unit above the team may provide insight into the team's rate of learning, because many of the norms CER team and software development team members learn may come from the departments in which they work. These department-level norms may structure the processes in the exocentric teams and may affect their start-up.

Transfer of Learning

The reconfiguration process also has implications for the transfer of learning. When the software development team disbands, there are probably lessons learned—perhaps about technical or organizing topics—that would be valuable for the next teams. Similarly, a WellMart–G&P team that goes out of business probably has learned a variety of lessons that might help other teams.

The question is, How can this knowledge be stored and shared, independent of any specific group or individual? When the WellMart–G&P group goes out of business, how can the general and unique learning about reducing supply outages be transferred? How can the organization learn?

For such a complicated issue, a detailed analysis is well beyond the scope of this chapter, but some of the central questions it raises can be addressed. One is the location in which knowledge may be stored. Possible "memory systems" include text, computer-based systems, and people (Olivera 1998). A second question concerns what information may be stored. For the WellMart–G&P example, information about how to deal with outages can be stored in terms of (1) content knowledge (specific processes about how to solve a problem) or (2) pointer knowledge (who knows how to solve the problem). The former deals with the information while the latter deals with where to go to get information. The decision to sort the information into content or pointer knowledge will depend on whether the underlying subject is explicit or tacit in nature (Nonaka 1994).

The reconfiguration feature thus poses two interesting learning issues that have not yet been addressed in group research. These two processes—short learning curves and transfer over time—are exciting topics for new research and practice.

Joint Optimization

Another feature of exocentric teams is that the members may not all come from the same organization (see Table 5.1). This was a defining characteristic of the WellMart–G&P teams: although members ostensibly shared a common group goal, they came from different organizations and were evaluated and rewarded against different criteria by their respective organizations. This is not characteristic of most traditional work groups, where all members work for the same organization with the same culture, goals, and sanctions.

The fact that in some new forms of groups, members may come from different organizations raises interesting questions about joint optimization, or the process of merging apparently conflicting interests in a synergistic way. The joint optimization process is defined by its result: an integrative solution or agreement that satisfies all aspirations to a greater extent than a simple compromise. Although the process of joint optimization has been applied to many different domains (Kolodny and Kiggundu 1980; Walton and McKersie 1965), our focus is on group members' conflicting goals.

Conflicting Goals

Conflicting interests and goals are not just a problem for cross-organization teams. These pressures are also common in distributed work groups. In the case of the software development teams, for instance, it would certainly be possible for the two members located in India to develop subgoals that conflicted with the goals of the members in the United Kingdom, or of the team as a whole.

Some might argue that these issues are similar to those encountered in more traditional cross-functional teams (Dennison, Hart, and Kahn 1996). Although some of what we know about cross-functional teams would apply to exocentric groups, we see some fundamental differences. In traditional cross-functional groups, for example, there is goal coherence at some level in the organization. Ultimately, everyone in the mining organization discussed earlier works to achieve some commonly accepted goal. This is not necessarily the case in exocentric groups. The highest levels of management in the parent companies of exocentric groups may have completely different goals for the team. Finally, traditional cross-functional teams can always identify a senior manager somewhere in the hierarchy who can resolve goal conflicts, but this is not possible when group members come from different organizations.

In some forms of exocentric teams, the goal of joint optimization poses some interesting challenges for group researchers and practitioners. Previously, we argued that the start-up process represents an important problem for exocentric teams primarily because of frequent reconfigurations of group membership. The start-up process is also complicated by the need to develop some shared understanding of joint optimization. Developing this shared understanding is difficult because (using the WellMart–G&P team as an example) members have spent their careers in different organizations and will return to different organizations. One force for moving the group toward joint optimization is the group leader, whose activities may range from direct training on facilitating group processes to helping members manage difficult external relationships. A second mechanism may be retaining members from prior teams to help current team members operate in a joint optimization mode. The problems associated with joint optimization in these groups challenge the researcher to explore new forms of socialization processes and the practitioner to try different approaches to training.

Re-entry

Joint optimization can also be examined in the context of the re-entry process. There are unique issues associated with leaving an exocentric group and returning to the parent organization. Members may have difficulty readjusting to the parent company's goals or norms; they may also have considerable difficulty transferring the knowledge they have gained in the group. Although there has been some research on the re-socialization and exit processes in groups (Moreland and Levine 2000), it has focused more on what happens within the original group than on what happens to members in the transition between the group and the organization.

Several factors may affect the success of the re-entry process. The relative strength of the members' attraction to the group and the parent organization is one. The stronger the identification of the members with the cross-company team, the more difficulties they may experience in the assimilation process. Members who remain highly identified with their parent organization may have an easier time in re-entry but a more difficult time operating in the cross-company team.

Another factor affecting re-entry may be the absorptive capacity in the parent company. Organizations with greater expertise in managing diversity in organizational goals may be better able to absorb members from cross-organizational teams. Indeed, the capacity to re-assimilate members may be related to the parent organization's past experience in dealing with different types of cross-organizational teams.

Thus, examining joint optimization at different points in the exocentric team's life—from initial socialization to re-entry processes—provides an opportunity to examine group processes that have not been fully explored in prior group research in organizations or in practice.

Conclusion

There is little question that groups have become a more important part of organizational life. If the thesis advanced here is right, they are not only growing in frequency. New forms—exocentric forms—are emerging that pose novel challenges to both organizational researchers and practitioners. Their diffuse and hard-to-measure goals, changing or physically separated membership, and multiple constituents increase the likelihood of conflicts and the need for negotiation skills on the part of both leaders and members. These different features require new constructs and methods in order to advance theory and practice. The research questions, variables, and findings generated on traditional groups do not easily generalize to these new group forms.

This argument raises a set of questions: How prevalent are exocentric groups? Are they really emerging phenomena? Some research on this topic exists (see Kraut 1994; Crandall and Wallace 1997; Kemske 1998), but there are no *systematic* survey data on the prevalence or growth of exocentric groups yet. This type of information would be informative to group researchers.

Nevertheless, it seems clear that some recently recognized trends should facilitate the growth of exocentric groups. Rapid changes in information technology support the development of distributed work, and increasing globalization of markets forces firms to operate in many environments. These two factors should encourage the frequency of distributed work, one element of exocentric groups. The emphasis on quality and customer satisfaction, and the new forms of customer-firm relationships are also trends that support the emergence of exocentric groups.

Another issue is, What makes a group exocentric? The distinction between exocentric and traditional groups does not lie on a simple continuum; rather it is spread across seven dimensions (see Table 5.1), and there are many different profiles among these seven dimensions. We could have a team that works together in the same space and time, for example, but constantly reconfigures. Or we could have a team that works separated by space and time but does not reconfigure. Which team is more exocentric is unclear.

This confusion seems quite compelling. However, our position is that the seven dimensions represent important, different group assumptions and that these assumptions have new implications for theorizing about groups. Our focus is on the assumptions underlying where a group fits in Table 5.1 and the implications of these assumptions for theory and practice. A group that bridges space and time creates a whole different set of challenges from a group whose members work together in the same physical space. In addition, a group that continually reconfigures raises critical socialization and transfer-of-learning concerns.

A third issue is whether research posed by exocentric teams is complementary to the body of research and practice on work groups that has been developing over the last twenty-five years. That is, will research on exocentric groups take us down a different theoretical and empirical path from this prior body of work? We believe that the research is fundamentally different, but it may complement or suggest new approaches for traditional work-group research.

Reconsider our discussion on whether a group is stable or continually reconfigures. Continual reconfiguration means that traditional concepts of effectiveness and related criteria do not fit. Processes such as socialization take on very different meanings. Methodologically, this may mean we need to compare samples of events, not group outcomes. In our discussion of the CER teams, for example, studying the effectiveness might mean focusing on the event of writing an advisory. We could examine the effects of different socialization processes on shared understanding of roles, goals, or the time it takes to write an advisory.

At the same time, there may be some interesting complementarity to research on traditional and exocentric groups. Studying events instead of group-level outcomes is a big switch. It requires us to learn what events to select and how to sample them. If we can learn more about event-based research, which is also being advocated in other areas of organizational research (Weick and Roberts 1993; Rousseau 1985), we may be able to translate some of these lessons to traditional group research. Reactions to events and performance outcomes may be critical indicators of group processes. Traditional group activities are, of course, merely a collection of events. Subsequently, an event-based approach might lead traditional researchers to a more fine-grained understanding of group processes.

The other example of potential complementarity concerns new processes generated by research on exocentric groups and their applicability to traditional groups, such as the processes of learning. That is, teams that are continually reconfiguring need to find ways to transfer knowledge from one group to another. While this form of learning is introduced because of the reconfiguration process, it may have some applicability to more traditional teams among groups that work in different time periods or shifts or groups that perform the same functions but work in different geographical areas. In both of these cases (those with time and space differences), transfer of knowledge may positively impact both group and organizational effectiveness. Understanding this type of learning is critical for exocentric group research, and some aspects of this learning process may inform traditional groups that are not distributed in time or space.

The implications for practice follow the basic arguments about the distinctions between traditional and exocentric groups. Identifying and improving coordination in "events" may be a new perspective for intervening in exocentric group processes. We have argued that focusing on long-term training of group processes may not work in groups where members are continually reconfiguring. Rather, practitioners need to think about ways to create fast start-ups. In addition, our identification of learning and transfer of knowledge as critical to the functioning of exocentric groups is important for both the practitioner and the researcher. Improving these learning processes will contribute to the viability of these new forms of groups.

Finally, we should note that the new types of groups likely to emerge in the future will be different from both the traditional and the exocentric groups discussed here. As in this case, practice is likely to be ahead of research in developing whatever new forms emerge. Thus, our task will be to remain open to seeing new developments as they emerge and to understanding the different assumptions in these new forms and their implications for theory and practice.

6

Leaning toward Teams

Divergent and Convergent Trends in Diffusion of Lean Production Work Practices

JOHN PAUL MacDUFFIE

The 1990 release of the summary report from MIT's International Motor Vehicle Program (IMVP), titled *The Machine That Changed the World*, prompted a variety of controversies but none more pronounced than that captured by the following pair of statements: "In the end, lean production will supplant mass production . . . to become the standard global production system of the twenty-first century," and "It is the dynamic work team that emerges at the heart of the lean factory" (Womack, Jones, and Roos 1990: 99, 278).

The evidence for these statements came from research in the auto industry, but this prediction was much broader in scope. The report's authors, and many others before and since, viewed the auto industry as a bellwether for other manufacturing industries. The research findings therefore sparked considerable debate over the future of work organization and production systems in other industries as well. As such, the auto industry provides a good laboratory for examining the forces affecting a major organizational change underway in many industries—the drive to introduce more team-based work systems and related human resource practices aimed at increasing productivity, quality, and

Robert McKersie was a strong supporter of the research described in this chapter and an invaluable advisor during my years at MIT and beyond. He always urged his students to pursue important problems and real-world data, and for that encouragement I am grateful. I am also grateful to my colleague Frits Pil for his continuing collaboration with me on the International Assembly Plant Study, and to the International Motor Vehicle Program (IMVP) at MIT for its past and current support for this research. Thanks also to Clair Brown, Takahiro Fujimoto, Susan Helper, Ulrich Jürgens, Thomas Kochan, Saul Rubinstein, Mari Sako, and Roland Springer for valuable conversations.

adaptability. In this chapter I use the research carried out with my IMVP colleagues to summarize the forces leading to convergence toward lean production across companies in Europe and North America, and suggest some factors that would predict continued variation in production systems and workplace practices. The result of this interplay of convergent and divergent forces will be influenced in the end by how the key parties involved—individual companies, workers, and their union representatives—negotiate their way through the issues associated with this particular form of organizational change. Indeed, debates over these production and work system design issues have been central to labor-management negotiations for the past two decades, both in the United States and abroad. Moreover, the debates are not yet over, the consequences are not fully known, and the choices made will have important bearing on the future of the industry and the work force. To illustrate this, I suggest three possible scenarios or patterns of development before offering a specific prediction of how the interplay of environmental pressures, strategies, and interests are likely to sort themselves out and shape workplace practices in the early years of the twenty-first century.

Mass and Lean Production Defined

To set the stage for this discussion I need to clarify the key differences between *mass production* as it has evolved since the days of Frederick Taylor and Henry Ford and *lean production* as it has evolved out of the Toyota Production System and associated human resource practices in Japan and the United States. In an earlier work (MacDuffie and Pil 1997a: 10–11), these terms were defined as follows:

> Mass production can be summarized along four core dimensions: (1) an extreme specialization of resources, including use of narrowly defined tasks carried out by people and/or equipment dedicated to each task; (2) a standardized product design that can be produced in large batches to achieve economies of scale and minimize setup time, coupled with large buffers of inventory, stock, repair, space, and utility workers to prevent any interruptions in production; (3) a centralized hierarchy that handles the control and coordination tasks that accompany a highly specialized and narrow division of labor; and (4) a separation of conception and execution, so that all "thinking" work associated with production is specialized and isolated from the doing work. . . .

Lean production inverts the four dimensions of mass production mentioned above: (1) more general resources are used (multiskilled workers, general-purpose machines, fewer functional specialists); (2) small buffers and lot sizes facilitate the handling of a greater variety of product designs and hence support a market strategy of offering niche products and responding quickly to demand fluctuation; (3) authority is more decentralized, and there is greater lateral communication across functional boundaries and faster response time; and (4) there is a higher degree of integration of conceptual activity with the execution of production tasks.

Explaining Patterns

The prediction in *The Machine That Changed the World* that existing patterns of work organization, so different across countries and companies in this important industry, would converge on a single dominant form—work teams, in this context typically a management-designated group structure designed to improve economic performance—seemed to defy certain immutable laws. Work organization is a repository of practices fixed by custom and technology, embedded in slow-to-change social interactions and institutional relationships (Kogut and Zander 1992). When faced with the latest management initiative to control and redirect discretionary effort at the workplace, workers can be very resourceful in preserving their preferred ways of working, concealing their knowledge from the prying eyes of supervisors and industrial engineers and often able to outlast the comparatively short managerial attention span for promoting workplace change. Unions and work councils often take action to resist unreasonable productivity demands and defend contractually established work rules. Managers can also be a source of inertia and resistance to work reforms that cede new responsibilities and discretion to workers. This "face" of work organization, then, is one of persistence grounded in social embeddedness and constrained by technology that can produce resistance to pressures for change. Any specific change is therefore the outcome of a series of informal negotiations among parties with different substantive concerns and power at stake.

Yet there was a deeper claim behind the easy rhetoric about lean production that points toward another face of work organization. Lean production, unlike mass production and other forms of bureaucratic control, obtains its economic advantage by setting into motion dynamic processes of improvement at the point where value is added. These processes take advantage of enhancements in individual human capital made possible by human resource practices that emphasize careful selection, extensive training, and motivation through contingent compensation. Yet these individual effects are necessary but not sufficient conditions. The advancement of production knowledge through the cognitive contribution of front-line employees is of necessity a collective activity. Only through dialogue and exchange can individuals exceed the limits of their own experience and perceptual biases. Such social interaction certainly draws on the informal network of workplace relationships that provides the source of persistence in work organization (and resistance to change) just described. But ultimately it is the channeling of group interaction into particular disciplined processes of problem solving—appealing to workers in their simplicity, their pragmatism, and their effectiveness—that generates the improvement capabilities differentiating lean from mass production.

Thus in its purest form, lean production points toward a second face for work organization: as a locus for innovation, the crossroads where the joint impact of the technical and social context is most strongly felt, and hence where the multiplicative effect of technical and social innovations is most clearly manifest. So when one is investigating the diffusion of the work practices of lean production into mass production settings, vital questions are raised: Which of these two faces of work organization will dominate the diffusion process? Will inertia and custom, institutional embeddedness, and the collective effort of workers and their representatives to resist managerial-driven change be the predominant pattern? Or will the organizational logic of these new systems prove persuasive to workers? Will workers' representatives get out in front of these changes and adapt them to address workers' as well as employers' concerns? To address these questions, I draw on Round 1 (1989) and Round 2 (1994) data from the International Assembly Plant Study that Frits Pil and I carried out. The focus here is a striking finding from past longitudinal analyses: a significant divergence between the United States and Europe in the implementation of lean production work practices from 1989 to 1994. Specifically, there was a rapid pace of adoption of practices related to work teams in Europe over that five-year period and an almost complete absence of such implementation in plants owned by General Motors (GM), Ford, and Chrysler—the so-called Big Three—in the United States and Canada.

During the time period studied, there were a number of similarities in the competitive situations facing domestic automakers in both regions. Both U.S. and European companies faced new competition from Japanese transplants that raised the bar for productivity and quality performance, and in response were working hard to master the intricacies of lean production. While certain forces for change were the same across these regions, others varied significantly. Yet the range of outcomes—such as the variation in adoption rate for new work practices—appeared to be much wider than the variation in facilitating conditions.

This wide range suggests the importance of understanding the economic, technological, and institutional factors affecting the introduction of these new practices. Factors at the national, institutional, and company level are important in explaining this pattern of divergence over the five-year period of 1989–1994, but their long-term effect must be balanced against the strength and durability of economic and technological pressures that might well reduce this divergence over the longer term. Based on this analysis, I offer three scenarios for the implementation of lean production work practices in these two regions early in the twenty-first century, and then make the case for which is most likely to occur.

The Backdrop: Work Organization Trends from 1989 to 1994

In the International Assembly Plant Study, Frits Pil and I have gathered data on work practices that allow us to identify where a plant lies on a continuum between mass and lean production. We combine these practices into a Work Systems Index for statistical analyses in which we examine how work practices interact with complementary human resource management policies (selection, training, and compensation, for example) and technical aspects of the production system to affect manufacturing performance (see MacDuffie 1995). The Work Systems Index and the practices underlying it supply the primary data for the next section. Table 6.1 provides details of the Round 1 and Round 2 samples. Unless noted, the data in this section are for the matched sample of forty-four plants, the identical plants in both years.

Table 6.2 shows the world sample means for the six work practices in the Work Systems Index in 1989 and 1994; differences in means are statistically significant at levels that vary from 90 percent to 99 percent for all practices except "Responsibility for Quality Inspection" (see the table for details). While these averages conceal tremendous variation across companies and countries, they do reveal a general trend toward the high-involvement work practices associated with lean production (Pil and MacDuffie 1996).

Figure 6.1 shows that despite extensive regional variation, the overall trend for the Work Systems Index from 1989 to 1994 is consistently in the

Table 6.1. Round 1 and Round 2 Samples for the International Assembly Plant Study

Regional Group	Round 1 (1989)	Round 2 (1994)	No. Matched across Both Periods
U.S./N.A.	16	25	13
Europe	24	21	12
Japan/Japan	9	12	6
Japan/N.A.	4	8	3
N.E.s	11	18	7
Australia	6	4	3
Total no. of plants	70	88	44
Companies	24	21	18
Countries	17	20	17

U.S./N.A. = U.S.-owned plants in North America; Japan/N.A. = Japanese-owned plants in North America; N.E.s = new entrants (in Round 1 = Mexico, Brazil, Korea, Taiwan; in Round 2 = these four plus South Africa and India).

Table 6.2. Changes in Work Organization Practices at Matched Plants: World Sample Averages for 1989 and 1994

	1989	1994	Significance Level of Change
Work force in on-line work teams (%)	16	46	**
Work force in off-line problem-solving groups (%)	29	49	***
Suggestions per employee (no.)	9	13	***
Suggestions implemented (%)	38	51	***
Job rotations (1 = none; 5 = within and across work groups)	3.0	3.2	*
Responsibility for quality inspection/SPC[a] (0 = staff specialists; 4 = production workers)	1.6	1.7	—

[a] SPC = Statistical process control
$*p < 0.1$. $**p < 0.05$. $***p < 0.01$.

direction of lean production work practices. As mentioned earlier, this chapter focuses on the most striking regional contrast, between U.S.-owned plants located in North America (GM, Ford, and Chrysler plants in the United States and Canada) and plants located in Europe (including both European-owned and U.S.-owned plants).[1] While the Work Systems

---

[1] For simplicity in nomenclature and for consistency over the time period in question, I use United States (U.S.) to identify plants in both the United States and Canada and include plants that were owned by Chrysler in 1989 and 1994 but are now owned by Daimler Chrysler. The U.S. category does not include any Japanese or European-owned transplants in North America.

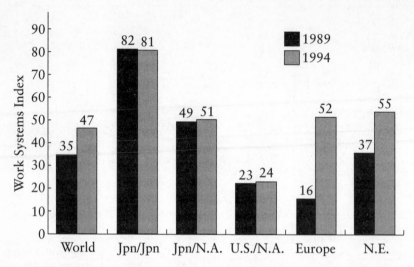

Figure 6.1. Steady movement toward work organization associated with lean production from 1989 to 1994. Jpn/N.A. = Japanese-owned plants in North America; U.S./N.A. = U.S.-owned plants in North America; N.E. = new entrants (in 1989: Mexico, Brazil, Korea, Taiwan; in 1994, these four plus South Africa and India)

Index average score is lower for Europe than for the United States in 1989, the European average score in 1994 is dramatically higher—roughly the same, in fact, as the Japanese transplant average—while the U.S. average remains low and unchanged. Figure 6.2 shows that the differences are located primarily in three practices: the percentage of employees in on-line teams and in off-line problem-solving groups, and the number of suggestions per one hundred employees.

Why are there such major differences in the work organization trends between the United States and Europe from 1989 to 1994? In particular, what explains this divergence in the face of strong economic and technological forces for convergence? In the next section, I discuss the forces for convergence and divergence, focusing on the comparison of the United States and Europe in the early 1990s.

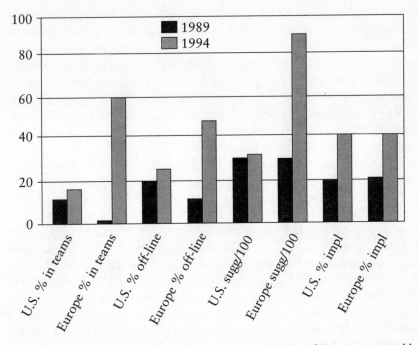

Figure 6.2. Implementation of lean work practices in U.S. and European assembly plants, 1989 and 1994. % in teams = percentage of employees in on-line work teams; % off-line = percentage of employees in off-line problem-solving groups; sugg/100 = number of suggestions per one hundred employees.

Forces for Convergence and Divergence: U.S. and European Assembly Plants in the Early 1990s

Historically, national-level differences in work practices have persisted over time because they are reinforced by national institutional factors affecting training, compensation, the way jobs are defined, and both union structure and the daily processes of labor relations. However, I (1996) previously argued that there are certain macro forces promoting a greater degree of convergence in work organization across countries today than was once thought possible—specifically, globalization, flexible automation, product market demands for variety and customization, and the influence of lean production ideas. These convergent forces will not necessarily be felt with equal force in different countries or regions. Indeed, a brief comparison suggests that this is one explanation for the differences between the United States and Europe. While a careful examination of globalization pressures is beyond the scope of this chapter, suffice it to say for our purposes that both U.S. and European assembly plants (regardless of their ownership) face similarly strong pressures from globalization. This is particularly true with respect to the continued investment by most automakers in new production facilities in developing countries, despite the wide perception of global overcapacity; the wave of consolidation in the global industry that has seen multiple cross-national mergers among both Original Equipment Manufacturers (OEMs) and first-tier suppliers; and the effort by automakers to establish a common production system across their global operations.

Flexible automation is also not an important differentiating factor. As Table 6.3 shows, U.S. plants and European plants have similar levels of overall automation, defined as the percentage of production operations (number of welds, square inches of paint, or assembly steps, for example) that are automated rather than manual. A second technology measure, the Robotic Index, shows a similar level for European and U.S. plants in 1989 and 1994, with both increasing their index score from 2.2 to roughly 3.3. This index is defined as the number of robots per vehicle produced per hour, so for a standard-size assembly plant producing an annual volume of 250,000 vehicles, this means an increase from 138 robots to 207 robots. (Note that U.S. and European plants do lag behind Japanese plants in the use of flexible automation; both plants in Japan and their transplants have scores around 6.7–6.8, indicating double the number of robots in a plant of a given volume.) Clearly the disparity in work organization between these two regions cannot be attributed to a technology "pull" toward flexibility (MacDuffie and Pil 1997b).

The story is different for the other two forces for convergence, however. Product variety is demonstrably much higher in Europe than in the United States. This is not so much true in terms of the number of different models built in a given plant, although the 1994 data do show a slightly higher number for European plants. The differences are more apparent in the number of countries to which export models are sent (only three to five countries for the United States versus well over twenty for Europe) and in measures of "under-the-skin" complexity—sources of complexity that are not readily apparent to customers. Wire harnesses proliferate as more and more electronic options are offered; U.S. plants only installed around twelve in 1994, compared with eighty-four in Europe. The number of paint colors is significant not so much for its impact on the paint shop, which is modest, but because of all the color-coded trim parts that must be organized in sequence in the assembly area. So the fact that European

Table 6.3. Extent of Flexible Automation and Product Variety in United States and
Europe, 1989–1994

	U.S./N.A.		Europe	
	1989	*1994*	*1989*	*1994*
Total automation (%)	30	34	26	31
Robotic Index	2.2	3.3	2.2	3.4
Models produced (no.)	2.7	2.2	2.6	2.5
Countries for export (no.)	2.9	5.6	23.7	26.6
Wire harnesses (no.)	15	12	83	84
Exterior colors (no.)	10	11	15	16
Engine/transmission combinations (no.)	30	29	83	86

U.S./N.A. = U.S.-owned plants in North America.

plants have, on average, sixteen different colors versus only eleven for the
United States must be multiplied many times over to capture the incremental complexity for the assembly process. Finally, European plants
have, on average, eighty-six engine-transmission combinations (versus
roughly thirty for U.S. plants), so they must cope with much more vari-
ability for this aspect of product mix.

The final force for convergence, I have argued, is the influence of lean production ideas, in particular the perception that lean production represents a
paradigm shift away from the principles of mass production that were dominant for most of the twentieth century. This perception has been fueled by
evidence of superior productivity and quality at lean production plants
(Womack, Jones, and Roos 1990). This is particularly true for the plants outside of Japan (both the transplants in the United States and the United Kingdom and the "greenfield" plants of Western companies built on the "lean"
model, such as Opel Eisenach) because they provide evidence that this production approach can be implemented in a wide variety of country and company settings. As a result, most automakers in the world have undertaken serious efforts to implement the work practices associated with lean
production. Nevertheless, there has been variation at both a national or regional and a company level in how strongly the influence of these ideas is felt.

In the United States, the influence of lean production ideas was felt most
strongly in the mid to late 1980s owing to the demonstration effects of the
Japanese transplants opening at that time. The Round 1 data show that
U.S. plants were already beginning to reduce their inventory buffers and
make other changes to the technical side of the production system (reducing set-up times, adding more preventive maintenance, and improving process flow). These trends continued strongly between Round 1 and Round 2.

This partial implementation of lean production, plus a drive to reduce levels of product variety at most Big Three plants, helped boost productivity substantially by 1994, narrowing the gap with Japanese competitors. Quality was improving during this time as well, owing to a variety of changes throughout the value chain, with assembly plant quality initiatives often implemented despite the persistence of traditional work practices. By the time the Round 2 data were collected, however, many Big Three plants were enjoying booming sales due to the strong recovery of the U.S. economy and felt little sense of urgency about pressing for further implementation of lean production practices.

Efforts to change work practices that did occur were often tentative and faced resistance, both active and passive, from managers and union officials at the plant level. As suggested elsewhere (MacDuffie 1996), this was often caused by company-level factors. It is also true, however, that the ambivalence of the United Auto Workers (UAW) toward work teams as a highly visible symbol of labor-management cooperation and the active opposition of the Canadian Auto Workers (CAW) to lean production affected the slow, often sporadic, attempts to implement new work practices—even if only by giving U.S. and Canadian managers who were similarly ambivalent a reason to avoid pressing ahead. One result is that many of the improvement efforts directed at production methods in the Big Three plants in the early 1990s were directed by industrial engineers and only rarely involved front-line workers. As evidence emerged that these efforts were helping to close the performance gap with Japanese competitors, once again there was little perceived need to change from this approach to implementing lean production.

The European situation was quite different during this time. Just as the U.S. economy began its recovery in the early 1990s, Europe began to face its worst recession in many years. The resulting financial crisis led many automakers to become newly receptive to the ideas of lean production. These ideas had had less impact in Europe than in the United States, partly because strong market conditions in the 1980s allowed many European automakers to claim that lean production was not applicable to them and partly because the Japanese transplants came later to Europe and then only to the United Kingdom; the first transplant to open out of the United Kingdom was Toyota's new plant in France, which began production in 2000. (As a number of observers have noted, Renault is an exception [see Charron 1999; Freyssenet 1999]). It is no coincidence that Renault had done more than any other European company to implement lean production in its plants when the Round 1 data were collected in 1989.)

Data from Round 1 of the International Assembly Plant Study revealed larger gaps between European and Japanese performance, in both productivity and quality, than had been generally suspected in Europe; this finding received wide attention at European automakers when the data were published by the IMVP in 1990. Finally, in 1989 Nissan and Toyota introduced Infiniti and Lexus products in the United States with great success, striking at the heart of a luxury product segment that European companies had dominated and meeting the quality expectations of consumers in this segment at dramatically lower production costs. Thus, the financial crisis coincided with evidence and events that convinced European automakers of the need to change their approach to production in fundamental ways.

In contrast with the United States, work practices were considered central to the changes that needed to be made in Europe. This is partially due to the very different stance taken by European unions, particularly in Sweden and Germany, to the idea of "group work." Semi-autonomous teams and "dock assembly" (whereby the moving assembly line is eliminated and vehicles stop at a docking station at which many tasks are completed during a long cycle time) had been central to the work reorganization experiments at Volvo, beginning with the plant in Kalmar in the 1970s and culminating with the opening of the plant in Uddevalla in 1989.

The Volvo experiences influenced German companies greatly. Attention focused on the "new production concept," handling high levels of product complexity with subassembly lines (or dock assembly) based on long cycle times and staffed with highly skilled workers (Turner 1991). This was not primarily a management initiative; it grew out of discussions in the early 1980s about eliminating alienation at work among union officials, government officials, company representatives, and academics in Germany. To reinforce this concept, the German metal-working union, IG Metall, developed a twelve-point list of principles for the implementation of group work (Eckpunckte zur Gruppenarbeit). While implementation of these ideas remained limited to pilot areas in many German plants by the late 1980s (as shown by the Round 1 data, which found a very limited use of work teams of any kind in Europe), the new Rastatt plant of Mercedes (which opened in 1992) was built initially along these principles. Thus, the stage was set on the union side in Germany by the end of the 1980s for a much more extensive implementation of group work than was actually evident. Indeed, at that time it was often management that showed more reluctance about moving in this direction (Jürgens 1997).

Thus, when competitiveness crises hit many European companies in the early 1990s, and with them the perceived need to move toward lean production, managers became backers of the implementation of work teams and other group activities. Union officials and other backers of new production concepts quickly recognized that lean production provided a very different structure for group activities, retaining the moving assembly line and short cycle times and offering relatively little autonomy to teams. Yet, for the most part, European unions backed the widespread implementation of lean work practices during the early 1990s. Possibly they felt this would be a "foot in the door" in moving away from traditional mass production methods and toward their conception of group work. Or perhaps they felt it best to support this initiative as part and parcel of negotiations to protect employment security and wages from strong concessionary pressures. Whatever the reasons, this confluence of support for implementing new work practices from both management and labor in the context of the competitiveness crises of the early 1990s is the reason why the average Work Systems Index score for European plants in the 1994 assembly plant data is so high. (For detailed accounts of these dynamics in Germany, see Kuhlmann and Schumann 1997; Roth 1997; and Katz and Darbishire 1999.)

The high levels of product variety in Europe also play a role in this story. Central to the new production concepts just described was the idea that standardized methods were only appropriate for standardized products and that high levels of product variety were therefore inconsistent with the assembly line and the narrow pursuit of efficiency. Thus, the question of whether dock assembly and long cycle times were more efficient than the assembly line was not the primary focus. The belief was that high-quality products offered in many variants should command a sufficient margin to justify such a production system financially. Indeed, highly differentiated production was seen typically as an important competitive advantage for European companies (see Sorge and Streeck 1988; Jürgens, Malsch, and Dohse 1993). As I note later, what ultimately undermined this view was not a shift away from high product differentiation by European companies but the discovery that high levels of product variety could coexist with high levels of productivity and quality on lean assembly lines.

In summary, U.S. plants did little to implement lean work practices in the early 1990s because (1) they faced few demands for flexibility due to product variety; (2) the earlier influence of lean production ideas, in the mid-1980s, had led to partial implementation, with a particular focus on changes in the technical system led by technical specialists; (3) performance gains combined with strong market conditions removed the pressure to pursue the implementation of new work practices; and (4) union ambivalence and/or opposition vis-à-vis new work practices slowed implementation in cases where new work practices *were* introduced, in part by providing a rationale for delay or abandonment for managers and engineers who shared the ambivalence.

European plants, in contrast, implemented lean work practices extensively in the early 1990s because (1) they did face high demands for product variety; (2) the influence of lean production ideas was beginning to be felt strongly; (3) many European companies faced a competitiveness crisis due to recessionary conditions and evidence of the performance gap with foreign (particularly Japanese) competitors; and (4) European unions had long been supportive of group work as part of a new production concept that eliminated the moving assembly line and lengthened cycle time (partially in support of high variety production), and thus chose to support managerial initiatives to implement work teams in the lean production mold, even though these fell short of their earlier vision.

Scenarios for the Future: Work Organization in the United States and Europe

I turn now to the question of what pattern of diffusion of lean work practices will be observable in the United States and Europe in the early years of the twenty-first century. I see three potential scenarios for what we might experience. The figure accompanying each scenario uses actual Work Systems Index scores for the United States and Europe in 1989 and 1994 and projects a third data point, labeled as 2004, to indicate the near future. We expect to collect further data that will allow us to confirm or disconfirm each scenario by that date.

Scenario 1

In the first scenario (Figure 6.3), Europe continues to increase its reliance on the work practices associated with lean production, at a rate that leads to convergence with the high level of lean practices at Japanese-owned plants. (I assume through all of these scenarios that Japanese-owned plants will continue to display similar levels of lean work practices in the future, with perhaps a small move away from lean practices in Japan and a continued increase in the use of these practices at Japanese transplants in the United States and Europe.) This scenario projects a continuation of the pace and direction of change found in Europe in the early 1990s. With the continued visibility of Opel Eisenach as a successful lean model for new plants (including the new Opel plant in Poland [see Mac-

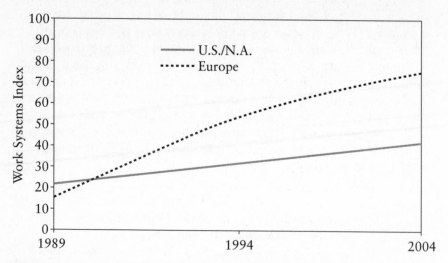

Figure 6.3. Scenario 1: Europe reaches a similar level of lean production work organization as Japanese-managed plants, while the United States continues to move more slowly. U.S./N.A. = U.S.-owned plants in North America.

Duffie 1999b]) and the opening of Toyota's first plant in continental Europe (in northeastern France), the argument here would be that lean production will continue to hold the "best-practice" pride of place, thus legitimizing the further implementation of lean work practices.

For this to happen, we would expect to see a further move away from the new production concept ideas of dock assembly and long cycle times. Many European companies have already abandoned this view, primarily because of evidence that lean production can achieve high product variety on regular assembly lines without sacrificing either productivity or quality (MacDuffie, Sethuraman, and Fisher 1996). In addition, the dock assembly experiments were not particularly efficient, requiring long training times and making it more difficult to cope with absenteeism or turnover. Furthermore, some observers argue that workers did not view these dock assembly jobs as a great improvement over assembly line work, even though improving job satisfaction and reducing alienation were a major rationale for the experiments (Springer 1999).

For this scenario to occur, European unions would need to support the continuing diffusion of lean work practices, even as they might work to establish certain conditions for how those practices would be applied. Recent changes in work practices and production layout at Toyota's Kyushu plant and retrofitted production lines at Toyota's Motomachi plant suggest efforts to increase attention to "humanization-of-work" issues within the Toyota Production System framework. Indeed, some have written about these changes as evidence that Toyota is moving toward the ideas implemented at Volvo's Uddevalla plant (Pil and Fujimoto 1999). This suggests there is ample scope for negotiation over the precise way in which lean work practices are implemented in order to accomplish certain humanization-of-work outcomes. Thus in this scenario, the focus of labor policy shifts away from new production concepts and toward defining the scope and process of what Adler and Borys (1996) call an "enabling bureaucracy" and what Springer (1999) calls "participative rationalization"—the active participation of workers in structured production-improvement activities.

Under this scenario, U.S. plants would also continue to implement lean work practices, but at a slower rate than European plants, thus leaving a substantial gap in the patterns of work organization found in these regions. The assumption here is that the same factors that slowed U.S. implementation in the early 1990s will continue to hold sway, yet they will not entirely overcome the power of convergent forces (competitive pressure from globalization, the pull of increasing use of flexible automation, and the continued legitimation of lean production as the best-practice path). This scenario also assumes that the United States will continue to face somewhat different product market conditions than Europe, with considerably less product variety needing to be produced in any given plant.

The North American union position (UAW and CAW) under this scenario is viewed as relatively consistent with what it has been—namely, skepticism about lean work practices but a pragmatic willingness to allow a certain amount to be implemented, particularly when a plant undergoes a major retrofit for a new model. Management, on the other hand, is assumed to be broadly supportive of lean production as an overall strategy yet more inclined to assign process-improvement responsibilities to technical specialists rather than to front-line workers. In the absence of a strong push from either party to get lean work practices implemented at the shop floor, this scenario sees the gap between the United States and Europe continuing for the foreseeable future.

Scenario 2

Under this scenario (Figure 6.4), U.S. and European implementation of lean work practices would converge at a level close to the current European average. This therefore assumes that the pace of adoption of lean work practices stalls in Europe and speeds up in the United States. There are several reasons why this might occur. Efforts to link production scheduling more directly to consumer demand, through new retailing models (build-to-order linked to Internet-based sales channels, for example), may pull U.S. plants toward higher levels of product variety, thus making flexible work organization more desirable. (The same trends would probably come to Europe, albeit a bit later, but European plants already have more experience handling high product variety and at least since the early 1990s, more flexible work organizations in place.)

Recent efforts by U.S. companies to promote the thorough adoption of a full production system modeled on Toyota's approach (the Ford Production System and the Chrysler Operating System, for instance) constitute a more systematic and intentional management strategy for the implementation of lean work practices than the technically oriented and decentralized plant initiatives of the past. In addition, several older plants are being completely retrofitted, not just for a new model but for a new approach to production. The second Saturn plant, which is located at the old GM plant in Wilmington, Delaware, for example, now builds an Opel-designed vehicle in a method said to be somewhere between GM's traditional production process and Saturn's unique approach. In addition, GM will build its first new North American plant in twenty years at Lansing, Michigan, based on a design that will be heavily influenced by GM's experiences in Europe, South America, and Asia.

The UAW and CAW will face the challenge of how to respond to these new initiatives, but recent history suggests that their response will be pragmatic and may well result in a much higher incidence of lean work practices. While there are still sufficient barriers to leave the overall level of implementation well below the U.S.-based Japanese transplants, it is certainly conceivable that U.S. plants could match the use of lean work practices in European plants.

Why, under this scenario, do European companies move no further than their 1994 level in their implementation of lean work practices? The assumption here is that the implementation efforts begun in the early 1990s will encounter various difficulties over time. Workers may react negatively to the short job cycles and pressure for performance in lean-design plants, and unions may continue to push for the alternate principles of group work that were established as policy priorities in the late 1980s. Difficulties at a "model plant" like Eisenach (or any of the Eisenach "clones") could weaken the legitimacy accorded to lean production approaches. Management resolve to pursue lean production could be diverted by other developments in the industry, such as consolidation in the supply chain, which is at a much earlier stage in Europe than in the United States. Finally, a company like Daimler-Chrysler may take some time devising a production system policy and a labor policy it can apply across its European and U.S. plants (assuming that it aims for such consistency), and this could slow the implementation of new work practices.

Scenario 3

Under this scenario (Figure 6.5), the use of lean work practices in the United States remains extremely low and the upward trend in Europe is reversed. Here, therefore, there is again some degree of convergence between the two regions but in the direction of traditional work practices. Given the strength of the overall trend toward lean production worldwide from 1989 to 1994, this seems unlikely. Yet it might happen, under the following conditions.

In the United States, the situation of partial implementation of lean production on the technical side, with process improvement given to technical specialists, would continue. If these changes were seen as leading to a "speed up" of work pace, worker and union resistance could be high in the absence of any mechanism that involves workers in the improvement process. Adversarial relations between the UAW and the Big Three, spurred by such events as the sale of Delphi and Visteon, an aggressive level of outsourcing, and whipsawing of plants to get local concessions, could provoke a more militant stance from the union and a withdrawal of support for the implementation of new work practices.

In Europe, there could be a similar souring of relations with unions that could make new work practices a battleground for larger disputes about outsourcing and terms and conditions of national labor contracts. Given that occupational boundaries such as those found in Germany that yield high levels of narrow but deep technical expertise are challenged by the emphasis of lean production on broad systems knowledge but relatively

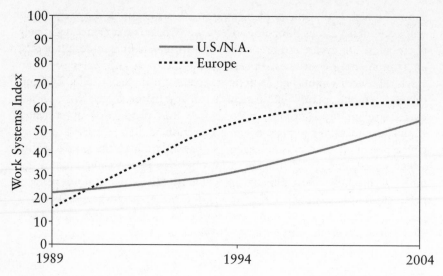

Figure 6.4. Scenario 2: Europe and the United States converge at a level somewhat below Japanese companies. U.S./N.A. = U.S.-owned plants in North America.

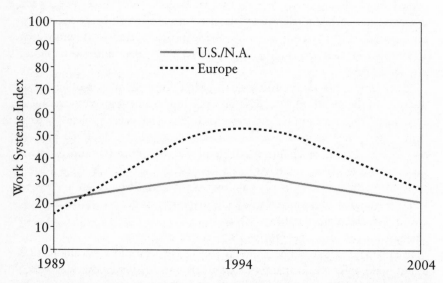

Figure 6.5. Scenario 3: Europe and the United States both move back toward traditional work organization and mass production. U.S./N.A. = U.S.-owned plants in North America.

shallow technical expertise, there could be a backlash against lean work practices as a perceived threat to occupation-based social identities. The developments mentioned in Scenario 2 as stalling the progress toward lean work practices in Europe could also fit under this scenario.

In addition, both regions could be affected by a broader technological trend that is already apparent in the semiconductor industry. Whereas the performance of semiconductor manufacturing plants was at one time partly dependent on problem solving by shop-floor workers, the increasing sophistication of the process technology reduces the role of workers and the problem-solving contribution they can make while increasing the reliance on the shop-floor role of engineers whose technical knowledge is much greater (Brown and Appleyard 2001). While the final assembly processes in the auto industry have proved stubbornly resistant to past efforts at automation, it is certainly possible that future changes in product and process technology could reduce the scope for worker contribution in this industry as well.

What Will Be the Face of Work Organization under Lean Production?

Here I weave together various strands of my arguments to justify my prediction concerning which of the three scenarios is most likely to prevail. In my view, it is the second scenario—the rapid pace of adoption of lean work practices in Europe slows (while still continuing), and the slow pace of adoption in the United States quickens, resulting in roughly similar levels of implementation in these two regions within the next several years. But this prediction is by no means certain or unalterable. Indeed, a key message here is that the parties can influence the future trajectory, just as their actions and strategies influenced changes and shifts from traditional patterns in the past. So in this final section I suggest how the parties themselves, by engaging in more direct dialogue and negotiations, might influence these trends.

The United States was an anomaly in the Round 2 data of the International Assembly Plant Study, with the lowest level of lean work practices and virtually no change from 1989 to 1994. Since that time, U.S. companies have been feeling a stronger need to increase product variety at their plants, which may pull them toward a stronger interest in flexible forms of work organization. U.S. companies have been among the earliest to conclude that there are benefits in moving toward a common production system and in transferring innovations back and forth from their home country operations to their plants in developing countries. The use of

cross-company teams in product development and in supplier development activities is becoming more common and legitimizing this approach
in production. Thus, the United States is now more extensively exposed to
the forces promoting the use of lean work practices than it was in the past.

In Europe, in contrast, a number of factors coincided in the early 1990s
to lead to a rapid implementation of lean work practices in most companies. These changes occurred in the context of major competitiveness
crises for individual companies and a volatile economic situation for the
region as a whole. Under these conditions, past approaches to reforming
work organization were discredited and lean production was often taken
up as a panacea. The work teams of lean production were seen as close
enough to the group work envisioned by European unions to be adopted
without much union resistance. Overall, implementation proceeded so
quickly because of the urgency of the crisis and the timing of the exposure
to lean production ideas at many European automakers, not on the basis
of extensive experience and careful study.

As European companies and unions have gained more experience with
lean production, the issues surrounding its implementation have become
much sharper, clarifying the parameters of a debate about the appropriate
labor policy. The pace of implementation will slow as a result, I believe,
but more because the earlier rate of change was unsustainable than because of any fundamental reversal in the factors supporting implementation. European companies still face high product variety and seek greater
flexibility in how their factories are run. They share the interest of U.S.
companies in standardizing the production system across their global operations, and they are exposed to innovations being achieved in their
plants in developing countries. Cross-company collaborations, which
came to Europe much later than to the United States, are now highly legit-
imized. Finally, there is some evidence (Springer 1999), based on data
from Mercedes-Benz, that participative rationalization is viewed neutrally
or positively by a majority of workers, and increasingly as a worker pre-
rogative that would be very difficult to take away.

Why is the second scenario more likely than the first? My assessment is
that the forces pressing for further implementation of lean work practices
will remain strong in Europe and intensify in the United States, but that
these forces will be sufficiently tempered in Europe so that the current implementation gap between the regions will be reduced. Why do I not expect the third scenario to be realized? Besides the reasons just given, I believe that both the UAW and the CAW in North America and the various
European unions will decide to take a pragmatic approach to lean work
practices.

This approach could take different forms, depending on the unilateral actions and joint interactions of the key parties. Unions (and works councils) could focus primarily on monitoring the implementation of lean practices for potential abuses, mainly at the shop floor. Or they could develop a more proactive policy on how such activities as participative rationalization by on-line and off-line work teams should proceed, making sure, for example, that safety and ergonomic issues are addressed as frequently as quality and productivity issues and that worker proposals are evaluated fairly and implemented promptly. In either case, I believe that the reaction from workers to lean work practices will be sufficiently positive (assuming that the practices are implemented with the proper respect for the worker's role in the production process) that unions will be more inclined to regulate these practices than to oppose them. In some respects, union leaders can influence not only the rate of change but also, as the German case (Katz and Darbishire 1999) and to some extent the Saturn case in the United States (Rubinstein and Kochan 2001) illustrate, the nature of the changes in ways that bring workers' interests more directly into the design of production and workplace practices and systems. But to do so, union leaders, in the United States and Canada in particular, would need to shift to a more proactive strategy and assert a more direct role in managerial decision making at both the shop-floor and higher levels of the corporation. This would be a substantial change for American unions but well within the traditions of at least some of their European counterparts.

Ultimately, then, what can we conclude from this thought experiment about the two faces of work organization? If, as I predict, automakers in the United States and Europe (and increasingly all over the world) are "leaning toward teams," it is because this form of work organization is a critical foundation for both the technical and the social innovations of lean production. As long as lean production continues to offer performance advantages over mass production (particularly the advantages related to quality and product variety, which will become more important than simple labor productivity), companies will put considerable (and persistent) effort into the implementation of some form of work teams and associated problem-solving activities. The transition period may be lengthy, with teams likely to be omnipresent at greenfield sites but entering brownfield sites only at a time of major product change or process retrofit. (Indeed, the oldest plants may well close without making this change.) But eventually I do expect work teams, which pool the cognitive efforts of individual workers and direct them toward process improvement, to be ubiquitous in this particular setting. The "locus of innovation" face will thus be clearly evident.

Yet, as the preceding discussion suggests, there will be new phases of negotiation and change in this setting, focused on the "how" and "why" of teamwork, rather than "whether" and "where." Here the "persistence from social embeddedness" face of work organization will be readily apparent. Divergent ideas about the importance and necessity of autonomy in team functioning (or, put differently, about the nature of management's role in directing team activities) and about the scope of problem solving will continue to be debated, both in daily work activities and in broader discussions between labor representatives and managers. The density and frequency of interactions in the social network will also evolve over time in particular settings. At this more fine-grained level of analysis—the nature of social interaction within and across teams, occupational groups, and hierarchical levels—considerable variation in team-related practices is virtually guaranteed.

There is ample reason to question, however, whether this "persistence" face of work organization will attach itself to geographical regions and national boundaries as much in the future as in the past. Indeed, if we continue to see the consolidation of the global automotive industry through mergers and acquisitions among the major automakers (like Daimler-Chrysler, Ford-Volvo, and Renault-Nissan), the question of regional differences may become less salient. Global multinationals will pursue different work practices in accordance with their production strategy, their corporate culture, their history of labor relations, and their technological capabilities. It will be increasingly valuable, in my view, to start any future assessment of work organization by applying a *company* lens first, and only subsequently a *national/regional* lens. While different national or regional patterns will always be apparent when implementation at the plant level is studied, company-level patterns are likely to be more significant in the future. The good news for students of industrial evolution and the labor process is that probing the two faces of work organization will remain as relevant to their inquiries as it ever was. The good news for managers and labor leaders who confront these issues on a daily basis is that by understanding the forces at work, they can gain better control over the destinies of the people and organizations they represent. An important lesson for all is that strategic choices over the design and implementation of production and work systems are key venues in which negotiations and change occur in this industry. If, as I argued at the beginning of this chapter, this industry is a bellwether for others, then debates over these issues will be "on the table" for many other industries as well.

7

Workplace Justice, Zero Tolerance, and Zero Barriers

MARY ROWE

CORINNE BENDERSKY

New Goals and Strategies for Conflict Management

The purpose of this chapter is to review the evolution and state of the art of dispute resolution systems in U.S. organizations. This field is evolving rapidly, but research is just beginning to catch up to the reality of dispute resolution practice.[1] In unionized and nonunion corporations, government agencies, academic institutions, professional and service organizations, school systems, and health care institutions, employers and employees are re-thinking the nature of dispute resolution and conflict management and reviewing their internal dispute resolution channels.

There are several reasons why this re-thinking is taking place now. One traditional motivation—the desire to provide workplace justice—is currently stronger than ever in some organizations, partly because of civil rights and workplace safety laws and partly because employers have found it hard to insist on fair and courteous treatment of customers without attempting to provide a fair and civil culture within their organizations.

Most employers also are attempting to prevent illegal behavior and to control costs. Many have established "zero-tolerance" policies for certain kinds of unacceptable behavior.[2] Some are trying to respond to pressures

---

[1] Readers may also be interested in the *Guidelines for the Design of Integrated Conflict Management Systems within Organizations*, produced by the Track One Committee of the Society of Professionals in Dispute Resolution (2001), and found at http://www.spidr.org, which drew in part from ideas presented in this article.

[2] Many dispute resolution experts do not like zero-tolerance policies and point to apparently unreasonable applications, such as the child suspended from school for saying, "Bang! Bang!" We are not advocates of zero-tolerance policies. We discuss them here as a proxy for all circumstances where employers try in a punitive way to outlaw specified behaviors.

to comply with laws and regulations in a way that does not expose them to public agencies or courts or burden their internal formal grievance procedures. These several goals to some extent have been in conflict when employers have interpreted zero tolerance to require mandatory punishment of proscribed behavior. This interpretation has often forced them to use formal procedures—inside and outside the organization—thus creating or leading to the very burden that employers want to avoid. In addition, mandatory reporting, investigation, and punishment do not seem to be effective in deterring proscribed behavior.

Private sector employers therefore have chosen to explore mediation, and arbitration in occasional cases (Lipsky and Seeber 1998). Similar pressure to use mediation has been felt in the public sector in an attempt to relieve the burden and backlog at the Equal Employment Opportunity Commission (EEOC) and other U.S. government agencies (McDermott et al. 2000; Kochan, Lautsch, and Bendersky 2000). Throughout North America there has been an ongoing discussion of alternative, also known as "appropriate," dispute resolution (ADR) mechanisms.

Employers reviewing their conflict management options have found that simply providing such external ADR mechanisms as mediation and arbitration does not deal with enough internal conflicts because relatively few of the day-to-day problems wind up outside the organization. Some therefore have turned to a consideration of internal systems. They also like the fact that effective internal systems help maintain employer control. Some believe, in addition, that a systems approach to conflict management improves productivity (Colvin 1999; Cutcher-Gershenfeld 1991).

In addition, employers are concerned with the fact that it can be difficult to get the members of their organization to act in a timely way when they find themselves with a problem. We believe that this may be especially true when the employer has punitive zero-tolerance policies. This chapter focuses on this issue. We discuss the challenge of getting individuals either to act on their own to resolve a matter or to come forward to use the conflict management system. We suggest that it is important for an employer to offer "zero-barrier" conflict resolution options. We begin by presenting the theoretical foundations for taking a systems approach to internal conflict management.

Theoretical Foundations

Some of the changes in conflict management practices over the past thirty years have come from the development of a theoretical understanding of the nature of interpersonal negotiations and conflicts. The language we use in this chapter derives from work in negotiation theory, which illuminates both *employer* conflict management strategies and the preferences of *individual* complainants. We believe these particular strategies and preferences are major reasons for the appearance of mediation and ombuds offices as conflict resolution options and for the new emphasis on a systems approach to conflict management.

In 1965, Richard Walton and Robert McKersie produced a seminal work on distributive, integrative, and mixed-motive negotiations (Walton and McKersie 1965). Distributive (win-lose) negotiations underlie competitive, rights- and power-based dispute resolution, which is oriented toward formal justice. Win-lose conflict management processes include formal investigation, advocacy, decision making and judgment, arbitration, and appeals. Integrative (win-win) negotiations underlie collaborative, interest-based dispute resolution, which is oriented toward problem solving between people who are concerned about fairness and want to maintain their relationship with each other. Win-win examples include helping people help themselves to achieve their own solutions through conflict coaching, informal shuttle diplomacy, formal mediation, generic solutions, and systems change (see appendix to this chapter).

Employees and managers may prefer win-lose or win-win strategies, or both, depending on the individuals and the situations. We do not mean to draw an absolute distinction between *rights* and *interests*. People may see acknowledgment of a particular right as one of their interests, and a particular conflict resolution option sometimes might serve both rights and interests. Our point is that since either strategy may be appropriate, both sets of options are needed in a system—indeed the existence of different options is part of what characterizes a system.

In their 1965 work, Walton and McKersie also described mixed-motive negotiations—those having both win-lose and win-win elements. They made clear that the inherent theoretical discord between distributive (rights-based) and integrative (interest-based) approaches to conflict could sometimes come to a head during the same dispute. The work of Walton and McKersie helps to explain the sometimes uneasy mix between handling rights- and interest-based complaints that now characterizes the variety of dispute resolution options in a modern conflict management system.

For example, there is occasionally tension between people oriented toward legal rights (some lawyers or union representatives) and people primarily oriented toward interests (complainants who "just want the problem to stop"). Employers who are interested only in defending themselves against legal vulnerability want hair-trigger responses to the least suggestion of illegal behavior. Some insist on mandatory reporting, investigation, and punishment of proven offenders. Individuals who are oriented toward interests (and especially toward their relationships) usually want a variety of informal options as well.

Many people in fact choose an option on the basis of how they think that option will affect their workplace and private relationships (Rowe 1990a). Walton and McKersie provided the theoretical foundation for understanding the importance of interpersonal relationships when one is considering a concern or a complaint.

Shifting to a Systems Approach

Over the past thirty years there has been a shift from thinking primarily about individual disputes, specified illegal behavior, or single grievance procedures to comprehensive consideration of all kinds of conflict management within an organization. Employers are integrating discrete channels into a systems approach. Such a system may include a pre-existing multi-step grievance channel. It often includes compliance, mediation, or arbitration structures, which originally operated relatively independently, on a case-by-case basis.

An integrated system goes well beyond traditional channels, however, to include other options (see the appendix); it includes training in first-party negotiations and conflict resolution, for example. An important contribution of Ury, Brett, and Goldberg's work on dispute systems design is to articulate this point (1988: xiii):

> Changing procedures alone . . . is not enough; disputants must have the motivation, skills, and resources to use the new procedures. The challenge is to change the dispute resolution system—the overall set of procedures used and the factors affecting their use—in order to encourage people and organizations to talk instead of fight about their differences.

This shift to systems thinking, which includes all kinds of disputes—not just employment concerns—is discussed in detail by Lipsky and Seeber (1998).

In effective systems, appropriate data-gathering structures link information from dispute resolution channels into the overall management information system. This is especially important where employers are insistent on zero tolerance for specified unacceptable behavior. "The most important check on waste and illegality is employee action . . . [and] if the mechanisms are good, the organization can respond promptly to challenges proved valid" (Ewing 1989: 50). Conflict management is, thus, about prevention of unnecessary conflicts, costs, and grievances; continuous improvement; and resolution of specific disputes.

There is no single ideal model for conflict management systems among organizations because their needs vary. Subject to different legal requirements and imbued with different missions and cultures, they are faced with a variety of internal and external reasons for having a conflict management system, and they need to design the system accordingly.

Internal Incentives to Consider a System

The traditional incentive for establishing a grievance procedure was to meet the demands of workers for workplace justice in disputes between the worker and the employer. Other internal motivations exist now, however (Costantino and Merchant 1996; Gwartney-Gibbs and Lach 1992; Lach and Gwartney-Gibbs 1993; Lynch 1996; Rowe 1984, 1988, 1997; Edwards and Lewin 1993; Center for Public Resources Institute for Dispute Resolution 1997; Slaikeu and Hasson 1998). Managers themselves are asking for justice and for help in dealing with conflicts. Peer disputes (manager versus manager, worker versus coworker, professional versus professional) have been found to be very costly. Organizations are seeking to keep valued professionals in a time of intense global competition. They are working hard to foster, and make the most of, racial and gender diversity. They are dealing with cross-national tensions and misunderstandings. They are hoping to enhance worker productivity and morale and to encourage innovative ideas and "intrapreneurship."

Lately many organizations have been moving away from hierarchical decision making to an emphasis on peer-to-peer and group-level problem solving. Of course, there have always been institutions that emphasized problem solving along with formal justice. Effective union grievance procedures, for one, have long included problem solving, as well as a determination of right and wrong. But problem-solving techniques are being implemented more and more widely because of the new emphasis on teams. One private nonunionized manufacturing plant we studied, for example, implemented a dispute resolution system that started with team-level negotiated dispute resolution agreements. They emphasized collaborative problem solving and interest-based negotiations to address any interpersonal or task-based disagreements that arose within a team. Only when the team members themselves were unable to work out a resolution were supervisors asked to step in. Best-practice systems approaches extend this idea, explicitly linking the dispute resolution options for people with problems.

In the past, dispute resolution focused primarily on negative behavior, such as dealing with difficult and unacceptable conduct from managers or employees. A well-designed conflict management system now explicitly seeks good ideas and constructive dissent, especially on teams, in addition to surfacing unacceptable behavior. A modern system fosters organizational learning from suggestions, questions, and concerns.[3] As an example, many savvy companies have been prompted to set up ergonomic workstations for computer users when faced with employee complaints of sore hands, arms, necks, and shoulders.

External Incentives to Consider a System

Under pressure from government agencies and public opinion, many employers are trying to eliminate destructive and illegal behavior by instituting zero-tolerance policies. They are seeking to reduce potential litigation and penalties for criminal behavior like waste, fraud, and abuse that arise from the U.S. Federal Sentencing Guidelines and similar laws and regulations (Furtado and Howard 1999). They are also trying to comply with regulations in areas such as safety and equal opportunity. Their purpose is both to limit unacceptable behavior and to prevent the need for whistle blowing. Thus, issues that used to be seen as matters of workplace justice are now also seen as matters of compliance. Employers wish to maintain control over how serious concerns will be handled by attempting to handle them internally in an effective way (Blake and Mouton 1984; General Accounting Office 1997; Lipsky and Seeber 1998; McCabe 1988; Slaikeu and Hasson 1998; Ury, Brett, and Goldberg 1988; Ziegenfuss 1988; Blancero and Dyer 1996; Edwards and Lewin 1993; Simon and Sochynsky 1995; Westin and Feliu 1988; Colvin 1999).

In short, there have been many reasons for employers to consider having both problem-solving and justice-oriented options available in their organizations. What about the needs of individuals? Their interests, which are especially important where there are zero-tolerance policies, affirm the importance of providing several kinds of options.

---

[3] This is one of the most consistent themes in the dispute systems–design literature. For some illustrative examples, see Slaikeu and Hasson (1998: 51), Costantino and Merchant (1996: 129), and Westin and Feliu (1988: 218).

Zero Tolerance and Zero Barriers

Individual employees and managers need to have choices about how they will address conflict and report misconduct. A single-channel system that emphasizes only one approach to dispute resolution will fail to address many conflicts. This is especially likely to occur when people are unwilling to come forward because they lack confidence that the organization will take any action or conversely, because they fear the kind of action their organization will likely take.

We call these two barriers to individual action "Type 1" and "Type 2" errors. Type 1 errors occur when individuals fail to report misconduct because they do not think the employer is serious about proscribing it. In other words, Type 1 errors result from not pushing hard enough to stop unacceptable behavior. Type 2 errors occur when an employer appears too draconian and individuals therefore do not come forward in a timely way, or perhaps at all, because of the perceived possible consequences of doing so. Type 2 errors result from pushing too hard to stop unacceptable behavior.

Imagine an example: The employer is committed to zero tolerance. It therefore sets up mandatory reporting, investigation, and discipline for certain types of misconduct,[4] and trains everyone to report the smallest infringement. The workplace learns that various kinds of misconduct will be seriously punished if proved. (We assume the best case here, that there is appropriate due process.) Type 1 errors—the failure to report misconduct because people think the employer is not serious about proscribing bad behavior—have been addressed. However, the employer learns that some people do not report the offenses and problems that they actually observe, suspect, or even endure. In our experience more than half of the observers of bad behavior do not act or come forward in a timely way if an employer pushes too hard (Rowe 1990a).

Many factors explain why this may be so. People may fear bad consequences, especially the loss of relationships, not only at work with the offender and with peers but also at home with family and friends, if they are seen as a complainer. People also fear a loss of privacy and dignity. These factors are especially potent if other employees in their organization have been seen to be complaining inappropriately, for example, to get back at a manager, to get someone into trouble, or to win nuisance settlements for equal employment opportunity (EEO) complaints. An excellent employee

---

[4] We do not recommend this path. The point of this chapter is that there are more effective ways to deal with unacceptable behavior.

in these circumstances may fear being seen as a frivolous, mischievous, supersensitive, or deceitful complainer. In some cases, employees may fear explicit retaliation for having blown the whistle on peers or especially, supervisors (Lewin 1990; Lewin and Peterson 1999).[5] In other words, an organizational culture that is hierarchical and oriented toward punishment, ironically, may inhibit the willingness to act or to come forward.

Other factors also keep people from seeking or cooperating with formal justice options. Many individuals feel they lack the skills to raise an issue, do not want to lose control over their concerns, or think it is pointless to complain. They dislike the processes of formal investigation that are required in formal procedures.[6] People often feel they do not have enough evidence and therefore will not be believed. They are very sensitive about the nature of "convincing evidence" and do not like to come forward with just suspicions. They especially dislike coming forward if their word is the only evidence—especially if formal due process with its emphasis on a standard of proof is really followed—because they understand the bind inherent in "he said, she said" situations. This is particularly likely if the employer's de facto standard of proof is high, that is, "clear and convincing" or "beyond reasonable doubt." Under these circumstances many people believe their word is not enough. So they do not act, or at least not in a

---

[5] Most honorable employers will do their best to prevent and deal with reprisal. Realistically speaking, however, it is almost impossible to prevent or deal with all forms of covert reprisal. This is especially true with respect to reprisal from people outside the organization. So the fact that retaliation is in many cases illegal does not necessarily reassure someone who is afraid to act responsibly or come forward openly.

[6] Many employers have discovered that there is no way to design a formal investigation that the whole workplace will like. Relatively "cooperative" people (those whose typical strategy in interpersonal relations is win-win) tend to dislike the dry, formal, tough methods of criminal investigation that have crept into the U.S. workplace for issues like sexual harassment. Win-lose people, however, who are oriented toward rights and power, paradoxically also sometimes dislike formal investigations. For example, the win-lose witness may feel "he who is not with me is against me," unless the investigator appears to side with that witness. Since a good investigator will strive to be and to appear to be impartial, the distrust that is sparked by impartiality happens quite often. In addition, the employer that protects privacy will discover that many employees think that "nothing is ever done" against those who behave illegally. (An employer that does not protect privacy in an appropriate way, and that speaks openly about individual offenders, may be attacked by all sides for several other reasons.) We believe, in sum, that there will always be some tension about investigation procedures. And this tension has implications for the design of complaint systems, since any tension about investigation procedures also increases the majority's general dislike of formal, win-lose, grievance options. This is yet another reason to offer problem-solving options in a complaint system, so that only the bare minimum number of concerns, those that must be investigated, actually go to formal processes.

timely way. These are some of the reasons for the Type 2 errors, those that occur when an employer is perceived as pushing too hard.

Harvard professor Howard Raiffa (1998) commented on Type 1 and Type 2 errors in the context of zero-tolerance policies.[7] Raiffa noted wryly that there are also quite a number of other possible errors. For example, he noted that overly strong zero-tolerance vigilance may result in solving the wrong problem. We can continue his analysis. Excessive pursuit of zero tolerance may solve the right problem too late or too early, or may solve the problem in a manner that is incomprehensible or repugnant to onlookers. Harsh vigilance may provoke a cascade of new problems, or its price may be too high. The machinery of mandatory investigation can be used easily to retaliate against management, avoid a lay-off, or shoehorn a mass of issues into an inappropriate venue, as sometimes happens with EEO complaints.

We believe that no employer can catch all—or even most—problematic behaviors if all it does is address the Type 1 error with a simple punitive policy of zero tolerance. The more the employer tries to insist on reporting, investigation, and punishment, the fewer Type 1 errors it will have but the higher the risk of Type 2 and other errors. If an employer wants to hear, on a timely basis, from people who are afraid of the consequences of coming forward, it must provide safe, confidential, accessible, credible, informal options for individuals who have concerns.

Of course, the reactions of people who observe bad behavior may vary, depending on the type of issue, the culture of the workplace, and the background of the complainant. We believe, however, that substantially more than half of the employees and managers who are concerned about a problem—whether it is conflict within a team, potentially criminal behavior, poor performance, or race or gender disputes—initially prefer private informal options to surface the issue. In theoretical terms, we believe that most individuals prefer integrative options based on interests, at least at the outset. On the other hand, perhaps a tenth or more want distributive options based on rights and power. Different people follow different negotiation strategies and have different values about conflict. They therefore require a *choice* of options if they are to be willing to act at all.

Observers sometimes think there is only one way to deal with serious problems, but this is usually not true. In a U.S. company, for example, where the law requires that harassment and discrimination be stopped,

---

[7] Howard Raiffa made these comments in the context of an earlier presentation of these ideas, at the 1998 McKersie Festschrift.

several routes can be offered. Harassment laws and regulations require employers to prevent discrimination and to take "effective corrective action" against this form of illegal behavior when it occurs. The basic elements of such action are seen as stopping the harassment, preventing retaliation, and providing an equitable work environment for the complainant. Contrary to popular belief, laws and regulations do not require punishment of an offender, though in any given case the employer may decide that punishment and disciplinary measures are appropriate and prudent. What the laws actually require is effective corrective action. Thus, the actions of a first party, of an informal third party, or of an ombudsperson—if the actions are effective—can fulfill the requirements of law.

In sum, we believe it is difficult to be successful with a single-option, zero-tolerance policy because many people simply do not wish to behave in a purely win-lose way in the workplace. They greatly value their relationships and may believe it is not in their interests to turn people in or to lodge a complaint. There must be interest-based, as well as rights-based, conflict resolution options, if most people are to react responsibly when they perceive a problem.

Current best practice, therefore, includes a focus on reducing an individual's reluctance to act in a responsible way about legitimate concerns. Effective discouragement of unacceptable behavior and effective conflict management require "zero-barrier options." The concept of zero barriers for responsible action thus joins the concepts of workplace justice and zero tolerance as metaphors for internal systems. As goals for a system, none of the three metaphors is totally achievable or even completely desirable, and zero tolerance is especially problematic.[8] These metaphors can help inform those who are thinking about system design, however (Costantino and Merchant 1996; Lach and Gwartney-Gibbs 1993; Lynch 1996; Rowe 1997; Edwards and Lewin 1993; Center for Public Resources Institute for Dispute Resolution 1997; Slaikeu and Hasson 1998).

Options in Parallel Rather Than Rigid Step Procedures

The linkages among dispute resolution options within a system also appear to be changing. Many writers think of a system as a series of steps from interest-based problem solving to rights-based arbitration. Ury,

---

[8] Justice can be defined in unduly harsh ways as well as desirable ways; zero tolerance can be harsh and forbidding, can infringe on the rights of perceived offenders, and can unnecessarily destroy relationships; and zero barriers can lead to unfounded accusations and chaos.

Brett, and Goldberg (1988: 169), for example, prescribe using interest-based resolution processes, like mediation, first and whenever possible. When interest-based processes are inappropriate or ineffective, they recommend low-cost methods of determining rights and power. Slaikeu and Hasson (1998: 47) go a step further. They prescribe a "preferred path of conflict resolution" that starts with "individual initiative, followed by negotiation, and then an assisted process such as mediation offered through a variety of informal and formal options, with higher authority next in line and power plays or force and avoidance or acceptance as last resorts."

Our own view is similar to theirs, but with one considerable difference. We believe that the best systems provide a choice of options at the same time, rather than in steps, for most problems (Rowe 1984, 1988, 1990a, 1997). Traditional step procedures usually require a direct approach between the parties, then informal intervention, then a formal determination of right and wrong, and then appeals or arbitration, if necessary. But many complainants prefer to have parallel (simultaneous) choices from the beginning.

Parallel choices are often possible, even if there are time limits for when a formal complaint must be initiated. Parallel options within a system can allow a formal claim to be filed and then put in abeyance while an interest-based process is attempted. This obviates risk to the claimant of losing access to rights-based options or of having to start over again from the beginning.

Parallel choices may also help those who are oriented toward rights and power. Our experience suggests that a significant, though small, proportion of the people in any workplace will not be satisfied by informal options. These individuals may prefer to skip informal problem solving and go straight to a formal grievance. In addition, some issues may be seen to demand formal justice as the first approach.

In theoretical terms, this means that in appropriate cases the parties may be permitted either to loop forward—or, in Ury, Brett, and Goldberg's terms, to loop back—to more or less formal options in an integrated complaint system. We believe that in many disputes the parties should be able to have choices, instead of having their options prescribed by a step procedure or by a third-party complaint handler. As Costantino and Merchant (1996: 121) note, the best systems "allow disputants to retain maximum control over choice of ADR method and selection of neutral wherever possible." We believe that providing this choice also helps to address the current ideological conflict between advocates for mediation and its detractors. The solution is not "either mediation or justice"; the solution should be for a system to provide both options—and a choice of options—wherever possible.

Elements of an Effective System

If, as we believe, it is essential to offer a choice of options, which options should be provided and how should they be chosen? Asking employees and managers which options they want is usually a good idea, for real and symbolic reasons, and much can be learned about how people feel about the organization from this process. However, the employer will not necessarily discover which options people will really *use* in their conflict management system just by asking questions in union discussions or focus groups.

It is necessary to track real-life behavior—what people actually choose to do when they are under stress—to understand which options people will use to raise a concern. In our experience most people in focus groups talk about rights and compliance options—and nearly everyone really wants these options to be provided. However, when in need, the majority actually *seek* interest-based options for most issues, even where an employer tries to require mandatory reporting for illegal behavior. It is essential to distinguish what people actually do from what they say they will do in conflict, and to recognize that this distinction may be different in different organizations (Bendersky 1998).

Many Functions and Providers

We think of options for complainants in terms of the multiple complaint-handling functions that are needed (see the appendix) and the multiple providers of those functions. The functions can be provided in different ways. Important providers of solutions based on rights and power include line managers, human resource managers, union officials and industrial relations managers, peer review panels, security personnel, and compliance officers of all kinds (safety, audit, animal care, ethics, EEO/AA [affirmative action], waste hazard, quality assurance, risk management, the legal department, inspectors general, and so forth). Important facilitators of solutions based on interests include line managers and human resource managers, union officials and industrial relations managers, team coaches, employee assistance and health care professionals, religious counselors, informal diversity advisors, in-house mediators, and ombudspeople.

People need a variety of options for gaining access to a conflict management system, as well as for actually dealing with conflict. Written complaints are appropriate for formal grievance procedures, but many employees and managers want interest-based access options as well. Confidential hot lines and ombuds offices can collect information in ways that may seem safer. Offering information anonymously sometimes leads to rights-based investigations, but from the caller's point of view, it is an interest-based option for the process of coming forward. In addition, it helps to have people of appropriate language groups, men and women, people of color and whites, and technical and nontechnical people scattered through the various offices of the system, available for those who need help. This is another important reason for having a system, rather than just one grievance process. A woman who would rather talk with a woman may be able to find one who seems to be approachable, attached to one complaint option or another. This factor alone may dictate her choice of option—and may influence whether she chooses to act at all.

In much of traditional grievance management, a designated manager decides how to handle any concern that comes forward, or the mode is specified in a contract. In our opinion, where the issue at hand is not covered under a contract, various options for raising concerns should be offered to complainants in all but the most serious cases. In addition, when a contract specifies a grievance procedure, there may be problems that are not covered under the contract, like coworker altercations, in which case options can be provided.

Appropriate Delegation to First Parties

Employers reviewing their internal systems are increasingly emphasizing first-party dispute resolution whenever possible. This means providing people with the skills to deal with their problems directly, where appropriate, without involving others. Of course, first-party solutions are not always appropriate, because of the nature of the issues or because the parties feel their skills are inadequate to handle the problem.

First-party solutions are often the best, however, for a number of reasons (Rowe 1993b). Those on the scene may know best what the facts are, may best understand the local culture, may understand the value of maintaining and building relationships as part of problem resolution, and may simply prefer their own methods of conflict management and their own solutions. First parties sometimes value being heard, and apologies between first parties are often powerful and cost-effective. They may value keeping some measure of control and may thus more strongly "own the resolution." First-party solutions may appropriately protect people's privacy and dignity. They may take less time. They may teach people how to prevent unnecessary problems in the future.

A first party who is a "responsible bystander" may nip illegal or inappropriate behavior in the bud. And first parties who believe that they can and should make a difference, and who are used to taking responsibility for direct action, may also be more likely to speak up in a timely way when management action is needed. Appropriate first-party action and first-party resolutions are therefore increasingly fostered as better solutions. Modern systems are providing ever more training in first-party negotiations—as well as conflict resolution—to all supervisors and to many or all employees.

The concept of third-party assistance is also broadening. In the past, the definition of third-party assistance was narrow and routinely included the presumption of intervention and of taking charge. It was often assumed that there must be an intervener and that this person would choose what kind of intervention would take place. Modern systems do provide formal third-party interveners of this kind. They also provide confidential support for first-party conflict management,[9] however, and confidential mediation, when appropriate, if requested by the parties.

Providing an Independent, Confidential, Internal Neutral

We believe that for an organization that wants people to act responsibly (who might otherwise not do so), a trained and experienced organizational ombudsperson can be the most accessible conflict resolution provider.[10] A backup to the ordinary line and staff channels, an organizational ombudsperson is an independent, confidential, designated neutral who works in an impartial way. The ombudsperson should report to the chief executive officer (CEO), or chief operating officer (COO), with access to the Board of Directors. One basic purpose of the ombuds office is to provide various options for fairness and justice. In effect, an organizational ombudsperson has all the common functions of any dispute resolver

---

[9] See the appendix for several examples of functions in a complaint system that are designed primarily to support first parties.

[10] Ombuds services can also be provided by trained, *external* ombuds practitioners. Though experience suggests that internal ombudspeople are more effective in most circumstances, external organizational ombudspeople may be quite suitable for franchises and other decentralized operations and for small organizations.

(see the appendix) except those of an advocate, formal fact-finder, appeals officer, arbitrator, judge, or peace officer. Ombudspeople typically work informally, with great flexibility. They make no decisions for the employer or for their visitors except in very rare emergencies.

The ombuds office should be seen as accessible and trustworthy—a zero-barrier office—to the extent that it really maintains confidentiality. For this reason it should not accept notice for the employer—that is, it should not be an office of record for reports of illegal behavior.[11] In consonance with current Ombudsman Association Standards of Practice, the organizational ombudsperson should not break confidentiality, except for emergency cases that pose imminent risk of serious harm for which there appears to be no other responsible option. What an ombudsperson can and should do, however, is to work with every visitor to devise acceptable options that both protect the confidentiality of the visitor and either get information where it needs to go or help to see that appropriate action is taken. Through helping to develop options and informal intervention, if requested, an ombudsperson should be able to foster resolution of most issues or get them appropriately referred (Rowe 1995; Rowe and Simon 2001).

An employer that has an organizational ombudsperson will catch, and can therefore deal with, more problems, suggestions, concerns, and misconduct. Costs (in terms of EEO, agency complaints, legal settlements, Freedom of Information Act, and so forth) are likely to drop, sometimes sharply. Although an ombuds office will not catch all problematic behavior, it is one of the useful counterweights to Type 2 errors. Furthermore, organizational ombudspeople report that about a third of the individuals who come to see them will choose to try to learn how to handle their con-

---

[11] The Ombudsman Association Standards of Practice assert that an organizational ombudsperson does not accept notice for the employer. This idea is not yet embodied in federal law and has been denied in one or two court cases. However, a considerable number of plaintiffs' lawyers, judges, and others with subpoena power *have* accepted this idea, in a variety of cases of record and cases settled informally. The idea has also been accepted for several other reasons, such as Wigmore principles, the right to privacy, implicit contract, and the similarity between ombudspeople and mediators. It seems likely that the confidentiality issue will be settled sooner or later by Congress: in 2002 the American Bar Association approved a report on this subject. At stake are a number of issues, such as the Type 2 error. Since society has an interest in getting people to come forward, it is hoped that legislation includes at least this one option through which most people can be granted well-protected confidentiality if they come forward about problems. In addition to several court cases that affirm a privilege, two encouraging signs are the emphasis in the Federal Sentencing Guidelines on what we call in this chapter "zero barriers," and the limited shield for neutrals granted by the Administrative Dispute Resolution Act as amended and re-enacted in 1996.

cerns themselves. This may help spread conflict resolution skills throughout an organization.

Integration into the Organization

An effective conflict management system should be fully integrated into the
organization. It should take every kind of problem; deal with problems in
and between groups and teams, as well as among individuals; and offer options to all professionals and managers, as well as all workers. The system
should be grounded in the core values of the organization, values such as
fairness and respect, teamwork, excellent service, and compliance with law
and regulation. The strategy underlying the conflict management system
should be part of the overall human resource strategy of the organization,
and the system should be mentioned in all relevant personnel policies.

Continuous Oversight by a Balanced Group

Effective systems need regular oversight. We believe that this can best be provided by a group of senior managers, not just one. The group can meet informally, but it should meet regularly and frequently—at least monthly, and
more often in large organizations. Subsets of this group can meet as needed
as crisis teams, but the oversight group should not be a crisis team. The
group should regularly seek input from all stakeholder groups and be explicitly attentive to the interests of all in the organization.

The oversight group should include some senior managers responsible
for rights and compliance and some—including the organizational ombudsperson—responsible for fairness and problem solving. An ombudsperson would have no formal role in decision making in such a group.
Many such groups in any case have no decision-making function. If decisions about processes are to be made, the ombudsperson might offer commentary on the fairness of the proposed process but would not vote or
participate in decisions. Typically, the ombudsperson would not discuss
the merits of a specific case in such a group.

Some of those who oversee the system should be managers who report
to the CEO, COO, or the Board of Directors. This group should not be
dominated by those representing compliance or conversely, problem-solving interests, but should be a team including both perspectives. Because
an effective, integrated conflict management system is itself a "mixed-motive" structure—in which people feel free to act informally to resolve
problems on the basis of interests or to seek formal justice solutions based

on rights and power—the structure of the oversight group should be developed and should function as a balance between rights and interests. The oversight group should exemplify, lead, and model this balance.

As Westin and Feliu stated in 1988 (p. 22):

> Any . . . firm that: (1) seeks to draw the greatest creativity and commitment from its workforce, (2) seeks to resolve employee complaints before they generate appeals to outside agencies and the courts, and (3) wants to meet both employee expectations of fairness and organizational interests in sound administration is—or ought to be—actively considering the creation of a multifaceted fair procedure system.

Employers are reviewing their dispute resolution systems for employment relations and other types of conflict. Their goals and strategies for conflict management are changing for both internal and external reasons. In many cases these goals now include workplace justice, zero tolerance for illegal behavior, and zero barriers for people either to act responsibly on their own or to come forward to use the conflict management system.

Multiple dispute resolution options, integrated together in a coherent system, provide the best chance for managers to deal with unacceptable behavior. The system should include zero-barrier options for people to come forward. In nearly every organization, effective conflict management now requires continuous training for first parties and considerable reliance on first parties in disputes. An organization using a systems approach will probably want to provide an organizational ombudsperson—to support first parties, to provide informal intervention and formal mediation, to offer all responsible options to those with problems, and to support fair processes. The ombudsperson should support the pursuit of justice, help prevent destructive and illegal behavior, help employees and managers learn and use effective negotiation and conflict skills, and provide a zero-barrier office. An effective system must also train and support the third parties that deal formally with conflicts. Effective systems permit individuals to choose fairness and problem solving, or formal justice, depending on the issues at hand, the nature of the situation, the wishes of the parties, and the culture of the organization.

Looking Ahead

As the workplace continues to change, so will the issues that give rise to conflicts. If this brief overview is any indication, there will be more change in the options and systems used to resolve these conflicts. Constant widespread training in negotiations and conflict management, and collaboration on global teams, may well bring more change to the culture of U.S. organizations. Thirty years ago, no student or practitioner in our field would have predicted the tremendous growth in the use of dispute resolution options within organizations. We suspect that Walton and McKersie, and others who contributed basic concepts about conflict management, also did not foresee the powerful reach of their ideas into this arena of organizational practice. Thus, we constantly need to be looking for new theoretical insights, and new ideas about new structures, in hopes of discovering or developing yet better ways of handling the issues and the injustices of the future.

Appendix: Functions Needed in a Conflict Management System (Adapted from Rowe 1997)

Interest-Based Options

Interest-based options for fairness and problem solving attempt to address the real needs of the complainant (and usually others), as distinguished from defining problems and their solutions solely in terms of legal rights or managerial power. Some interest-based options may deal mainly with how information gets where it needs to go, rather than how the information will be handled. For example, there should be several informal ways for surfacing credible information about criminal behavior, even though many allegations about criminal behavior will actually require formal procedures. Other interest-based options provide confidential third-party assistance to first parties to settle problems on their own. And some interest-based options provide third-party assistance to intervene, usually informally, to help solve problems.

Listening. An important option that a person may choose is just to talk, and for the manager, ombudsperson, union steward, or other resource person just to listen, in an active and supportive fashion that helps the speaker sort out the problem and reduce tension.

Giving and receiving information. Often a person needs information on a one-to-one basis. For example, an employee may not know what information or which records are by law available to him or her. A manager, ombudsperson, or a staff member answering a toll-free telephone line may also receive information about a problem in the workplace, such as a safety issue, evidence about a theft, harassment or potential violence, or equipment that needs repair.

Re-framing issues and developing options. A manager, ombudsperson, union steward, or other resource person may be able to help a caller or complainant develop new responsible options they might find acceptable as a means of dealing with a problem.

Referral. Many disputants and complainants need more than one helping resource; they need a helping network. The importance of this option is one of the major reasons for explicit integration of all the elements and resource persons in a conflict management system.

Helping people help themselves in a direct approach. An ombudsperson or other resource person, manager, or teammate may help someone with a problem deal directly with the perceived source of the problem (Rowe 1990b). The direct approach can be pursued by the person alone or with a colleague, in person or on paper or both.

Shuttle diplomacy. A person with a concern may choose to ask a third party to be a shuttle diplomat to go back and forth between A and B or bring A and B together informally to resolve the problem. The third party could be a supervisor, union steward, human resource officer, ombudsperson, or other staff member. Alternatively, a complainant might choose to ask a teammate, uninvolved colleague, senior mentor, or other appropriate person to intervene. This option is essential, and very frequently chosen, in many cultures outside the United States.

Looking into the problem informally. Most problems, especially if they are caught early, do not require a formal investigation. At least two kinds of informal data gathering may be performed by third parties, one by organizational ombudspeople and another by line managers, administrative officers, human resource managers, or other appropriate staff. Assistance from an organizational ombudsperson (except for classic mediation as described below) is informal and typically does not result in a case record for the employer. Line managers and staff people, such as administrative officers and human resource managers, may look into a problem informally, but they may also choose or be required to make management decisions as a result.

Classic formal mediation. Classic mediation is the only formal, interest-based option. This option is offered internally by some employers and externally by others. In classic mediation, the parties are helped by an organizational ombudsperson, or another person who is a professional neutral mediator, to find their own settlement, in a process that has a well-defined structure.

Generic approaches. A complainant may choose a generic approach aimed at changing a process in the workplace or alerting possible offenders to stop inappropriate behavior, in such a way that the apparent problem disappears without direct involvement of the parties. For example, an ombudsperson might be given permission to approach a department head about a given problem without using any names. The department head might then choose to distribute and discuss copies of the appropriate employer policy or encourage safety or harassment training, or legally correct billing behavior, in such a way as to stop and prevent the alleged inappropriate behavior. Generic approaches offer the advantage that they typically do not affect the privacy or other rights of anyone in the organization.

Systems change. People with concerns often simply wish to suggest a change of policy, procedure, or structure in an organization, to recommend re-orientation of a team project, or to start an orderly process of dealing with a policy, group, or department that is seen to be a problem. This function is especially important for problems that are new to the organization.

Training and prevention. The employer, if possible, should maintain ongoing training programs to teach the skills of teamwork, conflict management, and dispute resolution. This training should be about first-party negotiations, as well as third-party intervention, and should cover specific topics, such as diversity, ethics, and safety, as well as issues of dissent and reprisal. The employer should provide training that fosters individual responsibility and accountability at all levels. Four different groups need training about raising questions, about disagreeing, and about complaining: potential complainants and dissenters, potential respondents, potential bystanders, and supervisors.

Following through. Often a resource person or supervisor will undertake some action, as requested by a person with a concern. In other cases a complainant will decide after consultation to act directly. Complaint handlers can and should appropriately follow through on the problems brought to them.

A custom approach. Where none of the options above seem exactly right, a person with a concern or complaint may ask for or need unusual help. If all options seem inappropriate, an organizational ombudsperson or other resource person or manager may simply continue to look for a responsible approach that is tailor-made for a particular situation.

Rights-Based Options

Disciplinary action and adverse administrative action against a respondent require a fair investigation and decision-making process. Definitions of appropriate process differ. Our list of elements of a fair process contains many of the customary elements, including notice to the alleged offender, a reasonable opportunity for that person to respond to complaints and evidence against him or her, a chance to offer his or her own evidence, reasonable timeliness, impartiality of investigation and decision making, freedom from arbitrariness and capriciousness, the possibility of appeal, and the right to be accompanied by a colleague or coworker. The employer should have explicit rules about maintaining privacy and, if possible, should provide for follow-up monitoring on each case that is settled formally, to see if the problem has been fairly resolved and that there is no reprisal against any disputant or witness.

Investigation, adjudication, and formal appeals. Union contracts have their own formal grievance processes. For nonunion employees and managers, a supervisor, department head, personnel officer, inside or outside fact-finder, or other appropriate staff person or compliance officer may investigate, adjudicate a concern in a formal fashion, or deal with an appeal in a formal grievance channel. Final appeal might be to a peer review panel, senior manager, the CEO, or an outside arbitrator. Best practice in our opinion requires separation of fact finding from decision making in serious cases, and the possibility of appeal to a person or structure that is outside the relevant line of supervision.

Emergency action. Some organizations have their own security or sworn police force. This department may offer an option for emergencies based on both rights and power.

Part III

Transformations in Labor-Management Relations

8

How Process Matters

A Five-Phase Model for Examining Interest-Based Bargaining

JOEL CUTCHER-GERSHENFELD

The collective bargaining process is rarely mundane. Sometimes there is great tension as one party or the other realizes that it will fall short of the aspirations of its constituents. Sometimes there is great enthusiasm as inventive options emerge with the potential to deliver mutual gains. Sometimes seemingly minor or routine issues of contract language or working conditions have the potential to be explosive, based on how they are addressed.

In the highly charged atmosphere of collective bargaining, fundamental changes in the bargaining process promise to be complicated and controversial. The current experience in applying interest-based bargaining (IBB) principles to the collective bargaining process delivers on this promise. There are great complications introduced as contending parties attempt joint brainstorming around mutual-gains options while simultaneously demonstrating to constituents that they remain independent of undue influence by the other side. There is genuine controversy when one side or the other engages in a divisive, unilateral action that shatters the trust built up during interest-based, problem-solving dialogue. At the same time, there is a growing cadre of practitioners and trainers who advocate the use of interest-based principles in collective bargaining with a near missionary zeal.

In order to explore the strengths and limits of an interest-based approach to collective bargaining in the present era, I introduce a five-phase model for bargaining and use it as a framework for analysis. The model, which was jointly developed with Robert McKersie and others,[1] highlights

[1] The model is the central organizing framework for a seminar co-led by Robert McKersie and myself entitled "Negotiating Labor Agreements," which is offered through the Program

141

unique features and challenges associated with IBB in the labor-management context. These practical challenges are examined, along with links to relevant theory and data.[2] The core thesis of the chapter is that success in IBB at each step of the process depends on choices made in prior steps and that all of these process choices add up, having a powerful impact on substantive outcomes. In other words, process matters.

The analysis is focused on the context of collective bargaining, which itself is an important area of study. While unions represent only about 10 percent of the nonagricultural work force in the United States, key sectors of the economy are highly organized. Sectors such as autos, telecommunications, transportation, steel, utilities, health care, aerospace, and government are all highly organized and deeply affected when the collective bargaining process breaks down or delivers innovation. In addition, even at present levels of union density, the union remains a substantial social institution, considering that approximately forty thousand private sector labor agreements are negotiated every year. Implications for bargaining in other contexts are considered at the chapter's conclusion.

The Point of Departure: "Traditional" Bargaining

As an institution, U.S. collective bargaining has historically been dominated by what Walton and McKersie termed *distributive bargaining*. The process was defined in the minds of constituents and the public primarily by highly visible and vivid battles over wages and benefits and by periodic power contests involving strikes, lockouts, and more recently, the use of replacement workers. Labor and management negotiators were always well aware of the more "integrative" aspects of the process (to use the term from Walton and McKersie's *Behavioral Theory*), but historically this has not been its primary defining feature. Consider the list of what are termed *traditional bargaining behaviors* (Table 8.1).[3] When this list is presented to practitioners, there are always smiles of recognition—it is a set

---

on Negotiation at Harvard Law School. Others involved in helping to shape the model and its use include Marjorie Corman-Aaron, Elaine Landrey, Christina Sickles-Merchant, and Nancy Peace.

[2] In particular, this chapter revisits core concepts advanced by Walton and McKersie in their 1965 book, *A Behavioral Theory of Labor Negotiations: An Analysis of a Social Interaction System*. This chapter also summarizes findings from a recent national random-sample survey of labor negotiators sponsored by the Federal Mediation and Conciliation Service (FMCS).

[3] The list is part of the training materials in the seminar "Negotiating Labor Agreements."

Table 8.1. Traditional Bargaining Behaviors

Develop target and resistance positions in advance.
Overstate opening positions.
Commit to these positions early and publicly.
Channel communications through a spokesperson.
Give as little as possible for what you ge.t
Never "bargain against yourself."
Always keep the other side off balance.
Use coercive forms of power.
Mobilize support from constituents.
Divide and conquer the other side; protect against the same on your side.
An agreement reluctantly accepted is a sign of success.

of behaviors very familiar to labor and management negotiators. Moreover, these behaviors serve many critical institutional purposes, particularly in demonstrating to constituents that their representatives have achieved the best-possible settlement and in shielding bargainers from opponents' distributive power tactics.

Given that various forms of this traditional approach have endured and effectively delivered hundreds of thousands of agreements over the past half-century, the key issue to consider is, Why change the system? What is it that would lead parties to explore dramatic changes in this model for bargaining?

Broad Awareness and Experience with Interest-Based Bargaining

The exploration of alternative approaches to collective bargaining is driven by many factors (Cutcher-Gershenfeld 1994). First, the last two decades have seen broad diffusion of what are termed *alternative dispute resolution (ADR) principles* between nations and in such diverse domains as community, family, commerce, legislation, and the environment, among others. So the new ideas and approaches are "in the air."

Second, the agenda for labor negotiations includes an ever increasing array of issues not easily addressed via the distributive model. These include issues of quality, job security, continuous improvement, work and family issues, new pay systems, work redesign, benefit restructuring, training, new technology, and strategic investment choices. While some language on any of these issues can be achieved through more traditional power bargaining, it does not have the benefit that derives from joint problem-solving dialogues. Moreover, implementation of these issues can be seriously compromised when one side or the other primarily imposes the language. A union, for example, may force on an employer some language on job security, such as a restriction on outsourcing of work. But full implementation of such language depends on advance notice and dialogue around jobs that are at risk, which depends on voluntary initiative by the employer. Similarly, an employer may force a pay-for-knowledge reward system on a union as part of an imposed "modern operating agreement." Yet, full implementation will depend on the voluntary initiative of employees to work through a skills progression system. The implementation difficulties of imposed agreements on such issues are not new—only the growing number of issues that are at risk in this way.

Finally, the composition of the represented work force is shifting to include a broader range of office, service, and professional employees—all groups that are less institutionally tied to a traditional mode of bargaining. Similarly, the composition of the represented work force is more diverse in terms of race, gender, and even age. On the last issue, many unionized manufacturing settings experienced massive lay-offs during the early 1980s and again during the early 1990s, resulting in major swings in seniority. I was recently in one large auto components facility with more than 3,000 employees, for example. This facility experienced over 250 retirements for each of the past five years and over 300 new hires per year during the same time period. The result is that average seniority has shifted from more than twenty-seven years to less than seven years. It should be noted that these changes in the composition of the work force do not always point toward IBB—there are also cases of increasingly adversarial bargaining that can be traced to these shifts. Importantly, though, it is a period of unfreezing in which existing modes of interaction are being called into question.

In fact, data from two recent national surveys of lead negotiators in collective bargaining clearly indicate that interest-based approaches to bargaining are very much "on the agenda" for a substantial majority of negotiators. Based on these surveys, which were sponsored by the Federal Mediation and Conciliation Service (FMCS) and administered in 1996 and 1999,[4] between two-thirds and three-fourths of management and union respondents were aware of IBB and approximately half of those who were aware of the process reported utilizing it. Specifically, the survey asked about the negotiators' familiarity with "negotiation based on *Interest-Based Bargaining*." It was also indicated that this is "sometimes referred to as *win-win* or *mutual gains* negotiating." As Table 8.2 indicates, the experience is higher among union respondents, but the preference for

---

[4] These are selected findings from work reported in more detail by Cutcher-Gershenfeld, Kochan, and Wells (1998, 2001) and Cutcher-Gershenfeld and Kochan (2002).

Table 8.2. Experience with Interest-Based Bargaining (IBB):
1996 and 1999 FMCS Survey Data (%)

	Union		Management	
Characteristic	*1996*	*1999*	*1996*	*1999*
Familiar with IBB	76.0	79.3	62.0	66.7
Has used IBB[a]	35.0	47.0	21.7	36.2
Prefers IBB[b]	19.6	22.0	17.4	25.2

[a] Percentage of total sample (based on responses from the subset of respondents indicating familiarity with IBB).
[b] Percentage of total sample (based on responses from the subset of respondents indicating familiarity with IBB and past experience using IBB).

Table 8.3. Ratings of Interest-Based Bargaining (IBB) and Traditional Collective Bargaining (CB): 1996 and 1999 FMCS Survey Data (%)

	Union		Management	
	1996	*1999*	*1996*	*1999*
Rate IBB good, very good, or excellent*	69.9	53.6	76.0	71.2
Rate traditional CB good, very good, or excellent	77.5	73.5	74.3	52.3

* Question was asked only of respondents reporting experience with IBB.

this process is lower among them. Also, the rate of increase in use is not matched by a similar increase in the number of negotiators preferring IBB. The number of bargainers preferring IBB is growing, but at a slower rate than the growth in experience with IBB—with this trend most pronounced among union negotiators.[5]

The slower rate of increase in preference for IBB must be understood in context. In particular, it is important to also consider views on its relevant alternative, which is what can be termed *traditional collective bargaining*. The chief negotiators surveyed by the FMCS were asked how they would rate IBB and also how they would rate traditional collective bargaining. Their responses, which are presented in Table 8.3, point to a "yeasty" environment where views about both processes are shifting.

However, it is important to look beyond the general statements about awareness, experience, and preference for IBB. There is a broad range of behaviors that, in fact, might be contemplated when people discuss IBB. These behaviors, which are listed in Table 8.4, contrast quite strongly with

[5] All the statistics reported in Table 8.2 are weighted to adjust for over-sampling of cases involving mediation, larger bargaining units, and the ratio of union to management respondents.

Table 8.4. Interest-Based Bargaining Behaviors

Assess all stakeholder interests in advance.
Convert positional demands from constituents into interests.
Use subcommittees and task forces for joint data collection and analysis.
Frame issues based on interests—avoid positional statements.
Encourage open exchange of information and joint problem solving.
Generate as many options as possible on each issue.
Take on the constraints of your counterparts.
Ensure constituents are educated and knowledgeable on the issues.
Anticipate contract administration—"troubleshoot" agreements.
An agreement enthusiastically ratified by all parties is a sign of success.

Table 8.5. Reported Frequency of Behaviors Related to Interest-Based
Bargaining (IBB) in Most Recent Negotiation: 1999 FMCS Survey Data (%)

Variable	Union	Management
Pre-training in IBB*	43.0	42.9
Joint task force prior to IBB	24.7	19.6
Prior notice of IBB use to labor constituents*	21.0	5.7
Prior notice of IBB use to management constituents*	7.5	21.3
Management data sharing	60.9	66.4
Labor data sharing	60.9	26.8
Brainstorming/ problem solving	47.1	37.2
Consensus decision making	79.1	62.5

* Question was asked only of respondents reporting experience with IBB.

the behaviors listed in Table 8.1. They correspond directly to what Walton and McKersie termed *integrative bargaining*, and they are the focus of the analysis presented here. Throughout this chapter, contrasts and comparisons are made between what are termed traditional and interest-based bargaining processes. In these instances, the behaviors listed in Tables 8.1 and 8.4 comprise what is meant by each term. While the 1996 survey did not examine these types of specific behaviors, many of them were covered in questions in the 1999 survey (Table 8.5).

We see in Table 8.5 that the most common practices include the use of consensus decision making, sharing of data, brainstorming, and pre-training in IBB—though in all cases there are large numbers of negotiators who do not engage in these practices. Perhaps most striking, however, is the high proportion of negotiators who report not providing constituents with advance notice around the use of IBB. Admittedly, it is difficult to raise this issue in advance—a problem that I discuss in more detail below. Still, entering into a problem-solving approach to bargaining designed to surface "out of the box" options is likely to be seriously constrained when there is not a clear mandate from constituents to do so. In all, these behavioral data raise more questions than they answer, but they clearly suggest that the collective bargaining process itself is "on the table" for negotiation.

A Five-Phase Model for Bargaining

In order to better illustrate the strengths and limits of the interest-based process, I examine each of the five phases:

I. Prepare
II. Open
III. Explore
IV. Focus
V. Agree

This model could apply to the handling of a specific issue or to the phasing of the entire process. The first phase—preparing—involves all of the preparation prior to the formal opening of bargaining (overall or on a given issue). It is during this phase that constituents deliver a mandate to their representatives, and the representatives assemble relevant data and arguments to support bargaining on these issues. The second phase—opening—marks the formal framing of negotiations (again, overall or on a given issue). The third phase—exploring—is the point at which options are generated; this is followed by the fourth phase—focusing—during which linkages are made across issues, bargaining ranges are increasingly clear, and the contours of an agreement begin to take shape. The final phase—agreeing—can be a small step from focusing or a complicated interaction marked by threats and the potential for impasse.

Although the model is presented in temporal order, reality is never quite so simple. There can be some opening framing of issues during preparation, for example. Similarly, there can be some focusing interspersed with the exploring phase. It is possible that parties will skip the exploring and focusing altogether and jump to accept an agreement that has become apparent during the opening dialogue. The purpose of the model is not to impose an artificial structure on what is essentially a fluid and dynamic process, but to provide a framework through which to organize analysis. The model has also proved useful as a framework for action: even if reality is more complex, the model can help practitioners organize and structure their thinking about new approaches to bargaining.

In terms of analysis, there are two primary hypotheses developed in this chapter relative to the model:

Hypothesis 1: Success in each of these phases is sequentially dependent on results from the prior phase.
Hypothesis 2: Substantive outcomes are dependent on overall success with the process.

This chapter does not provide a formal test of these hypotheses, but it does provide analysis and some evidence to guide such tests. Where appropriate, links are made to bargaining strategies of forcing and fostering, which impact on the dynamics in distinct ways at each phase (Walton, Cutcher-Gershenfeld, and McKersie 1994).[6]

Phase I: Prepare

All bargaining requires preparation, but the importance of this step is increased multi-fold in the context of IBB. This is because constituents typically formulate the mandate for their representatives in positional terms—more of one thing, less of another, duplication of what others have, and so forth. In traditional bargaining, these mandates are a source of leverage. They become opening positions, where the fall-back position is along the same lines but less extreme. The challenge is not to dissuade constituents of their positions, just to ratchet down their expectations to a realistic level.

In contrast, IBB is dramatically undercut if the representatives accept a positional mandate. It is enormously difficult and risky to engage in creative, out-of-the-box problem solving if constituents' expectations are oriented around very specific positions. Their response at ratification is predictable—no matter how creative the bargaining, the hurdle of narrowly set expectations may be impossible to overcome. As a result, preparation for IBB requires two internal negotiations with constituents, neither of which is easy. First, it requires advance dialogue about the idea of bargaining in a new way—soliciting a mandate to utilize a nontraditional process. Second, it requires converting the positional mandates into interests.

For example, senior management may hand its representatives a man-

---

[6] For a more complete analysis of forcing and fostering as strategies, see Walton, Cutcher-Gershenfeld, and McKersie 1994. The two strategies are combined with the concept of "escape" (a third strategy) as self-reinforcing dynamics that emerge from the combination of various process behaviors (distributive, integrative, attitudinal, and intra-organizational—to use the terms from the *Behavioral Theory*). The theory represents a link between strategy and process.

date for a reduction in job classifications from one number, say twenty-five, to another, say three. If accepted, the focus of bargaining and the measure of success are quite narrow—was the number of job classifications reduced to three? Instead, the representatives might reject the specific mandate and urge that the bargaining seek flexibility in operations (an underlying interest), which may or may not require a specific new number of job classifications. Similarly, union members may insist on a specific dollar increase in pension contributions. Here, the underlying interest has to do with improved standards of living upon retirement, which might be achieved in many ways. Of course, the degree to which a stance is positional or interest-based is really one or more continua, where many positions are possible and many different interests can be highlighted. The examples cited here are offered to be illustrative of alternative ways of framing positions, not to be definitive on just how to do so.

The internal negotiations over just how positional or interest-based the mandate is would be an example of what Walton and McKersie termed *intra-organizational bargaining*. The bargaining at "second tables" within a given side is often more difficult than that at the "main table." Indeed, there is at least anecdotal evidence that internal negotiations represent one of the most common sources of failure in IBB. In one survey of participants in joint training on IBB, advance dialogue with constituents on the bargaining process was one of the least-common prior activities.[7] In this survey, many IBB preparation behaviors were quite common. Just over half of the respondents, for example, reported some prior use of IBB principles, just under half reported some degree of joint data collection prior to bargaining, and slightly more than 40 percent reported the use of joint task forces or subcommittees prior to bargaining. Of all the preparation behaviors examined, the smallest response—about 15 percent (a level generally consistent with the national survey data reported earlier)—was on the issue identified here: advance briefings to, and dialogue with, constituents on the bargaining process.[8] Not surprisingly, many of these individuals reported, in retrospect, that this lack of prior dialogue with constituents substantially hampered their efforts to bargain in new ways.

---

[7] This is a survey of participants in the seminar "Negotiating Labor agreements."

[8] In reflecting on this aspect of the training, Robert McKersie made the following comment: "I have been impressed by how many at the seminar have already been through some training on interest-based bargaining or something akin. So why are they coming to something that they already know quite a bit about? For some, it is a refresher. But for most, it is taking another small step toward actually putting these ideas into practice. I am convinced that the task of getting the respective bargaining teams and constituents aware of the process is monumental in most situations" (electronic mail from Robert McKersie, August 1998).

Having such a prior conversation with constituents is not easy. A negotiator who is persuaded that it is wise to engage in a more problem-solving stance with the other side takes a number of risks by seeking advance support from constituents. First, constituents may turn down the idea, resulting in a lost opportunity. Second, they may see even the suggestion as a sign of weakness. This is especially true within unions, where political opposition may try to exploit such an overture. Finally, constituents may support the problem solving only as a ploy to learn more about the other side's priorities, but still intend, or expect the negotiators, to try in the end to broker a power bargain. This is especially a concern in management organizations where senior leadership will authorize the problem solving but not relinquish its right to dictate the final terms of the agreement—a process that can seriously compromise the integrity of the problem-solving efforts and the reputation of the negotiator.

All these dynamics are particularly likely to occur when there is expected to be a combination of forcing and fostering behavior. In essence, the prospect of forcing occurring during the main negotiations polarizes the up-front internal negotiations with constituents and biases them against IBB. Since most negotiations feature a mixed agenda, the dilemmas are almost inevitable.

Many other challenges can arise during preparation. These include how much information to share, what topics lend themselves to joint task forces or subcommittees, and whether such joint preparation should draw from only the two bargaining teams or from a broader cross section of each side. My focus here, however, has been on the challenges in preparing constituents for a new way to bargain, because that area is most fraught with dilemmas and has such a large impact on what follows.

Phase II: Open

Breaking out the opening of negotiations as a distinct phase is more critical in IBB than in traditional bargaining. In traditional bargaining, the opening of the negotiations is generally marked by overstated initial positions. Though they are treated with skepticism, the statements are also carefully studied for clues about underlying priorities. In essence, the opening becomes the first move in a chess game: it is important in that there is some jockeying for position, but many more-critical moves are yet to come.

In IBB, the parties carefully avoid presenting an initial position. Their opening statements serve as powerful framing devices. Where issues involve a high degree of fostering, the opening statement shapes just how wide the range of brainstorming will be. Where issues involve more forcing, the opening statement plays a critical role in keeping the forcing sufficiently restrained so as not to undercut subsequent problem-solving efforts.

Crafting an opening statement draws on many of the concepts and principles Walton and McKersie examined in their analysis of what they term *attitudinal structuring*. That analysis preceded and anticipated in important ways much of the research currently taking place around the social psychology of negotiations—especially research on the concept of framing (Bazerman and Neale 1992). Of particular relevance in the context of IBB is the way a constructive framing of issues is dependent on the initial internal negotiations with constituents over the mandate. Where constituents support a broad statement of interest, there is quite a bit of freedom possible in how the issue can be framed. Where the mandate is largely positional, the framing is highly constrained. Thus, the opening phase serves to magnify dynamics that took place during the preparation phase—either further enlarging or further limiting the scope of bargaining that was defined in preparation.

Phase III: Explore

The process of exploring options characterizes both traditional and interest-based bargaining. The difference, as Ray Friedman (1994) has observed, is that most of the exploring in traditional bargaining takes place "back stage" in private dialogue between chief negotiators, whereas most of the exploring in IBB occurs in the "front stage" as a brainstorming process involving all the members of both bargaining teams (and sometimes other content experts on both sides). In either case, the parties are primarily engaging in what Walton and McKersie termed *integrative bargaining*,[9] but the dynamics are very different when this integrative bargaining is conducted as an open brainstorming process rather than as a

---

[9] One important contribution, and simultaneously an enduring source of ambiguity, is the way Walton and McKersie conceptualize the integrative aspect of bargaining. They use the term in two ways—referring to an integrative bargaining process and to the integrative potential of a given issue. The distinction between the two is important. All issues have some degree of integrative potential (as well as distributive elements), but the integrative potential will not automatically be realized. An integrative process, on the other hand, can be applied to many types of issues—even some that are primarily distributive in nature. (Note that this is also true of the way the term *distributive bargaining* is used.)

sidebar meeting between chief negotiators. In some ways, the dynamics are more favorable toward reaching the best-possible agreement—such as the way brainstorming focuses many minds on an issue rather than just those of the two chief negotiators. In other ways, participating in brainstorming may increase the risk of the chief negotiators and their teams being seen as having become "too close" to the other side. A further constraint is that it is more difficult to retract an option once surfaced when it is in front of both full teams—which may or may not be seen as more favorable. It is important to note that the exploring process is not merely a way of reaching a compromise between two competing positions. In addressing this issue (and introducing the concept of integrative bargaining), Walton and McKersie (1965: 128) drew on Mary Parker Follet's writing (1942): "The conflict in this case was constructive. And this was because, instead of compromising, they sought a way of integrating. Compromise does not create, it deals with what already exists; integration creates something new." Thus, the goal is for the process to add value by expanding or even transforming the understanding either side could generate, alone, on a given issue. The aim is to harness the collective knowledge of all parties to generate options that would not otherwise have been identified.

In describing this value-enhancing process, Walton and McKersie (1965: 137) offered a three-step problem-solving model and noted that there are significant dilemmas at each step of the model.[10] The first two steps of the model—"defining the problem" and "searching for alternate solutions"—correspond to Phase III, exploring.[11] The dilemmas they highlight in these two steps help to explain why exploring is at once a simple concept and a profoundly difficult challenge:

[10] The model is as follows: (1) Identify the problem. (2) Search for alternative solutions and their consequences. (3) Order preferences for solutions and select a course of action.

[11] Interestingly, in their analysis of the first step, problem identification, Walton and McKersie foreshadow the distinction between interests and positions that was popularized nearly two decades later by Fisher and Ury (1981). Walton and McKersie present two alternative conversations that a union leader might have in response to a concern about member loyalty to the union. The first, which is more integrative, would involve dialogue around a lack of internal union consensus, and the other, which is more distributive, would involve a union demand for a union shop. As they (1965: 146) point out, "The first approach focuses on a problem, the second approach on a demand; the first approach talks frankly about the union's needs, the second approach may even obscure the real needs; and the first approach does not prescribe the solution, while the second approach formulates the answer." Walton and McKersie not only point to problem identification as being very different from positional demands, but also highlight the political challenges that accompany a representative who assumes this sort of an open stance (see Fisher and Ury 1981).

- Just presenting a problem can reveal vulnerability.
- Preconditions constrain integrative bargaining, yet boundaries and interdependent issues need to be established.
- There is tension between an agenda with integrative potential and an agenda with partisan appeal.
- During brainstorming, it is difficult to shift from "caution and deliberateness to spontaneity and then back to caution and deliberateness, and so on" (Walton and McKersie 1965: 171).
- There is a tension between the fixed deadlines that are central to a distributive process and the open-ended exploration that is central to an integrative process.

Together, the dilemmas highlighted by Walton and McKersie suggest that integrative and distributive tensions are woven throughout the exploring phase. Even today, many labor and management negotiators are skeptical about entering into a brainstorming and problem-solving process during collective bargaining.

These tensions are further magnified when the integrative and distributive dynamics coalesce into concurrent forcing and fostering strategies. Take, for example, an issue such as employment security. Typically there needs to be initial forcing from the union for this issue to even be on the agenda and further forcing from management to link the issue to business outcomes. At the same time, concurrent fostering is required to explore fully the many scenarios and options with respect to subcontracting, outsourcing, skill development, cost accounting, new investment, business strategy, and other related matters. On an issue such as this, the dilemmas can be substantially tempered or exacerbated, depending on what has happened during the preceding two phases of the process.

Consider the situation where preparation has not produced a clear mandate to support a problem-solving approach, which has been further constrained by opening statements that create caution around working together to invent options. In this case, all the dynamics highlighted by Walton and McKersie are exacerbated. These dilemmas lead parties to be yet more cautious, which reinforces skepticism on each side regarding just how genuine the interest in a new process really is.

In contrast, consider the situation in which there has been strong constituent support for all negotiators to engage in brainstorming and the generation of creative options, as well as opening statements by both sides designed to signal clear areas of opportunity as well as points of concern. In this type of case, the dilemmas will still be operative, but it is more likely that they can be acknowledged and addressed explicitly. This difference is small, but it is crucial in counteracting the skepticism and enabling parties to entertain a broader array of options than would otherwise be possible. In sum, the inherent dilemmas associated with the exploring phase that is intended to be truly integrative are either tempered or exacerbated, depending on what happens during Phases I and II.

Phase IV: Focus

The concept of focusing as a distinct phase in the bargaining process is not well developed in the literature, but it is essential to a bargaining model designed to be relevant for IBB. Simply stated, there is no easy or immediate way to turn a large list of brainstormed options into an agreement—at least not without the risk of seriously suboptimizing the bargaining potential. If parties merely grab the first set of acceptable options (what social psychologists would call *satisficing*), they risk leaving a great deal of potential value on the table. In traditional bargaining, the risk is relatively small since the scope has already been artificially constrained by the opening positions. In IBB, if the exploring has been successful, there may be a dozen or more options, with countless variations possible.

Focusing is a deliberate process in which each party acknowledges that as much exploring as possible has taken place and that the focus is now shifting to narrowing toward agreement. Behaviorally, this may involve making linkages between issues, identifying potential ranges for settlement on a given issue (perhaps contingent on progress on other matters), specifying criteria to judge options, having "what if" discussions to clarify what agreement on a given issue would really entail, and other ways of defining the contours of what is to become a final agreement. Done well, the focusing truly optimizes the mutual-gains potential inherent in the many options generated during the exploring.

There are new risks and consequently, increased tensions associated with focusing. Walton and McKersie highlighted some of the risks in their analysis of step three of their problem-solving model, which they characterize in the language of economics as "preference ordering" to compare respective "utility functions." The dilemmas include the following:

- Both sides have an incentive to misrepresent their preferences.
- There is a paradox in the way threats are sometimes necessary to achieve consideration of integrative options.

- There is a shared interest in convergence at the same time that there are separate self-interests on substance.

Exacerbating these dilemmas is the long shadow cast forward from the first three phases. The less positional the mandate developed during Phase I—preparation—the less anxious the parties are about trying to steer the focusing toward one particular set of outcomes. Where the opening has been skillfully constructed during Phase II, many of the standards or criteria will have been articulated and will now become touchstones to refer back to. Finally, where the exploring in Phase III has been truly far ranging, there are many options to draw on. Conversely, a more positional mandate, combined with a narrow opening statement and limited exploring, may tip the focusing process away from an interest-based approach and into a positional dance that not only suboptimizes the potential for mutual gains, but even calls into question the validity of the entire process. In other words, Phase IV can either give real shape and direction to a robust interest-based process or reveal the limitations of a superficial or incomplete interest-based process.

Phase V: Agree

The promise of IBB is that agreements will be fundamentally different from those reached by traditional bargaining. Instead of a grudging agreement reached as an alternative to even less attractive consequences, particularly an impasse and collective action, the interest-based approach promises mutual-gains agreements that will be embraced by both sides. Reality is inevitably more complex.

The challenge in achieving a wise, mutual-benefits agreement is at least twofold. First, there is the art of actually constructing the agreement—building on the contours highlighted during focusing. Second, there is the often greater challenge of persuading constituents that this is, in fact, the best-possible agreement. Both challenges apply in both traditional and interest-based bargaining. Interestingly, addressing the first challenge is easier under IBB, where, for many of the same reasons, the second challenge is more difficult. The ability to discover and codify mutual-gains options is greatly enhanced by the combination of exploring and focusing behaviors in Phases III and IV. Yet, precisely because of the collaborative and highly personal nature of these processes, it is hard to persuade constituents that the greatest-possible benefit has been extracted from the other side.

During fostering, a more interest-based process means that parties are less likely to reach for the first plausible agreement they discover and instead continue the exploration of other options that may trigger yet better agreements. Even in the context of a forcing strategy, an interest-based process increases the odds of the parties' discovering a least-unfavorable formulation to the issues and, in some cases, favorable trade-offs or transformations of the issue. Take a highly controversial issue in the United States, for example—a management proposal for health care benefit co-payments, which encounters strong resistance by the union. Under traditional bargaining, the forcing on this issue makes it highly likely that one side or the other will be deeply dissatisfied with the outcome. Under IBB, the problem will likely be re-defined around overall containment of health care costs (with co-payments just one of many options). In this case a less objectionable, or even a favorable, agreement is possible.

The unfortunate irony here involves what happens after an agreement has been reached via an interest-based approach. Stay with the example of health care benefits. In traditional bargaining, the union representatives will resist any movement on this issue until the very end of negotiations. They may even go past the deadline and there may even be some concerted activity. Members will not like any concessions made on having to make co-payments, but they will at least accept the fact that maximum resistance was offered.

By contrast, in an interest-based approach, union representatives will have explored this issue at length with management during the middle stages of the process, including entertaining some highly objectionable options. They will then present as tentative agreements inventive ways to contain health care costs. Though these may be much more favorable to the members than co-payments, they risk being seen as having made the concessions too easily. The same dynamics can take place with management.

What is to be done? The answer lies all the way back in Phases I and II of the process. The only way to resolve the constituent dilemmas that arise in Phase V is to know in advance what issues the other side will be putting on the agenda. Then it is possible (though not easy) to educate constituents to a high level of awareness and understanding of relevant data. It is possible (though again not easy) to forge a mandate around the importance of exploring all options on this issue. Furthermore, it is possible to make sure the constituents (as well as the other side) hear how the issue is framed in opening statements.

There are also some pre-agreements that can be reached during Phase I that further temper the dilemma. For example, it is possible to agree that part of Phase I preparation will involve the establishment of a joint task force or subcommittee to collect data on key issues—such as the cost of health care benefits in the above example—and may include key opinion leaders from among the membership. Such a committee may even include in its mandate a responsibility to educate members early on regarding lessons learned from the data.

Another pre-agreement may be to set an artificial early deadline—say two months prior to the contract expiration. In this case the parties might calculate the anticipated costs that management would incur by allowing bargaining to go to the normal deadline. These include direct costs associated with building up extra inventory in manufacturing operations, developing a strike plan, and consulting with attorneys, among other things. Also included are indirect costs, such as reputational issues with customers and suppliers as they are notified of an upcoming contract deadline and the internal costs associated with uncertainty as the deadline draws near. By totaling these direct and indirect costs, it may be possible to approach constituents in Phase I and indicate that it might be possible to set up a signing bonus provided an agreement is reached by this artificial deadline (two months early). On the union side, constituents would be asked, is this worth pursuing? On the management side, constituents would be asked, is this a wise investment? If both groups answer in the affirmative, they then share responsibility for figuring out how to make sure that the best-possible deal is achieved in the absence of a strike deadline. Again, a Phase V dilemma is best addressed through options created in Phase I.

One final aspect of Phase V should be noted: the way the agreement phase of bargaining (and all prior phases) casts a shadow forward into contract administration. Under traditional bargaining, recall that a grudging agreement is a sign of success. In such circumstances, implementation and administration of agreements are also likely to be grudging by one party or the other. By contrast, an interest-based process that fully attends to the interdependencies across all five phases has a much higher probability for success when it comes to implementation and administration. As a result of Phase V, the agreement is likely to have more mutually beneficial dimensions. Reaching further upstream in the process to Phase IV, various "what if" scenarios and other troubleshooting will have been considered.[12] Due to Phases II and III, the matter will already have been con-

---

[12] Particularly relevant is anticipating a number of fostering challenges, such as building positive interpersonal relationships, maintaining internal consensus, ensuring measurable results, anticipating leadership turnover, and anticipating other potential sources of conflict—including possible future forcing.

structively framed and set in the context of many options that were considered. Finally, reaching all the way back to Phase I, constituents will have been sufficiently educated on the issues so that they will be able to constructively support implementation and administration. Thus, the bargaining process and even the ongoing relations that follow bargaining are all enabled or undercut by the interdependencies across the five phases.

Linking Interest-Based Bargaining with Substantive and Relationship Outcomes

Improving substantive and relationship outcomes is the most important way in which a bargaining process matters. In this regard, the evidence is simultaneously clear and complicated. It is clear that there is a long history of path-breaking collective bargaining agreements that emerged out of highly collaborative, interest-based processes—even if not all of them used the IBB terminology. It is also clear that there is an equally long history of joint partnerships in which interest-based principles have been at the heart of constructive relations. At the same time, there is no guarantee of such success just by virtue of utilizing an interest-based process. It can increase the odds of success, but economic, political, and social processes can swamp even the best of processes.

Moreover, the full value of an interest-based agreement may only be evident in context. Consider the widely publicized agreements between the Saturn Corporation and the UAW. The first contract, which was negotiated in 1982, covered the same range of issues as the 700-plus-page master agreement between the UAW and General Motors, yet the UAW-Saturn agreement was only 28 pages long. Instead of spelling out rights and responsibilities in elaborate detail, the parties established a comprehensive joint governance structure so that issues would be resolved appropriately in context. At the time, this approach was exciting for some and unsettling for others.

More recently, the master agreement for the Kaiser Permanente health care system represents a similarly tangible example of a very different type of agreement reached through an IBB process. This very complex negotiation involved over a dozen different unions and over a hundred different bargaining units in facilities across the United States. Nearly every aspect of the agreement represents a re-thinking of standard contract language. In addition to path-breaking language on work-life balance, joint staffing procedures, and joint initiatives aimed at improving patient and employee safety, the contract also provides new approaches to such traditional matters as the grievance procedure (with multiple processes depending on the nature of the issue). Implementation of this contract depends on the full joint governance structure these parties have established. This reality has proved a complication in other health care settings, where there are reports that the language of the Kaiser Permanente agreement has been advanced (by labor or management), but the infrastructure isn't there to support such provisions.

In order to address the impact of IBB on relationship outcomes it is helpful to return to the FMCS survey data. All respondents were asked whether their relationship was improving, getting worse, or staying the same. The majority of union (59.5 percent) and management (60.5 percent) negotiators reported no change in their relationship, with a small number reporting deterioration (8 percent and 4.9 percent, respectively) and the balance reporting improvement (32.6 percent for union respondents and 36.5 percent for management). On the basis of the negotiation behaviors listed in Table 8.5, and other relevant behaviors, a scale was constructed on which respondents doing none of these behaviors were coded as "no IBB practices" and those engaging in more than three were coded as using "IBB practices" in bargaining. The full list of behaviors includes joint training, joint task forces, agreements on ground rules, advance notice on IBB principles, sharing of data by union or management, consensus decision making, brainstorming, and use of external content experts. The cut-off of more than three behaviors was selected so as not to limit the definition of IBB to just a few practices, while also not prescribing any specific set of practices.

As Table 8.6 indicates, management negotiators reporting the use of IBB practices were substantially more likely to report improving relationships as well. The responses for union negotiators are in the same direction—with IBB practices positively associated with improved relations, although the effect is not nearly as large. These findings point to a positive impact of IBB on relationship outcomes, but highlight a potential gap between union and management perception of this impact.

Conclusion

Institutional change is rarely rapid. The data and theory presented here suggest that change is certainly on the table in the case of collective bargaining. However, the process of bargaining over how to bargain is far from complete. Awareness of new interest-based approaches is high, but there are fundamental practical and conceptual challenges in any simplis-

Table 8.6. Impact of Interest-Based Bargaining (IBB) and Traditional
Bargaining on Relationship Outcomes: 1999 FMCS Survey Data (%)

Variable	Union	Management
Relationship improving—no IBB practices	31.8	34.2
Relationship improving—3 or more IBB practices*	37.0	48.1

* Question was asked only of respondents reporting experience with IBB.

tic application of these principles in this context. In particular, a failure to attend to the interdependencies across the five phases of the process promises to limit or even fully undercut the interest-based initiative. Furthermore, there is evidence of substantial variation in the outcomes associated with preferences for the interest-based approach. Clearly, more research is needed into the relationship between these behavioral choices at each phase of the process and the outcomes—relationship and substantive. While the variation in outcomes makes for an interesting research topic, it is profoundly frustrating for practitioners who are faced with the challenge of re-thinking the process and depending on mutual-gains outcomes to justify their exploration.

By returning to the original Walton and McKersie framework, we find that today's challenges are not new. Moreover, we find helpful insights to guide us, including the basic insight that integrative bargaining is marked by countless dilemmas. In the end, Walton and McKersie (1965: 152) concluded that the integrative process of searching for options was more than a set of mechanical steps: "The secret to the search process is not any one or a combination of tactics but a certain frame of mind or orientation." The challenge, as we have seen here, is to hold on to this new mindset at every phase of the process. Choices made at the earliest phases are critical to success in later phases, which is the ultimate dilemma: a new mindset is needed at the outset regarding a process in which key learning takes place over time. It is only hoped that the comments in this chapter facilitate this great challenge of redesigning the institution of collective bargaining while living within it.

9

Collective Bargaining and Human Resource Management in Britain

Can Partnership Square the Circle?

PHILLIP B. BEAUMONT
LAURENCE C. HUNTER

Even more so than in the United States, collective bargaining was unquestionably the centerpiece of the national system of industrial relations in Britain for much of the post–World War II period up through the 1970s. In 1968 a report issued by the Royal Commission on Trade Unions and Employers Associations (commonly known as the Donovan Commission, after its chair, Lord Donovan) concluded: "Properly conducted, collective bargaining is the most effective means of giving workers the right to representation in decisions affecting their working lives" (1968, para. 212). The government requested this report at that time because there was great concern over the high degree of strikes and the perceived power of shop stewards within individual plants to use their leverage to disrupt production in unpredictable ways. Again, when the Advisory, Conciliation and Arbitration Service (ACAS) was placed on a statutory basis in 1976, its formal terms of reference were to promote the general improvement of industrial relations, in particular by "encouraging the extension of collective bargaining and the development and, where necessary, reform of collective bargaining machinery." Moreover, estimates of the coverage of collective bargaining in the 1970s varied between some two-thirds and three-fourths of the work force (Table 9.1).

In the last two decades we have moved from this industrial relations model (we might call it "Keynesian-collectivist" to reflect its economic and industrial relations ethos) through a phase governed by monetarist-type economic policies and an emphasis on the individual rather than the collective. We might possibly be standing on the brink of a further transition to a new model, which could be described as the "partnership-stake-

161

Table 9.1. Historical Estimates
of the Work-Force Coverage of
Collective Bargaining in Britain

Year	Percentage
1906	20
1910	20
1933	42
1939	51
1961	67
1970	68
1973	73
1978	70
1984	71
1990	54

Source: Milner 1994.

holder" model. This model is one in which business success is a common concern of both management and labor as key stakeholders, requiring a less adversarial, more problem-solving approach to industrial relations in the interests of both parties.

Such major changes in the industrial relations system, and in the role of collective bargaining, in a relatively short space of time raise questions about the conditions that both generate and support such shifts. Specifically, if there is to be a shift into the partnership paradigm (which many would see as the desirable next step for the British system), what conditions will permit it to develop, and what sorts of problems are likely to be encountered? These are the central questions we wish to address toward the end of this chapter. In the meantime we think it important to explore the factors that have influenced the most recent changes within the system and that established the base from which further development will start.

The outcomes of change during the monetarist-individualist period of Conservative government (1979–1997) are well summarized in the findings of the third national Workplace Industrial Relations Survey (WIRS), conducted in 1990:

The decline in the extent of union recognition naturally fed through into a fall in the proportion of employees covered by collective bargaining. This had shrunk to 54 per cent in 1990 from 71 per cent six years earlier. As most employees outside the scope of the WIRS series are almost certainly not covered, it is clear that only a minority of employees in the economy as a whole had their pay jointly determined by management and trade unions (Millward, Stevens, Smart, and Hawes 1992: 102).

In short, the former dominance of collective bargaining had sharply diminished and the size of the nonunion sector in Britain had substantially increased. Britain had moved from a situation in which the trade unions had begun to look seriously at joint involvement in problem solving within the productivity-bargaining framework, to one in which trade unions were increasingly finding it difficult to express an effective voice on fundamental matters of employee protection, far less to participate in the setting of a new, more expanded agenda.

A second finding from the same survey was that human resource management (HRM) practices, such as formal selection procedures, performance appraisal, consultation, communications, training, and employee participation processes, were a feature more of the union than the nonunion sector (Millward, Stevens, Smart, and Hawes 1992, particularly chapter 5; Sisson 1993). This finding provided empirical evidence for a raging debate among British academics that up to that point had been framed in terms of an "HRM model"—that is, the use of individually oriented, advanced, or "high-performance" practices such as those just listed, derived from the behavioral sciences and practices of leading U.S. nonunion firms—versus an industrial relations model based on traditional collective bargaining and union-management practices. Taking this finding from the survey together with the decline in union membership and the reduced coverage of collective bargaining, we might reasonably suggest that these developments are *inter-related*, stemming from management's increasingly skeptical perceptions of the value of collective bargaining. While some employers seemed to be saying, "Why bother with trade unions?" others were apparently building these and other HRM techniques on top of a collective bargaining framework. Did the latter firms have a sound industrial relations base that they were seeking to extend and develop through HRM practices? Or were they disenchanted with the unionized arrangements and seeking to develop HRM to overcome these perceived weaknesses?

Changing Management Views of Collective Bargaining

In marked contrast to the 1970s, management rather than labor undoubtedly has been the proactive agent in British industrial relations in the

1980s and 1990s. This was encouraged by a government stance that was anti-union, according to many commentators, or at best unsupportive of collective bargaining as a centerpiece of the contemporary industrial relations system.

It is essential to gain an increased appreciation of the reasons for management's changing attitudes toward collective bargaining. Various sources of information help us make a start in this regard. First, a number of individual companies and employers' representative bodies gave evidence to the House of Commons Employment Committee in 1993 on the future role of trade unions (*IRS Employment Review*, no. 556, March 1994). In essence their evidence was as follows: (1) collective bargaining is only one of a number of possible mechanisms for managing the employment relationship; and (2) individual employee-centered HRM practices are viewed as a potentially more important route to organizational effectiveness than is collective bargaining. Second, an experienced, lead management negotiator of one of the best-known employers' associations in Britain from an industry that is still one of the most highly unionized in the U.K. private sector told us that the membership composition and key personalities involved in his employers' association had changed quite noticeably. In the 1970s, he suggested, the position of the association would have been described as follows: "We all believed in the value and importance of collective bargaining, with the only disagreement being how could we make it work better from our point of view." In contrast, he described a three-way split among member companies in the 1990s: (1) collective bargaining is increasingly viewed as irrelevant to the current economic environment, and indeed as a major drag on the (all-important) speed of decision making; (2) we should consult with, but not negotiate with, trade unions; and (3) collective bargaining is still important and worthwhile. The changing competitive environment, the increased membership and influence of U.S.-owned companies, and the new breed of business school–trained HRM managers were the major factors held responsible for this change.

Discussions with other managers typically have yielded the following sort of spectrum of less positive opinions about collective bargaining:

1. Collective bargaining is increasingly less relevant to the changed economic environment.
2. Collective bargaining doesn't add value.
3. Collective bargaining is a necessary, but not sufficient, condition for organizational effectiveness.

4. Collective bargaining comes between employees and management and has diverted management from paying sufficient attention to the needs and interests of individual employees.
5. Collective bargaining generates performance costs for the individual organization.

What underlies these critical views on the part of management, almost certainly, is a range of factors, including legislative change and its influence on managerial attitudes, changes in product and labor market circumstances, and business cycle influences. Arguably, the fifth proposition has been the most intensively investigated, with most research following the essentially economic cost-benefit approach of Freeman and Medoff (1984). (See Table 9.2 for a summary of research findings on the union impact in Britain, findings that are not too dissimilar from those in the United States.) However, it is the fourth proposition that we are particularly interested in, for reasons that we seek to establish in the remainder of this section.

If HRM offers an opportunity for a strengthening of labor-management cooperation, will the union or the nonunion sector be more likely to follow this path? In the union sector, is the wider adoption of HRM techniques seen by management as a source of additional strength, or as a salvation from a problem-ridden collective bargaining experience?

In our next section we present a statistical test that addresses these questions. As background, and for more general reasons, we complete this section by briefly introducing some of the existing literature on the sources of industrial relations change. Which organizations are most likely to reform their industrial relations arrangements, and why?

In the United States, an examination of the adoption and diffusion process of Quality of Working Life (QWL) innovations across the plants of a single large company reached the following conclusion: "The correlations . . . between the industrial relations performance measures and involvement in QWL programs reflect the fact that plants with comparatively good industrial relations performance tend to develop relatively more extensive QWL involvement" (Katz, Kochan, and Weber 1985: 522). This particular pattern of findings would seem explicable in terms of an emphasis on the *ability* rather than the incentive to bring about change in industrial relations terms. That is, plants with "good" industrial relations can most easily introduce new innovations, through a simple, incremental, leveraging-up process. This emphasis is apparent in some of the prescriptive literature concerning industrial relations and

Table 9.2. Research concerning Union Impact in Britain

1. Unionized workplaces pay higher wages than comparable nonunion ones. This
    differential is particularly high when a closed shop exists, where multiple unions are
    bargaining separately, and where the product market is uncompetitive.
2. The size of the union-nonunion pay differential fell in the 1980s.
3. Unions have reduced the extent of wage inequality. As unions declined in the 1980s, the
    extent of pay inequality increased.
4. Over the 1980s, unionized establishments, companies, and industries on average
    experienced more productivity growth than their nonunion counterparts.
5. There is a strong negative relationship between unionization and financial performance
    or profitability at the workplace, firm, and industry levels.
6. There is no clear-cut conclusive evidence concerning the relationship between unions
    and investment.

Source: Metcalf 1993.

HRM change. Lawler (1981: 145–46), for example, has argued that gain-
sharing plans should only be introduced in organizations with the essential *prerequisite* of a highly cooperative union-management relationship,
while others have claimed that an initial high level of employee-management trust is necessary for the successful introduction and operation of
performance-related pay arrangements (Hills, Madigan, Scott, and
Markham 1990: 248–49).

In contrast to this perspective, most of the available literature comprises
single-plant case studies that have documented the introduction of industrial relations changes in plants with a history of "poor industrial relations" (Guest 1979; Ichniowski 1992). That is, they adopt a problem-
based view of the change process, with the emphasis being placed on
management's *incentive* to change, to overcome existing industrial relations difficulties and associated problems of achieving effective labor utilization in a more competitive economic climate.

One of the major areas of stress in labor-management relations in the
1980s stemmed from the search for greater labor flexibility in organizations, perceived as a route to greater efficiency. In practice, the evidence
suggests that British firms pursued the efficiency objective largely by a process of manpower economies, which took the form of permanent lay-offs
and replacement of standard by "nonstandard" contracts (for example,
part-time and temporary staff), and search for a reduction in wage costs
rather than an enhanced flexibility among high-skill, high-quality labor.
Against an unfavorable political and economic background, unions were
relatively powerless to resist either the lay-off and redundancy programs

or the various forms of work intensification that management felt able (and necessary) to introduce if they were to survive. Unions were increasingly bypassed or marginalized in these circumstances, and employers made increasing use of forms of participation that sought to engage the commitment of workers directly, rather than operating through the unions.

This illustration from British experience suggests that the drive for change has come from a perceived management and organizational *need*, rather than building on well-developed and effectively functioning collective bargaining structures that *enable* new opportunities to be opened up. In the next section we seek to shed further light on the British experience by referring to panel data derived from the 1990 Workplace Industrial Relations Survey.

Objective Indicators of Change: The Role of Management

We began this chapter by highlighting two important changes in the British system of industrial relations: (1) the increased size of the nonunion sector, and (2) the relatively greater presence of HRM practices in the union sector. The question we have posed is whether increasingly critical management attitudes toward collective bargaining can help account for both of these developments.

The Growth of the Nonunion Sector

Evidence of the role of management opposition to collective bargaining as a factor in the growth of the nonunion sector can be gleaned from a number of sources. For instance, evidence from the 1990 Workplace Industrial Relations Survey indicates that around a third of all nonunion establishments express hostile management views toward the possibility of a union presence in the plant; such plants have organizational and workforce correlates very similar to those of currently unionized establishments (Beaumont and Harris 1994). As with all attitudinal factors, however, it is important to try to document the particular ways in which such views have been *tangibly* manifested. Here, evidence from two reasonably comparable, company-level surveys indicates that the extent of both nonunion status and "double-breasting" arrangements (where some but not all plants in a multi-plant company recognize unions) has increased notice-

Table 9.3. The Growth of Nonrecognition[a] and Double Breasting[b] in Britain (Manual Workers Only): 1985 and 1992 Company Surveys (%)

1985		1992	
Recognition	89	Recognition	68
All establishments	50	All sites	25
Some establishments	39	Most sites	16
		Some sites	27
No recognition	11	No recognition	32

Source: Beaumont, Harris, and Phayre 1995: 111.
[a] Not recognizing trade unions for collective bargaining purposes.
[b] The practice of a multi-plant company to recognize trade unions for collective bargaining purposes in some but not all of its plants.

ably over the course of time in Britain. The relevant evidence in this regard is set out in Table 9.3.

Discussions with individual ACAS officers have indicated, furthermore, that where unions have been able to penetrate the growing nonunion sector, particularly among new plants, it has been much more on a *partial* recognition basis. That is, the unions have enjoyed some limited success in obtaining individual representation rights in relation to disciplinary or grievance procedures, but considerably less in the way of full collective bargaining rights. As the ACAS Annual Report for 1990 put it, "Some employers preferred to concede representational rights with a view to reconsidering their arrangements for full collective bargaining only if a positive relationship with the trade union had developed" (p. 20). Currently, many new union membership-recruitment campaigns appear to be concentrating on such partially recognized establishments, as illustrated by the example set out in Table 9.4.

The role of management opposition to collective bargaining as an important factor in the growth of the nonunion sector should surprise few people, particularly in a U.S. audience. We are much more interested, however, in trying to account for the relatively greater presence of HRM practices in the union sector. Specifically, we seek to test here a proposition suggested by our prior discussion of (1) management reservations about collective bargaining that are not fully and adequately captured by Freeman and Medoff's (1984) economic costs and benefits approach (see proposition 4, mentioned earlier); and (2) the types of plants (poor or good industrial relations performance) that are most likely to innovate in industrial relations.

Table 9.4. Results of a 12-Month Recruitment Campaign: Following the Line of Least Resistance

This union has some seven district offices.

In one district office there is a single officer responsible for both servicing existing members and recruiting new members.

The single officer's ability to recruit new members has been severely constrained by a combination of the wide geographical spread of membership, the small size of employment units, and servicing demands flowing from membership redundancies and plant closures.

In recent years the district concerned has had between 3,000 and 2,800 members, with overall membership numbers falling each year as membership losses (due to lay-offs and closures) have exceeded new members gained.

In 1997 a full-time officer (from another district) was seconded to the district concerned for 12 months to concentrate on new membership recruitment.

During 1997 the district recorded 194 members lost and 119 gained.

Of the 119 new members, 18 were recruited in a relatively newly established, nonunion, greenfield-site operation (some 300 employees in total).

However, the membership-recruitment officer overwhelmingly concentrated her activities on partially recognized establishments, because of less management opposition and the presence of union lay representatives, recruiting some 100 of the 119 new members in such establishments.

HRM Practices in the Union Sector

Prior to the publication of the 1990 Workplace Industrial Relations Survey results, a number of smaller, less representative surveys had come up with essentially the same finding: HRM practices were more a feature of the union than the nonunion sector in Britain (Milner and Richards 1991). The basic explanation offered for this finding was that the union sector has an existing institutional and authority structure for introducing and operating such practices; this interpretation seemed to emphasize the *ability* to change, leveraging up from an initial "good" collective bargaining relationship. Such an explanation fits very awkwardly with Storey's (1992) case study–based findings that (1) HRM practices were rarely introduced in unionized organizations via a "joint partnership" approach, and as a result, (2) the collective bargaining process had tended to be rather marginalized or even bypassed by managements enthused by a unitarist spirit.

Accordingly, in view of the discussion earlier in this chapter and of Storey's (1992) findings, we propose to test the following proposition: *the introduction of HRM practices will be disproportionately concentrated in unionized establishments where management initially reported relatively poor employee-management relationships.* This particular hypothesis is tested here utilizing the panel data set from the 1990 Workplace Industrial Relations Survey.[1]

The panel data set involves 537 individual employment establishments (data weighted by population yield 500 establishments) that were interviewed in both the second (1984) and the third (1990) national Workplace Industrial Relations Surveys; the panel contains more unionized establishments and more large establishments than the full, cross-sectional survey(s). Initially we constructed an index of HRM practices based on the following variables:

1. Establishments with any change in employee involvement in the last three years
2. Establishments with changes in working practices in the last three years that have reduced job demarcation
3. Establishments with a new consultative committee or more meetings concerning participation or communication in the last three years
4. Establishments with autonomous work groups, or reorganization of work, or increased responsibility given to employees, or quality circles, or training, or briefing groups, introduced in the last three years.

These variables were then subjected to cluster analysis, which allows for establishments to be classified according to groupings that have similar attributes. The outcome (for private sector establishments only) was the classification of some 70 percent of establishments (n = 341) to the non-HRM category and the remaining 30 percent to the HRM category. All establishments in the HRM category were characterized by increased employee involvement and changes in working practices; a large proportion also experienced increased levels of communication and work-group, task-related activities.

A logit equation was then estimated on the panel data using a set of potential explanatory variables based on the 1984 observations. The estimates were for private sector establishments only, weighted by population totals, with the key findings for present purposes being as follows (see Table 9.5 for other results): (1) A 10 percent increase in the proportion of the manual work force that comprises union members increased the probability of being in the HRM group by 1.8 percent. (2) Establishments recognizing unions for collective bargaining purposes for manual employees

[1] We wish to acknowledge here the role of our colleague, Richard Harris (University of Durham), in this analysis.

Table 9.5. Organizational Characteristics of the Human Resource Management (HRM) Establishments

A 10 percent increase in the employment size of the U.K. organization increases the probability of being in the HRM group by 5.2 percent.
Older establishments (those in existence for 20 years or more in 1984) are 9.9 percent more likely to be in the HRM group.
Belonging to the high-technology sector increases the probability of being in the HRM group by 28.2 percent.
Establishments with shift working arrangements are 17.5 percent less likely to be in the HRM group.
A 10 percent increase in the proportion of the work force that comprises unskilled manual workers decreases the probability of being in the HRM group by 2.8 percent.
Foreign-owned establishments have a higher probability of belonging to the HRM group.

and reporting that their management-employee relations were good or very good were 20.9 percent *less likely* to be in the HRM group.

Obviously there are some limitations in the measurement of our dependent variable: only a single management respondent (the individual responsible for personnel and industrial relations matters) provided a view on the quality of the employee-management relationship ("selective perception"?); and the *expectations* of the quality of the employee-management relationship may be systematically higher in unionized establishments than in nonunion ones. This being said, our results are strong and highly consistent with much of our prior discussion. In short, it appears that management's relatively poor perceptions of the existing employee-management relationship in unionized establishments were an important stimulus for the introduction of HRM practices over the period 1984–1990. Moreover if, as we suspect, management holds the unions to be in large measure responsible for this state of affairs, it will clearly go a long way to helping explain the limited use of the joint-partnership approach in introducing such practices (Storey 1992).

The Partnership Concept

The findings just reported are far from surprising in view of the unions' first reaction to the introduction of HRM practices in Britain. Many unions were initially hostile and critical of HRM. For example, it was only in 1991 that the Transport and General Workers Union voted to move away from their position of principled opposition to HRM practices.

More generally, one leading union official in Britain characterized the British union response to HRM as "incoherent, tentative, anxious, befuddled and uncertain" (*IRS Employment Review*, no. 552, January 1994). Some individual unions provided an exception to the general rule, but the predominant British union approach was to (1) express concern about the potential undermining of collective bargaining, and (2) leave the nature of the response to management initiatives very much up to the shop stewards in the individual plants. In short, throughout the 1980s and into the 1990s, few national-level union guidelines were forthcoming, enthusiasm for the concept and practice of HRM was conspicuous by its absence, and certainly no proactive union agenda was apparent. Furthermore, managers have frequently told us that any national-level union rhetoric in favor of HRM is rarely matched by tangible support further down the union hierarchy.

In more recent years the Trades Union Congress (TUC) has sought to orchestrate a change in this regard. Central to this proposed program of change has been the notion of "new unionism" and "new industrial relations" pivoting on the notion of a joint-partnership approach. As a recent TUC publication (1997: 8) put it:

A key test for social partnership will be how far unions and employers can give priority to jobs in practice. There are a number of ways, drawing on the best of experience in this and other countries, as to how this can be done. For example, a number of companies have reached agreements with trade unions which provide for job or employment security. In return, unions have agreed to much greater flexibility within the organization. In other areas when organizations have been faced with unavoidable technological and market changes they have been able to develop agreed policies which cushion the effects of redundancy and develop a better joint understanding of the business. The TUC is keen to develop the concept of best practice in this field: to show how unions and employers can develop the most effective models of work organization that both enhance productivity and competitiveness and also give protection to the individual.

More recently, the TUC has created a TUC Partnership Institute to promote a deeper understanding of what is involved in a partnership and to promote dissemination of best practices in implementing them. The TUC defines partnership in terms of six principles: (1) shared commitment to the success of the enterprise, (2) recognition of legitimate interests, (3) commitment to employment security, (4) focus on the quality of working life, (5) openness, and (6) adding value (TUC Partnership Institute 2001).

From the union point of view, the gains hoped for from a widespread adoption of the partnership concept appear to be (1) a re-assertion of the importance of collective bargaining (particularly in relation to increased job security), largely via a reduction in management concerns about collective bargaining, and as a consequence, (2) an enhanced union input to the design, implementation, and monitoring of HRM practices. The presence of a Labour government may assist in this regard. The government has stated that partnership, along with fairness and adaptability, is at the heart of their employment policies. Admittedly, tangible indications of this commitment to partnership are somewhat limited at this stage, although the government did encourage and facilitate discussions between the TUC and the Confederation of British Industry (CBI) on the subject of statutory recognition provisions, prior to announcing the details of proposed legislation.

In Britain, as in other countries with a history and tradition of adversarial distributive bargaining (like the United States and Ireland), numerous questions have been raised about the partnership notion. To some individuals it is such a vague general concept that it can mean all things to all people; others have viewed it as a recipe for "union incorporation"; and yet others have emphasized that the list of cited partnership cases in practice is very small, with the same names occurring again and again. Moreover, the frequently cited cases appear to fall into three extreme groups: (1) greenfield-site or new start-up cases in which a union-management partnership arrangement was consciously built into the initial design of these innovative organizations; (2) a highly unionized organization (with a strong adversarial relationship) that is facing an extreme crisis, possibly with the plant under considerable threat of closure ("reform or die"); or (3) an organization operating in a completely different economic or competitive environment, such as privatization. Such extreme cases can tell us very little about the road map that is involved in a relatively ordinary organization moving to, and sustaining, a partnership type of approach. Moreover, many practitioner-based publications and conference presentations of partnership cases present too rosy a view of the route to partnership, simply emphasizing mission statements and a change in attitude and providing too little detail about the difficulties and problems encountered during the process of change. We need more honest and realistic case study–based research which recognizes (1) that the institutionalization of partnership is likely to be a dynamic rather than a static process; and (2) that this process does not involve a smooth sequence of changes but rather the frequent confronting of issues, problems, and crises that periodically challenge the strength and commitment of the parties to the concept and practice of partnership.

This major deficiency in the existing literature needs to be addressed via a series of systematic comparative case studies focusing on the processes of change, with a view to generating a set of initial hypotheses for further development and testing. It is in this spirit that we present the findings of one case study (see appendix to this chapter). What this example shows is that even in the presence of both incentive and ability to move in the partnership direction, the path can be far from smooth. A deliberate linear strategy for a change program is unlikely to be fulfilled, owing to the dynamics of the process and the attitudinal restructurings that must be tackled along the way. At the very least, the achievement of partnership relations capable of yielding mutually beneficial results is a major challenge for all those involved.

Some Reflections on System-wide Reform Proposals

Given the starting point of our chapter, it is only logical that we begin this section with a look at the Donovan Report (Royal Commission on Trade Unions and Employers Associations 1968). This report essentially recommended a system-wide move to formal, single-employer (plant- and company-based) bargaining structures that would entail a heightened level of importance attached to the personnel management function, more formal recognition and involvement of shop stewards in negotiations, and enhanced procedural regulation. For those who created the Donovan Report, and for the productivity-bargaining phase that followed, the hope was that a new and more positive mutuality could be built between management and labor, expressed through a collective bargaining process that was still based in pluralism but offered scope for mutual gains through cooperative, problem-solving approaches to negotiation. Productivity bargaining proved to be relatively short-lived, however (burdened by its incorporation in incomes policy), and the remainder of the 1970s did nothing to establish the sort of mutuality the Donovan Report had attempted to instill. One can point to three major criticisms of this attempt at system-wide reform, admittedly with the aid of hindsight:

1. The commission's recommendations were overly influenced by experience in certain industries (such as engineering), and too little influenced by contrasting experience in other industries (such as the public sector).

2. The recommendation in favor of single-employer bargaining structures assumed that it was appropriate for all organizations and industries. It rejected a research-based contingency view of the determinants of bargaining structure (for example, that industries in highly competitive product markets, characterized by small firms, naturally favor multi-employer, industry-based structures).
3. The analysis and advice of the established external agent of change (the Commission of Industrial Relations) were able to produce little tangible movement in the required direction, in the absence of a strong internal awareness in individual organizations of a need for change.

By the end of the 1970s, and the advent of the Conservative government, Britain was moving into a new era (our monetarist-individualist model), which was to last until 1997. Far from building a stronger sense of mutuality and partnership, the system moved sharply in the other direction, with unions under attack from government and many employers anxious to regain control of the industrial relations agenda, union recognition in decline, and collective bargaining diminishing in coverage as well as moving in the direction of single-employer bargaining. As we have seen earlier, these changes were driven by an economic reform program set in a framework of national competitiveness in which Britain had become increasingly laggard. This was the context into which HRM entered in the 1980s, at a time when lay-offs were rife, job security was under threat for many employees who had regarded themselves in secure employment, and unions were in no position to offer more than token resistance. Both the labor market and the industrial relations systems were operating under a model characterized by individualism and flexibility, rather than the "Keynesian-collectivist" model that had prevailed in the 1960s and early 1970s. In this context "hard" HRM values driven by a managerialist agenda could be seen as an alternative to the mutuality of collective bargaining—especially of the distributive variety. Such a reading is highly consistent with the empirical findings reported in our section on the objective indicators of change, but what it does not bring out is that the new model created something of an industrial relations vacuum. The system was much more decentralized, as government wished, but it was based not on positive principles but on the ambition to remove perceived encumbrances to competitiveness.

This is the context for the emerging discussion of partnership, which may be seen as the keystone of an attempt to build a new industrial relations model, based on partnership and stakeholder values, under the new Labour government. In one sense, that might seem to herald a return to the sorts of values promoted by the Donovan Commission and approaches to mutuality in bargaining that might resemble some of the more genuine efforts to develop productivity bargaining. On the other hand, it has to be recognized that much has changed in the industrial relations and labor market environments. Whereas the Donovan Commission envisaged reform succeeding through voluntarism and mutuality, the experience of many managers over the past twenty years has been one in which they have enjoyed a new freedom to reshape work organization, deal with employees as individuals rather than a collective employee voice, and pursue a competitiveness agenda focused on low labor costs and flexibility in labor utilization. How willing a majority of employers will be to yield ground in this area in order to develop what our case study reveals as a hard road to partnership must remain open to doubt. Nor is it clear that many trade unionists, especially at the grass-roots level, will be convinced that this is the best way forward. We have already commented that "partnership" risks being all things to all people, and while from a managerial perspective, partnership might appear to embody a unitarist philosophy, it is in sharp contrast to the traditional British union approach to industrial relations based on pluralist values. If we sound skeptical of the prospects for partnership, we do not mean that the effort should be abandoned. But we do raise some fundamental issues: (1) there must be no fudging of what is involved in and implied by partnership, nor any impression that it is an easy ride; and (2) it is not clear whether industrial relations reform, and the deliberate transition from one system to another, can be left largely to voluntary forces and the diffusion of independently developed good practice. These are the final issues to which we turn.

The Voluntary Diffusion of Partnership

Our earlier discussion on the evidence relating to the adoption of new industrial relations and HRM practices suggests that at least in Britain the main driving force has come from the *need* (of organizations) to seek new solutions, and that in recent times a principal source of that drive has been economic pressure and the search for competitiveness. The changes that occurred in the 1970s were generally in the direction favored by the Donovan Commission, but the decisions were essentially made in the interest of the individual organization. We would argue that although the outcome was broadly what government desired, the driving force was not government exhortation or legislation. Rather the driving force was the pursuit of self-interest on the part of many organizations, which gradually altered the balance of the system. Similarly, in the 1980s, change was occasioned by economic necessity for organizational survival, and the moves toward flexibility and cost competitiveness were consistent with government's objectives, as well as being heavily influenced by government's *economic* policy. The implication is that unless organizations (and their management) see strong arguments for a partnership approach, there is unlikely to be a widespread and rapid adoption of partnership on a system-wide level, although it has the potential to be adopted in individual organizations. Given the story revealed in the appendix, our profile of the sort of organization most likely to adopt the partnership approach voluntarily would be as follows:

1. It is under considerable competitive and performance pressure.
2. It views HRM practices as a major means of responding to such pressure.
3. It is a relatively highly unionized organization.
4. The unions it deals with have not historically been strongly hostile to HRM.
5. Its existing collective bargaining relationship needs reform but has the potential of being moved in a joint problem-solving direction (it is not beyond redemption).
6. Management recognizes the importance of the distinction between the negotiating relationship and the larger employee-management relationship but is willing to commit time and resources to improving both.
7. Management appreciates that trade union representatives cannot be expected to sell changes to the work force if they have not been involved in the design stage of the changes.
8. Union representation in the design stage requires the plant to be opened up to the outside influence of the national union in the form of training, advice, and support.
9. The early concentration of the joint working parties is on issues of priority to the work force, with the parties' membership not being confined to a small cozy elite.
10. Early joint working party "successes" can be built on so that the relationship grows incrementally.

This may not be an exhaustive listing, but it is already a daunting one, emphasizing both the incentive and the ability to change. Accordingly the question—which only time and experience can help answer—is, Just what proportion of British organizations have the sort of requirements needed to walk down this particular route?

The obvious disadvantages of a voluntary diffusion process are that small numbers are likely to be involved, the process will be slow, and the voluntary adopters will not constitute a representative cross section of British industry. If a system-wide reform along partnership lines is a serious objective of government, it may decide that more positive prompting and supportive measures are essential.

Public Policy Encouragement of Partnership

A useful way to introduce the role of public policy in relation to the partnership notion is to consider the case of Ireland, a country with similar industrial relations traditions to those of Britain. In marked contrast to Britain (and indeed Europe more generally), however, Ireland has pursued for almost a decade a social partnership approach at the macro-economy level involving employers, unions, and the state. These tripartite (corporatist) agreements have been associated with considerable success at the aggregate economy level, although there have been growing criticisms and concerns, particularly from the trade unions, that the approach has no adequate micro-foundations and that there is little partnership at the individual organizational level. In an attempt to improve this situation, a relatively high-profile public policy initiative has been launched (Table 9.6). Although this initiative is still in its relative infancy, informed observers have already made two major points: (1) There has been limited diffusion of the partnership notion at the individual organizational level. (2) Important differences have emerged between unions and management about the partnership notion. These differences concern scope or coverage (strategic versus operational matters), the priority attached to representative structures as opposed to direct employee involvement, and the timing of rewards (up front versus contingent on improved performance).

Britain does not have anywhere near as formal a public policy initiative as Ireland, although the Labour government's white paper *Fairness at Work* (Department of Trade and Industry 1998) indicated that (1) government-funded research will be carried out to identify and publicize examples of good practice in work-based partnerships; (2) government funding will be made available to contribute to the training of managers and employee representatives in order to assist and develop partnerships at work; and (3) the government is encouraging ACAS to give more emphasis to their advisory work along such lines. Indeed, at least one ACAS region is currently seeking to establish a network of organizations interested in pursuing the partnership route, and some parts of the public sector (such as the National Health Service in Scotland) are seeking to encourage and facilitate sector-wide approaches toward partnership (Table 9.7).

Table 9.6. The National Centre for Partnership in Ireland

This center was set up in the prime minister's department.
It involves senior representatives of management and trade unions and public policy officials.
Its broad goal is to help transfer the spirit of national-level partnership down to the individual organizational level.
It explicitly recognizes the need for, and the value of, a diversity of partnership models at the individual enterprise level.
It has a sizable annual budget under its own control.
It seeks to encourage and facilitate change through the mechanisms of training and information dissemination based on best-practice company examples.

Table 9.7. Proposal Partnership Arrangements in the National Health Service (NHS) in Scotland

1. *National Framework*: A Scottish partnership forum will be established (by September 1998) and will report to the director of human resources, NHS in Scotland. It will consist of managers, staff, staff representatives, and independent advisors. The forum's goal will be to
   Support research and development in the areas of employment.
   Establish a common approach to new employment legislation affecting the NHS in Scotland.
   Provide advice on joint working and partnership.
   Develop a framework for managing human resources in the NHS in Scotland.
   Review key areas of employment practice to ensure consistency.
2. The forum will support the work of two temporary working groups, namely, the best-practice steering group (support services) and the organizational change group.
3. *Local Framework*: To demonstrate commitment to working together, the NHS in Scotland employers and Trusts and Health Boards will be required to develop a partnership agreement with staff and their representatives. These agreements will be subject to audit and will be reported to boards by joint staff/management groups. As a minimum, these agreements will contain
   Communication and consultation arrangements.
   Access to information and board meetings.
   Organizational change policies.
4. *Monitoring Arrangements*:
   Trusts and Health Boards will be required to report progress on the development of partnerships.
   Progress in implementing these plans will be monitored through accountability reviews and annual reports.

Some Final Reflections

These useful first steps are very much welcomed, at least in our judgment. The initiatives largely embody the implicit assumption that it is only a lack of knowledge, information, and training that is holding back a more extensive spread of partnership arrangements. We believe that the problem is much more complex than that, however, for four reasons:

1. As we have argued, "partnership" is a slippery concept, open to different interpretations, thus making it easy for the participants to talk past each other without really grappling with the issues that matter.
2. The experience of the Donovan Commission in the 1960s and the experience of the Labour and Conservative governments in the 1970s and 1980s suggest that for organizations to adopt changes in practice on a large scale, they have to see the changes as meeting a felt need: there needs to be adequate incentive.
3. The available public policy instruments tend to be limited, working most easily for those who are already converted but making limited inroads among those who are not—and the latter will include many below-average firms in terms of capability for change (though, objectively, they may need it the most).
4. Our case study demonstrates the difficulties that may exist in establishing and sustaining a partnership approach, even where there is a basis of mutual trust and a positive attitude toward such development.

If there is to be more positive action, there may be a need for leverage at three different levels:

1. The development of organizational and governance mechanisms that will give stronger effect to the voice of multiple stakeholders in the strategic direction of enterprises, including public sector organizations. This is consistent with the philosophy espoused by the Labour government, but it is not yet clear how it can be given concrete expression. Measures to curb the firms' focus on the short term and on shareholder benefit are likely to be potentially important in this regard.
2. There needs to be greater scope for employees as teams or individuals to participate more actively in decisions affecting their own jobs, work organization, and employment conditions. This is consistent with the participation ethos supported by many employers and trade unions, as well as with the extension of HRM concepts and tools.
3. Underpinning this, there has to be a developing sense of trust, which has to be founded on a stronger sense of employment security than has prevailed in recent years. This underlines again the importance of the macro-economic context in which industrial relations development is progressing (and which we have suggested has been influential in its previous transition). The trade unions have made it very clear that increased security is a critical factor in enlisting their cooperation (Monks 1998). Without it, widespread involvement of the trade unions and their members is unlikely.

This agenda is a large and demanding one for the Labour government—wider than is indicated in the 1998 White Paper. It is recognized, however, that the change may be slow: "Spreading good practice from the best organizations to the rest requires a change in the culture of employment relations. This will take time" (Department of Trade and Industry 1998: 12). Such a judgment is one we would not dispute.

Appendix: A Longitudinal Case: Steps toward Partnership?

The foreign-owned plant in this case study began operations in Britain in 1989. Prior to production, a single union-recognition agreement had been negotiated, resulting in some 90 percent of the production employees being union members. In the early start-up phase (1989–1990), there were few signs of any difficulty in the union-management relationship; a union-management consultative committee was quickly established, as was a joint health and safety committee, and annual wage negotiations proceeded smoothly. These early wage negotiations involved plant management and national and district officials of the union, *not* the shop stewards in the plant. The negotiated wage increases were above the local market's "going rate," and the union negotiators were both experienced and well disposed toward management, given the pre-production single recognition agreement that had resulted in such a highly unionized production work force.

After 1990 the full-time union officials withdrew from the negotiating process, to be replaced by the shop stewards in the plant. Problems began to emerge very quickly in the process of wage negotiations in 1991, which continued and in fact intensified dramatically in 1992 and 1993. In each round of negotiations the union's initial demands and management's initial offers were a long way apart, and there was little subsequent movement away from these initial positions. The process dragged on, with the national union officials having to be called in all three years to try to assist the attempt to reach a settlement. Management threatened to impose its offer in one year, the possibility of a strike ballot was raised in another, and on one occasion the work force rejected the agreement reached between management and the stewards. As a result of these problems, the post of chief union negotiator was held by three different individuals in four years. Moreover, alongside these problems in the wage-negotiating process, the shop stewards made continual reference to poor morale on the shop floor, supervisors reported limited work-force cooperation over certain issues (such as covering employee absences on shifts), and work-force grievances periodically "blew up" (regarding the extent of use of outside contractors, for example).

Both management and union representatives offered a variety of explanations for the occurrence of these problems. The most frequently heard concerned the continued failure of the plant to reach its profit targets; the high expectations of the work force, which resulted from "unrealistic" job previews during the course of an intensive recruitment process; and the overly extended use of a greenfield-site (or start-up) management mode involving tight, top-down control by production. Throughout the plant there was a widespread belief that the work force had lost, or was rapidly losing, confidence in both management and the trade union. The feeling was that both had failed to deliver on their promises.

The situation appeared to be deteriorating rapidly. Within management circles some individuals favored taking a strike "to sort the workers out," others favored a first-offer-equals-final-offer negotiating approach, and the national union officers were told that de-recognition of the union was being considered as a serious option unless things improved radically. At the same time, different parts of the work force were talking about resigning from the union or seeking a separate bargaining unit for themselves.

In late 1993 a new managing director for the plant was appointed. The plant was still not making a profit, and the route he chose to improve productivity and performance was to institute a program to change the work culture within the plant: there was to be less tight supervision, more teamwork, more open communication with the work force, and—above all else—an emphasis on *employee empowerment*. Within the context of this larger program, a joint working party was established specifically to examine the state of the existing union-management relationship. The working party, which contained both management and union representatives (full-time officials and shop stewards), broadly recommended the need for more early-stage union consultation prior to the processes of wage negotiation. This recommendation subsequently took three main tangible forms:

1. Management and union representatives held one or two off-site discussion sessions prior to undertaking the annual wage-negotiating process. These sessions (each lasting a day or so) were designed to consider the mood of the work force, share plant business plans, and indicate each other's negotiating expectations and priorities.
2. Once a month the senior shop steward would meet the managing director for coffee to discuss any particularly important or pressing developments on the shop floor.

3. Joint working parties would periodically be established to address any important, longer-term issues not deemed suitable for the annual wage-negotiating process.

These changes were followed by relatively smooth wage settlements in both 1994 and 1995 in which the full-time union officials did not have to get involved. In late 1995 a new head of personnel management was appointed in the plant. Initially he was favorably impressed by the appearance of the wage-negotiating process: "It was a non-threatening, non-confrontational process very different to what I had heard it was like before." His discussions with supervisors, involvement in supervisor–shop steward meetings, and examination of the details of the 1994 and 1995 wage settlements, however, led him to two major negative conclusions:

1. The improved negotiating process between management and shop stewards was essentially a discrete, self-contained entity that had not positively spilled over into the larger employee-management relationship.
2. Management was essentially "buying the improved union-management climate" in the wage-negotiating process by overly generous settlements, particularly in view of the continued failure of the plant to be profitable.

As a result of these conclusions, he initially sought a change in the composition of the management negotiating team: two supervisors were included in the team for the first time. Then he assumed a key role in the 1996 wage negotiations, which were reported as "a very tense affair," with the eventual settlement "being considerably below the level which the board had approved him to go up to." The 1996 settlement was viewed throughout the plant as a victory for management. The 1997 settlement again involved much tighter management control of the substantive outcomes,[2] albeit with much less tension involved in the process.[3] Indeed, the 1997 settlement contained a joint enabling clause "incorporating issues identified by both parties as being fundamental to the future success of the plant." This enabling clause was rapidly followed up by the negotiation of a three-year wage agreement; the clause had as its stated purpose "to re-

[2] Negotiated outcomes in 1994–1995 typically involved the retail price index (RPI) plus 1 percent plus "add-ons" (such as increased shift allowances). Since then, they have involved the RPI plus 0.5 percent with no add-ons.
[3] A new senior shop steward (chief union negotiator) was considered important in this changed process.

move the three months each year when everyone's attention is focused on pay, other issues are sidelined and the climate worsens. With a long term deal this time is saved, pay can be pushed into the background and we can jointly focus on the important changes facing all of us." The work force voted two to one in favor of accepting the three-year deal.

In addition to the three-year pay deal, in early 1998 the plant had nearly a dozen joint working parties in operation, addressing a variety of matters, such as possible changes in the shift pattern, re-grading, employee involvement, supervisor–shop steward relationships, shop steward development, terms and conditions update, and the union-management relationship. These joint working parties had the following characteristics: (1) They had four to six members, consisting of managers and shop stewards.[4] (2) They set their own reporting timetable, which initially varied from three to eighteen months. (3) They presented their recommendations to the board of directors or its management negotiating committee together with the senior shop steward, via the head of personnel management.

Table 9.8 presents one of the major tangible recommendations to emerge from one of the joint working parties; management accepted this recommendation.

An interview with the head of personnel management in early 1998 revealed the following points: (1) His initial prime concerns were to lower the level of work-force expectations by bringing the growth of wage costs (via the settlement process) under greater management control, while at the same time avoiding the union's having a bad reaction to any (proposed) unilateral introduction of HRM practices that might become an obstacle to their full implementation and effectiveness. (2) He believed the union could add value in both designing and selling the changes in HRM practices, particularly as a result of the increased involvement of the national union and the training of the stewards. (3) The recommendations of, and reactions to, the joint working party reports on employee involvement, re-grading, and changes in the shift pattern would be particularly critical to the viability and development of the partnership approach (Table 9.9). In addition, he made the following points about the status of the partnership notion at that stage: (1) It was more a *personalized*, rather than an institutionalized, concept, pivoting on a relatively small but growing number of committed individuals. (2) Some individual managers were experiencing personal, day-to-

---

[4] Currently there are eleven shop stewards in the plant. The current key role of stewards in the joint working parties is very different from the role of stewards in the 1994–1995 joint working parties; the previous approach was to call for employee volunteers, with only limited numbers being forthcoming.

Table 9.8. A Key Joint Working Party (JWP) Recommendation concerning Employee Relations Institutions

The existing joint consultative committee (for the unionized employees only) is to be scrapped.

It is to be replaced by a plant-wide council.

This council will deal with any and all employment matters, except individual discipline and grievances.

The council will comprise two directors, two senior managers, two line managers, two nonunion staff members, and four shop stewards, plus the plant's employee representative on its European work council.

The full council will meet only as required. Instead, each constituency will elect one member to constitute a quorum group, which will either (1) refer the issue to another management body for a decision; (2) settle the matter itself, if relatively minor; or (3) set up a JWP to examine and recommend.

These arrangements will be in effect as of May 1998.

day frustration, with any new initiatives being met with shop stewards' arguments about whether they were consistent with the partnership notion.[5] (3) There was a considerable gap between the shop stewards' personal commitment to the partnership notion and their ability to "sell" recommended changes to the work force ("we need to avoid a situation of shop steward commitment, but only work force compliance").

What are the key lessons from this particular case study regarding the journey toward partnership? Perhaps the most obvious point to make concerns the nature of the picture that emerges: it is certainly *not* a smooth, steady, incremental notching-up of a union-management relationship over time as a result of an initial well-designed strategy; linearity is not in evidence here! It seems, at least at first glance, a quite conventional story of organizational change: (1) the key *incentive* was the existence of very considerable competitive pressure on the plant to survive, providing a "felt need" for change (the plant was the second lowest performer in the company's internal league table of individual plant performance, with the lowest performing plant having recently been sold off to another company); and (2) the key *ability* factor was the change of personalities (a new managing director and head of personnel management), with values and priorities different from those of their predecessors.

Nevertheless, we again would argue that more than these two factors is involved. First, the case illustrates the importance of the distinction (drawn throughout the discussion) between the negotiating relationship

[5] A current proposal to pilot-test a "cafeteria-benefits" approach among (nonunion) staff is eliciting this reaction.

and the larger employee-management relationship, with plant management only gradually coming to appreciate the importance of this distinction and seeking to improve both. Second, some commentators have proposed a distinction between a *fostering* (integrative bargaining) and *forcing* (distributive bargaining) approach to change by management (Walton, Cutcher-Gershenfeld, and McKersie 1994). As they note, however, "A management whose long-term intentions focus on high commitment and union-management co-operation may also decide to use forcing as part of its broad change effort. Within this particular framework of intentions, the forcing strategy is employed periodically and for relatively limited purposes" (Walton, Cutcher-Gershenfeld, and McKersie 1994: 25). They suggest that this periodic, limited-purpose forcing approach will concentrate on constraining wage and benefit increases (and possibly broader rights to operational flexibility), but *not* usually on strengthening rights to get (and enforce) higher work standards or seeking an ongoing power advantage over the union(s).

Their description fits our case remarkably well. The new head of personnel forced the substantive outcomes of negotiation but fostered the process, particularly in regard to the introduction of HRM.[6] The shop stewards (perhaps more than the work force) appear to have accepted this trade-off or mixed approach, at least at this stage, largely for the following reasons: (1) the terms of reference of the joint working parties have focused on the work force's long-standing concerns; (2) the membership of the joint working parties has been very diffuse (not simply including the same small group of individuals represented on all of them);[7] and (3) management has effectively said to the trade union representatives on the joint working parties, "You are involved in both the design and selling of any recommended changes." This empowerment challenge to the plant union representatives has been critically supported by their access to the experience, guidance, advice, and training of the national union office, a union with a relatively long-standing endorsement of the partnership approach.

Two important but challenging steps for the long-term future in this plant will be moving the joint working party approach beyond purely HRM or employment-related matters, and moving beyond the discrete, periodic joint working party approach to building a partnership notion into the more regular, ongoing management decision-making processes of

---

[6] One of the first actions of the new personnel head in 1995 was to scrap an ongoing joint working party examination of re-grading. Two shop stewards resigned in protest over this action.

[7] The head of personnel has consciously refrained from being a member of a number of joint working parties.

Table 9.9. The Storm Clouds Gather?

By June 1998 all the joint working parties (JWPs) had reported.

The only union-management problems (but they were big ones!) centered around the response to the JWP on alternative work patterns. The JWP came up with two options: (1) move to a six-shift system or (2) maintain the present five-shift system but with a move to annualized hours.

The shop stewards rejected option (1) and were only willing to agree to option (2) in return for what management regarded as "an unacceptably high price tag," a major consolidation of overtime earnings. In management's view it was essential to change the shift pattern but only at a fair and reasonable cost.

Negotiations broke down over this matter, with the full-time union officials being called to the plant to discuss the issue.

Currently management is considering various options: restart negotiations; impose the changes; implement as far as possible and revisit the shift issue next year; cancel the three-year pay deal; and undertake a major communication exercise with the work force as a whole.

This important issue has been temporarily side-lined with the appointment of a new managing director and the need to establish a new board to cover this plant and another one in Britain.

Training and communication exercises are going ahead for the new team working arrangements that were recommended by another JWP, with no real problems or opposition from the shop stewards.

---

the plant. But such developments are still a long way off and certainly by no means guaranteed. Indeed there are challenges to be met before this stage is reached. This is dramatically illustrated in Table 9.9.

The attempt to negotiate over the proposed move to annualized hours was overtaken by a larger corporate-wide restructuring exercise. This exercise, which involved creation of the positions of vice presidents for three product groups and six (geographical) market segments, had the effect of linking the two U.K. plants under a common board. This board has three notable features: (1) all production units now have much less autonomy and power (relative to the newly created vice presidential positions); (2) the board is dominated by people from the sister (non-case-study) plant; (3) the personnel director on the board comes from the sister plant, which is very different from the case-study plant. (The sister plant is a high-volume, low-cost producer, which has consistently been profitable, largely due to an extremely effective marketing strategy. Its HRM strategy attaches relatively little importance to the notions of teamwork and employee empowerment.)

The immediate aftermath of the corporate-wide restructuring exercise was the declaration of some sixty lay-offs in the case-study plant, which caused the union to formally withdraw from the partnership agreement. The new board rejected the request by the personnel manager of the case-study plant for a dedicated budget to support the implementation of the joint working party's recommendation for employee involvement, the centerpiece of the new HRM strategy. Some managers have left or are proposing to leave the plant in the belief that the proposed initiatives and the general direction of change in recent years are underappreciated by the board and the new vice presidents and, as a consequence, will ultimately come to nothing. In short, we have here a classic case of a "strategic-level shock" to a plant-level initiative, beyond the knowledge, reach, and influence of the union and personnel professionals at the plant level.

10

Partnerships and Flexible Networks

Alternatives or Complementary Models of Labor-Management Relations?

SAUL RUBINSTEIN

CHARLES HECKSCHER

Over the past two decades, it has become clear to many U.S. labor and management leaders that the traditional labor-management relations system, in which collective bargaining stands alone or serves as the centerpiece, is no longer able to meet the needs of firms, employees, and their unions. Consistent with the British case described by Beaumont and Hunter in the previous chapter, a number of unions and employers have attempted to supplement traditional collective bargaining with a partnership model in which workplace relations are modified to support employees' value-adding participation in workplace problem-solving and decision-making activities and union leaders' involvement in high-level business strategy.

Recently, however, partnership models have experienced problems of sustainability and replication, especially in industries where technologies and markets are changing so rapidly and in such uncertain ways that flexibility becomes the dominant goal and a focus on core competencies and knowledge work becomes central. Management sees little value in forming a partnership with employees and union leaders when it wants to keep the firm's boundaries flexible as relative costs and technologies change.

The question is whether these models are competing or complementary. Is the partnership model a short-lived innovation destined to be destroyed by pressures for flexibility? If so, what will be the next generation of union-management institutional arrangements suited to the core-competency phase of industrial organization? Alternatively, will the emphasis on flexibility and focused competence be a relatively short-lived epoch in organizational history? Or will both models coexist in the future, fitted to the different circumstances of different industries?

In this chapter we first lay out the case for the two models, drawing on different sectors of the economy—automobiles and communications. Then we return to a discussion of the questions just posed and discuss the types of institutional development and research needed to determine which alternative, if either, will dominate, or how the two might coexist and find their appropriate places in the broad mix of industries and labor-management settings likely to characterize the economy of the future.

A Brief Historical Tour: Alternative Models for Working Together

As we examine the history of union-management joint efforts in the United States over the past century, we can identify four distinct forms aimed at supplementing the formal collective bargaining process, each with different outcomes for organizational and union performance. The first form, *off-line joint union-management committees* organized to solve business problems, has had a long history, going back eighty years (Slichter 1941; Golden and Ruttenberg 1942; Golden and Parker 1949). These efforts were widespread in industries such as textiles, apparel, and railroads in the 1920s and again during the Second World War, particularly among armaments suppliers. By *off-line* we mean labor-management committees that worked outside normal production or managerial activities. Since these committees were off-line and top level, they were often accommodated within the Taylorist model of organization as it fragmented the production process, separating thinking and planning (management activity) from execution and implementation (the role of labor). While these efforts succeeded in increasing product quantity and quality, with the exception of labor-management safety committees, most tended to be relatively short-lived rather than permanent. That is, they would arise to address specific pressures or crises (such as the need to bolster war-time production or adjust to a new technology or competitive threat), work for a period while the pressure or threat remained visible, and then slowly atrophy or fall into disuse as the pressure or threat subsided. Few of these, again with the exception of safety and health committees, became permanent features of labor-management relations. Even those that did continue did not alter the collective bargaining, management, or production systems in any significant way.

The second form, *off-line teams* involving bargaining-unit members in joint labor-management problem-solving efforts, emerged in the 1970s through programs such as employee involvement and Quality of Work Life (Kochan, Katz, and McKersie 1986). These efforts were in part a response to pressures felt by companies competing with Japanese manufacturers who were employing widespread work-force problem-solving efforts known as Quality Control Circles (QCCs). As with top-level off-line labor-management committees, these off-line efforts could be accommodated within the Taylorist model of production, because they did not change labor or management roles at the point of production.

In a search for new ways to increase flexibility and organizational responsiveness, however, more significant challenges to the classic organizational forms have emerged over the past twenty-five years. In particular, we have seen a vertical re-integration of management planning and labor execution and a horizontal re-integration of fragmented tasks that shifts the organizational focus from individual jobs to products and (as Goodman and Wilson and MacDuffie emphasized in their chapters in this volume) toward greater reliance on team processes. It is this horizontal integration that is the principle behind a third organizational form, which involves bargaining-unit members in self-directed work teams organized to produce products or services through an *on-line team-based* production process. This process involves rotation of jobs among employees who also assume many of the planning and coordinating tasks of supervision. Challenging the horizontal fragmentation of Taylorism, this form has become widespread since the 1970s (Walton 1975, 1985).

While these three forms of joint activity have produced significant results in areas such as improved quality or cost reduction (Ichniowski et al. 1996), many efforts either have not been sustained over time or have been inadequate in addressing the larger business issues increasingly faced by firms competing in a global economy. Much like collective bargaining, these workplace-focused initiatives alone are not able to influence the key strategic decisions made by top executives and line managers that determine the long-run income and employment security of the work force.

Strategic Partnership and Co-management

In response to these challenges, over the past fifteen years a few organizations have developed a new model that Beaumont and Hunter describe as a labor-management partnership, and which we are calling *co-management*. We use the term *co-management* because at the extreme this model represents a direct sharing of responsibilities heretofore reserved for managers. It involves the union on-line in representing the collective interests of the membership in the day-to-day process of running the business, and thus challenges the vertical fragmentation of Taylorism separating labor from management (the function). Co-management is the most far-reaching form of joint labor-management organization. By combining workplace flexibility, teamwork, and employee participation with active sharing of responsibility and influence in management and strategic affairs, those adopting this model hope to meet both the business needs of management for increased responsiveness and flexibility and organized labor's needs for voice and employment security.

Yet these new efforts at co-management pose enormous challenges for local unions, which typically have been structured in response to a clear separation in the roles and responsibilities of labor and management. Over the past fifteen years locals have struggled to develop organizational structures and capacities to help them function in these new roles in co-management. Along with colleagues at Rutgers and MIT, we have conducted research across North America looking at twenty of the most enduring, innovative, and successful cases of local unions engaging in partnership arrangements that provide opportunities for co-management and joint governance. We have some tentative findings to offer regarding the characteristics of these co-management arrangements. We illustrate these findings with examples from Saturn, our most extensively researched case:

1. Unions engaging in co-management have been significantly involved in business planning and strategy development, finance, product development, supplier selection, and operations management, all areas traditionally reserved for management. These unions see management as a function, an activity to be performed, not as a class of employees. Furthermore, the activity of running the business is considered a legitimate role for unions that are attempting to ensure the long-term job security of their members. In this way they are fulfilling their responsibility to represent the collective interests of the membership by being directly involved in the process of making key decisions, rather than negotiating over the impact of these decisions after they are made.

At Saturn, for example, over 400 union members, jointly selected by the local and the company, fill full-time operations and staff positions that would be considered management jobs in any other division of General Motors. The union has created a dense communications and coordination network among its co-managers at Saturn through a process of internal organizing, which is now embedded in the management systems (Rubinstein 1996, 2000). Our research has shown that over 50 percent of the quality improvement at Saturn could be explained by the communication and coordination activity of the union members who were actively engaged in jointly running the operation through the process of co-management.

2. Compensation tends to be contingent through a combination of risk and reward based on some aspect of performance. In some cases this may take the form of profit sharing; in others it may be an employee stock ownership plan as at United Airlines; or in still others it may be a more traditional form of productivity gain sharing. Saturn's risk and reward formula is jointly developed and based on targets for training, productivity, quality, schedule, and volume.

3. Co-management increases the influence and power of the union, largely through its knowledge and influence in running the business. However, co-management requires a new set of skills for union leaders, ranging from strategic planning to operations management and from organizational development to financial analysis. In the case of Saturn each employee, union and non-represented, must complete each year a minimum of ninety-two hours of additional training on production methods, team dynamics, leadership, and problem solving, or related topics. Furthermore, the local union must be prepared to leverage this new power both to sustain the partnership and to build the union. For example, early in 1998 the UAW local at Saturn forced General Motors to renegotiate the risk and reward contingent compensation plan to reflect the realities of a softer small-car market. Later in the year the local used a strike authorization from the membership to force General Motors to live up to its earlier commitments on joint decision making, new products, decentralized sourcing, and performance bonuses.

4. Strong support for this model of labor-management relations is required from both the corporation and the national union to create and maintain the partnership at Saturn. While the UAW International was instrumental in the creation of the partnership, its relations with the Saturn local union have been strained over time. Further, over the past few years General Motors has attempted to reduce Saturn's decision-making autonomy through re-centralizing supplier selection and creating a common platform for the next generation at Saturn to share with other GM small cars. This change would put Saturn at risk of becoming another division at General Motors rather than the "Different Kind of Company" it has sold to its customers and the public. As noted, however, the local union forced General Motors to bring new products to the Saturn business units involved in the partnership arrangement, and to reaffirm its role in supplier and product decision making. Further, the UAW International was involved in these negotiations, increasing its contact and communications with the local. In addition to managing its relationships with the corpora-

tion and the national union, the new local must also have the capacity to manage its organizational boundaries with other local unions, suppliers, customers, and the community.

5. The success of the partnership arrangements for the rank-and-file, and the ability to sustain co-management, depend in part on the local's ability to balance the resources it puts toward collective interests with those it devotes to individual representation in a manner consistent with the expectations of the membership. In the case of Saturn, after a year of debate over perceptions that individual representation was suffering from attention and resources both being devoted to collective representation through co-management, the union contract and structure were changed (in 1994) to allow for the election of fourteen members of a grievance committee. Internal tensions persisted, however, and in 1999 the local union leaders who had been in office since Saturn's inception were defeated by an alternate slate of candidates who promised to continue the partnership but to represent employees in more direct ways.

To date, this limited experience with a new form of labor-management relations—co-management—suggests that it may have the potential to increase organizational performance through flexibility and responsiveness. However, it requires new competencies, characteristics, and structures for local and national union organizations. This form is both more complex and more fragile than the structures and processes unions require to represent members in traditional production organizations. Yet, as we have seen in the case of Saturn, it also provides increased opportunities for the union to represent the collective interests of the membership through meaningful decision making and increased employment security.

While Saturn is clearly the most comprehensive model of co-management or partnership found in the country today, many of its essential features are found in other settings. The United Steelworkers of America negotiated partnership agreements with each of the major unionized U.S. steelmakers in 1993–1994. Harley Davidson has maintained a highly regarded partnership with its union locals for more than a decade; Xerox and the United Needletrades, Industrial, and Textile Employees had a twenty-year-long partnership that continued right up to its recent financial crisis and near collapse. Most recently, Kaiser Permanente and a coalition of six international unions and more than twenty local unions have embarked on a broad-based partnership that is every bit as ambitious and extensive as the one at Saturn. While all these differ in specific ways, they share a common set of features in that they include participation at both workplace and strategic levels of interaction and accept the union as a legitimate and valued partner in enhancing enterprise performance and employment security. In this respect, Saturn is not as unique as it is often perceived.

Under what conditions might this model be sustainable? Clearly, from the standpoint of the firm, co-management makes sense when the production work force can add value through participation and the union leadership can add value through direct participation in management. It also requires a view that the work done by union-represented workers fits into the "core competencies" or the areas of technological advantage of the firm.

Still, few, if any, firms are likely to initiate this type of co-management on their own. It is likely to occur only when union leaders initiate it based on their vision that the critical decisions driving the long-term security and related interests of their members are being made at strategic levels unreachable through traditional collective bargaining. Finally, it is likely to be sustainable only where union leaders and managers develop the capacity to balance their co-management roles with their more traditional responsibilities of representing employee and shareholder interests, respectively.

Beyond the Single Enterprise Model: Is a Network-Based Partnership Possible?

Although co-management in particular, and labor-management partnerships in general, have shown that they can significantly increase productivity and lower costs, they have hardly spread like wildfire. If anything, cooperation of all types is under increased pressure both in the United States and in the rest of the industrialized nations. Advocates often attribute this to resistance and old-line thinking on the part of managers and union leaders. But one should be cautious with such explanations—especially when, as in this case, the resistance has lasted for many years. If the efforts were so good for everyone, one would think that resistance would diminish over time.

Despite their successes, labor-management partnerships, even in their most extensive forms such as the co-management found at Saturn, are limited in part because the things they do well are not the things that many firms need today. Although productivity and costs are always important, in the current era of turbulence there is something else even more crucial: *flexibility*. Given that few industries are exempt from the enormous impact of microprocessor technology, combined with market shifts due to globalization, there is a premium on being light and fast on your feet. And this may be where partnerships fail.

It is true that co-management partnerships, and Saturn in particular, have developed degrees of flexibility in comparison with other unionized enterprises. Saturn has far fewer job classifications than the norm in its industry, for example. Perhaps more important is a less tangible factor: a level of commitment to the business on the part of workers, which yields a constant stream of benefits.

Yet in all these co-managed cases some key constraints on flexibility remain. The most important is that all cases of partnership rest on a strong presumption of job security. Although some cases have survived forced down-sizing in a crisis, none would survive in an atmosphere of regular employment fluctuation. A second inflexibility is around income levels: though Saturn has adopted some variable compensation, in practice it has become apparent through several experiences that any threat of income reduction causes major strains.

There are reasons to believe these are serious constraints, especially in the current economy. The familiar industrial labor-management system was designed to work in large, vertically integrated firms. Under those circumstances the stability brought by good collective bargaining contracts is a plus, and when that is achieved with positive feeling and commitment, the plus is even greater. But when the terrain changes, the values may change as well.

Today the notion of the large vertically integrated firm is widely in disfavor. What has replaced it is the notion of *focus*: companies try to get control over the things they can manage particularly well, that are core to their identity, and to get other companies to do the rest. So even large companies are divesting as much as they acquire and are entering into a bewildering set of alliances and links to other companies as a partial alternative to ownership.[1]

A second (though related) trend is to separate manufacturing from other

---

[1] These observations are based primarily on a close knowledge of the telecommunications service and equipment industries, augmented with more general knowledge of other sectors. The strategy literature is not consistent on this point, though there seems to be growing attention to the problem of focus. An excellent argument for the basis for a strategic shift is in Khanna and Palepu (1997). Focus, they suggest, essentially becomes more possible and more effective as societal institutions become more sophisticated, meaning that firms do not have to control so much in-house but can rely on effective performance by others. In particular, the better the societal mechanisms of trust and reputation, the more effective it is to rely on others for non-core parts of the business.

aspects of the business. The benefits of the same firm doing manufacturing and design and marketing used to be great because the costs of integration with outside contractors were high. Those costs have dropped rapidly with improved transportation and information-exchange capacities, so that now in many cases it is far more expensive to keep manufacturing in-house.

In effect many industries are bifurcating between high value-added *knowledge and relationship* businesses—doing invention, design, marketing, and working with customers to package new solutions—and lower value-added *production and distribution* businesses that focus on cost control and efficiency. In the former, margins are typically in the 20 percent range; in the latter, they are under 10 percent. Thus, on the low end, you have an Ingram Micro, which produces computers for Compaq, IBM, Hewlett-Packard, and other companies, all flowing from the same assembly line with minor variations and different logos at the end. On the high end, you have a Cisco Systems, an inventor, designer, and marketer of telephone and Internet equipment, which makes almost nothing in-house: its employees are largely software engineers and marketers, while the manufacturing is done through a wide network of subcontractors. Even the automobile companies are rapidly outsourcing increasing amounts of production and assembly. These examples involve overlapping and interpenetrating networks: one knowledge company uses many subcontractors, and each subcontractor works with many knowledge companies.[2]

In this phase of capitalism, in short, the business world seems to be doing two things: first, differentiating knowledge work from production, and second, within each category, shifting from a logic of simple combi-

---

[2] See "Is This the Factory of the Future?" *New York Times*, Sunday, July 26, 1998, Money and Business/Financial Desk; "Some U.S. Manufacturers Prosper by Easing Rise of 'Virtual' Firm," *Wall Street Journal Online*, August 18, 1998; "The Corporation of the Future" [Cisco], *Business Week Online*, August 24–31, 1998, www.businessweek.com. Here we cannot analyze the future of this trend or its details. It may be that the pressures against vertical integration are temporary and that we are simply in a transition on the way to a global, as opposed to national, oligopoly. But there are powerful reasons to believe otherwise: (1) the effects of technology have only begun to be felt, and there is little doubt that the continuing development of microprocessor technology will revolutionize industries and markets for quite a while to come; (2) markets have matured to a point where consumers are less interested in long-term mass-produced products than in novelty and customization—there will be continued pressures for innovation; (3) the institutional systems of capitalism have also matured so that less of the monitoring, human development, and reputational management needs to be done within hierarchies, and more can be done in trans-firm systems; (4) the major economic source of added value in these circumstances is intellectual capital rather than physical investment.

nation to a logic of *recombination*—from trying to dominate stable markets or industries to developing the ability to adapt and refocus as markets and industries shift. In this landscape companies don't want to develop everything internally; they want to acquire abilities that they find they need and get rid of the ones they don't. That way they can move much faster, stay at the leading edge of development, and offload many of their costs to the wider market. They want to be able to bring in employees with the latest skills, not try to re-train people who have been doing other things for years. They want to be able to form alliances, task forces, and outsourcing relationships quickly—and get out of them equally quickly.

Of course this is not a clean or total change. Though it is now fashionable to speak of everything as a "paradigm shift" sweeping away the old in a flash of imagination, the real world is full of partial cases and transitions and leftovers. It is also possible that these trends are industry specific or temporary signs of transition to new integrated monopolies. But let's for the moment take seriously the logic of recombination and the move from vertical integration to focus, which seem to account for a great deal of what is really happening around us.

Consider a Saturn-type partnership from the perspective of a manager in the rapidly changing environment of information technology—a good manager, one not bound up in old habits and a lust for control. If you invest the time and effort needed to achieve a high level of trust, what do you get? The partnership may be able to bring costs down compared to other unionized plants, but that's not the benchmark: if cost is really what you're after, you may do better with nonunion arrangements. In that case the incentives are to avoid partnership commitments and work toward subcontracting out as much as possible. On the other hand, you think, maybe the amount of responsiveness and customer focus you would get from a partnership would be worth higher labor costs. But whatever benefits you could pick up there would be in a narrow frame: you would still be committed to employment security, you can't adjust the pay levels (except in a crisis), and you therefore can't do much about the skill mix of employees (except through training). A whole range of possibilities—partnering with other companies, radically new production methods or technologies, and so on—is basically shut off.[3] Plus, you've invested a large amount

[3] For example, in 1999 General Motors reached a deal with the UAW to build three new plants in the United States, using one-third as many workers as the ones they replace ("GM and Union Are Near Deal on New Plants," *New York Times*," January 8, 1999, C2). This agreement is an outcome of collective bargaining, but it would be unlikely in the kind of embedded participation represented by Saturn—that is, the Saturn local would not easily reach

of capital that could be put into acquiring the intellectual assets that actually drive profits. Do you really want to tie yourself down that way?

In the scenario just presented, the only way it would make sense to take on the limitations inherent in partnerships is if you had no alternative. If your choices were a traditional and inflexible union-management relationship or a partnership, your duty as a good manager would clearly be to build the latter. But that's not really the choice for many managers today: given how fast things are changing, there are plenty of opportunities to shift away from the traditionally unionized aspects of the business. In negotiating terms, they believe they have better alternatives to negotiating a partnership and sharing managerial decision-making power. Their alternatives are either a strategy focused on high value-added at the leading edge of innovation, in which case they want to invest their resources into intellectual capital and not manufacturing, or a low-cost strategy, in which case they want to avoid unions. Partnerships fall into the crack, or rather chasm, between these.

So where does that leave us? Is partnership possible in a turbulent economy?

Labor-management partnership or co-management as described in the case of Saturn is only one of the possible alternatives to traditional forms of labor representation through collective bargaining. In some sense, *it represents the acme of the traditional union-management relationship.* Despite its radical nature, it maintains the assumptions of a stable work force organized in a permanent union under a long-term collective bargaining contract with a steady employer. Those are all assumptions within the logic of simple combination.

If we step outside that logic to think about a recombinatorial system, we can imagine other forms of connection between employees and employers. Though employers can easily take advantage of it, recombination is not necessarily a way for employers to increase their power: there are real historical examples of balanced systems in which workers do well in a constantly shifting network. Take construction, for example: workers are hired as project teams to do a building and then recombined for the next project. But where a union exists, it has an important role in making sure that the conditions of work are fair and that workers are committed to the task. Professional associations sometimes play the same kind of role for high-tech engineers and the like. These structures and mechanisms are

---

an agreement to replace its paint line, say, with another using one-third the workers, unless employment security could be maintained through transfers to other departments or attrition.

quite different from those of standard industrial unions, and we don't often classify these relationships as "partnerships"; however, in the abstract they meet many of the new requirements of industrial organization in an environment of rapid change better than the features of a labor-management partnership within a single firm.

In a recombinatorial system, in short, employee representation must look different. Employee bodies will survive in the long run only if they contribute not only to their members but also to the strength of the overall system; thus, industrial unions grew when it became clear that the stability they provided made sense for business as well as employees. What could "new unions" provide in the emerging order?

The answer to this question may be different depending on whether one is looking at the "knowledge-relationship" sector—technicians, engineers, and their support—or the production sector. In the latter, the challenge is that the level of unionization is low and the skill demands are generally not as high. Under these conditions management's desire for stringent cost control is in direct contradiction with unions' basic interests. Any new union-management relation in this sector must start with large-scale organizing, which will be anything but a partnership phenomenon in its early phases.

In the higher value-added sector there is a clear conceptual place for a partnership, though of a new kind. First, if a flexible (or recombinatorial) economy is really a good thing, then employees need support for flexible careers. Without it, they will naturally continue to hang desperately onto existing jobs and fail to develop new skills, which will mean that there will be unnecessary obstacles to the ideal match of problems to skills. To help employees in a flexible economy, employee institutions need to provide information, help with job movement, support access to improved skills, and so on. These are in fact the sorts of things that craft unions and professional associations have traditionally provided through hiring halls, apprenticeship, and certification programs.

Second, a flexible economy requires a high degree of business understanding and involvement from employees. Although most employers today recognize this rhetorically, they have a lot more trouble implementing it in practice. Hence another role for employee bodies: to pressure employers to live up to their own rhetoric.

Both of these functions—providing the infrastructure for real employee mobility and pressuring for real participation—benefit employers as well as employees, but employers can't perform them on their own: the constraints of competition as well as old habits inevitably push them to try to maintain tight control, even when this runs counter to their own understanding and preaching about what needs to be done. This paradox is exactly what enables employee organizations to grow and flourish.

This kind of unionism provides a basis for a partnership that *helps* the manager whose perspective we imagined earlier. It can contribute to flexibility instead of freezing an old system in place; it can contribute precisely by helping employees have decent work lives in the new order.

This model, however, is clearly not a partnership of the Saturn type. The Saturn model seeks a relation of permanent equality between two stable and tightly interdependent institutions—a single local union and a single plant, division, or firm. This new model might better be called an alliance among multiple independent institutions that can contribute to one another; *alliance* carries the connotation that the relation can be continually reviewed and must be continually justified.[4]

Despite its conceptual fit in a rapidly changing environment, we would not want to underestimate the difficulty of implementing this alliance model. It would require major changes in at least three institutions: corporate management, labor unions, and government and allied societal institutions. All these institutions are currently built to support a traditional logic of combination and would need reorientation.

Management would need to recognize that if it seeks an economy with a lot of mobility, it must take responsibility for helping to build its foundations. The current approach is, for the most part, one of "Let's have our cake and eat it, too": companies want to have flexibility when they need it and to maintain traditional loyalty when they want that; and they seek to draw on a pool of trained and skilled workers without contributing to their development. This arrangement is not tenable for long. Management must also take seriously its own rhetoric of involvement and teamwork and put in place the conditions for its development. Specifically, employers will need to participate in a network of relationships that involves some form of union, employee association, or web of employee organizations that work together to facilitate the movement of people to where changing technologies and market conditions take the work they do. This will require efforts to rebuild local and industry-wide institutions capable of supporting the movement of people across organizational boundaries.

For government and societal institutions the problem is to put in place the policy framework for a genuinely open labor market. Too many of our

---

[4] There has been too little analysis of the concept of "partnership" and its variants. Michael Maccoby (1997) has developed an interesting continuum of relations between firms, which, in a longer work than this one, could be adapted to the labor-management context: commodity supplier, preferred supplier, value-added supplier, alliance, cooperation, and strategic partnership. The notion of continual justification is central to his view.

laws are still written with the assumption that employees should draw most of their benefits from their employer; workers are actually penalized for building their own funds, though this is slowly changing. Even more important is the need for relatively low unemployment and relative wage equity: without these two key conditions the foundation of trust underlying true flexibility is eroded.

Industrial unions have a Herculean task as well. Their internal structures are designed to support collective bargaining contracts with stable employers; as soon as they move away from that structure, they run into jurisdictional battles that are unresolvable in the existing system. They are also weak on the skills and the leadership knowledge needed to represent a more mobile membership.[5] To make this adjustment, industrial unions will need to learn from the experiences of their counterparts in craft unions and professional associations.

A few partial models have started to develop, despite the obstacles. Working Partnerships in Silicon Valley and Working Today in New York are new organizations with loose links to organized labor that offer training, portable insurance, and other benefits to facilitate mobility while trying to establish standards for particular industries. Some professional associations, such as the Institute of Electrical and Electronics Engineers (IEEE), have extended their activity to the representational arena. Some unions, especially those close to the professional or craft ends—the building trades and the teachers, for example—are exploring innovative ways to represent people where collective bargaining contracts are lacking. None of these is "the answer," but they are examples of the range of creative exploration under way today.

There is no question that a co-management partnership of the Saturn type is better than a traditional labor-management relationship for all the stakeholders. But it is not yet clear how it will fare over the long term in an economy with a significantly increased rate of change. When we explore the implications of late-capitalist development—the focus on value through knowledge, the new information capacities, the growing sophistication of consumers, and the advanced educational levels of the work force—it seems that there is potential for a major leap in differentiation, innovation, and choice, but only if we develop a labor market system with

---

[5] There is, of course, danger in the transition. For example, it could turn into a kind of professional sports–style struggle in which a few benefit hugely from "free agency" and many more struggle. Fortunately the creation of knowledge and economic value is not really like sports, where mass markets can be focused on a single person such as Michael Jordan; it is necessarily more distributed and collaborative. So there is at least room for employee bodies to create a more equitable system.

considerably more flexibility than in the past. Thus, if there is to be a next-generation partnership model, it is likely to be one that is able to cross organizational boundaries and support the recombinatorial processes in which firms and workers find themselves as technologies and markets change rapidly in unpredictable ways.

Alternatives or Complements?

We have described two very different partnership models—one based on a single-firm and single-union relationship and the other suggesting more of a network structure involving multiple firms, more than one local, and perhaps more than one national union. The question is whether these are *evolutionary* models, with the network model eventually replacing the single-firm model, or *complementary* models, with each finding its appropriate but relatively long-lasting place in the industrial organization landscape of the future. The answer to this question must, of course, await the future. It is clear, though, that while the industrial union model and the forms of collective bargaining and union-management partnership described in the first section of this chapter rose to dominance in tandem with the rise of the large multi-division and integrated corporation, the industrial model did not completely displace the "older" craft union model. Instead, craft unions continued and expanded into new professional occupations in settings where the features of the second model described in this chapter were present. Now, the conditions giving rise to network models that are more similar to the traditions of the craft and professional unions appear to be growing once again. But we are unlikely to see the complete demise of the large corporation or large organizations that need to gain value from their full work force, not just an elite and mobile set of "knowledge" workers.

Furthermore, eliminating in-house manufacturing as a core competency of the automotive industry assumes that production is not knowledge work. The key issue is where the line is drawn between core competencies that give firms competitive advantage and therefore must remain in-house, and the non-core competencies that can be subcontracted. Subcontracting core competencies risks the loss of critical knowledge and creates dependence on suppliers for crucial decisions. For example, Toyota is seen as a strategic leader in the automotive industry, yet it continues to rely on vertical integration and long-term relationships with suppliers to which it is tied through equity interests. Chrysler, on the other hand, has struggled with its manufacturing quality as it has become the domestic manufacturer with the lowest level of vertical integration. One could argue that in the auto industry manufacturing is as important as design and marketing in maintaining a loyal and satisfied customer base over the long run. Contracting out major portions of the manufacture of automobiles runs the risk of poor engineering integration, inferior quality, and the loss of knowledge that can help in future design decisions, innovation, and product differentiation (Babson 1999).

Unlike computers, automotive components do not have standard interfaces that make them interchangeable. Therefore, manufacturing and assembly are as critical as design to the performance of components in the final product. It is unlikely that auto manufacturers will standardize components across the industry, as this would result in the erosion of brand distinctions. Thus, most companies will retain control over the manufacture and assembly of their key components (MacDuffie 1999a). Flexibility will be required to bring new products on line quickly and to shift production between a variety of products as market preferences change. The key to flexibility has been multi-skilling and adequate knowledge of the business to allow new production configurations for new products, and effective communication and coordination to identify and solve problems. These conditions require trust between employees and management, however, as well as substantial investment in training, both of which are unlikely in short-term employment relationships.

In summary, partnerships between labor and management at the company level will continue to be important and relevant in environments where the work force has the knowledge and skills needed to add significant value to the enterprise and union leaders have the skills and the power needed to support this type of model. While not all partnerships will have the full features of the Saturn model, and there is no assurance that once created they will last forever, we are likely to see more experimentation along these lines in the years ahead. Where the boundaries of organizations are unstable or uncertain, however, new models, perhaps along the network lines suggested here, will have to be invented. The question, however, is how many firms will be in the type of environment that led General Motors and the UAW to create Saturn, and their counterparts to create the other partnerships mentioned here, versus the more turbulent and uncertain technological and market settings characteristic of today's communications and information technology sectors. The relative importance of these two types of environments is likely to be the final arbiter in the debates over the viability of the alternative models of labor-management relations and partnerships outlined here.

11

The Truth about Corporate Governance

LEE E. PRESTON

Corporate governance, a topic long regarded as arcane and of little practical relevance, is currently the focus of intense attention and controversy all over the world. Managers and employees subject to down-sizing, institutional investors choosing between "fight" and "flight," shareowners confronted with merger and leveraged buy-out (LBO) proposals, constituents of state-owned enterprises undergoing privatization and domestic enterprises subject to foreign takeovers—all are raising the same set of questions: How, and for what purposes, are corporations governed? How *should* they be governed, and why? These are questions of growing importance in the fields of labor relations (Hunter 1998) and organizational theory and practice. These topics are not yet "put on the table" explicitly for debate or negotiations, however, since most organization theorists, economists, and managers continue to take for granted that the U.S. model of the shareholder-maximizing firm is the optimal approach to corporate governance. If, as other chapters in this book suggest, the key decisions driving employee welfare are now more likely than in the past to be made at the highest level of the corporation, then it is likely that governance issues will take an increasingly visible and important place on the agenda of labor and management. In this chapter I review the different models of corporate governance available to choose among, and then in the final section offer some ideas on what will be needed if employees and their representatives are to participate successfully in corporate governance processes in the future. Not surprisingly, making these adaptations will require considerable skill in negotiations and the management of change, since they imply a shift in the distribution of power within organizational decision making, among other things.

An earlier version of this paper was published as "Les parties intéressées et le gouvernement d'entreprise" in *Gestion: Revue internationale de gestion* 23, no.3 (1998): 13–20.

The Nature of "Governance"

Whether or not there is a "crisis in corporate law" concerning governance issues, as an American legal scholar (Millon 1993) recently declared, there is clearly a breadth and intensity of interest in the subject not seen in the United States since the Great Depression and never, to my knowledge, in the rest of the world. What is all this discussion and controversy about? In commonsense terms, *Corporate governance* may be defined as *the set of institutional arrangements that legitimates and directs the corporation in the performance of its functions.*

Writing from an Italian perspective, Barca (1998: 490) defines governance as "institutions that take care of the conflict between the interest of investors to get the 'warranted' return on their invested funds and the interest of 'managers' to exert control over the use of those funds." Within the context of transactions-cost economics, which recognizes the dual principles of conflict and mutuality in every transaction, Williamson (1998: 76) defines governance as "the means by which order is accomplished," so that conflict can be reduced and mutual gains realized.

According to the U.K.-U.S. tradition, the private for-profit corporation is conceived of as a pool of assets (including "goodwill" and "going concern" values) belonging collectively to its shareowners. In the conventional arrangement (depicted in Figure 11.1), the shareowners elect members of a board of directors, who in turn select the management and direct the affairs of the enterprise. Most of the contemporary corporate governance literature is framed within this model and focuses on the composition and structure of corporate boards and on principal-agent relationships.

This view needs to be challenged, though, if employees are to be viewed as legitimate stakeholders and brought into the governance process. Moreover, even setting the question of the role of employees aside for the moment and accepting this limited scope, the conventional model is of dubious value. A recent survey of board-related research finds "no convincing evidence" that board composition has any specific impact on corporate performance (Bhagat and Black 1998). And an economics-based critique of the board-focused literature begins with this declaration: "Corporations are not governed by the process that corporate law would seem to imply" (Hermalin and Weisbach 1998: 96). Even the most conservative authorities agree that board composition and procedures are merely the surface, not the core, of the matter. As the recent Business Roundtable *Statement on Corporate Governance* emphasizes, "The *substance* of good corporate governance is more important than its *form*" (1997: 1, italics added).

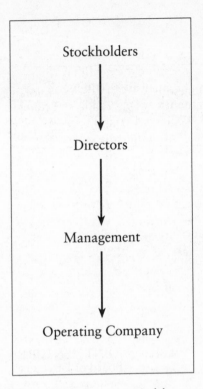

Figure 11.1. U.K.–U.S. Corporate Governance Model

Like most of these recent commentaries, I begin with the assumption that the arrangement depicted in Figure 11.1 is inaccurate as a picture of the actual structure of corporate governance, even within the United Kingdom and the United States, and grossly inappropriate as a general model of corporate governance around the world. In all known settings and situations, corporate governance involves complex relationships among numerous and diverse constituents, both internal and external. In some cases, employee constituents are formally and explicitly represented in the governance structure, whereas in others, employees, like other nonrepresented constituencies, still exert influence depending on how critical a resource they are to the firm. Therefore, we need to expand this view of governance mechanisms. We can do this best by comparing the standard U.S. and U.K. models with those found in other parts of the world. To illustrate the range of corporate governance mechanisms that are, in fact, in place in the global economy at the present time, Figure 11.2 presents a model of the governance structure of international joint ventures in China. This model identifies a number of stakeholders, each with distinct governance

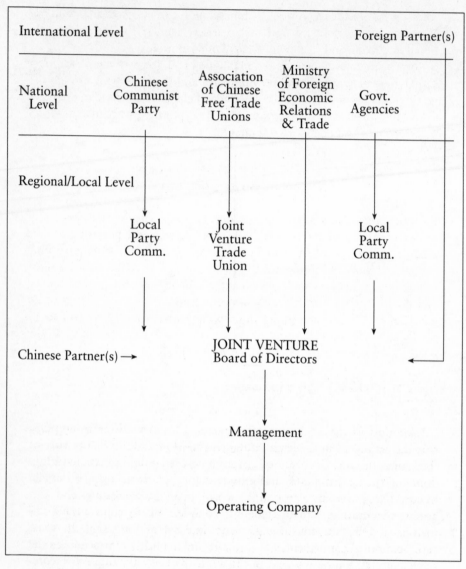

Figure 11.2. Multinational Joint Venture in China Governance Model

roles: the sponsoring entities, Chinese and foreign; national and regional/local governments, and their various agencies; trade unions, national and local; and Communist Party units at all levels.

Both of these models (Figures 11.1 and 11.2) are extreme cases; most actual governance structures now in place, and those evolving around the world, involve combinations of the kinds of elements depicted in them. (A third, and again very different, proposed corporate governance model is described in the appendix to this chapter.)

A Corporate Governance Typology

For purposes of this discussion, corporate governance encompasses any institutions or arrangements that affect the selection of directors, or that alter the decisions and behaviors of directors or managers from what they otherwise would be. (Alternatively, referring back to Williamson's definition, any feature of the *order* that regulates the balance between mutuality and conflict among the constituents of a corporation is an aspect of its governance.) Before presenting the typology of corporate governance, I briefly comment on two of its critical aspects: the role of the state, and the nature and implications of the stakeholder concept.

The Role of the State: Necessary but Not Sufficient

In all political jurisdictions, formal recognition by the state provides the foundation for the legal status of the corporation and the framework for its governance, including the rights and responsibilities of owners and directors. The importance of chartering conditions is frequently overlooked in advanced countries, where such formalities are routine and rarely onerous. In other settings, however, state recognition can be controversial and problematic. Even in advanced countries increased competition, deregulation, and privatization are raising new governance issues (as, for example, in the case of telecommunications in both the United States and Japan). The status of newly privatized enterprises in transitional economies requires the creation of entirely new corporate governance mechanisms, although there are often relevant antecedents of one sort or another in the communist and pre-communist past. Even in Maoist China, "cooperatives," which differed only in trivial ways from employee-owned private corporations, were legally recognized. Now they provide a basis for evolving transitional institutions. However, in spite of its foundational role—

and dramatic importance in conspicuous cases—state recognition alone is not the whole story. The social legitimacy of the corporation is derived primarily from its policies and practices, specifically including its governance arrangements and its relationships with significant stakeholders. Recognition by government is a necessary, but not sufficient, condition.

The Stakeholder Concept and Its Problems

In a famous article published more than sixty years ago, Harvard Law Professor E. Merrick Dodd asked, "For whom are corporate managers trustees?" His answer was that managers are trustees "for the institution rather than for its members" and further that "society may properly demand that [business] be carried on in such a way as to safeguard the interests of those who deal with it . . . even if the proprietary rights of its owners are thereby curtailed" (Dodd 1932, reprinted in Clarkson 1998: 46). Although this position was considered highly controversial at the time, and still is in some circles, most contemporary analysis equates the interests of the corporate institution with the interests of some or all of its multiple stakeholders, nonowners as well as owners. One commentator describes the 1992 American Law Institute (ALI) report as "the death of property rights" (Carney 1993). And in a "Looking Ahead" symposium commissioned to mark the seventy-fifth anniversary of the *Harvard Business Review*, Charles Handy (1997: 7–8) declared,

> The old language of property and ownership no longer serves us in modern society because it no longer describes what a company really is. . . . The idea of a corporation as the property of the current holders of its shares is confusing because it does not make clear where power lies. . . . A public corporation should now be regarded not as a piece of property but as a community . . . created by a common purpose.

In spite of broad agreement about the existence and importance of stakeholders within the corporate system, the troublesome questions raised by Dodd are still at the center of the current debate.[1] The key issues are as follows: Which stakeholders are to be recognized, and in what ways? How are the interests of multiple stakeholders, whoever they are, to be incorporated into corporate governance and decision-making pro-

[1] See Steere 1998 and references cited therein. See also Clarkson 1998, for a comprehensive collection of the current stakeholder theory literature, and Wheeler and Sillanpaa 1997, for a survey of contemporary stakeholder management practices.

cesses? The first of these questions is easy to deal with in general, although difficult to resolve in specific cases. The second is easy to deal with in specific circumstances, but hard to resolve in general. Each requires a brief comment.

Who Are the Stakeholders?

The notion that corporations have stakeholders—persons or institutions that have something to gain or lose as a result of corporate activity, and hence that merit some consideration in corporate decision making—has become standard doctrine by now. Conventional lists of stakeholders include employees, customers, suppliers, communities in which the firm operates, the governments having jurisdiction over its operations, and so forth. Problems arise, however, when a specific corporation attempts to identify its particular stakeholder constituencies and to recognize their particular concerns and interests within the multi-dimensional corporate performance matrix. (The problem of identifying stakeholders seems to be the principal concern of Pfizer CEO William Steere, although his suggestion that the term *constituencies* be substituted does not appear to resolve the issue. See Steere 1998.)

How Are Multiple Stakeholder Interests to Be Served?

Although it may be readily agreed that most broad categories of stakeholders derive benefits from the general "success" of their common corporate "community"—profitability, growth, and so forth—it is very easy to spot sources of potential trade-offs and conflicts. Should there be more retained earnings for investment, higher dividends for shareowners, or higher wages for employees? Should there be greater corporate contributions to social services (including higher tax payments to governments) or lower prices for customers? In the face of such examples, it is not enough simply to list the stakeholders of an enterprise. Some mechanisms must be found to focus their joint efforts on mutual benefit and to prioritize, balance, and mediate their disparate, and potentially conflicting, interests and objectives.

The balancing of diverse objectives (stability versus growth and risk versus security, for example) is a routine task—indeed, one might say it is the primary function of corporate governance and of management at the "institutional" level. (Again, we may refer to Williamson's notion that governance establishes order between *mutuality* and conflict.) In the simplest case, diverse stakeholder interests may simply be "taken into account" on an ad hoc basis by whatever boards and management structures happen to be in place. At the opposite extreme, formal mechanisms guaranteeing "voice," and perhaps even voting or veto power, to particular stakeholder interests may be established by law. Hertig (1998) notes that such protective arrangements are much more common in Europe than in the United States, and questions whether the conventionally emphasized "fiduciary duties" of U.S. corporate officials are, in fact, sufficient to protect minority interests.

The Spectrum of Stakeholder Representation

Our analysis of the diverse modes of stakeholder representation in corporate governance arrays them along two dimensions (Figure 11.3): (1) *compulsory-voluntary*—are the arrangements for stakeholder representation required by law, or adopted voluntarily by autonomous bodies?—and (2) *collaborative-adversarial*—do the arrangements adopted assume, or attempt to establish, collaborative behavior among stakeholders, or do they reflect recognition of a fundamental diversity of interests and adversarial postures? Although the extremes of each of these dimensions are easy to identify, both of them are subject to gradations, and the two dimensions interact with each other as well. Legal requirements, whether general or highly specific (either to particular organizational features or to particular industries or companies), establish the framework within which individual, and to varying degrees "voluntary," arrangements evolve. And recognition of "best-practice" standards by official bodies—for example, endorsement of the Cadbury Commission's recommendations by the London Stock Exchange, or of the Business Roundtable's suggestions by the Securities and Exchange Commission—creates a middle ground between voluntary arrangements and formal requirements. In addition, both voluntary and compulsory arrangements may be intended to strengthen collaborative behaviors within situations that might otherwise be highly adversarial. I now turn to a brief commentary on each of the clusters of corporate governance structures noted on the two-dimensional grid in Figure 11.3.

Board Committees

Board committees and related forms of consultation within a conventional shareowner-director governance structure reflect a broad policy of "taking into account" diverse stakeholder concerns without introducing institutional modifications. The 1981 Business Roundtable *Statement on*

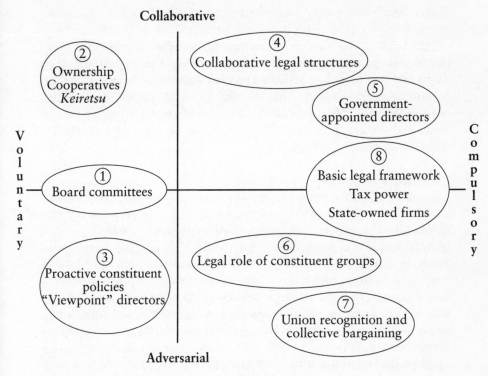

Figure 11.3. Spectrum of Corporate Governance Mechanisms

Corporate Responsibility (various pages) describes the motivation involved as follows:

> Corporations operate within a web of complex, often competing relationships. . . . Carefully weighing the impacts of decisions and balancing different constituent interests . . . must be an integral part of the corporation's decision and management process. . . . Many companies now include the whole spectrum of corporate social objectives in strategic planning. . . . Some companies have established committees of the board of directors to deal with corporate responsibility issues.

Board committees, accompanied by staff support and other mechanisms for obtaining stakeholder input, may reflect either adversarial or collaborative expectations about corporate-stakeholder relations. Indeed, their frequent purpose may be to anticipate stakeholder concerns and either respond to them before they become serious or defuse them through increased communication and participation.

Stakeholder Ownership, Cooperatives, and Keiretsu

Stakeholder ownership structures and the interlinked corporate structures known as *keiretsu* appear to be quite different on the surface. They reflect practices in widely separated parts of the world. They share the important similarity, however, that they build on and attempt to strengthen ties and behaviors of mutual interest and benefit among voluntary participants and, hence, increase the power of *specific types* of stakeholders within governance structures.

Employee Ownership

Occasionally at the outset, but usually after a going concern has become established, all or part of the ownership interest in a corporation may become vested in active employees. Employee stock ownership plans (ESOPs) and similar arrangements have been widely adopted in the United States, sometimes for purposes of motivation and gain sharing and sometimes in order to transfer responsibility for troubled enterprises to the control of persons with the strongest interests in their recovery and survival. Whether employee ownership is complete or only partial, so long as it represents a significant ownership bloc, it opens the way for greater employee involvement in governance. Yet, the evidence suggests that only a very small proportion of the firms in which employees own a sizable portion of the stock actually provide a role for employees in governance processes. Instead, most firms use ESOPs either for their tax incentives, as a protection against hostile takeovers, or as a means of profit sharing. As I note later, where employees purchase stock through wage concessions negotiated by unions, however, ESOPs generally have been accompanied by providing employees one or more seats on the board of directors.[2]

Producer Cooperatives

The form of producer cooperative familiar from the North American and U.K. experience involves the establishment of some type of service or distribution enterprise to perform functions commonly required by initial producer or supplier entities. The most common use is in agricultural industries.

---

[2] For a general overview of employee participation alternatives, see Kaufman and Kleiner (1995). Recent experience with Scanlon Plan gain-sharing arrangements, which have some of the same governance implications as employee ownership, are examined by Collins (1998). The Chinese version of cooperatives—small enterprises owned and controlled by their own workers—is another variation in the employee-ownership repertoire.

Consumer Cooperatives

The Swiss and Scandinavian experience with consumer cooperatives, imported into North America with mixed success, involves the creation of a common "purchasing agent" for a group of customers with similar needs or tastes. These owner-customers, in turn, create the governance structure for the organization. The Swiss cooperative Migros, which operates on both consumer and producer levels, even has its own general publications and national political party.

Keiretsu

Japanese *keiretsu* are made up of between twenty and fifty financial, production, and distribution companies that are linked together by common ownership, managerial, customer, and supplier relationships (see Morris 1996). Their relevance here is that they combine diverse vertical and horizontal stakeholder interests to focus on mutually beneficial objectives (often, it is believed, to the detriment of would-be challengers or market entrants). In North America, institutional investors—which in the aggregate account for at least half of all public corporate ownership—may play both an ownership and an alliance-partner role. A recent study showed that when institutional investors have no other links to an enterprise, they appear to act as self-interested shareowners (specifically, to hold down executive compensation levels and increase emphasis on long-term performance); however, when inter-corporate customer-supplier (*keiretsu*-type) relationships exist, such effects are not found (David, Kochhar, and Levitas 1998). The governance impacts of various kinds of inter-corporate alliances, now increasingly common in both domestic and international businesses, appear not to have been systematically examined beyond the descriptive level.

Proactive Stakeholder Policies or Viewpoint Directors

Corporations confronted with potentially adversarial relationships with various stakeholder groups may try to neutralize or co-opt them by means of proactive policies. These include efforts to anticipate and meet stakeholder expectations before conflicts arise. A commitment to match or better any relevant set of union-bargained employee benefits has long been standard labor relations policy in many nonunion companies in the United States. The idea is to meet employee-stakeholder objectives (as revealed by the results of union negotiations elsewhere) voluntarily, without introducing employee stakeholders into the formal governance structure. This general approach was associated historically with General Electric and has been attributed more recently to the new Japanese automobile plants in the United States. Undoubtedly such preemptive and co-optive tactics can be (and have been) adopted with respect to stakeholder groups other than employees as well.

Another option is to include stakeholder interests within formal governance structures by appointing directors who are either "representative" members of the relevant stakeholder groups themselves or nonstakeholders chosen to "represent" the relevant stakeholder interests. This approach has been explored most extensively with respect to employee stakeholders and is often associated with employee ownership (for a general survey, see Kaufman and Kleiner 1995). Where substantial employee ownership is *not* involved, formal employee or union representation on boards is not customary in the United States and is certainly not mandated by law (see later discussion of compulsory union-employee representation in other countries). A recent study of union-nominated directors in three industries—airlines, transport, and steel—identified eleven people, holding eighteen directorships, who were *not* active or retired union officials or members but who were expected to introduce employee-related concerns into board deliberations (Hunter 1998). Similar appointments might also be (and probably have been) made to take account of the interests of other stakeholders—institutional investors, environmental or community groups, and so forth—although on a less formal basis. The impact of such "viewpoint" directors is unknown. Hunter (1998: 573–75) concluded that "with only a few exceptions, the boardroom did not become a vehicle for truly joint governance" simply because union-nominated directors were present; however, their presence may introduce a "more pluralistic perspective" into otherwise hostile environments. In any event, these types of "boundary-spanning" board memberships can be expected to become problematic when matters of extreme confidentiality or critical inter-stakeholder conflict arise.

Collaborative Legal Structures: European and American

Both European and U.S. law have produced innovations designed to increase the likelihood of representation of nonowning stakeholders in corporate governance. The best known and most powerful of these is the German two-tiered board structure. The French arrangement, although also mandatory, appears to be weaker. Contemporary U.S. "constituency statutes" are somewhat vague and essentially permissive rather than compulsory.

Two-Tiered Boards

The German constitution states that the use of property should "serve the public weal," and in pursuit of this objective German corporate law specifically mandates a two-tiered board structure for all large corporations. The management board (*Vorstand*) is similar to the executive committee of North American, U.K., and Japanese firms. It consists entirely of internal management personnel and has responsibility for the regular operation of the enterprise. The supervisory board (*Aufsichstrat*) consists entirely of persons ineligible to serve on the management board, half of whom are elected by the shareowners and the other half (which must include union representatives in some cases) by the employees. The chairman of the supervisory board is chosen by the owner-elected directors and has tie-breaking power. The function of the supervisory board is to focus on "the long-term health of the company," including the welfare of all stakeholders but with particular emphasis on shareowners and employees (Lorsch and Graff 1996). Others argue that these arrangements, usually referred to as aspects of "co-determination," weaken firm-level corporate governance structures, and Roe (1998) believes that they have deleterious effects on securities markets as well.

Comité d'Entreprise

Since 1983, French labor law has mandated the creation of a *comité d'entreprise* in all large firms. Such a committee is composed of one or two management representatives and a sufficient number of labor members "to assure representation of the diverse categories of personnel" involved in the firm. The committee is authorized to receive information about the financial condition of the firm, employment, social programs, and other matters relevant to employee welfare. It is to be represented in various "councils" of the firm and *must* be consulted on matters of expansion, contraction, and structural change (Assemblée Nationale 1983). The role of these committees appears to be entirely advisory, and no study of their impact has been found in my search of the literature. An overview of French corporate governance in comparison with other European and U.S. models is presented by Windolf (1998).

Constituency Statutes

Corporate constituency statutes, now adopted by more than half of all U.S. states, purport to expand the traditional responsibilities of directors of private for-profit corporations to include the welfare of nonowner stakeholders. Variously phrased, these statutes either permit or require directors to consider the welfare of employees, customers, local communities, and others when making some or all important strategic decisions. Some commentators view these statutes as fundamental changes in corporate law, while others see them as inconsequential or nothing more than affirmations of accepted practice (Orts 1992). The legal impact of these statutes has not been significantly tested as yet, but it is certain that they provide evidence in "black letter law" that the fiduciary responsibility of directors may extend beyond the economic welfare of shareowners.

Government-Appointed Directors

Although uncommon in North America, the appointment of "public" directors to the boards of nongovernmental corporations is routine in many other parts of the world. Such persons are not typically government employees or officials, but rather members of academic or professional "elites" who are expected to exercise oversight on behalf of the society at large. For example, national banking authorities may designate such persons as a means of control or supervision for banks of a certain size or with particular roles and functions within the national banking system. In the transitional economies of Central Europe, the boards of state-created "investment funds," similar to the mutual funds familiar in North America, are typically composed of government appointees, and some of these people have moved onto the boards of operating companies as well. The roles taken by "public" directors vary widely, but their general purpose is to ensure that the particular public policy goals for which corporate privileges are being granted—financial stability, privatization, and so forth—are being pursued. Of course, in state-owned firms, all directors are either appointed by the government or chosen through some government-mandated mechanism (such as employees' election of directors in state-owned firms in Ireland).

Legal Role of Stakeholder Groups

During the last couple of decades, the courts have emerged as a major source of stakeholder power in the United States. Consumer-interest lawsuits and environmental challenges brought by activist individuals and groups have forced both corporations and units of government to broaden their consideration of stakeholder concerns. Increasing judicial recognition that such individuals and organizations have "standing to sue" has given them increased recognition and influence within the governance process, even if the lawsuits themselves are ultimately lost, abandoned, or settled without serious consequences.

Union Recognition and Collective Bargaining

From the U.S. perspective, national labor relations policy put in place in the 1930s provided for a very limited form of stakeholder participation on the part of employees and their union representatives, namely, the right to negotiate over the effects of governance decisions made by the board or by executives on wages, hours, and conditions of employment. In fact, a considerable body of labor law focuses on protecting the rights of management to govern the firm without direct involvement of workers or unions in strategic decisions or governance processes. But the law is not the only factor limiting employees from gaining a stronger direct voice in governance through collective bargaining. The norms of labor relations built up under the New Deal collective bargaining system—both on the management and on the union side of the table—largely accept the separation of management rights from any direct union role. This is changing now, however, at least on the union side of the labor-management divide. Thus, for employees in the United States to take a more active role, both the legal doctrines and the norms governing labor relations will need to change.

Basic Legal Framework, Tax Power, and State-Owned Firms

As noted at the outset, the ultimate power of the state over the corporation is established by the basic legal requirements for incorporation, access to capital markets, public reporting, and the power to tax. Although corporate chartering requirements are not onerous in most advanced countries, their *potential* impact is unlimited. And control over chartering, along with the tax and other regulatory powers, gives units of government unique status among stakeholders, with the power to assert or protect other stakeholder interests as well.

The power of the state to govern corporate activity reaches its maximum level in state-owned firms, which are in principle *entirely* under governmental control. In advanced countries the objectives of such enterprises generally include some combination of providing essential public services (such as postal and transport) and providing benefits for specific stakeholders (such as housing loans). (State investment in "flagship" enterprises has also been significant in Europe and elsewhere.) In spite of a decade or more of active "privatization" in advanced countries, state ownership is still widespread. It is very common in all the transitional economies, where demand for the protection of specific stakeholder interests (particularly by employee groups and communities or regions) has proved to be a serious barrier to economic rationalization and adaptation to international competitive conditions.

Conclusion

Corporate governance provides the foundational structure and purposeful direction for the business enterprise. It establishes *order* among the potentially conflicting interests of corporate constituents, so that their opportunities for mutual benefit can be realized. Contemporary governance mechanisms, many of which are prescribed by law in various jurisdictions, involve the interaction of multiple stakeholders. Some analysts (Reich 1998; Kochan and Rubinstein 2000), for example, argue that additional mechanisms giving formal recognition and greater protection to diverse stakeholder interests *should* and *will* become more prevalent in the future. Others (such as Handy 1997) believe that firms will voluntarily adopt proactive stakeholder policies in order to strengthen and preserve their value as productive "communities." With specific reference to the roles of employee stakeholders in corporate governance in the United States, it would appear that the trend is away from traditional collective bargaining over the effects of managerial decisions and toward efforts on the part of some unions to gain a more direct role in managerial decision making and corporate governance structures and processes. This movement is still rather tentative, however, and is limited by traditional norms of labor relations, by legal doctrines protecting managerial rights, and perhaps most of all by managerial and investor resistance to sharing power in this way with employee stakeholders and their representatives.

If those arguing that pressures to involve more multiple stakeholders in general, and employees in particular, in corporate governance will continue to grow are correct, this issue is likely to move to a more visible and explicit position in both processes of organizational change and labor-management relations. If it does, it would be well to consider the multiple models of governance reviewed here in choosing options for bringing stakeholders into corporate governance. Putting these issues, which have all the ingredients of what Walton and McKersie labeled as mixed-motive situations, on the table will tax the negotiating skill of the parties involved. Attempts to bring new interests into what was in the past a shareholder-dominated structure and process imply a sharing of power. Hence, negotiations about recognizing any new stakeholders and including them in governance processes are likely to be highly contentious and to set the stage for highly adversarial interactions. But the dilemma involved here is that once a stakeholder achieves a position in governance processes, to be successful and to make the new role work successfully for all stakeholders requires considerable use of integrative bargaining tactics and tools. Otherwise, as various case studies have shown, the parties run the risk of simply replicating adversarial relations in the boardroom or other governance forums. When that happens, the governance process ceases to function effectively and sometimes the enterprise itself may be threatened.

So the stakes involved in debates over the future of corporate governance are high. If this issue is to be joined in ways that achieve the benefits anticipated by its advocates, all the skills and tools of modern negotiations will need to be brought to bear with considerable skill.

Appendix: A Proposed Stakeholder Governance Innovation

The contemporary corporate governance literature is filled with pleas for greater employee ownership, greater shareowner democracy, more extensive stakeholder representation on corporate boards and committees, and so forth. In the United States, many of these suggestions are also accompanied by demands for federal chartering. Although the latter might be bureaucratically neat, providing a basis for greater standardization of incorporation requirements that would be useful in the multinational environment, none of these ideas adds new dimensions to the repertoire of corporate governance arrangements described in this chapter.

One suggestion put forward some time ago by a prominent business leader (and systematically ignored ever since) does introduce a new and stakeholder-oriented idea, however. Writing in the *Harvard Business Review*, Abram T. Collier (1979), retired chairman of the board of New England Mutual Life Insurance, proposed the creation of a new "class" of corporations which he referred to as "Co-Corps." In these entities, "the powers normally vested in the owners of common shares" would be given to the "members of the corporation," consisting of customers, managers, and employees, and individuals or institutions who chose to participate in the venture on the given terms. The objective of the Co-Corp would be to serve the interests of the "members," with primary attention to customer interests (product quality, service, and price) and secondary emphasis on "the interests and goals of the staff." Investors would be converted into secondary debt holders, with stability of returns the primary goal. The transformation of existing for-profit corporations into Co-Corps would have to be legally recognized as a nontaxable event and would be purely voluntary.

Collier's suggestion was based on his career with a mutual insurance company in which policy holders (customers) are also viewed as owners. His contention was that this transformation of corporations would result in improved governance because it would re-join ownership and control, with a new definition of corporate "success" (that is, satisfying the customer). He also argued that moderate-sized companies would be able to prosper under this regime and to protect themselves from takeovers because the shareowners would have a strong interest in preserving existing relationships. His suggestion obviously flies in the face of the contemporary emphasis on shareowner primacy and the accompanying wave of mega-mergers. It does, however, suggest that there could be significant (stakeholder-oriented) additions to the repertoire of corporate governance options currently observed. Similar, although less detailed suggestions for greater formal recognition of long-term employees within governance structures are contained in the recent work by Blair (1995).[3]

---

[3] A more recent proposal, originating in 1996 with then Secretary of Labor Robert Reich and introduced into the U.S. Congress by Senator Jeff Bingaman (Democrat, New Mexico), would grant tax advantages to a new class of "A-Corps" on the condition that they (1) made substantial commitments to employee pensions, training, health plans, and so forth; (2) adopted profit- or gains-sharing plans for employees; and (3) developed compensation structures that limited the high-low salary ratio to 50:1 or less (Bingaman 1996). This proposal would clearly provide substantial employee benefits and also put a cap on executive compensation; it does not contain any innovations in corporate governance, however.

12

Union-Nominated Directors

A New Voice in Corporate Governance

ROBERT B. MCKERSIE

As Lee Preston suggested in the previous chapter, the nature of the American corporation in general, and corporate governance in particular, is a subject of considerable debate today. Some of this debate is playing out in practice as firms explore alternative ways to meet the needs of both traditional shareholders and other stakeholders. The purpose of this chapter is to report on one such nascent development—the role of union-nominated directors (UNDs) on boards of American companies. There are no more than thirty to thirty-five instances in the United States where unions currently have UNDs serving on boards. Despite their small numbers, however, these individuals' experiences may be of major significance as a signal of the types of opportunities and challenges organizations will face in the future if they choose to bring multiple stakeholders directly into corporate governance at this level of the firm.

Other UNDs did exist in the past, in the automobile industry (at Chrysler as a feature of the "bailout"), the airline industry (PanAm, Western, Republic, and Eastern), the trucking industry (during the 1980s approximately six companies that experienced "crisis restructuring" employed Teamster-nominated directors), and the steel industry (prior to the 1993 New Directions agreement in basic steel, where the presence of UNDs emerged as part of a restructuring process to avoid bankruptcy). For the most part, the companies just mentioned have since vanished, however. One development that merits special attention is the emergence of UNDs in all the integrated steel companies as a matter of conscious policy—initiated by the United Steelworkers of America (USW) and not as a result of crisis. In addition, the Airline Pilots Association (ALPA) has established a policy of seeking board seats whenever it is feasible.

In the airline industry, several examples of companies with UNDs cur-

223

rently exist: United, Northwest, TWA, and Hawaiian. And while ALPA seeks board representation wherever possible, it has only been successful where employee stock ownership is involved. (For additional documentation regarding the extent of union representation on boards see Hunter 1998 and Strauss 2001.)

Although management resists UNDs, when employees own substantial amounts of stock (via trust arrangements), the case can be made that directors nominated by the union *should* be included since the primary role of any board of directors is to represent stockholder interests.

Before I examine the experience of UNDs more closely, a personal observation is appropriate. I have served in the role of UND for thirteen years, first in the trucking and now in the steel industry. Clearly, I am not a disinterested observer, and I should state at the outset my strong belief in the importance of stakeholder governance.

By stakeholder governance, I mean that workers and their representatives should be involved at the front end of the decision-making process, not as co-decision-makers but as participants having effective input into strategic decisions before they are made so that the consequences, and plans for handling the consequences, can be considered at the outset.

Workers and their representatives should be involved especially at the strategic level when down-sizing and restructuring are involved, to help shape transition programs. An increasingly pervasive characteristic of the recent knowledge-based economy is that workers have acquired considerable industry-specific skills. In some cases (especially manufacturing), this base of skills is not directly transferable to other industries. In addition, given the fact that employment in many manufacturing industries is shrinking, it is unlikely that a worker displaced from one company would be taken on at another firm in the same industry. This underscores an important premise of this essay: that workers' voices need to be heard at the strategic level of the business.

Much of the material in this chapter is drawn from discussions among UNDs at two meetings held at the Institute for Work and Employment Relations at MIT in 1996 and 1998 as part of a larger project examining changes in America's labor market institutions.[1] Before providing an ac-

[1] I would like to thank Thomas Kochan of MIT's Sloan School and Lynn Williams, formerly of the USW, for serving as convenors of the project, as well as the union-nominated directors who attended the two seminars and shared their experiences. An earlier version of this paper was prepared as a working paper for the Task Force on Reconstructing America's Labor Market Institutions, November 1999. Support of the Ford and Rockefeller Foundations for the Task Force is gratefully acknowledged. Quotations in this chapter are from the two meetings at MIT and from personal communications.

count of the experiences of these UNDs, however, it is appropriate to put this development in context. Given the vitality of laissez-faire capitalism in all parts of the world—and the role corporations play in that arena—and given that a modified form of capitalism may emerge beyond the pure market form we now are experiencing, an examination of the role played by UNDs with an allegiance to unions or workers, as well as shareowners, may provide some clues about what kinds of economic structures lie on the horizon.

Perhaps the most important reason for examining this subject is that it provides a window into the highest level of corporations, where important strategic decisions are made about such matters as mergers, down-sizing, and policies with respect to union representation. Currently, a sharp debate has arisen over the appropriate model for evaluating corporate governance—a debate between those advocating a model of enhanced shareholder value and those advocating the harmonizing of the interests of many stakeholders, including owners, employees, customers, and community members. By examining the role of the UND, I hope to further the discussion of who should be involved in the decision-making process at these highest corporate levels and of what standards should be used to evaluate the results of these decisions.

The Major Dilemmas Facing UNDs

The life of a UND can be quite difficult, given the fact that he or she serves as a director in the same fashion as the directors elected by stockholders, yet at the same time carries a special portfolio of expectations from the rank-and-file and union leadership. Stated another way, UNDs operate within and across two distinct cultures. As a result, they are constantly wrestling with the dilemma of how to be effective in both domains, when the values and standards for success are so different.

Certainly, the obligations of UNDs are no different from those of other directors. In today's business environment that responsibility means emphasizing stockholder interests. Although there may be some support within corporations for the notion that UNDs should serve the interests of all stakeholders (especially employees), the orientation of top management increasingly reflects the notion that shareholder value should be the overriding consideration.

Over the long run the interests of shareholders and other stakeholders generally coincide, but in the short run a considerable divergence in benefits can often take place among the primary interest groups that constitute the modern corporation. This divergence can remain for extended periods of time when, for example, such events as the introduction of new technology, restructuring of operations, or the implementation of new alliances and mergers are executed.

The task facing a UND is to be effective when measured against the criteria of both the board and the union. There are many examples of UNDs who have fallen off this high wire. The missteps come in two forms. On the one hand are directors who are seen by top management and other directors as union agents, pure and simple. These directors either are not taken seriously or, much worse, are excluded from important meetings. Thus, in carrying out perceived obligations to the union, such UNDs may fail to gain standing and to be effective within the culture of the board.

On the other hand, a danger exists that the UND will become so much a part of the board's culture that the union doubts the effectiveness of the director in serving labor's interests. In these cases, the directors are seen as having been co-opted by the requirements of confidentiality. Recently, the USW asked a steel company not to re-elect a particular UND for precisely this reason.

Effectiveness within Management and Board Councils

Compared with other "outside" directors, UNDs bring a different perspective to board discussions. Typically, directors come from the ranks of bankers, marketing experts, and executives of other companies and are able—based on their extensive experience—to have substantial input in board deliberations.

By contrast, since UNDs are in touch with the union, they bring expertise from the "inside" of the organization, and are sometimes in a position to contradict the chief executive officer (CEO) and other management presenters in particular situations. How this expertise is presented can make a considerable difference in the effectiveness of a UND. One UND's approach is to focus on the expected reception of the rank-and-file to a proposed decision, and by such a presentation to encourage management to shift its thinking: "If a UND believes that an issue is not going to be received well by the membership, he or she might ask management, 'How do I explain this so that a worker will understand it?' After framing an input in those terms, management sometimes changes its perception of an issue, and it gets revisited."

Generally, a confrontational style in the boardroom does not produce desired results. To support this point, it is necessary to say a few words about the modus operandi of top management vis-à-vis the deliberations of boards of directors. Generally, proposals are developed and examined in a variety of management meetings and deliberations before they are presented to a board. The board is never told about the process and generally does not ask how a particular report was prepared. While those associated with the preparation of the report are on hand to make the presentations and to answer questions, UNDs are not able to penetrate or to participate in the "management board"[2] except through informal contacts and conversations.

The assumption that undergirds the way in which boards operate is that "management is on top of the situation." If management were to come and ask for advice before proposing solutions, it would indicate inadequacy on their part. This perspective is in line with how most companies operate: once a problem has been identified, a solution must also be proposed.

For the most part, the style of a board meeting could be characterized as "show and tell." It is not the custom—to use the academic model—to hold a workshop at which questions are posed and a freewheeling discussion takes place. Some unstructured brainstorming does occur at planning sessions, but 90 percent of what takes place in board meetings follows the format of formal presentations, with board members asking questions and making comments. Most UNDs thus do not openly challenge members of management at board meetings; rather, they raise questions or make comments that indicate that more analysis is required on the subject at hand. Some UNDs may contact individual managers off-line to share their thoughts on the basis of their firsthand knowledge.

A UND at one airline stated his approach as fostering a relationship of trust with the CEO: "Unless you have the trust or support of the CEO, you're not going to get very far in terms of the management process. It can serve as an absolute earliest warning system on different initiatives that will have significant effect—not only on union contracts but on any action that you want to influence early on." It took this UND some time to establish a level of trust, which he fostered by providing information and background materials to the CEO; these actions, in turn, prompted the CEO to communicate with him directly.

Another UND in the steel industry has developed trust by alerting man-

---

[2] It is helpful to draw the distinction, as is done in the governance of German corporations, between the supervisory board and the management board. Clearly, the board of directors at a typical U.S. company is analogous to a supervisory board. While a de facto management board exists, it is not formalized as such.

agement prior to board meetings when he planned to raise controversial issues; he believes management truly appreciates this gesture: "If you do offer some prior notice, you get recognized and appreciated for it."

Participation on Committees

Membership on committees can be another forum for UNDs to make a difference. Like other directors, UNDs serve on audit, compensation, finance, and other specialized committees. One UND who serves on the audit committee proposed, for example, that as part of the company's internal audit program, special experts (retired personnel from the Occupational Safety and Health Administration) be retained to determine whether the joint union-management safety initiative was up to standard.

Another UND, who chairs his board's audit committee, believes that this role has offered a unique opportunity for him, particularly since he is privy to a great deal of information. One significant contribution was his testimony on behalf of the company before the Securities Exchange Commission (SEC). He found the SEC staff to be skeptical of foreign-owned companies (his company being a case in point) and to be wary of their potential for misleading the investing public. They were curious about his role, and he was able to lend credibility to the company, preventing lawsuits by shareholders and minimizing adverse SEC action.

A UND from the airline industry has found that membership on the finance committee provides considerable leverage. He made the point as follows: "All roads in this company lead to the finance committee," where all of the company's major projects are decided on and launched. He has found that many problems can be resolved prior to board discussions through finance committee meetings; this strategy has been very effective for him, particularly since management does not appreciate being confronted in the boardroom.

Another UND who serves on his board's social responsibility committee, which deals with safety, health, and environmental issues, noted that his company has one of the best records for environmental safety. This same director reported on how major decisions were made in the company. Recently, the board voted to close a mining operation. They had established a committee to investigate the situation, weighing potential costs for workers against overall revenue concerns. The committee consisted of seven independent members (mostly retired politicians), five union representatives, and the chair of the board of directors. The decision to close the operation thus was made by union representatives and management together.

Executive Compensation

No subject represents a greater gulf between the two cultures than the question of executive compensation. UNDs can serve as "watchdogs" to ensure that compensation agreements are upheld, since many labor-management agreements contain "equal sacrifice clauses" insisting that management take pay cuts when labor is asked to accept wage reductions. One UND, who serves on the compensation committee of his board, had a hand in determining the percentage increase for executive compensation and also shared this information with the local union. In addition to helping set the level of executive compensation, UNDs can also help to influence the *structure* of compensation packages—linking the behavior of top management to incentives that reflect true performance, as well as reassuring union members that compensation is fairly distributed. For example, a UND on an airline board was able to have an impact on executive compensation at his company by convincing the compensation committee to make changes in managerial bonuses, making them less subjective by requiring managers to meet specific targets based on performance.

Another UND—in the steel industry—was able to influence debates on executive compensation in two fundamental ways: first, by promoting the idea that managers should have a stake in the performance of a company and accomplishing this feat by tying managers' salaries to that performance, as well as stipulating that stock options not be available until executives had reached a certain tenure level; and second, by comparing executive compensation with benchmarks within the industry to avoid setting exorbitant rates.

A UND from the airline industry has had an impact on the reception of compensation packages by his union constituency in several ways. First, by publishing a comparison of his airline's executive compensation rates with those in the airline industry as a whole, he was able to demonstrate that regardless of how high executive compensation levels were, they still fell within the industry's mean. Second, he was able to explain the nature of the incentive structure of compensation, which the union members did not understand. Although management took a 20 percent wage reduction, there were management bonuses, which served as incentive pay and which sounded more like giveaways to the unions. There was an uprising when they were reported in the year following concessions. The UND was able to help the membership understand what function this portion of the compensation package served. Finally, he was instrumental in influencing management to adopt an executive compensation plan which stipulated that any executive pay raises would parallel general increases negotiated by the unions. As a direct result of all these actions, which occurred during concession bargaining, management at this airline adopted a self-imposed discipline regarding compensation—even after the company's lean years ended.

The experience at another airline offers a slightly different perspective on the UND's role regarding executive compensation. When the board was structured, executive compensation was a critical issue, and a larger percentage of union representatives were placed on the compensation committee than on the board of directors itself. By charter, the committee must approve management compensation, and the UNDs were even given the option to block compensation packages. As one director commented, "Although it seemed like a good idea, we did not expect the sheer amount of time that boards and this committee would spend on this issue. We found that we do not have a coherent compensation philosophy that affirmed our corporate philosophy—it was more a case of reaction than proaction. It's a challenge for us now to develop an affirmative compensation philosophy for this large company that needs to attract talent to remain a successful company."

Roles in Collective Bargaining

What should be the role of the UND when contract negotiations arise? Management at one company solves this issue by not discussing any contract negotiation strategies during board meetings. A type of management board operates de facto, largely behind the scenes. In this case, one of the non-UNDs, who has extensive experience in labor-management relations, serves as an advisor to these discussions aimed at coalescing a plan for contract negotiations.

In other companies, the CEO and other members of the board may attempt to solve the dilemma by asking that the UND be excused from discussions. A UND from the steel industry recounted his experience with board deliberations during a strike, mentioning that—at first—he was asked to leave the room when the board arrived at this item on its agenda: "I said I would leave, but under protest. They said it was inappropriate for me to be a part of their discussion about strike strategies. I said that I was appointed to the board of directors and had every right to be involved in all of their conversations." After having his lawyer write a letter to the board protesting its actions, he was "never kicked out of a meeting again." However, the board also never again discussed strike strategies in the boardroom; they simply moved those conversations elsewhere, convening the core members of the board at headquarters and conducting conference calls with the remaining members. "The distinction I made was that I was not functioning as a union leader and not involved in their bargaining strategy, but acting in the interest of stockholders," this UND said.

At one airline, all four union representatives agreed to excuse themselves from the boardroom during discussions of corporate strike strategies, but this concession was a trade-off for greater latitude regarding confidentiality. The UNDs were able to report all of the content of board meetings to their union governing bodies.

Many of the UNDs in the airline industry are also high-ranking union officials and as a result are often directly engaged in bargaining. This role has placed these UNDs in the middle of a difficult conflict: as chief negotiators, they are still held responsible by their unions to arrive at a contract, yet they must also continue to serve in the role of corporate directors—and are still briefed on corporate strike strategies.

In the case of a UND from the basic steel industry, while his company has not entered into any formal collective bargaining during his tenure on the board, he has participated in discussions of the approach that company intended to follow in arbitration of a wage re-opener: "I am a director. I sit in on all of the meetings; no one asked me to leave. I was there when we heard what the company was intending to propose in arbitration. I think every director represents some constituency, except truly outside, independent directors. If some directors represent vendors and other constituencies, why should the role of a director who represents the interests of workers have any less prominent a role?"

One UND, who has developed a rather close working relationship with the CEO of his company, is openly consulted on the company's strike strategies. In his role as UND, he does not formally engage in bargaining, but he does offer input on what direction the company should take in the negotiations—guidance that reflects his views on what is beneficial for the company as well as for workers. On one occasion, as the bargaining continued, he brought in outside mediators, with the goal of encouraging both sides to reach an agreement.

How far can a UND go in performing any type of mediation? One UND described his experience in the following way: "At the time of the re-opener, I spent quite a bit of time talking with union leaders and top management, exploring ideas and proposing solutions—for example, expanding the agenda, shifting negotiations to the local level, and considering ideas for financing an improved pension from savings generated by not filling vacancies—so that the parties would not invoke binding interest arbitration. All of these efforts took place informally behind the scenes. While nothing came of the efforts—the terms of the re-opener were set by the arbitrator—given the importance of contract negotiations, it was important for me to attempt to help the parties find common ground."

Union Organizing

No subject is of greater interest to a union than the company's response to union organizing drives. One UND involved himself in critiquing his company's strategy and tactics during several campaigns. After one of the elections was over—and the company had won by a significant margin—he asked to review the literature that had been distributed by both sides. (It should be noted in passing that this tool, namely, requesting information, is always available to a director.) Management was quick and forthcoming with binders that provided a full picture of the literature that had been distributed by both sides. While the union, in its campaign material, used some strong language to characterize management, the UND chose not to criticize the union handbills but rather turned his attention to the statements and techniques used by management in their communications. Since certain statements did not represent a high-road campaign by the company, he sent a letter detailing where he thought the literature could be improved.

The UND's role in union organizing is critical when a company contemplates opening a nonunionized facility. One UND was instrumental in keeping the discussion on the board table for two years. Most of the other directors were staunchly anti-union, and the dispute was bitter. He was accused of not considering the interests of stockholders, but argued that opening the plant would ultimately not be in their best interest. He was helpful to the union, which engaged in a corporate campaign once the new facility was announced, and he has continued to advise management that the fight over "union flight" was not going to disappear.

Effectiveness with the Union Constituency

Given the reality that UNDs would not occupy their seats without nomination by a union, the task of keeping in touch with this constituency presents special demands and challenges. One UND from the steel industry commented on his approach:

> I am in frequent contact with the union president and, to some extent, with the vice president and several other officers. This relationship has evolved to the point where I connect with the union president primarily by telephone. When the agenda for a particular board meeting contains an item about which I would like to alert the union president and solicit his reaction—for example, a capital appropriation—I will call him ahead of the board meeting. More often, I contact the union president after a board meeting to brief him on what has just occurred. In terms of content, when I attend union membership meetings, a wide range of issues are surfaced, and sometimes individuals will corner me on the side and ask if I can do something about their particular problems. My stance has been one of being willing to listen and to understand their concerns so that I am better informed, but I emphasize that answers to problems raised will come down through management to the union leadership and not from myself. In other words, I want to be sure that they do not see me as a "super steward."

Another UND from the steel industry spends time "making the rounds" at local unions before board meetings to identify what they want to know. He also convenes meetings with these locals and with the labor-management participation teams, emphasizing to participants that this role is a "two-way street." He is not sure, however, "to what extent information is flowing outward and what I might need to do to more actively promote channels of communication to local union personnel."

A former UND for a trucking firm noted that most union leaders did not have a strategy regarding the UND's role. In fact, there was little expectation of information to be channeled from the UND to the rank-and-file. This UND commented, "To the extent that a UND can be influential in representing workers' concerns in board decisions, you need to extrapolate what the membership reaction will be. You are really acting as a resource; more than any other board member, you understand work force issues better, but in order to do that, you need to know what's happening with the rank-and-file."

How accurate can a UND's assessment be of the rank-and-file's perspective on an issue? For very large companies, it is difficult for a UND to know what the rank-and-file is really thinking. As one UND said, "If I attend a local union meeting, I'm speaking to 40 or 50 people—out of 3,000 members. I shouldn't substitute my judgment for that of the staff representative or district directors that are charged with speaking for the rank-and-file."

A UND from the airline industry attends local governing body meetings and local council meetings and has found that his presence makes a real difference in the perception of his role: "Everyone knows who I am. The membership sees me at these meetings; they ask questions and feel they have input. They not only want to know what I do, they also want to express concerns to me and feel confident that I'm going to take those issues to the board. Polling has demonstrated that it's really important to them. Although I have a great deal of latitude in reporting information, one thing I don't do is put anything in writing."

Another UND commented, "Your position is improved if the UND is recognized by other directors as being current and able to assess the mood of the rank-and-file." To maintain this perspective, he has regular contact with the national union and writes a yearly summary of what has happened in the company. He also meets with the international representative twice each year and speaks with him by phone both before and after each board meeting. It is important for this UND to know what the union's concerns are in order to represent them in the meetings—but he does not necessarily consider the opinions of a few members at a local meeting to represent the concerns of the union at large: "When we meet with union leaders, we have to assume that they speak for the workers—this is representative democracy. When I meet with the local executive board, they often want to tell me more than they want to know from me. It ultimately improves my situation on the board of directors; when I go to a board meeting, the other directors perceive that I have my finger on the pulse of the company. It's a source of strength."

A UND can exercise another option to get in touch with rank-and-file workers and with members of management—the plant tour. Viewing operations and understanding the plant's technology present a natural setting for learning about the work force and general issues that affect labor-management relations. In the experience of one UND, a familiarization tour turned into a constructive, tripartite fact-finding mission. The trip was to an ore mine and included the UND, the staff person for labor relations, and the vice president of the union. As it turned out, local union leadership at the mine felt out of touch, and considerable tension had developed between that leadership and local management. Upon its return to the mill, the delegation suggested that a joint union-management team from the mine visit the steel mill to learn about the positive developments taking place at the blast furnace—the customer for the iron ore they supplied.

Other examples indicate the range of activities in which UNDs engage union officials and the rank-and-file. One UND maintained contact with the local of a plant when it was targeted for shutdown. He helped to represent workers' concerns to the board by fostering a discussion of whether there should be a "golden handshake" for this facility's workers, particularly since they went above and beyond expectations to meet two deadlines and extend the life of the plant. The UND wanted to make sure that workers were compensated somehow for exemplary service while facing the eventual loss of their jobs.

A participant from Canada described differences in the perception of UNDs according to whether they are nominated by the local government or from the shop floor. Government-nominated UNDs, who are placed in response to broad union initiatives rather than through the efforts of a specific union, are often seen as having "cushy jobs" by the rank-and-file. It is difficult for these directors to report back to their respective constituencies. Those nominated from the shop floor, on the other hand, tend to report to local officers and staff, as well as to the regional coordinator or district director. Before a board meeting, they often conduct conference calls with officials and other UNDs. The Canadian UND believes that the infrastructure for communication is inadequate, however, and presents a future challenge.

A major challenge facing all UNDs is to demonstrate to union leadership and rank-and-file that something different is happening as a result of the role they play. Generally, union members refer to UNDs as "their directors"; UNDs, however, find it difficult to be specific with their union constituencies about the range of questions and probes they have initiated within their boards or with top management, since many of their activities as directors are governed by confidentiality rules and involve details that are not easily communicated.

One UND found himself confronted with the following question at a union meeting: "So, Mr. Director, how much did we give up in our last agreement to get you on the board?" In other words, this member was asking: Are we receiving enough value to offset whatever was traded for this arrangement?

One participant described a unique idea for bridging the two domains—having employees attend open board meetings as a way of increasing confidence in the UND role. This small company conducted two open board sessions, which this director believed had changed the direction of the company. Employee-owners were able to address the board directly; they expressed the concerns the UND had been trying to convey. As a result, the board could no longer deny their relevance.

Directors' Compensation

The issue of directors' compensation can bite back at UNDs in several ways. First, directors are generally well paid, and for that reason alone they may have difficulty convincing union leaders and rank-and-file that they have not been co-opted by the board's culture.

At one airline, though, UNDs receive no compensation and cannot trade in stock above and beyond what is provided through the ESOP. One UND noted, "It's true that, for employees who own stock, they're not going to question the votes I've made when it goes up or down. All of the employees and directors benefit at the same level." This UND mentioned, however, that the rank-and-file are very sensitive to the benefits UNDs receive as part of the "world of the mahogany desk." The membership is concerned that a UND will be transformed from the "fire-in-the-belly union man" whom they want to represent their concerns.

Another UND reported that when he attended a union meeting at which a merger proposal was being discussed, he was asked: "So, how much stock do you own?" In this case, he did own some company stock because a part of the compensation package was paid in shares. He had followed a self-imposed guideline of not buying any additional stock, however, as other directors had done over the years.

Some UNDs contribute a portion of their compensation to the union in lieu of dues, but while such a symbolic act may help align the UNDs with the union constituency, it can simultaneously be a source of concern to management and other directors who expect UNDs to be truly independent.

Confidentiality

No issue so strongly illustrates the dilemmas and tensions created by the conflicts between the two worlds within which UNDs operate as does the issue of confidentiality. A sharp divergence in style and approach to information disclosure and decision making occurs across the two domains. The culture of top management and the board of directors is one of consensus and working things out behind the scenes. Information about strategic plans is kept confidential, as is often said, "for stock market considerations." On the other hand, the culture of a union is considerably more open and insistent on access to critical information.

UNDs shared their experiences in negotiating the difficult confidentiality issue. "I'm continually torn between the role of mediator between two parties, of advocate for union expansion, and a 'whisperer' to union leadership about what needs to be done," said one participant. "This is particularly true during discussions of acquisitions and mergers. I can raise the question of how the merger will affect employees, but what do I do about alerting the union membership?"

In one case of a major joint venture, the problem of confidentiality went beyond the UND role to include union officials as well. One partnership agreement involving a joint committee of union officials and management was never fully realized because the officials refused to sign a confidentiality agreement that would preclude them from discussing corporate policies and information on mergers and acquisitions with rank-and-file members.

One UND discussed how a series of leaks about merger and acquisition discussions undermined his standing with the union leadership and rank-and-file. When discussions of these possible strategic moves started at the board level, the UND urged management to brief the union as soon as possible. In fact, the UND made a special trip to company headquarters and outlined a procedure whereby confidentiality could be ensured on the part of both the local and the national union leadership. The response of management was, "We're sensitive to this and we're willing to run the risk of a leak, but we don't think the time is right for consultations with the union." When a rumor appeared on the Internet, the local union president was asked about the news. He gave the report little credence since he believed that something of this magnitude would have been mentioned to him by management or by the UND.

As it turned out, the UND was scheduled to speak at a monthly membership meeting just a week after the embarrassing situation developed, and he was put on the spot. In fact, the chairman of the grievance committee, a very professional and mild-mannered individual, stood up and asked two questions: "Did you know about these merger discussions?" The UND answered that he did. Then the chairman followed with another question: "Why did you not tell us?" The UND did not have a good answer, other than the defensive routine about confidentiality. The UND was also called to task by union headquarters for failing to carry through on what they saw as the key function of a UND: to keep them informed about important strategic matters, especially if the company executives chose not to bring union leaders into the loop on a timely basis.

Some partnership agreements "legislate" the terms of confidentiality, but management does not always honor them. One partnership agreement states, "Without limiting the foregoing, the company shall provide the union with early notification of any contemplated significant transactions involving mergers, acquisitions, and regular updates regarding dispositions, joint ventures, and new facilities." Even when management officials sign such agreements, in the view of many UNDs, managers do not disclose strategic information in a timely manner—if at all.

A top union leader observed that "our membership is more concerned with whether or not we [union officials] know about something, rather than whether or not we tell them. Unions have never faced this as a policy issue; I think we should sign these confidentiality agreements and explain this to our local leadership and membership. I think they would feel comfortable that someone at least knew these plans were happening."

Another participant questioned whether confidentiality agreements simply move the burden down one more level, from the UND to the union official: "The union president then has to carry the burden of not telling union membership about this information. At whose desk does this buck stop?" A further issue, says this UND, who was unable to alert a facility of the date it was targeted for shutdown, is whether or not management is telling UNDs what they need to know when they are communicating directly with officials who have signed these agreements: "If we are responsible agents within the company, should we be satisfied with the fact that union officials are told? Does that mean that the system is working? Or, are we absolving ourselves of our responsibilities?"

A UND from the airline industry believes that because of legitimate SEC regulations, mergers and acquisitions represent the only situation for which a company can insist that confidentiality be maintained: "The UND board seat changes the issue: Are you there just to monitor what's going on, or are you there to affect the outcome—to help it or stop it?" For example, in the development of an alliance between the company where he was a UND and another airline, he was involved at the planning stage, six or seven months prior to the public announcement. At ninety days prior to the announcement, he insisted that the deal be disclosed to union leadership, who had signed a confidentiality agreement. He believes that his role goes beyond simply being informed; he must help to decide the fate of the deal, based on the issue of job security for all workers.

And during the 1990s when United Airlines first considered acquiring US Airways, employee input actually "killed" the acquisition. United's board was prepared to make an offer, but the employees, led by the pilots' union, felt that the time was not right. All of the SEC concerns were honored, but the decision process included more than the members of the board of directors.

Another participant believes that the airline industry offers an interesting model regarding confidentiality. Given the structure of the industry's unions, it has been easy to establish a "cone of silence" for very confidential information that includes not only the UNDs but also the union leadership and the local governing body. This arrangement has been effective for alerting local governing bodies about major decisions, while preventing the information from being leaked to the membership more generally. He believes that there are lessons within the airline industry that can be applied elsewhere—both in the structure of the unions themselves and as an example of management's ability to "live with less secrecy than they thought they could."

An official of the USW underscored the primary reason for placing UNDs on boards of directors: "The fundamental point to having a UND is for the union to have more access to information and influence. We needed this in steel, because companies were doing wild things without the unions being able to influence the result. We talked about 'closing the circle' of participation—by achieving union involvement at every level of the company—because we wouldn't be able to keep an eye on what top management was doing." The primary reason why the USW pressed for UND representation was to improve communication, increase access, and reduce confidentiality. He related this motivation to the future of the UND role itself, stating that it is threatened by excessive confidentiality: "I think that the maintenance and growth of the UND concept will depend on UNDs' erring more in the direction of telling unions, irrespective of any other consideration. The most effective union people know who they can tell things to; you just have to test that out."

The Power of the Lone Dissenter

The question is often asked, "What difference can one director make in the deliberations of a board?" A UND at one airline has found that—unlike the tenor of union decision making, where splits in decisions are more acceptable—corporate boards are reluctant to maintain dissent: "If you work within the system, you can either get a lot accomplished or get some projects struck down, even though your opinion may at first be in the minority." A UND from the steel industry offered his experience with consensus: "On what I thought was a fairly minor issue, but one that I felt strongly about, I cast the only opposing vote on the board. It caused a great deal of problems; the other directors could not understand how I could be opposed after hearing their point of view. Because there is a tendency to move only on unanimity, it gives UNDs much more influence than I ever expected we had."

Another UND from the steel industry noted that when it came time to vote on a takeover bid, his opposition was taken very seriously. Considerable pressure was exerted on him to abstain if he could not support the proposal. Because the CEO and other directors place a high value on unanimity, he was able to garner considerable airtime for sharing his concerns about the impending strategic move.

Of course, taking a stand has to be done in a way that does not cast UNDs into "one-issue" directors. UNDs try to contribute on a wide range of topics. At the same time, UNDs report that whenever a subject arises in which the union is involved, the attention of the board turns in their direction.

The Future of the UND Concept

In sum, where does the UND concept stand? Where will it go? Where *should* it go as a matter of social policy?

Based purely on the empirical test of the market—that is, how widely the role is employed in industry today—we should not be too optimistic about its expansion. As I mentioned at the beginning of this chapter, the concept is used rather infrequently, and it does not appear to be expanding in any significant fashion. In fact, the idea does not have many champions. Management, for the reasons alluded to earlier, finds the role of a director who holds a special mandate for worker and union concerns as out of synch with the way in which boards of directors operate. As an example of this strong opposition, in the 2001 negotiations between Delta and ALPA, management was willing to go to impasse over the union's demand to have an ALPA representative be a *voting* member of the board of directors (ALPA has the right to have an observer at board meetings).

Similarly, some union leaders are wary of the idea for fear that the presence of a UND may create a competitive channel of communication, thereby diminishing their own contact with top management and the board. An important advantage for a union in having a UND, however, is that the arrangement enables the union to remain somewhat independent and to maintain an adversarial posture, if desired, at the same time that it has someone on the "inside"—on the board—who is working for more shared solutions to major challenges.

Realistically, the concept and practice of UNDs in the United States will only expand significantly when public policy endorses the concept, much as what happened in Germany with the requirement for union representatives on supervisory boards, instituted at the end of World War II as part of the reconstruction strategy. As of early in the twenty-first century, the outlook for any shift in public policy that would support union-worker engagement at the strategic level as a new right of the workplace is indeed quite bleak.

The next question is whether the added value of UNDs has been substantial enough to advocate an expansion of the concept. At the moment, this question is impossible to answer. There are no controlled studies that let us judge whether the presence of such individuals makes any difference in terms of improved economic performance, enhanced effectiveness of the union, higher morale among the work force, and any of a host of other standards that might be used in evaluating this development.

Even without a nudge from public policy, however, it is quite possible that the number of UNDs will slowly expand. Here unions have a need and an opportunity to provide support in the form of training and on-going assistance to the individuals who find themselves playing roles both as directors responsible to stockholder interests and as voices for union concerns and principles.

But while the route to greater worker and union influence via the UND may not be highly traveled for the foreseeable future, other developments under the banner of labor-management partnerships are bringing union leaders into much more active roles at the top of corporations. The path-breaking agreement signed in 2000 between Kaiser Permanente and its eight unions is a case in point. This large health organization, based on the West Coast, with approximately 80,000 employees, signed a framework agreement with the unions establishing principles of partnership very similar to those in place between Saturn and the UAW. The unions are assured of consultation and input on all strategic matters. In addition, joint working parties provide guidance on such important topics as staffing and standards for patient care.

Summary of Key Functions

The functions performed by the UNDs who attended both the seminars mentioned earlier can be summarized as follows:

1. *Facilitating communication.* Ideally, a UND wants to avoid becoming a messenger who runs back and forth with information. Instead, it is important to surface issues that are of central concern for union membership and leadership and to ask management to respond

through proper channels. It is also especially important for management to communicate sensitive information to union leadership and
for a UND to be a catalyst for this practice.

2. *Formulating proposals and facilitating the process of finding common
   ground across the two institutions.* When one plant was unable to get
   a new work system designed because of differences within management, one UND suggested letting workers advance their own proposals. Once the new system was organized into self-managed teams, the
   plant broke every company record. The effort has allowed the UND to
   develop a good working relationship with plant management.

3. *Monitoring management performance and critiquing it where appropriate.* An example given earlier—one UND's scrutiny and analysis of
   how management handled a union representation campaign with
   feedback to management—illustrates this role well.

4. *Addressing issues that may be overlooked in the union-company relationship.* After a company experienced four fatalities in six months,
   one UND raised safety as an issue at a board meeting, and the subject
   received immediate action.

Specifying the Role

One question that will only be resolved through more experience is
whether active union officers should serve on the board, as is the case with
ALPA nominations, or whether it is more advisable to follow the policy of
the USW, which precludes nominating active union officials. It is important
to select individuals who will bring value to a company as directors, according to one USW official, and not serve as official union representatives.

A further point is that even though the individual has been nominated
by the union, the UND cannot be seen as the *primary* spokesperson for the
union's concerns. Such a view undermines the influence of the individual
on issues other than labor-management relations and also creates the impression that this person speaks for the union leadership and the rank-
and-file. No one individual should carry that much weight in the deliberations of the board. Many channels need to be used to select input and
perspectives from union leaders and workers.

Some commentators argue that the purposes served by UNDs can be
replicated by appointing to boards individuals with substantial experience
in human resources and industrial relations. While many boards have such
individuals, and their presence is to be encouraged, they do not possess the

same credibility as a UND to speak about the concerns of a company's work force.

A brief historical digression is in order at this point. Early on, most boards were composed of insiders, specifically, key managers of the enterprise. They brought to strategic discussions the advantage of considerable detailed knowledge about the operations but often lacked the objectivity and ability to stand up to the CEO since these inside directors were also employees of the company. With the changeover of board membership largely to outside directors, often executives of other companies, objectivity and perspective have been achieved but detailed knowledge of the operations has been lost. A UND, who in some cases is literally an employee of the organization or even a retired union official, brings considerable inside knowledge but at the same time a point of view that is quite different from other directors.

Concluding Perspectives

What reasons exist for advocating an expansion of the UND concept? *First, such a role can add a corrective force to the deliberations at the top of corporations today.* There are many examples in which boards of directors are forced to move in extremis to change a CEO or implement dramatic change, and insufficient equilibrating arrangements exist at the top of corporations—given the way boards of directors are selected and given the extensive discretion that is accorded to CEOs. An individual nominated by a union who brings an independent perspective is in a position, as one of our participants said, "to raise the bullshit flag." Or, to cite the more typical metaphor, a UND can "tell the emperor [the CEO] that he or she has no clothes."

Second, this role has the potential for forcing management—as it formulates strategy and engages in change—to do so in a restrained and effective manner. UNDs can be a moderating influence by pointing out the pitfalls in precipitous down-sizing, in dramatic shifts of activity to subcontractors, and in shifting facilities overseas—steps that may produce short-run improvements but often turn out to be long-run disasters. Thus, the UND might ultimately serve to keep a corporation from stumbling.

These points are merely other ways of saying that if at the board level, human considerations are placed on a par with financial considerations, then the long-run results for all concerned are likely to be much more satisfactory.

13

Negotiating Equality?

Women, Work, and Organized Labor in the European Union

KIRSTEN S. WEVER

As suggested in the introductory chapters of this volume, the effectiveness of negotiations in any given arena is contingent in large part on whether and how leaders of social institutions and economic organizations manage the forces for change. This chapter, like the others, explores how changes in the world of work affect negotiations. Specifically, this chapter focuses on developments concerning employment-related outcomes for women in the paid work forces of the member countries of the European Union (EU). Pressures to improve these outcomes derive from changes in the nature of work and from broader social changes, such as changes in perceptions about "women's work" against a backdrop of rapidly growing service sectors, high and protracted levels of unemployment, and some shrinkage in the welfare states of most EU member countries. These pressures for change have been reflected in, and augmented by, the EU's systematic devotion to the incorporation of "women's issues" into its social policy agenda, especially in the past several years.[1]

Many of the EU's policies are meant to reduce differences across EU member countries. Certainly EU-wide differences with respect to employment-related outcomes for women are stark (Charles 1995; Blau and Kahn 1996). In Sweden, for instance, women's relative earnings are about 85 percent of men's whereas in Britain that figure is roughly 64 percent.

I am deeply grateful for the intelligent and diligent research work, data analysis, and conceptual contributions of my research assistant, Debra Davis.

[1] Because men remain advantaged relative to women on such dimensions as the provision of child care and care of other family members, these are generally dubbed "women's issues." While this may be descriptively accurate, it is normatively problematic: there is no intrinsic reason why these issues should be of less concern to men than to women.

Even holding skills and education constant, the gender wage gap on average remains significant and is especially high in some countries, such as Germany (European Foundation for the Improvement of Living and Working Conditions [hereafter European Foundation], January 1998). Occupational segregation and the crowding of women into generally "feminized" (low-skill, low-pay) jobs and occupations remain significant problems throughout the EU, with especially high levels of segregation in the Scandinavian countries (Grimshaw and Rubery 1997). The incidence of atypical work—which is also called contingent or irregular employment) and is quite common—and work in "informal" sectors—which is somewhat less common—is especially high in the Latin countries: Italy, Spain, Portugal, and Greece (International Labour Office of the United Nations 1998). While the situation has improved slowly for women in most places, there are still stark differences across the EU with respect to the most basic issues, like women's relative earnings and occupational segregation by gender. Even where progress seems to be more significant, a careful analysis reveals a range of obstacles to women's employment gains. For instance, the worldwide average for female participation in managerial jobs hovers around 20 percent, but promotions do not necessarily guarantee wage increases: women who shatter the "glass ceiling" tend to remain fixed to the promotion wage floor (*Financial Times*, August 4, 1998). Needless to say, this exacerbates the overall gender wage gap.

Interest in addressing these problems at the EU level has met with ambivalent responses from unions and employers. The Social Partners (including the Employers' Confederation of Europe [UNICE], the European Centre of Enterprises with Public Participation [CEEP], and the European Trade Union Confederation [ETUC]) generally resist the imposition of political deals and EU directives, preferring instead to negotiate agreements on their own. Yet with regard to many of the issues of particular concern to women in the paid labor market, it is either particularly difficult or particularly impractical to reach agreement through collective bargaining or political labor-management negotiations. Consider child care, for example, which tends to be provided privately or by the state; or atypical workers, who are generally not unionized; or atypical work, which does not figure prominently on the traditional labor-management agenda. In addition, formal pacts or agreements negotiated by the Social Partners are less likely to affect women to begin with, because women are less likely to be unionized or covered by collective bargaining contracts.

The effective result of all this is that important employment outcomes for women are less influenced by national or subnational labor-management negotiations. This chapter briefly reviews the main EU-level initiatives of the past decade that were meant to influence labor market outcomes for women as the EU has consolidated its power, to some extent at the expense of the power of national actors and nation-states. It then considers specifically why government, employer, and even trade union responses to these initiatives have usually been ambivalent. It argues that the institutions of negotiation that are used to further women's equality in employment may be ill-suited to achieving this goal, in part because they were originally developed to serve substantially different ends. The greatest successes of the Social Partners entail negotiations over improvements in workers' wages, hours, and working conditions so as to take the cost of labor out of competition among employers (usually through encompassing meso-level bargaining). But the institutions structuring these negotiations can neither compensate for women's lack of collective bargaining power nor include substantive issues that may be inappropriate subjects for labor-management negotiations. This chapter concludes by considering an alternative, occupation-based, two-pronged strategy for representing and furthering women's interests through political channels as well as collective bargaining at the EU level. The success of such an approach would appear to require that women's groups take over some of the interest representation and negotiation functions traditionally carried out by trade unions.

The EU and Employment-Related Outcomes for Women

During most of the postwar period and virtually everywhere in the advanced capitalist world, the institutions of labor-management relations have been most highly developed in manufacturing, male, manual-worker régimes. Wages, working conditions, possibilities for advancement, and other terms and conditions of employment for service workers, nonmanual workers, and thus women in particular have been more or less strongly influenced by negotiations in the traditional arena. The strength of this influence has depended, first, on the cohesiveness and centralization of employment relations institutions in each country, and, second, on the relative conservatism or egalitarianism of national political cultures. As a result, scholarly "discussions of the quality and form of collective bargaining still often relate primarily to industrial and manual work-forces" (Rubery and Fagan 1995: 210).

Indeed, employment outcomes for women are still largely determined in this way, especially in countries in which the male-breadwinner model still strongly informs employment structures and policies (Lewis 1993) or in which politicians are more likely to insist that the principle of national "subsidiarity" trumps EU policies and directives, especially in such "social" matters as labor policy (Ostner and Lewis 1994). Recently, however, EU-level social policy debates have highlighted and begun vigorously to address long-unresolved problems of gender inequality in employment.

In April 1998 the European Commission adopted a communication on its Social Action Programme 1998–2000, in which employment policy was moved to the center of the EU agenda. The force of this development is underscored by the commission's call for National Action Plans on employment, which are to serve as the basis for an integrated European employment strategy (European Foundation, May 1998). Regarding the National Action Plans at Cardiff, the EU found (among other things) that further work is required in the areas of "strengthening actions on equal opportunities by ensuring that equality between men and women is mainstreamed in all employment policies; [and] promoting family-friendly working practices, including suitable childcare and parental leave schemes" (European Foundation, June 1998).

In its meeting at Essen in 1994, the European Parliament had declared that equal opportunities for women and men should be as important a priority as the (still severe) problem of unemployment (European Foundation, March 1998). The European Commission's first annual report on equal opportunities contains the theme of "mainstreaming," or "the systematic consideration of the differences between the conditions, situations and needs of men and women in all Community policies, at the point of planning, implementation and evaluation." This was a key priority at the Fourth UN Conference on Women held in Beijing in 1995 and has been at least rhetorically raised to prominence in all aspects of EU policy debate and policy making (European Foundation, March 1998).[2] In addition, allocations from the EU Structural Fund are beginning to take the target of mainstreaming into account: for over five years the European Social Fund (ESF) and the European Regional Development Fund have been trying to incorporate equal opportunities into their funding of training programs (European Foundation, March 1998).

At the Luxembourg Summit on Employment in March 1998, the European Women's Lobby (EWL) and the ETUC suggested that member states' national employment plans pay close attention to the qualities of women's employment and unemployment (women comprise a disproportionately

---

[2] Article 6 of the 1997 Amsterdam Treaty also affirms the principle of nondiscrimination in employment matters, and Article 3 includes the principle of mainstreaming (European Foundation, January 1998).

large portion of long-term unemployed workers in many EU countries).[3] The Luxembourg guidelines call for stronger public sector policies at the national level to ensure (1) equal opportunities at work, (2) further movement toward the goal of equal pay for work of equal value, and (3) greater child care availability (ETUI, March 1998).[4]

According to the EWL and the ETUC, however, women's needs are not adequately mainstreamed in the Luxembourg guidelines on work reorganization, training, and unemployment (ETUI, March 1998). Also not addressed at the Luxembourg Summit is the prevalence of both undeclared work and large informal sectors in many EU member countries. Workers in the informal sector usually are not covered by collective bargaining agreements or even by most national labor policies. Undeclared work (much of it in the informal sector) has approximately doubled since the 1970s (to account for between 7 and 16 percent of the gross domestic product [GDP] in EU member countries). In Greece, Italy, Portugal, and Spain, undeclared work accounts for between 20 and 35 percent of national GDP—most of it performed by women working out of their homes or in the informal retail trade, private services, and textile and agriculture sectors. Because women are more strongly represented than men in the informal sector, they are less likely to benefit either from protections coming directly from the Social Partners *or* from EU directives, however egalitarian they may be. In April 1998 the European Commission finally adopted a communication on undeclared work, calling for debate on this growing problem.

A related problem is atypical employment, also concentrated among women and notorious for its low pay and poor benefits. Atypical employment has grown at an enormous pace throughout the EU in the past decade. The vast majority of these workers are women working part-time. In June 1997 the European Social Partners concluded agreements about regularizing part-time work, which gave some part-time workers some of the benefits and job-security provisions afforded to most full-time workers. The unions remain dissatisfied, however, with the extent to which part-time workers are protected by these agreements.[5]

---

[3] The Luxembourg Summit also emphasized the need to support higher levels of female labor-force participation; policies on career breaks, parental leave, and part-time work; and good quality care for children and other dependents.

[4] The European Commission in 1996 adopted a code of practice on the implementation of equal pay for work of equal value for women and men, as well as a directive (adopted in December 1997) that reverses the burden of proof in cases of alleged sex discrimination, thus requiring that employers must now show there has *not* been discrimination (European Foundation, January 1998).

[5] In March 1998 negotiations were opened on the rights of workers employed under fixed-term contracts. The ETUC aims to establish the maximum duration of fixed-term contracts,

"Women's Issues" and the Limits of Trade Unionism

What can unions do to address these problems? The image of the male breadwinner, assuming a family wage, remains dominant in most EU countries. Rising male unemployment and changing family practices undermine this assumption, but its vestiges are still visible in both collective bargaining processes and wage structures. Women continue to be underrepresented in collective bargaining and on the decision-making bodies of trade unions, employers, and employer associations (European Foundation, January 1998).

The European Commission's report on equal opportunities found that "while *some* trade unions have instituted positive action measures to address the imbalance between men and women in their own structures, employers' organizations doubt the necessity for positive action" (European Foundation, March 1998, italics added). The ETUC has also complained that the Social Partners are inadequately involved, and that business is insufficiently interested, in helping to draw up National Action Plans. The ETUC wants to negotiate over training, working time, and work organization. In advance of the European Council's meeting at Cardiff in June 1998, however, UNICE expressed its view that, especially with respect to employment policies, national sovereignty should take precedence (European Foundation, June 1998).

The public rhetorical position of the ETUC seems rather removed from these realities. Emilio Gabaglio, general secretary of the ETUC, believes, for instance, that "subsidiarity and solidarity go hand in hand" and that "it would be intolerable if the Union were to find itself after completing the Internal Market and Economic and Monetary Union with no powers to take effective action articulated with that of other Member States in areas like taxation, social policy, workers' and citizens' rights" (European Foundation, June 1998). But do subsidiarity and solidarity go hand in hand, in practice? So far, the evidence remains unconvincing.

It is not hard to understand why the Social Partners have not made greater strides on women's employment-related issues—given the incentives established by current institutional structures. Employer associations

---

the number of times they may be renewed, and the bases for collective bargaining agreements on fixed-term contracts (European Foundation, February 1998; ETUI, March 1998).

In December 1995 the EU Social Partners reached an agreement on minimal parental leave provisions. However, part-time workers, 80 percent of whom in the EU are women (ETUI, July 1997), are not as likely to have access to such leave. Moreover, unions and women's groups remain dissatisfied with this agreement because it fails to include even minimal provisions for *paid* leave. Thus, even if part-time workers were to have access to parental leave, the question remains whether they would be able to afford to take it.

and governments generally negotiate regularly with collective representatives of workers, in part to take some of the costs of labor out of competition among employers. This has been most successful in the northern European ("Germanic") countries with relatively centralized institutions of employment relations: Germany, Denmark, Sweden, and Austria. The EU is also designed to take some of the costs of macro-economic policies out of competition among EU member countries. The goal has been to create social and economic institutions that could increase productivity and national competitiveness by loosening restrictions on the movement of capital, goods, and labor (that is, by expanding the market). Regarding employment relations, the EU has focused on the institutions and dynamics associated with the Germanic countries, not the more political approaches of labor movements in the Latin countries or the more fragmented Anglo "free market" economies. The EU has made its most impressive progress with regard to *economic* issues (the single market and currency, for example). It has made less notable gains on the political or social front. Since labor issues are considered to be social issues, progress on these has been comparatively slow. Where progress is evident, it usually reflects the extension of national or subnational (usually Germanic) institutions to the EU level (such as European Works Councils, maximum working hours, minimum parental leave provisions, and industry-specific negotiations).

There are no tried and true models, solutions, or institutions to address most of the problems facing women in the paid labor force (or women who might like to be). This is partly because outcomes for women not only vary substantially across countries but also appear to entail significant negative trade-offs. Relatively high levels of occupational segregation are accompanied in Sweden, for example, by a relatively small gender wage gap. In France, good national child care provisions apparently have not had much of an effect on occupational segregation by gender. These trade-offs confound searches for European-wide solutions to women's labor market problems in existing national or subnational approaches. In addition, women are handicapped by a lack of collective bargaining leverage. Finally, some widespread "women's issues" (child care, for instance) may not allow for negotiated solutions between the Social Partners.

I have argued elsewhere (Wever 1998) that these circumstances offer an opening for unions to boost membership among women workers by tackling gender inequalities in employment. Analysis of the problems considered in this chapter casts doubt on this proposition, however. Labor-union density has declined in almost all the advanced capitalist economies in recent decades. Part of this decline reflects the shift from employment in manufacturing (mostly unionized, male) to employment in the service sector (largely nonunion, female). Unions trying to gain new members among the service sector work force have not had much luck, however, when using traditional organizing techniques. Unions might be able to start to reverse membership declines by appealing to women on the basis of women's issues and "new" employment issues (the regulation of contingent work and the formalization of informal work; see, for example, Bronfenbrenner and Juravich 1995; Crain 1994). If this were possible, and if national unions could gain bargaining leverage that could be applied at the EU level, employer associations might be more willing to use the channels of negotiation created by the EU to bargain over, regularize, and improve employment outcomes for women.

The mere coexistence of unmet demand (for collective representation among women) and ready supply (unions eager to increase membership rolls) does not necessarily create the impetus to link the two. Among other things, the conservatism of many large industrial unions casts doubt on their ability to meet the specific needs of working women. Many women rightly perceive unions as performing functions not aligned with their interests in reducing gender inequalities. Even if women did join unions in droves, and even if the costs of their demands could be spread across employers, it is not clear that employers or their associations would give in to the demands of the representatives of a collective whose members' labor market positions (low skills and high unemployment) are generally weak. Thus, it is hard not to conclude that EU-level efforts to address gender inequalities in employment outcomes require new institutions and new forms of negotiating.

Many of the obstacles mentioned here could hypothetically be avoided or overcome if women were organized by women's groups, pursuing coordinated political *and* bargaining demands, along occupational lines. Consider, for example, the classic alternatives to the Germanic model: the craft-occupational unionism of the Anglo-American, and to some extent the Latin (especially the French), cases. If women could be organized by type of job (such as cleaners or low-level clericals) and by women's groups or new women's unions, their representatives could bargain simultaneously over wages and working conditions and lobby for improved basic labor standards.

The EWL has spurred many of the EU-level initiatives catalogued here. In France and Canada, labor and government have negotiated with employers to secure basic work standards and improved benefits for temporary workers (Carré 1995). What has not been systematically tried is the coordination of political lobbying with collective bargaining, aimed at improving conditions for women in particular types of jobs. Political pressures could target EU-wide standards regarding atypical work, for instance, while women's collective representatives tried to engage employers and employer associations in negotiations over basic working conditions and wage floors (based on the euro).

It would not be hard to identify collectives of women whose common cross-national employment-related interests could be quickly ascertained and articulated. The EU itself has commissioned research identifying the occupations into which women are crowded, and detailed information on these exists in the public domain (see Grimshaw and Rubery 1997). Linkages across these occupational groupings could develop on the basis of shared, or even universal, concerns (equal employment opportunities, equal pay for work of equal value, equal access to high-quality training programs, improvements in national child care provisions, and so on).

At least some of the women who might join the new occupation-based collectives would already be represented by unions, probably industrial unions. This is another reason why new women's organizations might be better suited than traditional unions to attacking employment-related equality policies and occupation-specific collective bargaining demands. After all, these new organizations would not have to compete with unions for membership.[6] Furthermore, because of the concentration of women in certain types of jobs throughout the EU member countries, it would be relatively easy to coordinate efforts across national boundaries. Differences across unions, in industrial structure, union structure, or political-religious affiliation, for instance, would not arise. Jurisdictional disputes could be limited by the fact that this approach would require the establishment of new institutions that could anticipate such difficulties.

This approach would certainly run into some fairly obvious difficulties. One would be the problem of forcing policy compliance among member countries. Another would be that women's weak leverage in collective negotiations would not automatically be strengthened, making the simultaneous pursuit of a political lobbying strategy all the more important. Third, negotiations with the existing EU-wide employer associations would be complicated by the fact that they are not organized along occupational lines. This could work for, as well as against, occupationally defined collectives of women, however. While it would probably be difficult for existing employer associations to adapt their organizational structures to occupation-specific bargaining, the bargaining itself might be eased by the fact that virtually all member associations and individual employers

---

[6] For instance, membership in Holland's Women's Union often coincides with membership in a traditional industrial union engaged in regular collective bargaining.

represented would be involved. After all, most large companies in Europe employ cleaners and low-level clerical workers, the occupations most EU women are in.

Three factors speak most forcefully for the adoption of an approach such as that just outlined. First, the European Social Partners have not been especially effective in managing the forces for change affecting women in the paid labor market. Familiar approaches are not working, at least not working quickly enough. Second, there is the inevitable continuing growth of the service sector in all EU member countries, especially those in which it remains relatively underdeveloped. Thus, women's potential bargaining leverage is bound to increase, if not through skills at least through sheer numbers. Third, by pursuing this two-pronged approach, occupation-based women's collectives could perform a function analogous to taking the cost of labor out of competition among companies at the national or subnational level: they could take some of the costs of reducing gender inequalities in employment out of competition among countries, as well as companies.

Part IV

Negotiations in Other Arenas

14

Applying the Insights of Walton and McKersie to the Environmental Context

MAX H. BAZERMAN

ANDREW J. HOFFMAN

Ben Cone used sustainable forestry techniques on his 6,200-acre woodland in North Carolina for over sixty years. Yet, in the 1990s he clear-cut a large segment of his land when he feared he would find the endangered red-cockaded woodpecker on his property. Concerned about losing the rights to freely manage his land, he liquidated its value by cutting down all the trees. He did this in anticipation of a dispute with the government over the Endangered Species Act (ESA). The ESA protects endangered or threatened species and attempts to restore them to a secure status in the wild. Once a species is listed, the act forbids the killing, harassing, possessing, or removing of that species from the wild. Cone's response was not the one desired for species protection, but it was consistent with the distributive mentality of negotiation described by Walton and McKersie (1965).

Like Cone, it is not uncommon for many negotiators in the environmental arena to base action on overly simplistic assumptions. Some adopt a distributive lens. Others adopt an integrative lens. The result is a political debate, at the expense of mutually beneficial discussions. We argue that this was the general state of the negotiation literature prior to Walton and McKersie's 1965 classic work. Walton and McKersie provided the critical understanding of the simultaneous nature of integrative and distributive processes, as well as the need for attitudinal structuring and intra-organizational bargaining. As they (1965: 8) noted, "While it is important to acknowledge previous contributions to our understanding of these (the four subprocesses) aspects of negotiation, it is equally important . . . to state what we regard as the limitations of these contributions. They have tended to deal with the dynamics or results of only one of these processes." As we will see, a third of a century later the environmental literature has been limited by the same myopia. We seek to bring Walton and McKersie's wisdom to the environmental domain.

Why did Cone cut down his trees? He assumed that anything desired by the government would be bad for him—what is now often referred to as the "mythical fixed-pie" of negotiation (Bazerman 1983). The most common reason why negotiators fail to find optimal outcomes is that they do not look for trade-offs that can enlarge the pool of resources to be distributed. It is important to note that it was not the implementation of the ESA that caused Cone's hasty actions, but rather his misperceptions of it. After the story became a touchstone for ESA critics, it was revealed that considerations for endangered species influenced only 15 percent of Cone's land. He was free to continue thinning trees on the remaining land as he had done for years. Furthermore, the U.S. Fish and Wildlife Service repeatedly offered Cone proposals that would have insulated him from future ESA responsibilities. He refused to cooperate, however, fearing that if the environmentalists want it, it must be bad for his business. Cone's fear of the complete economic loss of his assets led him toward a radical protective strategy. His belief in the win-lose nature of endangered species protection guided his unfortunate actions. We surmise that similar beliefs by many protagonists in environmental disputes end up with similar dysfunctional results.

Solutions existed to Cone's situation. In fact, the ESA provides a framework for finding a solution—Habitat Conservation Plans (HCPs). HCPs provide the opportunity to enlarge the pie by giving private landowners a permit to violate the specifics of the ESA, by allowing the "incidental taking" of listed species in the course of lawful development activities, provided that the landowner follows certain steps to provide for conservation of that species. HCPs can break the win-lose mentality by creatively developing plans that serve the interests of both endangered species protection and economic interests.

Before assuming that Ben Cone is unique in making such simplistic assumptions, it is critical to realize that many brilliant scholars committed errors similar to his in the negotiation literature prior to Walton and McKersie (1965). In fact, competing perspectives on the relationship between economic competitiveness and environmental protection are part of an active, highly visible debate today. Splitting into polarized camps, protagonists argue whether this relationship is inherently "win-lose" or "win-win." Win-lose proponents argue that environmental protection must reduce economic competitiveness (Walley and Whitehead 1994; Palmer, Oates, and Portney 1995). Win-win proponents argue that this framing of the issue is a false dichotomy, that economic competitiveness improves through environmental protection (Gore 1992; Porter and van der Linde 1995a, 1995b). We find it fascinating to see such impressive writers arguing for one incomplete process or the other, rather than recognizing the simultaneous nature of these alternatives.

On the win-lose side, Palmer, Oates, and Portney (1995) argue that environmental demands "must," by their very nature, result in reduced profits for the firm. Walley and Whitehead (1994) add that the existence of a win-win, or cost-free, solution to environmental problems neither makes sense nor is recognized. Walley and Whitehead further argue that any euphoria over the win-win scenario is not only "unrealistic" and "misleading" but also "dangerous." Fundamentally, they state that "ambitious environmental goals have real economic costs. As a society, we may rightly choose those goals despite their costs, but we must do so knowingly. And we must not kid ourselves. Talk is cheap; environmental efforts are not" (Walley and Whitehead 1994: 2–3).

In contrast, the win-win side sees environmental gains as complementing economic objectives: "the costs of addressing environmental regulations can be minimized, if not eliminated, through innovation that delivers other competitive benefits" to the firm (Porter and van der Linde 1995b: 125). These authors go on to argue that "emissions are a sign of inefficiency and force a firm to perform non-value creating activities such as handling, storage and disposal. . . . Reducing pollution is often coincident with improving the productivity with which resources are used" (Porter and van der Linde 1995a: 105). Gore (1992: 342) adds that "some companies have found that in the process of addressing their environmental problems they have been able to improve productivity and profitability at the same time. . . . An emphasis on environmental responsibility makes good business sense." Win-win proponents hold that the key to realizing benefits lies in "a new frame of reference for thinking about environmental improvement" (Porter and van der Linde 1995b: 127).

Consistent with Walton and McKersie (1965), we argue that these contrasting frames of reference are not only unnecessarily polarized but also fundamentally incomplete. Conflict between economics and the environment is a mixed-motive situation, where the balancing of environmental and economic interests is neither purely cooperative nor purely competitive. While the present debate is forming as an ideological conflict between intractable positions, we see an alternative model (adapted from Walton and McKersie) that offers a more productive outlook on resolving this issue—one in which elements of both positions can be integrated. Within this mixed-motive perspective, we argue that too many opportunities are missed that could move the contentious debate out to a more efficient set of solutions. That is, we argue that it would be healthier for the protagonists to argue over a more optimal set of possible solutions.

In the rest of this chapter we consider a mixed-motive model of the economic-environment debate that we developed with colleagues (Hoffman et al. 1999), based on the work of Walton and McKersie. In the spirit of their original inquiry, we seek to survey the unique character of the environmental context. Specifically, we focus on the cognitive barriers to accepting our mixed-motive perspective in the environmental arena. Finally, we offer some concluding thoughts about future research on the interaction of economic and environmental objectives.

The Mixed-Motive Perspective

We argue that instead of engaging in an empirical debate concerning the frequency of win-win opportunities, scholars and practitioners are better served by recognizing the inherently mixed-motive nature of environmental disputes. Win-win and win-lose perspectives have the advantage of simplicity. They have the disadvantage of being wrong. It has become an easy task for each side to provide counterexamples that show that the other perspective is incomplete. We (Hoffman et al. 1999) have argued that a mixed-motive perspective can facilitate the negotiation of more efficient agreements.

Virtually all negotiations involve a distributive element. As Figure 14.1 shows, one party's gain comes at the expense of another. The pool of resources is considered fixed and parties negotiate over their allocation.

The most influential and controversial legislation on the use of property is the ESA, which exemplifies legislation that has led parties to focus on a win-lose perspective to negotiation. Many people see the ESA as pitting economic interests against environmental protection. To anti-environmentalists, the idea of giving up jobs to save owls sounds absurd. The economy is the central concern. To environmentalists, economic sacrifices are unfortunate but necessary to protect endangered species. The most extreme environmentalists see the protection of the natural ecosystem as priceless.

As parties fight to enhance or weaken endangered species legislation and the interpretation of such legislation, environmental and economic interests establish intractable positions and fight a win-lose battle. Recently, for example, the Sierra Club voted to oppose all logging on all federal land, allowing no room for integrative negotiations (Hoffman et al. 1999). Many advocates for the timber industry have equally extreme positions, advocating their absolute rights to harvest land. Such debates are couched in win-

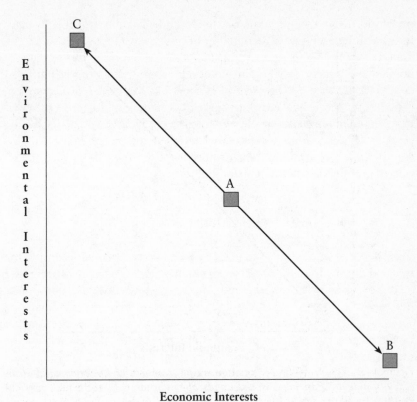

Figure 14.1. The Win-Lose Negotiation. From *Competitive Environmental Strategy: A Guide to Changing Business Landscape* by Andrew J. Hoffman. Copyright © 2000 by Island Press. Reprinted by permission of Island Press, Washington, D.C. and Covelo, California. All rights reserved.

lose language. If species protection is weakened, we move from point A to point B in Figure 14.1, helping economic interests at the expense of environmental interests. If species protection is strengthened, we move to point C, helping environmental interests at the expense of economic interests. Both sides, of course, believe in the appropriateness of their position.

In contrast, most negotiations also involve an integrative element—the pool of resources is not fixed and parties can work to increase its size. Some land is more valuable to environmental interests, and some land is more valuable to economic interests. Timing of harvesting, the form of harvesting, specific habitat protection efforts, and many other issues increase the opportunity to create mutually beneficial trades. Once multiple issues are identified and the values the parties involved give each issue are explored, opportunities for integrative trade-offs arise. Any negotiation in

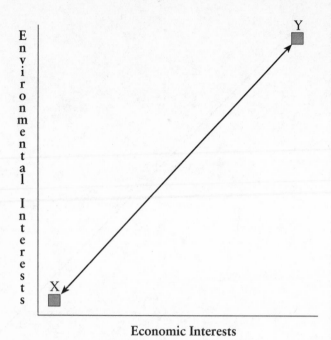

Figure 14.2. The Win-Win Negotiation. From *Competitive Environmental Strategy: A Guide to Changing Business Landscape* by Andrew J. Hoffman. Copyright © 2000 by Island Press. Reprinted by permission of Island Press, Washington, D.C. and Covelo, California. All rights reserved.

which there is more than one issue, with each party valuing issues differently, has integrative potential. Both parties can gain by integrating each other's interests into the agreement, as shown in Figure 14.2.

The distributive tug-of-war between economic and environmental interests will always persist, but so will opportunities to expand the scope of the debate, finding solutions that will improve the potential outcome simultaneously for both sets of interests. The chance to expand the realm of possible outcomes by merging the win-win and win-lose perspectives is illustrated in Figure 14.3, which shows that expanding the pie from point A to point D allows the parties to argue over whether to move toward points E or F, each an improvement for both sides (Hoffman et al. 1999).

Bazerman and Neale (1992) provided ample evidence that parties frequently fail to pick up the easy integrative gains because of a myopic focus on distributive gains and losses. Most readers can easily audit their own

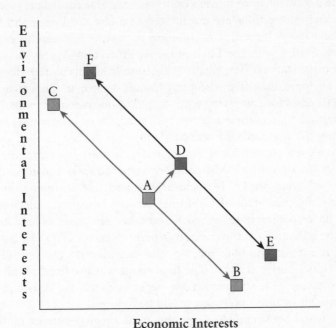

Figure 14.3 The Mixed-Motive Negotiation. From *Competitive Environmental Strategy: A Guide to Changing Business Landscape* by Andrew J. Hoffman. Copyright © 2000 by Island Press. Reprinted by permission of Island Press, Washington, D.C. and Covelo, California. All rights reserved.

houses, for example, to find energy-efficient improvements that are good for the environment and will save money. The mixed-motive model highlights the opportunity to realize gains that make all parties better off, without ignoring the need to divide the larger pie (Walton and McKersie 1965).

Endangered species protection is the area in which the win-lose perspective appears to predominate most in the battle between economic and environmental interests, even though implementation of the ESA provides opportunities for mixed-motive solutions to enhance both environmental and economic interests. Win-win advocates are ignored by those who focus on clear examples where the environment has economic costs, and win-lose advocates unfortunately dominate the debate. Opportunities to expand the pie are missed.

These win-lose positions, which are often based on misperceptions, prevent the argument from moving out to a more efficient debate (see Figure 14.3). Such interactions are not limited to a few vivid examples like the Ben Cone story. Indeed, it is common for major polluters to engage in win-lose battles with the Environmental Protection Agency or environmental organizations. Yet, creative deviation from this pattern does occur. In one example, the energy company Unocal created an innovative way to reduce its costs for complying with the pollution standards in the Los Angeles basin, by integrating interests with the State of California: Instead of following the standards for reducing emissions at their facility, the company achieved the required emissions reductions by scrapping older, higher-polluting vehicles. The company removed more pollution than required by buying pre-1971 cars at $600 apiece and scrapping them. The company and the State of California created emissions reductions that would have cost ten times as much and taken ten times as long had they made the reductions at the company's plant (Stegemeier 1995). Before declaring this a win-win outcome, we must note that the outcome also possessed a distributive element. The final result was not fixed simply by the creative solution; it still required a negotiation on the distributive side concerning how much pollution would be reduced.

Walton and McKersie's focus on the simultaneous existence of distributive and integrative dimensions reminds us that even after a mutually beneficial trade is created, environmentalists are able to identify an outcome that would further sacrifice economics for the environment, and economic interests are able to identify a preferred outcome that would further sacrifice the environment for the economy. It is better for the parties to have this battle along the efficient frontier, however. Integrative negotiation tactics allow for solutions that can only be found by expanding the realm of possible outcomes. We all stand to gain by approaching environmental issues with an eye toward their inherently integrative and distributive aspects. This mixed-motive perspective can lead to more effective searches for optimal outcomes that maximize both environmental and economic gains.

Cognitive Barriers to Efficient Environmental Trades

Disputants often fail to reach the efficient frontier of Figure 14.3 because of the assumption that their interests directly oppose the other party's. This is particularly true when the other side is viewed as the enemy, which is the prototypic case in environmental contexts. Bazerman (1983) labeled this assumption the "mythical fixed-pie." Floyd Spence, Republican member of Congress from South Carolina, demonstrated the mythical fixed pie when he stated, "I have had a philosophy for some time in regard to SALT, and it goes like this: the Russians will not accept a SALT treaty that is not in their best interest, and it seems to me that if it is in their best interests, it can't be in our best interest" (Ross and Stillenger 1991). This confused reasoning is both common and dangerous.

Spence's attitude is often seen in environmental disputes. A recent article advocating tighter regulation of hazardous waste dumps, for example, declared, "We must pass an effective Superfund law. If the polluters win, then we lose our tax money, our environment, and our health" (Pandya, Rosenfeld, and Caffee 1998). Yet, the government has spent more money trying to force polluters to clean up Superfund sites than it has spent on the clean-up itself (Bazerman, Moore, and Gillespie 1999). The mythical fixed pie leads people to the conclusion that they cannot gain by working with the "enemy." When one of us asked executives from corporate and environmental organizations attending negotiation seminars why they failed to make a mutually beneficial trade-off in simulated negotiations, the common response was that they did not know trade-offs were possible. Their fixed-pie assumptions kept them from seeing potential trade-offs.

The mythical fixed pie of negotiations is exacerbated by a series of other systematic cognitive mistakes, such as pseudosacredness, egocentrism, and overconfidence. *Pseudosacredness* refers to the false perception that an issue is not viable for a trade, when in fact that party would trade the issue with a good enough deal. The perception of sacredness eliminates the possibility for any discussion that would allow the discovery of that trade. *Overconfidence* is the tendency of negotiators to overestimate the likelihood that their judgment is correct (Bazerman and Neale 1992). *Egocentrism* refers to a self-serving bias in an honest assessment of what would be fair (Messick and Sentis 1985; Wade-Benzoni, Tenbrunsel, and Bazerman 1996). We see each of these attitudes as creating added barriers for reaching the efficient frontier of environmental negotiations. In fact, other biases could be added to the list, particularly in the case of environmental disputes.

Pseudosacredness

In most complex environmental negotiations, value includes not only the market value but also a component for an emotional or sacred attachment or unique appreciation of the item. We often hear words like *priceless* and *sacred* in environmental negotiations (Thompson and Gonzalez

1997). Tetlock, Petersen, and Lerner (1996) define sacred issues as items that the negotiator sees as unavailable for compromise or trade. It is useful to distinguish between two classes of sacred issues, however. Bazerman, Moore, and Gillespie (1999) argue that there are issues that a party would never trade under any realistic circumstance. These items are seen as so critical that to trade them is seen as morally reprehensible. There exists a second group of issues, however, that are labeled sacred, but for which the potential for trade does exist—items for which the negotiator does not ever expect to receive an offer that is good enough. This latter group is called *pseudosacred*. Bazerman, Moore, and Gillespie (1999) argue that the use of the sacred label can create a barrier to the discovery of a mutually beneficial trade. That is, when a party claims an issue to be sacred or nondiscussable, this may eliminate the search in that area for integrative options.

Douglas Medin (personal communication) tells of the Lacandon Maya population that believes that when a tree is cut down, a star falls from the sky. Despite this seemingly sacred view, the Lacandon obtained an agreement with the Mexican government for selective harvesting of the forest. When the tribal leader was asked how an agreement could be reached, the response was that the agreement was the best alternative for keeping as many stars in the sky as possible.

Claims of sacredness often stand in the way of finding integrative solutions. If a party will not discuss an issue, it is very difficult to find an agreement that requires that they give up part of that issue. The result can be a strike, a lawsuit, or armed conflict. We see pseudosacredness as a barrier to the discussion of issues that could create wise trades for all parties.

Overconfidence

Research shows that negotiators tend to be overconfident that their positions will prevail (Neale and Bazerman 1983; Bazerman and Neale 1982, 1992). They also tend to be overconfident in estimating the position of neutral third parties and in estimating the likelihood that the third party will accept their position. In the labor context, negotiators in final-offer arbitration consistently overestimate the probability that their final offer will be accepted.

We argue that overconfidence inhibits settlements in environmental disputes, despite the existence of a positive bargaining zone. Overestimating the likelihood that a particular position will be accepted reduces the willingness to compromise and the search for integrative trades. Overconfidence leads organizations and individuals to take inappropriately aggressive stances in environmental disputes. A critical ingredient in the search for integrative agreements is the need to find added value. When the parties falsely assume that they will prevail in the legislative or judicial process, the motivation to search for integrative trades is reduced.

Egocentrism

Substantial research shows that people make egocentric judgments in negotiation (Messick and Sentis 1985; Babcock, Loewenstein, Issacharoff, and Camerer 1995; Thompson and Loewenstein 1992). Negotiators justify their assessment of fairness by changing the importance of the attributes affecting what is fair (Diekmann, Samuels, Ross, and Bazerman 1997). As a result, negotiators judge that it is fair for them to have more of whatever is being allocated than an independent advisor would judge. This leads environmentalists to believe that the corporation is responsible for the pollution it creates, while leading the corporation to believe that its responsibilities are limited to its legal obligations.

Egocentrism acts as a barrier to the resolution of environmental conflicts. For example, a simulated social dilemma based on the real-life crisis in the fisheries of the northeastern United States found higher harvesting levels to coexist with higher levels of egocentrism (Wade-Benzoni, Tenbrunsel, and Bazerman 1996). The ongoing negotiations on global climate change also show egocentrism to be an obvious problem. Developed nations want the developing nations to share the burden, whereas developing nations feel the burden should be on the developed nations since they caused the problem. Developed nations see a cessation of the destruction of the rainforests as the most important solution to the issue of carbon dioxide emissions, while developing nations see the reduction in the burning of fossil fuels in the north as a more obvious solution. The different positions in economic development lead to egocentric interpretations of fairness.

The critical issue for this discussion is that these egocentric views lead to a debate on who will do how much, rather than a discussion of what trades can be made. The discussion of who is to blame ends up being a barrier to a wiser search for solutions.

Conclusion

Convincing parties in environmental disputes (and perhaps in other social arenas as well) to follow the guidance of Walton and McKersie (1965) on how to introduce integrative bargaining in mixed-motive situations will not be easy. The fixed-pie assumption is strong and impedes the recognition of the mixed-motive state of most complex negotiations. There is some evidence, however, that exposure to the other party's interests may help improve insight into the potential for integrative trades. It is necessary for the parties to understand integrative trade-offs for this experience to be beneficial, however. Thus, environmental disputants should learn about strategic and integrative issues in negotiation and think carefully about the potential for integration in their own disputes.

There are many reasons why outcomes to environmental disputes will be suboptimal. The fixed-pie assumption interferes with the identification and exploitation of opportunities for negotiators to integrate their interests. Pseudosacredness interferes with parties' ability to think clearly about their valuation of, and their willingness to trade on, value-laden issues. Egocentrism and overconfidence are likely to bias disputants' perception of a fair outcome and lead them to overestimate the righteousness of their own position, as well as their chances of winning in court. Trained negotiators will be more able to avoid these biases and come to more efficient agreements. It is critical, however, that negotiators break away from their assumptions about the nature of the conflict and approach negotiations with the anticipation of finding agreements that integrate interests. While the barriers are significant, disputants, society, and the planet all stand to benefit from wiser resolutions to environmental disputes.

15

Collective Bargaining and Public Policy Dispute Resolution

Similarities and Differences

LAWRENCE SUSSKIND

Community and regional planners in the United States have a difficult job. They not only are expected to prepare plans and formulate policies to shape future growth and development but also are expected to take account of the interests of "all affected parties" in everything they do. Thus, for several decades the planning profession has been trying to find ways of involving everyone in the process of setting goals, considering policy options, formulating detailed implementation strategies, and monitoring progress. Recently, planners have been forced to confront the downside of their success in promoting such citizen participation. Public involvement efforts have worked too well—everyone is now at the table demanding to be heard! Each interest group expects to have a hand in determining what is and is not done. So, planners are currently struggling to invent ways of dealing with the conflicts of their own making—disputes that are a by-product of increased public involvement.

Let me give some examples of public dispute resolution efforts. In one instance, a downtown veterans' hospital announced that it could no longer function effectively at its long-time location and that the scale of its operations (the number of beds) would have to be reduced dramatically. The prospect of reduction in size and relocation of the hospital, which also happened to be the largest employer in the city, was frightening to the predominantly elderly population. As the hospital considered alternative sites in the suburbs, veterans and residents responded angrily. Neighbors in most of the areas being considered as possible new sites were also unhappy—they did not welcome the traffic, the ambulance noise, and the other likely impacts of a new facility. After months of futile political bickering, the hospital engaged the assistance of a mediator. Three-dozen "representatives" of key stakeholder groups, which chose the representatives, met regularly (in public sessions) for more than a year with hospital and political officials. In the end, the group was able to recommend a new site in the city (which the state provided at almost no cost), a scaled-down but financially feasible facility, a plan for re-use of the old facility, and a strategy for ensuring that elderly residents would have immediate access to the round-the-clock medical assistance to which they had become accustomed. The joint problem-solving efforts were not easy, especially since few, if any, of the participants had ever been involved in anything similar, where merely voicing complaints was not sufficient.

A second case involved the U.S. Department of Housing and Urban Development (HUD). Congress pressed HUD to come up with a new formula for allocating what are called Section 8 certificates—subsidies for low- and moderate-income renters. Billions of dollars are allocated annually to thousands of qualified housing authorities so that qualifying households can afford to live in appropriately sized and priced units. Unfortunately, the "system" for allocation of Section 8 certificates seemed to be short-changing many agencies while others ended up with money in the bank and too few qualified households or units. With huge sums at stake, and Congress demanding that HUD move quickly, a mediation team was asked to help identify several-dozen representatives of key stakeholding groups, generate agreement on a consultative process for formulating new regulations (called *rules* in federal parlance), and then get agreement on the formula itself—all within eight months. What began as a zero-sum game (any gains to some agencies meant losses to others) quickly expanded in scope to include a wide range of concerns regarding HUD's administration of the Section 8 program and a series of contingent commitments. Agreement was reached in time, by consensus, to stave off further congressional action. These two examples are typical of the public disputes that are now mediated regularly, at every level of government, in the United States.

Fifteen years ago, I set out to determine what planners could learn about managing such conflicts and settling public policy disputes by studying the lessons that have been learned in international relations and in labor relations. One of the most important people I met along the way was Bob McKersie.[1] At that time, I faced three difficulties. First, the pro-

---

[1] Bob McKersie's insights and support have been crucial to the long-term development of the Program on Negotiation. As the first executive director of the program, I was always able to

cesses I wanted to study were themselves in flux. No sooner had I gotten a sense of the dynamics of labor relations than I realized that the processes of contract bargaining were being transformed and reinterpreted. The same thing was true in international relations. For an outsider trying to master two rapidly changing fields, the chances of missing the forest for the trees were great, so I turned to Bob and several other colleagues for guidance. Second, to make sense of what I was learning I needed a theoretical frame in which to place the insights that Bob and others were offering. The theory of interest-based (or what I call mutual-gains) negotiation, developed through the inter-university Program on Negotiation, provided that frame.[2] Some of the key ideas at the heart of interest-based negotiation grew out of the published work of Bob McKersie and his colleague Richard Walton (Walton and McKersie 1965). When my efforts to extrapolate from labor relations and international relations to the world of public policy foundered at various points, the differences in context overwhelming the similarities, Bob provided valuable support and advice.

Now, as I look back on the entire experience, it seems amazing to me that there was a period when I (1) did not see the important overlaps between the worlds of collective bargaining and public policy dispute resolution, (2) did not understand the significance of the differences between the two, and (3) did not understand the contribution to negotiation theory that a comparative analysis of these separate worlds had to offer. It is now a good time to reflect on what I have learned about these three points.

---

count on Bob for advice and encouragement. The task of building an organization straddling three universities was no small challenge, and Bob always understood how to weave a sufficiently tight institutional web so that we could hold things together without binding ourselves too tightly and cutting off opportunities for innovation. As we tried to balance our commitments to both theory building and practice, Bob helped to set the tone. He has a great feel for the advantages of such interaction and a wonderful capacity to envision these connections before they come into focus for the rest of us. Finally, for me personally, Bob has been a supportive tutor as I tried to make sense of the changing world of labor relations. Every time I thought I knew what I was looking at and how it was changing, Bob offered one more bit of interpretation to challenge my all-too-simplistic attempt at synthesis. All of us working in the field of negotiation have benefited enormously from Bob's clarity of mind, his long-term perspective, and his wise counsel.

2 The Program on Negotiation at Harvard Law School was created in 1983 by faculty members from Harvard, MIT, and Tufts University. The consortium is still in operation. More than two-dozen faculty members from at least a dozen disciplines and professional fields are working to improve the theory and practice of negotiation. A great many books—including *Getting to Yes* (Fisher, Ury, and Patton 1991), *The Art and Science of Negotiation* (Raiffa 1982), *Social Conflict* (Rubin, Pruitt, and Kim 1994), and *Negotiating on Behalf of Others* (Mnookin and Susskind 1999)—have helped to make the case for an interest-based or a mutual-gains approach to negotiation.

The Similarities between Collective Bargaining and Public Policy Dispute Resolution

There are several important similarities between dispute resolution in the collective bargaining world and dispute resolution in the world of community planning and public policy. First, distinct interest groups within the same community *must* find some accommodation or neither will be able to reap the benefits of community membership. Obviously, in the collective bargaining context, if labor and management are unable to find common ground, a unionized work setting will fall apart, causing a company to lose market share and ultimately its competitive advantage. When this happens, both management and labor invariably suffer. Somewhat less obviously, if the factions in an urban area fail to agree on how their community should develop, and spend all of their time trying to thwart one another, that place will lose its competitive appeal and ultimately fail to attract or retain investment and residents. It is only recently through the work of Michael Porter (1998) and others that city leaders have begun to realize that "social capital," represented by a consensus on how public resources should be used, can be crucial in attracting new investment and expanding the local labor pool.

The second similarity concerns the need to establish procedures that help to institutionalize useful ways of dealing with conflicting interests. The history of industrial relations is primarily a story about the ways in which competing interests (labor and management) have adopted rules that make it possible for them to move forward together in spite of their differences. In the public policy arena, the electoral and administrative machinery of government should facilitate the search for common interests, but it rarely does (see Susskind and Cruikshank 1987). Some additional means of brokering agreement on how to use scarce resources or set priorities is required. Slowly, as the results of numerous experiments have accumulated, consensus building in the public arena has emerged as a supplement to the fundamental processes of representative democracy.

In various ways, consensus building in the public sector parallels the key features of collective bargaining in unionized work settings (Susskind, McKearnan, and Thomas-Larmer 1999). Representatives of key stakeholding groups must come together in an extended joint problem-solving process. These representatives must take responsibility for keeping their constituents informed about the progress of the negotiations and must be accountable to those constituents. There is typically a range of issues that must be packaged in some way. The product of the conversation needs to take the form of a written agreement that spells out the responsibilities of

all parties. And, along the way, the parties often need the help of a professional mediator. The key is to find a way of exploiting the fact that everyone has what McKersie and Walton called *mixed motives*. In fact, if negotiators work together they can create value, even as they seek to claim for
themselves the largest share of the value they have helped to create.

Third, when the parties in a collective bargaining context seek only to
win at the expense of the "other side," acting as if all choices can only be
handled in a zero-sum fashion—and arranging the dynamics of their bargaining process accordingly—they will almost always miss opportunities
to "create value" and inevitably, will achieve suboptimal results. In the
public policy arena, the same is true. Nevertheless, it has taken an enormous effort to win credibility for the notion that public policy making
need not be a zero-sum process and that consensus-building techniques
(that go beyond lobbying and voting) can be used to invent positive-sum
outcomes. In the land-use planning field, for example, the presumption
has been that if a group succeeds in preserving open space, the economy
will suffer, and that if economic development is allowed to go forward,
environmental quality must be forsaken. However, there are numerous examples of "assisted negotiation" producing sustainable development plans
that protect fragile environmental resources while promoting economic investment (see Susskind, Levy, and Thomas-Larmer 1999).

The fourth similarity concerns the help that neutrals can offer. The role
of neutrals (mediators, for example) in collective bargaining is so well established (in practice and in law) that participants in labor relations hardly
think twice about it. They understand how a neutral "adds value" both
before and after a bargaining process reaches impasse. Now, after nearly
two decades of experimentation in the public dispute resolution field, the
success of mediation is clear. Indeed, the contributions of mediation have
actually helped to recast the theoretical metaphor of planning—moving
from an image of the planner as expert offering technical advice, to the
planner as mediator, facilitating a public dialogue leading to informed
agreement.

This change has created some confusion, however. Mediators in the
labor relations field are clearly not part of either labor or management.
They exist as a separate category of actors with their own organizational
and professional identity. That is not the case, yet, in the public policy mediation field. Most of the people who mediate public policy disputes have
a planning or public administration background. While they identify
themselves as mediators and belong to umbrella organizations like the Society for Professionals in Dispute Resolution (recently renamed the Association of Conflict Resolution), they continue to maintain their affiliation

with professional planning and public management associations. This means that the interveners who seek to mediate public policy disputes are sometimes part of the city's planning staff. From the standpoint of a neighborhood upset with what the government has proposed to do in its area, the idea that someone in city hall, regardless of the skills he or she might have, could be neutral is almost impossible to accept. So, as planners pursue the notion that they can mediate public policy disputes, they need to separate themselves from their former government identities.

Public dispute mediators have learned a lot from their counterparts in the labor relations field. Foremost, they have learned that a dispute resolution process cannot be rushed, and that mediation must unfold in a way that takes account of both the internal and the external relationships of the parties. In addition, mediators with relevant experience in a particular sector are more likely to be able to "add value" there than those who do not have appropriate background and experience. Third, while the parties to an agreement have to "own it" and feel that it is theirs, they also may need the neutral to take part of the responsibility (or blame, as the case may be) when it comes time to sell the agreement to a particular constituency. Finally, public dispute mediators have come to appreciate the diversity and eclecticism of labor mediation. No single approach to mediation always works or is even always appropriate.

The Differences

Planning involves a lot more than two parties. Indeed, planning often involves a great many interest groups (with enormous asymmetrical power) that are poorly organized and unable to articulate their concerns. While the same internal debates within stakeholder groups exist in both collective bargaining and public dispute resolution, the process of selecting representatives to speak for each "side" is not at all developed in the public policy world. Efforts to select ad hoc representatives to participate in consensus-building efforts in the public arena are sometimes thwarted by elected officials who feel that they are the only legitimate spokespeople (to say nothing of their claim to being guardians of the public interest). It is not at all obvious that an organized system of bargaining agents that works in the collective bargaining arena will work in the public policy world. In addition, the number and scope of issues on the agenda in a community or public policy setting can be staggering. And the agenda is constantly changing. In a collective bargaining context, the range of issues may be significant, but ultimately patterns develop. I don't think the same can be said for public policy or community disputes. This kaleidoscope of issues presents all kinds of obstacles to the institutionalization of public dispute resolution. As policy questions change, so too do the boundaries of the policy arena. This makes it extremely difficult to design effective and stable dispute-handling systems. While the practice of mediation in the world of collective bargaining has solidified, this has not been (and may never be) the case in the public dispute resolution field.

Long-time industrial relations experts take for granted the system of representation that has evolved (by law) in the United States. The rank-and-file accept the legitimacy of their bargaining agents (even though there is always jockeying to see who will take over as head of the union). The se-lection of ad hoc representatives (nonelected leaders) to participate in pub-lic dispute resolution efforts is still quite controversial. And corporate rep-resentatives in public disputes (unlike their counterparts in collective bargaining situations) tend to question whether spokespeople for environ-mental advocacy and other unofficial groups can, in fact, represent their members' interests.

The number of parties involved in public policy mediation efforts is startling to long-time labor mediators. It is not uncommon, for example, to have thirty or more participants (even up to one hundred!) at the table in a public dispute resolution effort. Each expects to speak for himself or herself, and they are not organized into a small number of sides or cau-cuses. Indeed, caucusing in the world of public dispute resolution is quite chaotic. Mediators often have to work in teams just to handle the prob-lems of scale that really have no parallel in a collective bargaining context.

One other difference—the importance of scientific or technical informa-tion—is also worth noting. In a great many public disputes, particularly those involving standards of environmental or human health and safety, it is crucial that the parties get the science right. Merely satisfying the con-cerns of the parties at the table is not sufficient. A mistake could literally kill people! So the mediation process in the public policy world has to en-sure careful consideration of scientific and technical input (Ozawa 1991). Again, there is no parallel in collective bargaining.

The Theoretical Importance of the Similarities and Differences

For those of us interested in the link between theory and practice, the sim-ilarities between efforts to resolve public policy disputes and the mediation of collective bargaining disputes are interesting—suggesting new ap-proaches to try and opportunities for possible improvement. The differences, however, are daunting. How far can we go in applying the ideas from one field in a very different setting?

From a theory-building standpoint, there are two points that have struck me as especially important about these similarities and differences. First, the internal conflicts within the union side and within the management side (and how they are handled) are absolutely essential to explaining how any labor-management negotiation works out. We must understand how to translate this insight into the application of mediation in the context of community and public policy disputes. Second, it is possible for an "organization" to learn to negotiate in new and more effective ways. In the collective bargaining context, this often requires joint training in a mutual-gains approach to negotiation for bargaining-team members from both labor and management. While this is a difficult task, we know it can be done. We are slowly importing the idea of joint training in the mutual-gains approach to negotiation (and more generally the concept of organizational learning) into the world of public policy disputes. There are serious problems, though, to be solved.

For one thing, organizational memory in the public arena is getting shorter and shorter. This is partly a result of the politicization of the civil service. Every new administration that comes into office replaces additional layers of experienced administrators to ensure that they are supported by individuals who are loyal to them. In addition, fewer people seem committed to life-long public sector careers. It is now common for trained managers to move back and forth between the public and private sectors. Finally, there is an increasing level of cynicism in the public sector that seems to permit, if not encourage, changes in policy and the throwing-off of promises made by others. All of this means that many of the players involved in public disputes have to learn anew how the process of mediation works. There are few long-standing relationships in the public policy arena, such as those that exist in the labor relations world. This does not provide much to build on.

What Roger Fisher (1989) dubbed "the inside-outside problem" has special significance in the public dispute resolution field. Unlike labor leaders, most of the participants in public policy disputes are not empowered, let alone obliged, to speak for their members. This is as true for official agency representatives as it is for the spokespeople for ad hoc coalitions, like a new neighborhood association that has sprung up in response to a recent government proposal. So while individuals arriving at a mediation session in the public policy world may have canvassed their "constituents," the odds are they have no systematic way of doing this and no sense that they are obligated to do so. In the labor relations setting, we know that the union leadership can work with management to generate a proposal, but ultimately a vote of the membership will be required. Voting, however, won't work in the public policy arena. Many of the "constituencies" are not organized well enough to poll their members uniformly. Indeed, in many situations supposed members do not even know that they are being represented in an ad hoc negotiation.

Bob McKersie and I (along with Charles Heckscher and others) undertook a rather elaborate study for the Department of Labor in which our goal was to see if the strategy of "joint training" could be used to reduce the adversarial nature of the collective bargaining process (Susskind et al. 1990). We were invited into three collective bargaining situations—one in a university, one in a high-tech communications company, and one in a traditional manufacturing firm. We developed tailored training programs for all the members (on both sides) of the bargaining committee in each of the three situations. Over a period of months, we introduced the idea of mutual-gains negotiation and helped to formulate changes in the way the upcoming round of contract bargaining might be handled (to better maximize mutual gains). We had some success in two of the three situations, although subsequent rounds of contract bargaining did not reflect the level of institutional learning we had hoped might result.

For the past several years, I have tried through a not-for-profit entity called the Consensus Building Institute (CBI) to do the same thing in the public dispute resolution world. In one state CBI managed to get all the relevant environmental regulators (local, state, and federal) in a multi-session joint training program with regulated (chemical) companies and environmental advocates. The idea was that joint training might lead to a reduction in the adversarial nature of regulatory negotiations. Relationships were certainly enhanced as a result of the training. Whether this made a difference over time, however, is much less clear.

In the labor relations context, McKersie, Heckscher, and I were able to use joint training to generate a shared commitment to alter the bargaining process for the next round of contract negotiations. In the most successful cases, the modifications and improved relationships remained intact for two rounds of contract bargaining. After that, new leadership on one side or the other thought there might be some advantage to going back to the old model. Although this shift never produced especially good results for those who advocated it, it was a way to make a case for pushing aside the previous set of leaders.

In the public policy arena, it was very hard to get agreement even to participate in a joint training effort. Regulators were suspicious of and worried about any behind-the-scenes interactions with the regulated community. (Indeed, in one state CBI needed to get permission from the attorney general's office for joint training to take place.) When McKersie, Heckscher, and I were successful in mounting joint training, the results were modest. The players involved in the negotiations that followed were not in a position to decide whether to use a mutual-gains approach. Newly elected or appointed officials (most of whom had not participated in the joint training) did whatever they felt would advance their political interests at the time. In the few situations where we really managed to change relationships, the results faded rapidly.

Thus, as efforts are made to transfer dispute resolution methods from one context to another, mediators and others must be attentive to both similarities and differences. My experience has been that the most useful application of the ideas from labor relations in the public dispute resolution field has been through the "bridging" efforts of a facilitator or a mediator. Individuals in a neutral role can use what they have learned through comparative analysis without naming what they are doing or highlighting the effort to transfer an idea or a technique. If it works, the parties will accept it. If it doesn't, they will complain. In either case, it is probably not useful for the neutral to discuss the whys and wherefores of the transfer effort with the parties. Public dispute mediators can learn a lot more from labor mediators, and additional cross-contextual learning should be encouraged.

16

Negotiating Identity

First-Person Plural Subjective

LAVINIA HALL
CHARLES HECKSCHER

Negotiating Identity, Recognizing Equality

For a long time now, in our roles both as third-party helpers and as students of negotiation, we have wondered why so many integrative negotiation opportunities are not turned into successful agreements. Since, in a number of the cases we followed, mutual-gains processes were used to conduct the negotiations, we began to think that there was some basic flaw in that process.

These difficult cases shared a key element: a history of domination or oppression between the parties. We began to recognize that the dynamics of the dominator-dominated relationship were barring stable integrative agreements. Part of*f* what was missing in the negotiation dialogue was an acceptance of each side's sense of identity, especially as revealed in its interpretation of the past.

Our argument is that the source of these problems—the dynamics of identity development among the parties—is a dimension not often dealt with in the negotiations literature. An unchallenged assumption of most theories in our field is that parties approach the negotiating table as "players" with secure and independent identities and identifiable interests. This assumption is blatantly violated in dominator-dominated negotiations. In these instances the parties start from a historical relationship of inequality, which can be rebalanced only through uncovering and developing new collective identities. The parties literally communicate through a thick distorting screen in which the issues are not only about different values but also about different significances, with the result that they cannot negotiate effectively.

Characteristics and Dynamics
of Identity Negotiations

Negotiations in which identity is an issue are extremely long and tortuous, often continuing for generations, taking a step and a half backward for every two steps forward. They are highly volatile, subject to emotional explosions at unexpected moments. They seem regularly to miss opportunities for mutual-gains agreements, falling repeatedly into destructive patterns of mutual recrimination even under the guidance of experienced mediators and negotiation advisors.

History and memory, particularly the litanies of past wrongs perpetrated by the group across the table and the caveats that they necessarily hold about that group, are central subjects to the dominated group. The historically dominant group responds by allegations that the dominated group is wasting inordinate amounts of time and perhaps is not serious about negotiations. While the dominator group wants to "get on with it" and work on the present and future, the dominated group wants to revisit the experiences and inequities of the past. As a result, both groups feel unlistened to and unacknowledged, alleging that their chief purposes in negotiating are being undermined.

Here, we want to explore how both sides distort the negotiation process: the dominated by obsessively plowing the ground of collective past wrongs and the dominators by trying to ignore them and pretend that the issues are purely pragmatic matters of "real" interests. The problem is not that the interests are so divergent that there is no common ground for integrative solutions; rather, the parties' divergent identities demand that their painful histories of who they are and what they have done be resolved before they can move into a problem-solving space.

This approach is closer to an anthropological view than to standard negotiation theory. Anthropologists argue that (1) identity is defined in frames by specific relationships and words; (2) ethnic identities are defined in social interaction, not by cultural differences; and (3) individuals define themselves during presentations of rhetorical definitions of reality.

In this view when parties say "this is our tradition" or "this is what we believe," they "usually want to define the identity of their social group in order to assert its importance or to defend it against somebody else. Culture or tradition in this sense, therefore, is a rhetorical rather than analytical device" (Buckley and Kenney 1995: 213).

Equality

Permanent inequality teaches how to "enforce inequality, but not how to make the journey from unequal to equal" (Miller 1976: 5). The problem, as we see it, is to help both sides (1) have self-confident identities that include an understanding and acknowledgment (though not necessarily agreement) of each other's history and memories and (2) recognize each other as necessary and equal partners for a positive, interdependent future. Looking to our core questions of why integrative solutions are so often left on the negotiating table and what can be done to improve the outcome, we find that the parties' identities are divergent and that without resolving painful histories, their interests are "supercharged" as symbols of who they think they are and of claims of moral superiority.

A facilitator or mediator in such a situation faces difficult choices, particularly about whether to take a forward-looking approach or to explore the historical background. Our hypothesis is that in these cases there needs to be, prior to interest-based discussion, a phase in which the parties create at least the beginnings of a relationship of self-confident equality.

Collective Identity and Memory

The notion of collective identity is an old one, and in the twentieth century it was a core concept of classic sociology.[1] Only much more recently, however, has attention turned to the ways in which these memories and identities affect movements for liberation. Practical efforts came first, and interestingly, they originated with the dominators: it was they, in case after case, who recognized the importance of trying to root out all sources of collective memory among those they controlled. Thus, for example, in the case of the American Indians, whom we will use to illustrate our points, the governments of both Canada and the United States strove systematically to exterminate their native languages and to prevent the teaching of their traditions in the schools.

Dominated groups have begun trying consciously to recapture their heritage, especially since the 1960s. The Civil Rights movement changed its character fundamentally when "black power" advocates began to seek a history and identity separate from that of their relation to whites. The

[1] An important contribution of Durkheim (1947) was the tie between shared values, which hold a society together, and defining historical moments.

same theme was later taken up by the women's movement and then by a growing number of ethnic and regional independence efforts.

From this practical activity followed scholarly studies. Frantz Fanon's powerful 1967 exploration of the psychology of colonialism was one of the earliest ventures into this territory. Another early strand came from those who studied the Holocaust and its effect on survivors. The women's movement has also been a fertile source of studies: Jean Baker Miller's works (for example, Miller 1976) are among the earliest and most subtle efforts to explore the ways in which women's identities, defined in relation to men, hold them back from self-expression and keep both parties from exploring new ground. Among African-Americans, bell hooks (1994, 1995), Audre Lord (1984), and Cornel West (1993) have been eloquent analysts of the power of repressed memory. Experimental social psychologists have pursued the issue in their own way, testing for the empirical connection among group identification, collective memory, and self-esteem. All of this has culminated in the past few years with an explosion of studies of collective memory—still nascent, uncoordinated, a set of specific observations more than a theory, but clearly opening a new terrain.[2]

From this literature we can draw three major themes for our purposes. The first is the power of the basic need to express shared memory, and the pain that is felt when it is suppressed. Holocaust studies are particularly forceful in this respect, but for all "liberated" groups, whether survivors of genocide or gays emerging from the closet, the intensity of emotions that comes from discovering and expressing shared memories is literally extraordinary—something that lifts them above their normal lives and gives them a new sense of excitement and power. This signals to us that the early negotiations must distinguish themselves from the "business as usual" and "normal" frames that bury the history of domination.

The second point is the converse of this: for subordinate groups, the lowering of group identification and the suppression of shared memory are clearly related to lowered self-esteem.[3]

Finally—and most important—a group of studies showed the way in which the dominator-dominated relation is *self-reinforcing*: the dynamics of hierarchy create vicious circles that lock everyone into place (Smith

[2] For an excellent review of recent studies of collective memory, see Zelizer (1995).

[3] Social psychologists have repeatedly reproduced this phenomenon in the laboratory. Roger Brown, one of the most eminent, showed that when you create groups without a history, they will see themselves as superior to those outside, but as soon as you bring in those with a real history of superior-subordinate relations, the latter will put down their own group and elevate the out-group (Brown 1986). Similarly, Ethier and Deaux (1994) showed that in integrated settings, students with lower initial group identification fare far worse.

1982).[4] This puts in high relief the problem for the set of negotiations we are discussing: the problem of *breaking* the patterns of domination through negotiation is increased by the interlocking nature of the defenses of the parties.

A few writers from different fields have taken the next step and begun to discuss ways of *reconstructing* identities in situations of domination. This discussion has developed very little, however, especially in terms of practice: there is more exhortation ("It is important to rebuild identities") than useful advice.[5]

Identity and Negotiation Theory

Though some of the authors and fields we have just described talk of "negotiating identity," their work does not focus on the negotiating theory: they use the concept of negotiation in a very loose sense. The analytical study of negotiations, for its part, has gone in three major directions: the rationalistic game-theory approach; the individualistic/psychological approach in which one tries to understand the other side's motives; and the "interest-based" approach. Of these, the first clearly has no space for the kinds of issues we have just sketched. The second is more concerned with matters of identity but not in the *collective* sense.

The interest-based approach is in principle most open to this dimension, but the door has largely been closed by a rationalistic bias. "Separate the people from the problem," Fisher and Ury (1981) famously exhorted in *Getting to Yes;* this amounts to trying to move the discussion as quickly as possible to the grounds of public interests and objective principles. From our perspective this language makes the dominant group comfortable but

---

[4] Other studies similarly stressed the conservative effect of unrecognized and informal dynamics in hierarchical relations: see, for example, Bartunek, Kolb, and Lewicki (1992), especially the concluding chapter. These analyses of the conservative dynamics of repression echo the themes of Freud from a century ago.

[5] Among relevant pieces with which we are familiar, we would cite Touraine (1985) for his extended discussions of the dynamics of new movements. We have also been intrigued by Eviatar Zerubavel's sociological reflections on the structuring of history, in particular the ways in which historical time can be "split" and "bridged" in order to highlight particular events meaningful to the construction of identity (so far these ideas have been developed only in lectures). And, for a completely different take, Charles Taylor's (1989) philosophical treatment of the making of modern identities may have much to teach us. Various treatments of identity construction are also scattered through works already cited, including the literatures of the women's movement, of black consciousness, and so forth. This topic has not become an entity in itself but can be found in bits and pieces in a wide variety of places; we cannot pretend to cover it all.

not the dominated; it denies the latter's chance to be heard and to develop their own and different identity. Thus, the interest-based training for the Indian negotiations, to which we have referred, often ran into resistance from First Nations reluctant to enter (as one chief referred to it) "the white man's game."[6]

What the interest-based approach has obscured is that interests cannot be explored and expressed except within a framework of mutual respect and understanding. Without such a framework, one side's interests are seen as unimportant or illegitimate by the other side. This then kicks in a powerful emotional dynamic of alternate self-abasement and self-assertion, obscuring the "rational" interests at play. Our experience has been that solutions that are clearly rational from the position of an outside observer are frequently rejected because of the dynamics of identity. Those who have been dominated in the past do not want to be "invited in" to the dominator's frame; they want a *new* frame and relationship.

In the remainder of this chapter we want to advance the discussion a little further by specifying, first, the ways in which the interplay of collective identity and memory concretely affect negotiations between dominators and dominated and, second, various alternative ways of dealing with them.

The Impact of Identity Dynamics on Negotiation

We have already referred to a number of ways in which the problem of inadequate identities can distort a negotiation process; let us expand briefly and add to them.

In general, the parties are locked in a self-reinforcing and intertwined relationship that blocks open expression of interests. The dominators have generally committed acts of which they would be ashamed in "normal" circumstances and which they often justify by denigrating those they have dominated. The latter have adapted to their subordinate position in part through self-denigration, with suppressed rage in the background. In order to achieve a relationship of mutual respect and equal partnership, the parties must go through complementary and painful developments in

[6] A few writers in this tradition have extended the boundaries a bit. Notably, Herb Kelman's (1997) treatment of the Israeli-Palestinian conflict explores the need for renegotiation of identities in exactly the way we are proposing, though he concludes by saying the social scientists need to figure it out. John Forester's (1989) work, applying a Habermasian layer to interest-based bargaining, similarly runs up against these issues and says they need further treatment.

which both come to deal with moral failings. The dominators, from a position of self-satisfaction, must accept responsibility for illegitimate repression; the dominated have to come to terms with their history of weakness and servility.

This phase of the negotiation centers on *confidence* in self and others—or as many of the movements of the dominated put it, *pride* ("black pride," "gay pride"). Such confidence is the coin of identity. A solid identity is one that results in pride rather than shame; we would all like to be proud of ourselves and our associations. But it is also a word with a wide range of connotations and an inflammatory edge. The "pride" movements have an "in-your-face" quality that makes them highly controversial, and the word has been associated since biblical times with arrogance and self-aggrandizement.

These conflicting meanings reflect the unstable dynamics of the assertion of identity. One way of achieving pride—one embedded in our nature[7]—is to put down other groups. This is the equivalent of a "win-lose" negotiation, with the well-known dynamics of a negatively reinforcing spiral. A typical example in these negotiations is when the subordinate group seeks to have the historically dominant party go through extended self-abasement for the wrongs it has done; this sparks resentment and a self-justifying reaction among the latter, which then spirals into increasing mutual misunderstanding and mistrust.[8] The converse is also common: the dominant group's resistance to any admission of guilt may increase the anger and demands of the subordinate group.

It is possible to achieve a relationship, however, in which *both parties can be proud of who they are*. This is the equivalent of a mutual-gains (or "win-win") negotiation. But like most such negotiations, it requires going beyond the positions that are brought to the table: if the parties simply try to assert their traditional sense of self-worth, they will end up in a mutually destructive cycle. They need to explore territory "beyond" the traditional relationship, where both groups can accept new levels of responsibility. This is necessary if the parties are to construct a new relationship as

[7] This is a central theme of Roger Brown's text (1986).

[8] One can interpret much of the history of race relations in the United States since the 1960s in this framework: First, white liberals began to accept and express their shame for historical wrongs, and blacks developed movements around cultural pride. But rather than moving to a new level of relationship, this turned into a win-lose spiral: the whites became more and more defensive and apologetic, the blacks more demanding and assertive, with no resolution that could make both parties proud. The result was a severe backlash from whites, which fueled much of the conservative movement from the early 1980s. Similar dynamics may be developing in the case of Germans and Holocaust victims (see "Germany Searches for 'Normality,'" *New York Times*, November 29, 1998).

equals. Getting beyond the frame of being reactive in dominator and dominated roles is critical to creating positive negotiations for change and an interdependent future of equality. The need is to create a basis for confidence and a partnership in which the parties reinforce each other rather than putting each other down.

It is common, for example, for the dominant group to have constructed a myth—either that the subordinates are happy with their lot, or that they deserve it.[9] This enables the dominators to avoid shame; indeed, they can often feel pride in the way they have "taken care of" the others. In order to achieve a mutual relationship, however, they need to listen to and understand the contrary view of the dominated themselves, to accept that their actions have caused pain, and to understand the dominated as capable of equal responsibility.

The dominated may have an even more difficult task. They naturally tend to demonize the "oppressor." In order to negotiate, however, they need to understand the dominators' actions as those of human beings—or, to put it another way, they need to forgive. At the same time they have to construct a *new identity*, one of which they can be proud, not that of a subordinate group. It is this need that pushes them to resurrect forgotten traditions and history. The dominated, in other words, need to *develop* an independent identity that did not exist before.

The dominators usually have a far stronger degree of independence; their problem is the less complicated (though still painful) one of *opening* to incorporate another perspective.

These dynamics play out in practice through a myriad of particular patterns in the negotiation process that prevent the open exploration of shared interests.

---

[9] In some cases, these "myths" may be close to reality—as in the case of the oppression version of the Holocaust or American slavery. But even in these instances aspects of the truth are covered to maintain the clear identity of the oppressed: for example, the role of collaborationist Jews or blacks is buried. To bring these into the open is explosive. Sometimes—especially where historical conflict has been too obvious—the oppressor's myth is not of harmonious hierarchy but of just subjugation.

Substantial social-psychological research on the tendency of offenders to relieve their guilt by maligning the victim and denying responsibility includes the seminal work (to our knowledge) of Sykes and Matza (1957); other works cited by Haley (1998) include Macauley and Walster 1971; Walster and Berscheid 1967; Walster, Berscheid, and Walster 1970; and Walster, Berscheid, and Walster 1973.

The myth of the "happy slave" is found wherever the masters have a bad conscience about slavery; it still endures today and poisons race relations. See, for example, "Class Teaches That Slaves Were Happy," *New York Times*, November 16, 1998.

Taking Offense

These kinds of negotiations are particularly subject to outbursts of "irrational" anger and hurt—expressions of wounded pride—that are hard to predict and manage. The problem is all the more difficult because the basis for the pride is constantly shifting as the parties redefine their identities. To take a currently familiar example, it is difficult to know today whether or not a reference to "blacks" will stir outrage among some who have redefined themselves as "African-American."

In the creation of labor-management partnerships, one can often see an issue that has been muted in a traditional framework suddenly activated as a hot button within the emergent relationship. For example, lay-offs, which have historically been subject to standard negotiations, suddenly become a symbol of lack of partnership and respect and thereby become much more volatile. At a much simpler level, the way management walks into a room and positions itself around a table—something that has never been a contentious issue before—may touch off union feelings of being disrespected and bring dialogue to a halt.

History Games

The sense of offense and the search for respect frequently center on assertions of history and tradition. In both the Canadian First Nation negotiations and in labor negotiations going beyond the routine, the subordinate group seeks to explore the historical relationship and the dominant group seeks to avoid it. Thus, in land-management negotiations, the Indians want to spend a great deal of time explaining the relationship of the First Nation to that land, the history of how they and their ancestors have used it, and how they continue to want to maintain it. They sometimes bring a talking stick to the negotiations—a historical artifact used by chiefs to manage discussions. They may conduct lengthy traditional tribal ceremonies at the beginning of the negotiation process. And over and over they come back to the notion (even among those who have served in the army or who are members of the bar) that first they are members of a clan (bear, turtle, wolf) and that historically Canada has all too often cheated them of their land, their culture, and their language. The government negotiators, meanwhile, accept these behaviors with discomfort; they may take the talking stick or listen to opening ceremonies with outward respect but express bewilderment and irritation in hallway conversations. Their repeated refrain is an impatience to move on, to get past these distractions, to focus on the "real" problem at hand.

At best, these displays of tradition and culture are irritations to the historically dominant, a visible reminder of misunderstanding. Sometimes they can become more serious flashpoints for conflict if, for example, the dominant group tries to cut them off or if it tries to respond with its own traditions, which reopen old wounds. The display of the Confederate flag in the South is the kind of symbol that can make dialogue impossible.

A Mohawk Tribe dispute in Oka, Canada, in 1990 over whether a developer should build a golf course on a traditional, sacred burial ground serves as another warning of the power of historical symbolism. The government's attempt to frame the issue narrowly on economic grounds, far from limiting conflict, led to a greater explosion: various First Nation groups involved themselves in major protests, including stopping traffic on the main arteries into Montreal.

Internal Splits

Walton and McKersie's analysis of the need for *intra-organizational* negotiations is justly famous (Walton and McKersie 1965). In dominator-dominated negotiations, however, these internal negotiations typically become far more difficult, not infrequently leading to major splits. These are essentially manifestations of a changing identity. Because the dominated group is the one that has the most new construction to do to achieve a sense of full equality and self-respect (the dominators being happier with the status quo), it is they who most frequently begin internal battles that can derail negotiations.

The First Nations in Canada, most notably some of the Mohawk First Nations on both the Canadian and U.S. sides of the St. Lawrence Seaway, often split bitterly between warrior groups trying to preserve traditional identity and those promoting economic development, including the building of casinos or involvement in contraband, such as cigarettes brought across the border. The arena of labor-management partnerships is full of similar battles between those who want to hold on to an adversarial posture and those who support cooperation. It is typical for early steps in a dialogue to spark a reaction from militant groups who claim that the new form of negotiation is "selling out" the true nature of the union or giving away advances hard won over many years by their ancestors. The possibility of interest-based negotiation then becomes a hostage to the resolution of this internal battle.

It is easier to maintain a sense of identity when one is "separatist" than when one is trying to engage the other party in dialogue and tackling issues of interdependence. This basic tension—separatism versus engagement—reappears in every negotiation of this type that we are aware of. These battles can even come to the point of internecine violence, as in the case of the assassination of Prime Minister Rabin in Israel.

Resistance to Understanding

All negotiations involve some danger of miscommunication, but in these there is a *motivated* resistance to understanding. Each side's sense of self is built around a picture of the world that is radically different from that of the other party. To confront the other perspective threatens this coherent self-image. Thus, the parties often do not want to listen to each other.

This resistance is seen most strongly around issues of moral rightness. Nothing establishes identity like moral judgment. People often seem to feel that even to listen to the other side, or to try to understand the other side, is an immoral act. To take a dramatic instance, Holocaust survivors cannot have a dialogue with those who deny the reality of the genocide: they feel that to discuss the deniers' point of view is to legitimate evil.[10] When the barriers are this high, interests are not discussable, and every move in negotiation becomes a contest for moral authority rather than a sober analysis of interests.[11] These interchanges can take on a winner-take-all quality, each side trying to make the other kneel to its interpretation of the truth. We return to this dynamic in our discussion of apology.

Intertwining of Issues

An important tactic in interest-based bargaining is to take issues apart and recombine them in new packages that satisfy both sides. In these dominator-dominated negotiations, though, the parties have a tendency to

[10] See Vidal-Naquet (1992), summarized in Hutton (1994). Catholics asked to enter into dialogue about the church's teachings, as in Cardinal Bernardin's Common Ground Initiatives, have a similar (though less dramatic) uneasy feeling that they are being asked to put matters of faith into the realm of negotiation and dialogue, and thereby to legitimize error (O'Brien 1997).

[11] Religious believers also often make the argument that their faith is beyond dialogue—that by definition a revealed truth cannot be changed through humanistic processes of discussion; see, for example, O'Brien's (1997) summary of the debates on the Catholic Common Ground Initiatives.

stubbornly resist the unbundling of issues because, once again, such taking apart is a threat to their moral view. A frequent example in the Indian negotiations has been the attempt by the whites (and sometimes the facilitators) to separate out issues of financial compensation from the problems of self-government: they argue (in accord with rules of good negotiation) that it would be easier to take these problems one at a time, to see what the core interests are and to seek new combinations. The Indians, however, do not see them as separable: to treat money by itself, apart from self-determination, is to accept a cheapening of their claims. Their negotiation demands, in other words, represent not an "interest" in the rational sense most frequently used, but rather symbolize a moral code. This can be a very hard matter to discuss.

Dealing with History and Identity: Some Approaches

We believe these dynamics are so powerful in these negotiations that it is necessary to pay direct attention to the establishment of new identities that can support a relationship of mutual respect *before* one can try standard interest-based discussions. But this is dangerous ground—a minefield, in fact: even the most experienced diplomats find it difficult to avoid explosive missteps as they try to explore feelings of hurt and historical wrong. When they succeed, it is often by a clever obscuring of issues, allowing the two sides to understand the same thing in different ways, and so on. Such tactics are often useful in keeping an agreement from flying apart, but they contribute to the atmosphere of frustration and the interminably slow progress that characterize so many of these negotiations, and they do not lessen the danger of later misunderstandings.

Thus the dilemma: if one leaves history and identity alone, or obfuscates the issues, one remains trapped in a circle of misunderstanding; if not, one risks blowing the lid off. Is there a way out?

We cannot offer any assurances of an escape—that is, we haven't found one, either in our own practice or in the literature. Only a few efforts have really attempted a direct approach to the issues of identity,[12] and to our knowledge, there has been no careful analysis of what we can learn from such efforts.

[12] One useful strand of literature is the "idea from urban anthropology that the interaction that gives rise to identity takes place within relatively discrete situations, relationships, or 'worlds.' . . . [A] person's identity is a 'social construction' and from moment to moment is subject to negotiation" (Buckley and Kenney 1995: 1). But this approach is largely descriptive, with little systematic help to someone searching for guides to action.

Our comments here are just a first cut, trying to outline some of the issues that a more extended study would need to consider: What are the basic types of intervention on identities? What do they accomplish? And what are the main conditions that affect the outcomes?

Separate Consciousness-Raising

So far in the real world, identity issues have been dealt with predominantly in *separate* processes—in particular, through "consciousness-raising" within the dominated group, such as the "black power" or "queer" movements. This clearly has a powerful effect in releasing people from self-hatred. The obvious weakness is that it does nothing to construct a new relationship. In fact, when people engage in separated consciousness-raising, the process sometimes encourages them to build their self-esteem by denigrating the other party; it creates a win-lose dynamic of pride.

This dilemma underlines the fact that the process we are trying to define is a relational one—one in which both parties create new identities of which they can be proud. This requires that they listen to each other and make the effort to understand what it would be like to be in the other side's shoes.

Applied specifically to a negotiation situation, separate meetings can be useful at the margins when one side merely needs a little push to build up its self-confidence; we have used it in labor-management situations with some effect. But when the identity needs to change significantly (when the parties need to develop new capacities and self-definitions), the process needs to be predominantly one of interaction in which both sides work on defining their new relationship or what they will do together.

Symbolic Assertion

By symbolic assertion we mean the kind of action we have already discussed, where one side—typically the dominated—forces its symbols on the other. Examples include the Indians using the talking stick or engaging in lengthy opening ceremonies. The dominators generally tend to force their way of viewing things in quite an unconscious way: they may wear suits or insist on legal procedures or drink wine instead of beer. When the dominated push back, there is generally a sense of shock, which can be effective in opening dialogue and showing that there really are different ways of looking at the world.

By itself, however, such assertion does not get very far. At best it evens the discomfort level of the parties and makes the dominated feel better, but it does not significantly reduce the "irrational" dynamics we have discussed or ease the process of defining interests and interdependence.

Mutual Listening

Sometimes facilitators structure periods in which the parties move away from formal negotiation and talk about their core concerns—moral outrage, historical remembrance, and so on—in the presence of the other party and in a way that creates a real interaction. This can be done casually, through social interactions, or in a more structured exercise. In the formal versions the key is for the listening side to "double" the presenters by repeating back what it thinks it has understood of what the others have said.

Either way, in our experience, this can have a powerful effect. As many social-psychological studies have shown, just the feeling that someone is really listening, really trying to understand what you have experienced, is very calming for those who have been hurt. This approach sometimes produces dramatic progress in negotiations, the ability to consider types of agreement that were previously blocked.[13]

These moments of interaction support our basic hypothesis: direct focus on problems of identity and history can make possible normal dialogues about interests that were previously blocked by the "supercharging" of issues.

At the same time, however, mutual listening is clearly insufficient for the most serious tensions because it does not in itself lead to a reconstruction of identity. It may be the first step, but it leaves undone the task of incorporating the reality of different perspectives into identities built on denying them.

Ordinarily, in our experience, mutual-listening exercises end with a feel-good moment at which both sides say, "We are really not so different after all; we really want the same things." The problem is that this statement itself denies reality: one can look at the stories and perspectives that have been exchanged and see enormous unresolved differences. Thus, the positive outcome of the exercise is a preliminary opening to the other side, a

[13] In labor-management settings we have often used an exercise in which the two parties separately write down the major obstacles to trust, then look at each other's lists and discuss them. This is regularly remembered months later as a breakthrough moment in the relationship.

recognition of shared humanity. Left there, however, it allows the parties to obscure the real problems and avoid the work of redefining themselves.

In more volatile cases, mutual listening is essentially impossible—it is rejected because, as suggested earlier, the act of listening involves accepting the legitimacy of what the other is saying and the possibility of empathy with it. When one's sense of self is tied to moral rejection of that position, one cannot be open to it. Some African-Americans and some Israeli Jews have begun to question their people's emotional attachment to the symbols of oppression, arguing the need for building something positive: they see historical grievances as a crutch for crippled identities.[14] Listening in such a situation therefore requires that the parties re-invent themselves.

That is about as far as our experience takes us. It is relatively rare for a structured discussion of identity and history to occur at all in a negotiation framework, and we have not seen it put in practice beyond this last approach: a phase of organized mutual listening. If it is inadequate to the problem, as we have argued, then we need to get beyond what we have already seen and to structure new techniques.

Exploring New Ground

There are a few instances we are aware of in which groups have engaged in extensive and intense dialogue that has significantly changed their sense of history and identity. A first category is that of face-to-face small groups. There are many efforts today to bring together the sides from highly flammable disputes for ongoing discussions: these include dialogues between children of Holocaust survivors and of Nazi guards (Bar-On 1995; Anonymous 1995), or between Palestinians and Israelis.

The most important lesson from these cases is that mutual understanding is possible across extraordinarily wide gulfs. There is no question that for the people directly involved, these processes *can* make possible at least

---

[14] See for example Steele (1998) and Confino (1997). Of the African-American community, bell hooks (1995) wrote, "The contemporary crisis of identity is best resolved by our collective willingness as African Americans to acknowledge that there is no monolithic black community, no normative black identity. There is a shared history that frames the construction of our diverse black experiences. Knowledge of that history is needed by everyone as we seek to construct self and identity." The damaging effects of holding onto a sense of injury are quite independent of whether the moral position is "right" or not. One can believe at the same time, for example, that the Holocaust was morally unspeakable *and* that certain Jews have built wounded identities around nursing the injury.

a peaceful coexistence that was previously impossible. Dan Bar-On (1995) summarized the transformation: "Once the victimizer could be recognized, in oneself, in others, the quality of the discourse changed drastically and became 'richer' in the variety of emotional meanings." Desmond Tutu (1998) wrote of some of the sessions of the South African Truth and Reconciliation Commission in the same way, recounting moving stories of new understanding created around intense interpersonal experiences.

But the South Africa commission recognizes the limitations of even this kind of deep personal dialogue. It is not enough for a few members of the parties to learn to speak to each other, for in the background are large social groups who carry collective memories of wrongs, guilt, and pain. In all of the dominator-dominated negotiations, in fact, the constituency problem—common to all negotiations—is greatly increased. The leaders not only need to meet the interests of their constituencies and to persuade them that the best deal has been struck, but also need to bring them to share in the emotional process of identity building that is necessary before the legitimacy of negotiation is even acceptable.

There have been a number of efforts, including the South African one and a series in South America, to structure experiences at this large level. The verdict at this point is completely inconclusive. The South African commission broke down at its end into squabbling. On the other hand, it is amazing that the races in that situation have been able to communicate and work together reasonably well, and there is some reason to think the South African commission's hearings have helped to prevent a vicious spiral of misunderstanding and violence (Anonymous 1997; see also Adam 1998; Hayes 1998; Tutu 1998). The various commentators generally end with more questions than answers—they cannot yet say whether or under what circumstances victims can accept truth rather than vengeance, or how much digging-up of the past is the right amount, or what is "reparative justice" rather than "retributive justice."

Mechanisms of Reconciliation

At this point we can just begin to outline some mechanisms worth exploring in further studies. There are several types of action that recur frequently in these negotiations, but without any agreement on their effectiveness: this should give us pointers about what we need to look for.

Among mechanisms that can help move negotiations beyond the phase of identity construction are joint exploration of the past (as in the Truth and Reconciliation Commission), restoration of rights, and restitution.

Each of these is often used or explored, and each of them is controversial and poorly understood.

Apology is one of the most complex and inflammatory mechanisms. In the last few years it has been a central aspect of the kind of long-running dominator-dominated disputes we are discussing: Tony Blair's apology for England's role in the Irish potato famines may have helped move the peace process forward, but nothing similar has emerged from the Israeli-Palestinian negotiations;[15] the Canadian and Australian governments have apologized for their abuse of aboriginal populations, though with considerable conflict around it; the Japanese apology to China for their actions in World War II only increased tensions and misunderstanding (Lies 1998; Ching 1998). These and many other major emotional debates in just the past few years are further evidence that the dynamics of reconciliation are not resolvable by interest-based negotiation in its usual sense, but call out for better understanding of a murkier area.

Our approach would put apology in the context of the construction of new identities. We therefore would emphasize that apology needs, first, to help the dominated see the dominators as human beings rather than as moral monsters and, second, to affirm a new set of norms that both sides can share. Above all, we would stress that apology should be analyzed as a process of interaction, not as a single act. The apology is a moment of vulnerability and change, and it can only be offered if there is an expectation that the other party will accept it and will take on its own responsibility for a changed relationship in the future.

Thus, the act of apology is subject to the same "prisoners' dilemma" dynamics as any negotiation: the dominant party hesitates to take the first step for fear of being humiliated and rejected, which leads the dominated to increase the stridency of its demands in an attempt to assert itself, and so on into a vicious win-lose circle. The lessons from mutual-gains negotiation should be able to give us, in a longer analysis than this one, some help in structuring the interaction.

Apology, in short, needs to be put in the context of the identities being created in the emergent relationship, with both parties taking on new obligations. It cannot merely reinforce the victims' sense of victimhood, nor can it leave untouched the dominators' sense of rightness: it needs to point forward to a relation both can accept. It therefore cannot be a single mo-

---

[15] "Each side has tended to consider the Oslo accord a kind of apology from the other, an acknowledgment that it had done wrong. But each side sees only the other's misdeeds, not its own" (Ethan Bronner, "Filling in Peace's Details Is the Painful Part," *New York Times*, October 25, 1998).

ment, over and done with, but needs to emerge and change as the understanding of the relationship between the parties itself changes.

Conclusion

Negotiations between dominators and dominated at whatever level—whether it be black-white tensions on local school boards or the resolution of armed conflicts between nations—are generally extremely partial and frustrating types of processes. At best they eke out small concrete gains without doing much to address the underlying mistrust, and therefore remain highly vulnerable to explosions that can instantly undo the hard-won gains.

It often appears, especially to the dominators, that nothing will satisfy the historically dominated side, and in a sense that is true. For the key issue is not about money or land or numbers of hires; it is first about establishing ongoing relationships of mutual respect. Without that, no concrete solution is satisfying or stable.

The rationalistic approach to negotiation—one that runs through almost all versions of the theory—assumes that one can ignore such problems and move on to "hard" interests. We have just sketched our reasons for believing, on the contrary, that a conscious, focused period of attention to the reconstruction of identities (on both sides) is needed before interests can even be understood or separated out. We know very little so far about how that process can best be managed. The enormous current concern and confusion in many national and international disputes around problems of reconciliation, apology, vengeance, and collective identity are a call for attention from those of us who hope to improve such negotiations.

We need, in effect, to create an analysis of moral negotiation, in which the stakes are the self-respect and mutual respect of parties. If they engage in a winner-take-all contest for moral authority, there is little hope for any resolution of disputes. Our problem is to transform the negotiations into mutual-gains discussions around building identities that both can accept.

Steps in this negotiation of identity include the following:

1. Acknowledging the past and the historic perspective of each side.
2. Recognizing each side's orientation to time: the dominateds' tendency to look to the past and to have trouble seeing positive opportunities in the present and the future; the dominators' tendency to want to look only to the future.

3. Acknowledging the need for and interest in a continuing relationship on a new basis that recognizes interdependence and equality.
4. Recognizing each side's needs: the dominateds' need to have autonomy and recognition of their particular needs for self-determination—be they cultural customs or historical political problems; the dominators' need to be open to looking at the past from the dominateds' experience and recognizing the need for interdependence.

This process requires the reconstruction of the moral terrain on a new level, in which the parties by their interaction can renegotiate their relationship and create new, interdependent identities and ways of interacting.

Part V

The Future of Negotiations

17

From the Behavioral Theory to the Future of Negotiations

ROBERT B. MCKERSIE
RICHARD E. WALTON

The papers in this volume attest to the tremendous amount of progress made in the research, teaching, and practice of negotiations over the past half-century. Indeed, the arrival of a new century is perhaps a good occasion for us to take stock of this progress.

We begin by focusing on what attracted us to the study of collective bargaining and, more particularly, to the process of labor negotiations in the first place. In the mid-1950s a number of us were convinced that collective bargaining was the wave of the future. The era was characterized by some elements of high drama: a major strike at Westinghouse in 1955 and a very long stoppage in the steel industry in 1959. The labor movement was on the move—it had grown steadily during the immediate postwar period. Contracts being signed articulated the rights of the parties and established grievance systems to resolve and adjudicate disputes rather than resorting to slowdowns and strikes. By 1960, the Supreme Court decided that grievance arbitration had matured to the point where it could defer to the judgments of arbitrators on substantive workplace issues. A type of industrial jurisprudence that was in the making foreshadowed by nearly thirty years the development of the alternative dispute systems described by Rowe and Bendersky in this volume. In terms of the substance of collective bargaining, many milestones were being achieved: pensions had been declared proper subjects for bargaining, for example, and long-term agreements embodying cost-of-living clauses and annual improvements in wages linked to production were coming into vogue.

But beyond the establishment of a counterforce to managerial authority and the negotiation of labor agreements that accompanied collective bargaining, the union movement of the 1950s exhibited some other important features. Workers in the mass-production industries had been recently or-

ganized, and in addition to the oft-repeated bargaining demands for simply "more," the leaders of these CIO-affiliated unions espoused a social vision of a better society. The whole gamut of social issues—pensions, housing, health care, and race relations—were high on the agenda, if not to be
realized in collective bargaining, then to establish the ground on which political action and legislative proposals would be developed. Walter
Reuther, then-president of the UAW, typified the labor leader who embodied the leadership qualities that we admired: high energy, articulateness,
and social vision. We attended the 1958 convention of the UAW that grap-
pled with the agenda the union would place before the auto companies.
We saw "the redhead" in action and marveled at the skill with which he
shifted direction from a previously touted idea of a shorter work week
(which was undercut by the launch of Sputnik and the outpouring of concern that we were falling behind the Soviet Union militarily and economi-
cally) to a newly crafted proposal of profit sharing as a means for spreading the fruits of a prospering economy.

For us, the labor movement and the institution of collective bargaining
represented industrial democracy in action. In a recent book, Amartya Sen
(1999), the 1998 Nobel Prize winner in economics, argues that democracy
and its associated freedoms are an indispensable arrangement for fostering
sustainable economic development. We saw the labor movement as having
a profound impact not only on the unionized sector of the economy but on
all reaches of society.

So why, then, did we concentrate more narrowly on the labor negotiation process? When we commenced our doctoral studies in industrial relations in the mid-1950s, most of the attention in the coursework at Harvard Business School focused on contract administration and the
companion process of grievance handling. The subject of negotiations
concerned itself primarily with outcomes (the terms of the new contract)
and, to the extent that there was any attention given to the process, the
focus was on strikes and national emergency procedures for settling these
big disputes.

Two faculty members, Benjamin Selekman and Steven Fuller, taught a
course on the negotiation of labor agreements in which they used actual
transcripts to analyze the behavior of key negotiators in a variety of industries. Selekman brought to the subject his deep knowledge of conciliation programs for dealing with labor unrest. He described negotiation as a
process for taming and structuring "raw" power in the book *Power and
Morality in a Business Society* (Selekman and Selekman 1956). Fuller,
who had been trained at Harvard Business School, viewed negotiation as a
process that management could use to establish constructive relationships.

During the 1970s, he served as vice president of Human Resources at General Motors (GM) and was instrumental in bringing the quality-of-work-life concept to GM.

With one of us (R. E. W.) based at Purdue University and the other (R. B. McK.) approximately one hundred miles away at the University of Chicago, it was feasible to work collaboratively on a five-year project to develop a framework for understanding labor negotiations. This was a time of considerable ferment in the disciplines that had something to say about the process of negotiations. For example, the *Journal of Conflict Resolution* was creating considerable interest in the subject. Economists (Thomas Schelling [1960]), psychologists (Sidney Siegel and Larry Fouraker [1960]), game theorists (Anatole Rappaport [1960]), and practitioners (such as Edward Peters [1955]) were producing extremely relevant works. And, of course, important contributions such as the pioneering work of Mary Parker Follett (1942) were already available in the literature.

Our book, *A Behavioral Theory of Labor Negotiations*, was published in 1965 in the Economic Handbook series of McGraw-Hill, with a second edition produced in 1991 by ILR Press of Cornell University. Over the three and a half decades since then, the framework for analyzing labor negotiations has held up quite well. Thinking about the prominent features of the various decades is instructive.

The 1960s witnessed an explosion of union organizing in the public sector. While the focus of *Behavioral Theory* centered on the private sector, the theory applied equally well to the new setting for collective bargaining. Thomas Kochan (1974) extended the framework to the multi-lateral elements that are so pervasive in public sector labor negotiations. The 1960s also saw a wave of work stoppages over local issues. These developments illustrated the increasing challenges faced by labor leaders in the intra-organizational process and foreshadowed many of the developments that became more pronounced later in the century, namely, the challenge of achieving alignment between the expectations of the constituents and the realities as experienced at the bargaining table by their representatives.

The decade of the 1970s brought forth the quality-of-worklife movement and a variety of programs that emphasized worker involvement and the introduction of high-performance systems. The search for integrative solutions and the structuring of positive working relations were increasingly emphasized as components of negotiations in the efforts of the parties to find common ground and to work together on a continuing basis.

The 1980s began with the air traffic controllers' strike and the clarion message sent to employers by the action of President Reagan in firing all of the strikers: management could take the initiative to change labor relations as well as the fundamental arrangements of the business. In industry after industry, management came to the bargaining table demanding concessions and prepared to use such coercive tactics as hiring permanent replacements for striking workers. Not common in industry for the previous two decades, this was a type of reverse collective bargaining, where management was the moving party seeking to extract or to retrieve distributive gains that had been won by unions and their members over the years.

What started as an effort by management to reduce costs gradually blended into a strategy of seeking to increase value through a variety of restructuring moves. This became the overriding theme for the 1990s and certainly continues now at the turn of the century (when we are taking stock of the journey just completed and the road ahead). In terms of *Behavioral Theory* this period can be thought of as illustrating the mixed-motive nature of labor negotiations. The parties have a lot in common because they both want to achieve a viable enterprise that satisfies stockholders and provides employment for as many members as possible. Yet, at the same time, considerable conflict exists over the avenues chosen for the realization of joint gains over the long run. Plants are shut down, workers are displaced, subactivities are outsourced—all of these creating substantial conflicts of interest, at least in the short run.

While the emphasis in our book was on labor negotiations, we suggested that the subprocesses in the theory and their interrelationships applied to other social and political negotiations as well. We used the civil rights arena to illustrate this point. The chapters in *this* volume on societal-level conflicts using current examples from environmental, public policy, and ethnic or racial settings demonstrate that negotiators can indeed learn a great deal from those operating in different settings. The key, however, is to recognize that the broad principles need to be adapted and used in ways that are sensitive to the different institutional contexts and cultural norms operating in these distinctive arenas.

Negotiations Go Generic

While we suggested that certain negotiation principles should apply broadly, little did we anticipate that the field of negotiation research and education would become a growth industry. And it does not show any signs of let-up. To cite several items attesting to the explosion of interest in negotiations, courses carrying this label are invariably oversubscribed; research and teaching centers have been established across the country, many with funds from the Hewlett Foundation; and moving to the cyber level, a recent search of the Web turned up over 1,300,000 listings for the word *negotiation*.

To understand this phenomenal growth, we need to highlight several developments that have spurred this "success story." Some of the developments include the following:

- Increased interest in empowerment and participation by all stakeholders in organizations. Today very few organizations operate with the dictum, "The boss decides everything." Acceptance of initiatives by the people involved is key, and this means bringing them into some type of negotiation process.
- Reliance on policies and rules to settle a question is also not as relevant in today's environment. Given the rapidity of change and the complexity of the available options, it is not possible to use the "policy manual" to resolve matters.
- The restructuring of business into supply chains, joint ventures, and business alliances means that decisions can only be made by having the relevant parties "at the table."
- Diversity and the presence of many stakeholders with different perspectives generate a requirement for a process of collaboration and negotiation.

One of the healthiest developments in the field of negotiation is that it is no longer limited to the highly stylized and periodic routines of formal contract negotiations. Instead, as Part II of this book attests, the more common forms of negotiation are those that are informal ongoing parts of everyday organizational life. The fields of organizational change and negotiation have come together over the years to enrich both fields of study and practice. All change involves interests, power, and some interpersonal tension. Resistance is to be expected, but, again, while some broad principles of negotiation transfer well to the arenas of organizational change, some caution is needed in applying them too automatically. Change in organizations is a multi-faceted phenomenon that requires more than a negotiation lens. The psychological or social contract discussed by Denise Rousseau, for example, broke down in the 1990s not because of conscious negotiated efforts to do so, but because economic and technological changes led to an era of restructuring, often beyond the control of any single organization or set of decision makers or negotiators. Negotiation theory helps to understand, and perhaps to guide, organizational change if the parties involved have a well-grounded understanding of their environment and how it is changing and can make explicit how their interests are affected. Then the search for common ground or integrative solutions or the necessary trade-offs can be made. In our more recent book exploring the application of these principles to negotiating change (Walton, Cutcher-Gershenfeld, and McKersie 1994), we emphasized the importance of mixing distributive and integrative processes in ways we call "restrained forcing" or "robust fostering." The point is, going too far in either distributive or integrative directions in an era of significant change can blind parties to the need to balance short- and long-run pressures.

The Continuing Relevance of *Behavioral Theory*

In developing the framework for *Behavioral Theory*, it was our belief that all negotiations between social entities, whether groups of organizations or nations, contain four subprocesses and their associated dilemmas. Here we want to examine several sets of these subprocesses and dilemmas against the backdrop of a number of current developments. We start this discussion with the set of dilemmas that has received the most attention—the intersection of distributive and integrative bargaining as the parties address the explicit agenda at the main table.

The Tension between Distributive and Integrative Bargaining

Too often in the lexicon of those who teach negotiations, the ideal outcome is touted as "win-win." Such an image of the process is not faithful to the reality of most situations. Major conflicts of interest do exist, deadlocks do develop, and the parties are often prone to utilize coercive forms of power. Anyone familiar with collective bargaining understands these realities, but at the same time there is a recognition that conflict can sometimes set the stage for a transformation of the relationship. The point is that a more nuanced view of the process is necessary, and that the mixed-motive nature of the engagement holds the potential for breakdowns as well as breakthroughs.

Over the past four decades, the terms "distributive bargaining" and "integrative bargaining" have been widely incorporated into the lexicon for studying and teaching negotiations. Some have used alternate terms, such as "claiming" versus "creating" gains (see Lax and Sebenius 1986: 29–45) or "shares" versus "the size of the pie."

Both of these subprocesses appear to be very much alive and present in contemporary collective bargaining. On the integrative side, as Joel Cutcher-Gershenfeld suggests in his chapter, there is considerable use of interest-based bargaining in labor negotiations today, a development that took off after the publication of *Getting to Yes* by Fisher and Ury (1981). (We turn to this perspective shortly when we describe an educational program for union and management negotiations.) On the other hand, some notable impasses and major strikes have occurred, indicating that distinct conflicts of interest and associated distributive bargaining are still present. These include the 1997 confrontation between the Teamsters and UPS over the issue of part-time workers, and the strike in 2000 between the engineers union and management at Boeing over parity of treatment with the blue-collar workers. The spate of union mergers that occurred in the 1990s has enabled union leaders to commit resources and to engage in corporate campaigns when negotiations break down and strikes ensue, thereby expanding the use of distributive techniques away from the bargaining table.

The contrasting outcomes just cited can be linked back to a number of developments that hold the potential for increasing both cooperation and, to a limited degree, protracted conflict. Regarding the forces that suggest the parties are finding common ground, we would mention decentralization (which enables the wage and effort bargains to be coupled), day-to-day problem solving of work-system issues, new compensation arrangements (contingent pay and gain sharing that link the fortunes of the company to benefits for workers), and programs for enhancing career employment. On the other side of the ledger, we find a rise in vigorous union-avoidance programs (thereby creating considerable tension at the highest levels of the labor movement), an increase in outsourcing, and the continued disruptive aspects of down-sizing and plant relocation.

Certainly the forces of competition can heighten both cooperation and conflict. And we are clearly in an era of industrial competitiveness. Management's agenda today emphasizes cost containment, flexible assignment of labor, improvement of quality, and responsiveness to customer needs. For its side, labor's substantive agenda emphasizes job security, protecting past gains, ensuring institutional security for the union, and in some instances enlarging the union's role in business decision making. These respective agendas guarantee that collective bargaining will retain its mixed-motive character for the foreseeable future.

Intra-organizational Bargaining

The subprocess of intra-organizational bargaining came into the framework as the final piece of the puzzle. Originally, in our formulation, we concentrated on the three subprocesses taking place at the main table: distributive bargaining, integrative bargaining, and attitudinal structuring. In our fieldwork, however, it became clear that much of what was happening at the main table could be understood only with reference to the negotiations that were taking place within each organization. Thus, we added a new venue to the conception of the labor negotiation process.

Others have referred to intra-organizational bargaining as negotiations at the "second" tables. John Dunlop, in his classic statement (1984: 10, 12) noted that before any agreement can be reached, there has to be agreement in three negotiations: one each within the labor and management organizations, and a third across the main table.

The tensions that exist between chief negotiators and their constituents (or clients, to use a legal term) have been explored during the 1990s with the help of agency theory, a hot topic in economics. This perspective delves into such questions as how principals instruct and control the behavior of their agents and structure incentives to ensure acceptable performance. A working group under the auspices of the Program on Negotiations published a study in 1999 that examined negotiations in a variety of settings using this conceptual framework (see Mnookin and Susskind 1999).

Achieving internal consensus within management and within the ranks of the union has always been a challenging task. It has become increasingly demanding as a result of a number of new developments, however. First, the work force in a typical employment relationship today is much more diverse and brings a wider range of interests and priorities to the negotiation of a new contract. Second, employment relationships in many sectors of the economy are much less enduring. Third, values have changed, and many workers want a much more direct say in how the bargaining agenda is framed and the contract finally approved.[1] Consumerism has come to the ranks of union members and shapes the content and urgency of the messages they send to their representatives.

Some unions have seized on the opportunities provided by information technology to communicate more effectively with their constituents by keeping them updated on the progress of negotiations. Various devices, such as hotlines, Web pages, and videoconferencing, have increased the alignment between the agent and the principals. But note that these new

[1] Recently, one of the authors talked with the chief negotiator for a group of clerical employees working for a large pharmaceutical company. This person reported an episode that illustrates the increased voice that union members and their representatives insist on exercising during negotiations. The management attorney, at a critical stage in the negotiations, asked her to join him in an off-the-record, sidebar discussion. She countered by saying, "Whatever you have to say must be said to the whole committee—all twenty of us."

technologies can also easily be used by constituents to mobilize coalitions against proposals or tentative settlements they do not like. The airline pilots experienced this in their 1999 negotiations with American Airlines over the use of regional jets. Before one of the tentative settlements could even be communicated to the rank-and-file, opponents mobilized and dispatched their reasons for opposing it over the Internet. Clearly, both theory and practice on intra-party negotiations and relationships have advanced far beyond what we could have expected.

The alignment challenge also exists on the management side, although with very different dynamics. Most companies today feel the pressure of shareholders' expectations. This has keyed the behavior of management to the financial performance of the firm as viewed by security analysts. This orientation is passed down through the management organization to the chief management negotiator. In a sense, Wall Street is the silent partner at the bargaining table, and increasingly it is not even silent. While many labor relations academics and other professionals are reluctant to comment on ongoing negotiations out of a sense of professional courtesy and ethics, Wall Street analysts do not hesitate to weigh in with newspaper comments on what should or should not be done in negotiations before or during the process. So the "internal" negotiations within management now extend to those who profess to speak for the firm's owners and investors. To the extent that some of their expectations for cost reduction or flexibility to outsource work are at variance with the operational objectives of building a more committed work force, the task of the negotiators becomes even more complex.

The Importance of the Social Contract

In the original *Behavioral Theory* the term that we used for this subprocess was "attitudinal structuring." Originally, we envisioned the process primarily as a companion activity to either distributive bargaining or integrative bargaining. We believed that to carry out distributive bargaining effectively, it was essential to have a certain attitudinal context that would enable effective deployment of coercive sources of power. Correspondingly, we believed that integrative bargaining succeeded when a working level of trust was present, which could only be achieved with a conscious program of behaviors that developed a working rapport.

As the restructuring era unfolded during the 1990s, we became convinced that the relationship dimension of negotiations was extremely important and that the social contract should be viewed as a distinct outcome, separate but related to the substantive contract between labor and management. Thus, we embarked on a research project (with Joel Cutcher-Gershenfeld) to augment *Behavioral Theory* with two books (Walton, Cutcher-Gershenfeld, and McKersie, *Strategic Negotiations* [1994, 2000] and Cutcher-Gershenfeld, McKersie, and Walton, *Pathways to Change* [1995]). In so doing we noted that when distributive bargaining is required, it should be restrained—the parties should pursue their objectives vigorously but at the same time recognize that at some point they will have to implement the agreement, and that this phase will require a strong working relationship that must be preserved during the negotiation of the desired changes.

Another way of making the point is that in many situations today the character of the labor-management relationship is as important as the substantive agenda. The latter tends to have a short-term focus and may be driven by cost pressures and stock market considerations that prompt companies to insist on specific changes. By contrast, the quality of the relationship shapes the ability of the parties to work together over the long run to find solutions to their conflicting, as well as common, interests. Greenhalgh explores this subject very effectively in *Managing Strategic Relationships* (2001).

The counterpoint to the growing awareness that distributive bargaining needs to be restrained is the premise that integrative bargaining (often referred to today as "labor-management partnerships") must be robust and focused on achieving concrete benefits for all parties. One reason why so many efforts at labor-management cooperation have floundered in the past is precisely that they have been unable to produce real gains for the parties, such as increased productivity, additional union members, and enhanced employability for the work force.

The emergence of partnerships is not a development limited to the United States, as Hunter and Beaumont underscore in their chapter. Anyone steeped in the lore of labor history would quickly note that what we call partnerships today were once called cooperative agreements or joint committees to deal with new technology, production, and imports—to name a few of the more prominent examples.

The main lesson from all these efforts that seek to identify common interests and to work collaboratively is that many risks have to be managed in order for productive relationships to be sustained. Changes in leadership, skepticism from constituents, and lack of tangible benefits, to name three, are factors that must be anticipated and attended to for joint endeavors to remain robust.

With increased recognition of the importance of long-term, productive relationships between labor and management, a new frontier for research has emerged. While partnerships can produce benefits for all the parties, they can also go sour. This sometimes occurs when leadership changes or when various expectations are not met. In any event, these "experiments" provide fruitful ground for research for a new generation of scholars.

The network of social contracts that exists in a typical labor-management relationship today is far more extensive and complex than was the case when we developed *Behavioral Theory*. In those days (the 1950s and early 1960s), the social contract, if it could be called that, existed primarily between the two chief negotiators from management and the union, and among the supervisors, workers, and their stewards. The potential connections between management and labor were limited to these avenues. By contrast, today the relationship patterns are much more extensive. Let us illustrate this point by examining the three levels of a typical current labor-management relationship.

At the strategic level today, many companies provide union leadership with regular briefings on strategic developments. In a limited number of instances, unions have nominated representatives to serve on the respective corporate boards of directors. McKersie's chapter in this volume ("Union-Nominated Directors: A New Voice in Corporate Governance") explores this development and reports on the experiences of a score of union-nominated directors.

Moving to the level of collective bargaining, a variety of joint committees and task forces exist in many situations. Rather than negotiations being characterized by an intense period of activity leading to a new agreement, followed by a three- or four-year period of implementation of the agreement, negotiations in many relationships today are much more continuous. The original distinction of only dealing with issues of interest at contract negotiation time and issues of rights in the implementation period is being considerably blurred.

At the level of operations, the emphasis on teams and involvement has led to a wide range of new patterns of interaction. In some cases, supervisors are no longer on the scene and the operations are performed by self-directed teams.

Our purpose in enumerating the complexity of organizational relationships is to underscore the pervasiveness of social contracts and to reiterate the point that the shaping and nurturing of social contracts represents a much more intricate and demanding set of activities, given today's organizational context, than when we developed the framework for *Behavioral Theory*. Again, this points to the reality that negotiations and organizational change are highly intertwined processes.

The Tension Points between Internal Bargaining and Building Social Contracts

When we bring the two subprocesses just discussed together, a very intricate picture of alignments and gaps emerges. For example, the more constituents force their expectations into the behavior of their representatives, the more difficult it is for these agents to develop a social contract with each other. Put in the parlance of adversarial bargaining or distributive activities, when a representative is tightly aligned with the interests of constituents, the only significant bargaining that takes place is across the main table. The internal bargaining has already been accomplished as a result of this tight alignment.

On the other hand, consider a contrasting situation: two chief negotiators have dealt with each other over an extended period of time, have bonded, and have developed a working rapport (or, in our language, a social contract) that enables them to deliver a new agreement that makes sense, given the interests of both sides. They will have considerable internal work to do to make sure that expectations and acceptance levels within their respective organizations are such that the terms arrived at will be ratified by their respective principals and constituents.

Summary and Perspective for the Next Generation of Scholars

The four subprocesses have stood the test of time, and our theoretical understanding, as well as the implications for applying each of these distinctive types of social processes, has advanced steadily. Less attention has been given, however, to the challenges of managing pairs of these processes that are sometimes mutually reinforcing and sometimes mutually defeating and therefore capable of presenting minefields of dilemmas.

The multiple roles that negotiators must assume and pursue can be summarized as follows:

- Negotiators are competitors with their counterparts in claiming scarce resources.
- Negotiators are collaborators with their counterparts in creating value.
- Negotiators are relationship shapers.
- Negotiators are coalition managers and consensus builders within their own party, and sometimes purveyors of divisiveness within the other party.

So a challenge to the next generation of scholars is to explore the intersection of these various subprocesses—to the end that the dilemmas and the concepts and behaviors that are necessary to conduct effective negotiations are much better understood.

Coming Full Circle—or Back to Understanding the Behavior of Effective Negotiation

Our research work was not designed to be prescriptive; rather, it was meant to be descriptive and theoretically positive. Over the years, others developed prescriptive principles (Fisher and Ury [1981] being the best known). Given the very distinctive features of what we think of as the institutional relationship of labor-management relations, starting in the mid-1990s, Joel Cutcher-Gershenfeld pioneered the design of an educational program for practitioners that would help them understand and practice effective negotiations. Drawing on the theoretical material contained in *Behavioral Theory* as well as *Strategic Negotiations*, Cutcher-Gershenfeld fashioned an integrated program of conceptual material and simulations around the theme of interest-based negotiations. The concept of interest-based negotiations and the deployment of forcing and fostering strategies have served well as a framework for a two-day seminar that, in addition to Joel, has involved Nancy Peace, Phyllis Segal, and one of us (R. B. McK.). As of early 2000, almost 1,800 practitioners had been exposed to the fundamentals of effective labor negotiations in this seminar. In applying these ideas, the seminar participants have reported back to us a number of successes and some major challenges, including the following:

- Convincing constituents and principals that interest-based negotiations will deliver agreements that are superior to those reached via traditional bargaining methods—this task being especially difficult when there has been a history of deep adversarialism.
- Approaching distributive issues such as wages in a constructive fashion, or avoiding a win-lose scenario.
- Developing sufficient trust so that brainstorming and other techniques of integrative bargaining can be used with minimal risk of exploitation.

In developing the original *Behavioral Theory* and its successor, *Strategic Negotiations*, our aim was to provide students with a map of the bargaining process as practiced by skilled negotiators. So it has been heartening to us that our ideas, derived from field observations, have proved useful in exposing many, many professionals to the possibility that labor-management relations can be structured differently and with beneficial outcomes for all the parties.

What is more important is that these educational programs (and scores are being conducted annually by a variety of educational institutions and government agencies) hold the promise of advancing our understanding of how skilled and experienced practitioners resolve the many dilemmas they encounter in their pursuit of effective negotiations.

What makes our field so rewarding is the interplay between theory and practice that continues to take place—now facilitated by educational programs offered in hundreds of venues around the country. As the saying goes, there is nothing so practical as good theory, and it should be added that there is nothing so stimulating to new theory as a deep understanding of practice, or of negotiations as practiced by experienced professionals.

References

Adam, Heribert. 1998. "Trading Justice for Truth." *World Today* 54(1):11–13.

Adler, Paul, and Brian Borys. 1996. "Two Kinds of Bureaucracy: Enabling and Coercive." *Administrative Science Quarterly* 41(1):61–89.

Advisory, Conciliation and Arbitration Service (ACAS). 1991. *Annual Report 1990*. London: HMSO.

American Law Institute. 1992. *Principles of Corporate Governance: Analysis and Recommendations*. Philadelphia: American Law Institute.

Ancona, Deborah G. 1990. "Outward Bound: Strategies for Team Survival in an Organization." *Academy of Management Journal* 33(2):334–65.

Ancona, Deborah G., and David. F. Caldwell. 1992. "Bridging the Boundary: External Activity and Performance in Organizational Teams." *Administrative Science Quarterly* 37(4):634–65.

Anonymous. 1995. "An Overdue Apology." *Psychology Today* 28(5):19.

Anonymous. 1997. "Burying South Africa's Past." *Economist* 345(8041):21–23.

Argote, Linda, and Joseph E. McGrath. 1993. "Group Processes in Organizations: Continuity and Change." In *International Review of Industrial and Organizational Psychology*, vol. 8, edited by C. L. Cooper and I. T. Robertson, 333–89. New York: John Wiley and Sons.

Assemblée Nationale. 1983. *Code du Travail*. Paris: Assemblée Nationale.

Babcock, Linda, George Loewenstein, Samuel Issacharoff, and Colin Camerer. 1995. "Biased Judgments of Fairness in Bargaining." *American Economic Review* 85(5):1337–44.

Babson, Steven. 1999. "An Overview of Lean Production and Modular Assembly." Presentation at the UAW Local 595 Conference on Changing Work Rules and New Technology, Linden, N.J., January.

Baldwin, Carliss Y., and Kim B. Clark. 1997. "Managing in an Age of Modularity." *Harvard Business Review* 75(5):84–93.

Barca, Fabrizio. 1998. "Some Views on U.S. Corporate Governance." In *Corporate Governance Today: Columbia Law School Sloan Project*, 489–507. New York: Columbia Law School.

315

Bar-On, Dan. 1995. "Personal and Historical Catastrophe. Four Encounters between Descendants of Survivors and Descendants of Perpetrators of the Holocaust: Building Bonds out of Silence." *Psychiatry* 58(3):225–45.

Bartunek, Jean M., Deborah M. Kolb, and Roy J. Lewicki. 1992. "Bringing Conflict out from behind the Scenes: Private, Informal, and Nonrational Dimensions of Conflict in Organizations." In *Hidden Conflict in Organizations: Uncovering behind-the-Scenes Disputes*, edited by Deborah M. Kolb and Jean M. Bartunek, 209–28. Newbury Park, Calif.: Sage.

Bazerman, Max H. 1983. "Negotiator Judgment: A Critical Look at the Rationality Assumption." *American Behavioral Scientist* 27(2):618–34.

Bazerman, Max H., Don A. Moore, and James Judson Gillespie. 1999. "The Human Mind as a Barrier to Wiser Environmental Agreements." *American Behavioral Scientist* 42(8):1277–1300.

Bazerman, Max H., and Margaret A. Neale. 1982. "Improving Negotiation Effectiveness under Final Offer Arbitration: The Role of Selection and Training." *Journal of Applied Psychology* 67(5):543–48.

———. 1992. *Negotiating Rationally*. New York: Free Press.

Beaumont, Phillip B., and Richard I. D. Harris. 1994. "Opposition to Unions in the Non-union Sector in Britain." *International Journal of Human Resource Management* 5(2):457–72.

Beaumont, Phillip B., Richard Harris, and Roger Phayre. 1995. "Large, Multi-establishment Companies and Opposition to Unions in Britain." *Review of Employment Topics* 3(1):111.

Bellotti, Victoria, and Sara Bly. 1996. "Walking away from the Desktop Computer: Distributed Collaboration and Mobility in a Product Design Team." In *Proceedings of the Conference on Computer Supported Cooperative Work*, edited by M. Ackerman, 209–18. Boston: ACM Press.

Bendersky, Corinne. 1998. "Culture: The Missing Link in Dispute Systems Design." *Negotiation Journal* 14(4):307–11.

Benford, Steve, Chris Brown, Gail Reynard, and Chris Greenhalgh. 1996. "Shared Spaces: Transportation, Artificiality, and Spatiality." In *Proceedings of the Conference on Computer Supported Cooperative Work*, edited by M. Ackerman, 77–85. Boston: ACM Press.

Bhagat, Sanjai, and Bernard Black. 1998. "The Uncertain Relationship between Board Composition and Firm Performance." In *Corporate Governance Today: Columbia Law School Sloan Project*, 291–316. New York: Columbia Law School.

Bingaman, Jeff. 1996. "Scrambling to Pay the Bills: Building Allies for America's Working Families." Unpublished paper, United States Senate.

Blair, Margaret M. 1995. *Ownership and Control*. Washington, D.C.: Brookings Institution.

Blake, Robert, and Jane S. Mouton. 1984. *Solving Costly Organizational Conflicts*. San Francisco: Jossey-Bass.

Blancero, Donna, and Lee Dyer. 1996. "Due Process for Non-union Employees: The Influence of System Characteristics on Fairness Perceptions." *Human Resources Management* 33(3):343–59.

Blau, Francine, and Lawrence Kahn. 1996. "Where Are We in the Economics of Gender? The Gender Pay Gap." Working paper no. 5664:1–37, National Bureau of Economics, Cambridge.

Brewer, Neil, Carlene Wilson, and Karen Beck. 1994. "Supervisory Behavior and Team Performance amongst Police Patrol Sergeants." *Journal of Occupational and Organizational Psychology* 67(1):69–79.

Bronfenbrenner, Kate L., and Tom Juravich. 1995. "Overcoming Barriers to Organizing Women Workers in the Private and Public Sectors." Paper prepared for Workplace 2000: Women's Rights, Workers' Rights, Cornell University/New York State School of Industrial and Labor Relations, New York City, May.

Brown, Clair, and Melissa Appleyard. 2001. "Employment Practices and Semiconductor Manufacturing Performance." *Industrial Relations* 40(3):436–71.

Brown, Roger. 1986. *Social Psychology*, 2d ed. New York: Free Press.

Buckley, Anthony, and Mary Catherine Kenney. 1995. *Negotiating Identity: Rhetoric, Metaphor, and Social Drama in Northern Ireland*. Washington, D.C.: Smithsonian Institution Press.

Burnham, James. 1941. *The Managerial Revolution*. New York: John Day.

Business Roundtable. 1981. *Statement on Corporate Responsibility*. Washington, D.C.: Business Roundtable.

———. 1997. *Statement on Corporate Governance*. Washington, D.C.: Business Roundtable.

Carney, William J. 1993. "The ALI's Corporate Governance Project: The Death of Property Rights?" *George Washington Law Review* 61(4):898–925.

Carnoy, Martin, Manuel Castells, and Chris Benner. 1996. "What Is Happening to the US Labor Market? Part 1: A Review of the Evidence." Unpublished manuscript, University of California, Berkeley.

Carré, Françoise. 1995. "Policy Responses to the Growth of Unstable Employment Arrangements: The French and Canadian Experiences." In *47th Annual Proceedings of the Industrial Relations Research Association*, edited by the Industrial Relations Research Association (IRRA), 422–29. Madison, Wisc.: IRRA.

Castells, Manuel. 1997. "Sustainable Flexibility." Unpublished manuscript, University of California, Berkeley.

Center for Public Resources Institute for Dispute Resolution. 1997. *Employment ADR: A Dispute Resolution Program for Corporate Employees*. New York: Center for Public Resources Institute for Dispute Resolution.

Chamberlain, Neil W., and James W. Kuhn. 1965. *Collective Bargaining*, 2d ed. New York: McGraw-Hill.

Charles, Maria. 1995. "Cross-national Variation in Occupational Sex Segregation." *American Sociological Review* 57(2):483–502.

Charron, Elsie. 1999. "FASA Renault: Innovation in Productive Flexibility and Job Security." In *Between Imitation and Innovation: The Transfer and Hybridization of Productive Models in the International Automobile Industry*, edited by Robert Boyer, Elsie Charron, and Ulrich Jürgens, 235–59. Oxford: Oxford University Press.

Ching, Frank. 1998. "World Leaders Vie to Say Sorry." *Far Eastern Economic Review* 161(7):34.

Cialdini, Robert B. 1993. *Influence: Science and Practice*, 3rd ed. New York: HarperCollins.

Clark, Vivian S. 1999. "Role Negotiations for Professionals Moving into Part-time Roles." Unpublished dissertation, University of British Columbia, Vancouver, Canada.

Clarkson, Max B. E., ed. 1998. *The Corporation and Its Stakeholders*. Toronto: University of Toronto Press.

Coff, Russell, and Denise M. Rousseau. 2000. "Sustainable Competitive Advantage from Relational Wealth." In *Relational Wealth*, edited by Carrie R. Leana and Denise M. Rousseau, 27–48. New York: Oxford.

Cohen, Susan G., and Diane E. Bailey. 1997. "What Makes Teams Work: Group Effectiveness Research from the Shop Floor to the Executive Suite." *Journal of Management* 23(3):239–90.

Collier, Abram T. 1979. "The Co-Corp: Big Business Can Reform Itself." *Harvard Business Review* 57(6):121–34.

Collins, Dennis. 1998. *Gainsharing and Power*. Ithaca: Cornell University Press.

Collins, James C., and Jerry I. Porras. 1994. *Built to Last: Successful Habits of Visionary Companies*. New York: HarperBusiness.

Colvin, Alex. 1999. "Citizens and Citadels: Dispute Resolution and the Governance of Employment Relations." Doctoral dissertation, Human Resources Management Department, School of Industrial and Labor Relations, Cornell University, Ithaca.

Confino, Alon. 1997. "Collective Memory and Cultural History: Problems of Method." *American Historical Review* 102(5):1386–1403.

Costantino, Cathy A., and Christina S. Merchant. 1996. *Designing Conflict Management Systems*. San Francisco: Jossey-Bass.

Crain, Marion. 1994. "Gender and Union Organizing." *Industrial and Labor Relations Review* 47(2):227–48.

Cramton, Catherine. 1997. "Information Problems in Dispersed Teams." In *Academy of Management Proceedings*, 298–302. Boston: Academy of Management.

Crandall, N. Fredric, and Marc J. Wallace. 1997. "Inside the Virtual Workplace: Forging a New Deal for Work and Rewards." *Compensation and Benefits Review* 29(1):27–36.

Cutcher-Gershenfeld, Joel. 1991. "The Impact on Economic Performance of a Transformation in Workplace Relations." *Industrial and Labor Relations Review* 44(2):241–60.

———. 1994. "Bargaining over How to Bargain: Addressing the Limitations of Interest-Based Bargaining in Labor Negotiations." *Negotiations Journal* 10(4):323–35.

Cutcher-Gershenfeld, Joel, and Thomas Kochan. 2002. "Taking Stock: Collective Bargaining at the Turn of the Century." Working paper, MIT Sloan School of Management.

Cutcher-Gershenfeld, Joel, Thomas Kochan, and John Calhoon Wells. 1998. "How Do Labor and Management View the Collective Bargaining Process?" *Monthly Labor Review* 121(10):23–31.

———. 2001. "In Whose Interest? A First Look at National Survey Data on Interest-Based Bargaining in Labor Relations." *Industrial Relations* 40(1):3–20.

Cutcher-Gershenfeld, Joel, Robert McKersie, and Richard Walton. 1995. *Pathways to Change*. Kalamazoo, Mich.: W. E. Upjohn Institute.

———. 1996. "Strategies for Negotiating Fundamental Change." Unpublished working paper, Massachusetts Institute of Technology, Cambridge.

D'Aveni, Richard A. 1994. *Hypercompetition*. New York: Free Press.

David, Parthiban, Rahul Kochhar, and Edward Levitas. 1998. "The Effect of Institutional Investors on the Level and Mix of CEO Compensation." *Academy of Management Journal* 41(2):200–8.

Davidson, Martin N., and Leonard Greenhalgh. 1999. "The Role of Emotion in Negotiation: Reflections on Race and Anger." In *Research on Negotiations in Organizations*, vol. 7, edited by Robert J. Bies, Roy J. Lewicki, and Blair H. Sheppard, 3–26. Greenwich, Conn.: JAI Press.

Davis-Blake, Alison, and Joseph Broschak. 2000. "Speed Bumps along the Way: Developing Roles for Labor Intermediaries." In *Relational Wealth*, edited by Carrie R. Leana and Denise M. Rousseau, 91–115. New York: Oxford.

Denison, Daniel R., Stuart L. Hart, and Joel A. Kahn. 1996. "From Chimneys to Cross-functional Teams: Developing and Validating a Diagnostic Model." *Academy of Management Journal* 39(4):1005–23.

Department of Trade and Industry. 1998. *Fairness at Work*, Cmd. 3968, May. London: HMSO.

Derber, Charles. 1994. *Money, Murder, and the American Dream*. Boston: Faber and Faber.

Development Dimensions International (DDI). 1997. "Teams and the People Who Keep Them Going." Research Bulletin 3. Pittsburgh: DDI.

Diekmann, Kristina, Steven Samuels, Lee Ross, and Max Bazerman. 1997. "Self-Interest and Fairness in Problems of Resource Allocation." *Journal of Personality and Social Psychology* 72(5):1061–74.

Dodd, E. Merrick, Jr. 1932. "For Whom Are Corporate Managers Trustees?" *Harvard Law Review* 45(7):1145–63. (Reprinted 1998 in *The Corporation and Its Stakeholders*, edited by Max Clarkson, 31–46. Toronto: University of Toronto Press.)

Dunlop, John T. 1984. *Dispute Resolution: Negotiations and Consensus Building*. Dover, Mass.: Auburn House Publishing.

Dunlop, John T., and John J. Healy. 1953. *Collective Bargaining: Principles and Cases*. Homewood, Ill.: Irwin.

Durkheim, Emile. 1947. *The Division of Labor in Society*. New York: Free Press.

Edwards, Richard, and David Lewin. 1993. *Rights at Work: Employment Relations in the Post-union Era*. Washington, D.C.: Brookings Institution.

Ethier, Kathleen A., and Kay Deaux. 1994. "Negotiating Social Identity When Contexts Change: Maintaining Identification and Responding to Threat." *Journal of Personality and Social Psychology* 67(2):243–51.

ETUI (European Trade Union Information On-line). www.etui.org.press. July 12, 1997; March 5, 1998; July 16, 1998.

European Foundation for the Improvement of Living and Working Conditions.

www.eiro.eurofoun. "Big Pay Gap Remains between Men and Women," January 17, 1998; "UNICE Opens Door to Negotiations on Rights of Fixed-Term Contract Workers," February 18, 1998; "First Annual Report on Equal Opportunities Published," March 11, 1998; "Commission Issues Communication on Social Action Programme 1998–2000," May 10, 1998; "Cardiff Summit Debates Next Steps in Employment Strategy," June 10, 1998.

Ewing, David W. 1989. *Justice on the Job*. Boston: Harvard Business School Press.

Fadil, Paul A. 1995. "The Effect of Cultural Stereotypes on Leader Attributions of Minority Subordinates." *Journal of Managerial Issues* 7(2):193–208.

Fanon, Frantz. 1967. *The Wretched of the Earth [Les Damnés de la Terre]*. Translated by Constance Farrington. Harmondsworth, U.K.: Penguin.

Fichman, Mark, and Paul S. Goodman. 1996. "Customer Supplier Ties in Interorganizational Relations." In *Research in Organizational Behavior*, vol. 18, edited by B. Staw and L. Cummings, 285–329. Greenwich, Conn.: JAI Press.

Fisher, Kimball. 1993. *Leading Self-Directed Work Teams: A Guide to Developing New Team Leadership Skills*. New York: McGraw-Hill.

Fisher, Roger. 1989. "Negotiating Inside-Out: What Are the Best Ways to Relate Internal Negotiations with External Ones?" *Negotiation Journal* 5(1):33–41.

Fisher, Roger, and William Ury. 1981. *Getting to Yes: Negotiating Agreement without Giving in*. With Bruce Patton. Boston: Houghton Mifflin.

Fisher, Roger, William Ury, and Bruce Patton. 1991. *Getting to Yes*, 2d ed. Boston: Houghton Mifflin.

Federal Mediation and Conciliation Service (FMCS) Collective Bargaining Surveys. 1996 and 1999. Washington, D.C.: FMCS. Data available on request from the author (Joel Cutcher-Gershenfeld), subject to approval from the FMCS.

Fogarty, Gay M., and Denise M. Rousseau. 1999. "Spillover in Psychological Contracts: The Case of Rehired Workers." Technical report, Heinz School of Public Policy, Carnegie-Mellon University, Pittsburgh.

Follett, Mary Parker. 1942. *Dynamic Administration: The Collected Papers of Mary Parker Follett*, edited by H. C. Metcalf and L. Urwick. New York: Harper and Row.

Fondas, Nanette. 1996. "Feminization at Work: Career Implications." In *The Boundaryless Career: A New Employment Principle for a New Organizational Era*, edited by Michael B. Arthur and Denise M. Rousseau, 282–94. New York: Oxford.

Forester, John. 1989. *Planning in the Face of Power*. Berkeley: University of California Press.

Freeman, Richard B., and James L Medoff. 1984. *What Do Unions Do?* New York: Basic Books.

Freyssenet, Michel. 1999. "Renault: From Diversified Mass Production to Innovative Flexible Production." In *One Best Way?: Trajectories and Industrial Models of the World's Automobile Producers*, edited by Michel Freyssenet, Andrew Mair, and Koichi Shimizu, 365–94. Oxford: Oxford University Press.

Friedman, Ray. 1994. *Front-Stage, Back-Stage*. San Francisco: Jossey-Bass.

Friedman, Stewart D., Perry Christensen, and Jennifer DeGroot. 1998. "Work and Life: End of the Zero Sum Game." *Harvard Business Review* 76(6):119–29.

Furtado, Thomas, and Charles L. Howard. 1999. "The United States Sentencing Guidelines—What an Organizational Ombuds Might Want to Know and Share with Management." Dallas: Ombudsman Association.

Galbraith, Jay. 1977. *Organizational Design*. Reading, Mass.: Addison-Wesley.

Gardner, B.B., and William F. Whyte. 1945. "The Man in the Middle: Position and Problems of the Foreman." *Applied Anthropology* 4(2):1–28.

General Accounting Office (GAO). 1997. *ADR: Employers Experience with ADR in the Workplace*. Report GAO/GGS-97–157. Washington, D.C.: GAO.

George, Jennifer M. 1990. "Personality, Affect and Behavior in Groups." *Journal of Applied Psychology* 75(2):107–17.

George, Jennifer M., and Art P. Brief. 1992. "Feeling Good—Doing Good: A Conceptual Analysis of the Mood at Work-Organizational Spontaneity Relationship." *Psychological Bulletin* 112(2):310–29.

Gilkey, Roderick W., and Leonard Greenhalgh. 1986. "The Role of Personality in Successful Negotiating." *Negotiation Journal* 2(3):245–56.

Golden, Clinton S., and Virginia Parker. 1949. *Causes of Industrial Peace under Collective Bargaining*. New York: Harper and Bros.

Golden, Clinton S., and Harold Ruttenberg. 1942. *Dynamics of Industrial Democracy*. New York: Harper and Bros.

Goodman, Paul S., and Steve Garber. 1988. "The Effects of Absenteeism on Accidents in a Dangerous Environment: Empirical Analysis of Data from Underground Coal Mines." *Journal of Applied Psychology* 73(1):81–86.

Goodman, Paul S., and Dennis P. Leyden. 1991. "Familiarity and Group Productivity." *Journal of Applied Psychology* 76(4):578–86.

Goodman, Paul S., Elizabeth C. Ravlin, and Linda Argote. 1986. "Current Thinking about Groups: Setting the Stage for New Ideas." In *Designing Effective Work Groups*, edited by Paul S. Goodman, 1–33. San Francisco: Jossey-Bass.

Gore, Albert. 1992. *Earth in the Balance*. Boston: Houghton Mifflin.

Greenhalgh, Leonard. 1986. "Managing Conflict." *Sloan Management Review* 27(4):45–51.

——. 1987a. "The Case against Winning in Negotiations." *Negotiation Journal* 3(2):167–78.

——. 1987b. "Interpersonal Conflict in Organizations." In *International Review of Industrial and Organizational Psychology*, vol. 1, edited by Cary L. Cooper and Ivan T. Robertson, 229–71. Chichester, Sussex: Wiley.

——. 2001. *Managing Strategic Relationships*. New York: Free Press.

Greenhalgh, Leonard, and Deborah I. Chapman. 1995. "Joint Decision Making: The Inseparability of Relationships and Negotiation." In *Negotiation as a Social Process*, edited by Roderick M. Kramer and David M. Messick, 166–85. Thousand Oaks, Calif.: Sage.

Greenhalgh, Leonard, and Roderick W. Gilkey. 1993. "Effect of Relationship-Orientation on Negotiators' Cognitions and Tactics." *Group Decision and Negotiation* 2(2):167–78.

Greenhalgh, Leonard, and Thor Indridason. 1998. *The Economic and Strategic Imperatives for Labour: A Relational Perspective*. Working paper, Templeton College, Oxford University.

Grimshaw, Damian, and Jill Rubery. 1997. *The Concentration of Women's Employment and Relative Occupational Pay: A Statistical Framework for Comparative Analysis*. Labour Market and Social Policy occasional paper no. 26:1–93. Paris: Organization for Economic Cooperation and Development.

Guest, Robert H. 1979. "Quality of Working Life—Learning from Tarrytown." *Harvard Business Review* 5(4):76–87.

Guzzo, Richard A., and Marcus W. Dickson. 1996. "Teams in Organizations: Recent Research on Performance and Effectiveness." *Annual Review of Psychology* 47:307–38.

Gwartney-Gibbs, Patricia A., and Denise H. Lach. 1992. "Sociological Explanations for Failure to Seek Sexual Harassment Remedies." *Mediation Quarterly* 9(4):363–73.

Hackman, J. Richard. 1983. "A Normative Model of Work Team Effectiveness." Technical report no. 1, Research Program on Group Effectiveness, Yale School of Organization and Management, New Haven, Conn.

Hackman, J. Richard, and Greg R. Oldham. 1980. *Work Redesign*. Reading, Mass.: Addison-Wesley.

Haley, John O. 1998. "Apology and Pardon: Learning from Japan." *American Behavioral Scientist* 41(6):842–67.

Handy, Charles. 1989. *The Age of Unreason*. Cambridge, Mass.: Harvard Business School Press.

——. 1995. "Trust and the Virtual Organization." *Harvard Business Review* 73(3):40–50.

——. 1997. "The Citizen Corporation." *Harvard Business Review* 75(5):26–28.

Hayes, Grahame. 1998. "We Suffer Our Memories: Thinking about the Past, Healing, and Reconciliation." *American Imago* 55(1):29–50.

Heider, Fritz. 1958. *The Psychology of Interpersonal Relations*. New York: Wiley.

Hermalin, Benjamin E., and Michael S. Weisbach. 1998. "Endogenously Chosen Boards of Directors and Their Monitoring of the CEO." *American Economic Review* 88(1):96–118.

Hertig, Gerard. 1998. "Corporate Governance in the United States as Seen from Europe." In *Corporate Governance Today: Columbia Law School Sloan Project*, 509–25. New York: Columbia Law School.

Hills, Frederick S., Robert M. Madigan, K. Don Scott, and Steven G. Markham. 1990. "Tracking the Merit of Merit Pay." In *Human Resource Management: Perspectives and Issues*, 2d ed., edited by G.R. Ferris, K.M. Rowland, and M.N. Buckley, 243–48. Boston: Allyn and Bacon.

Hoffman, Andrew, James Judson Gillespie, Don A. Moore, Kimberly A. Wade-Benzoni, Leigh Thompson, and Max H. Bazerman. 1999. "A Mixed-Motive Perspective on the Economics versus Environment Debate." *American Behavioral Scientist* 42(8):1254–76.

hooks, bell. 1994. *Outlaw Culture: Resisting Representation*. London: Routledge & Kegan Paul.

——. 1995. *Killing Rage: Ending Racism*. New York: Henry Holt.

Hunter, Larry W. 1998. "Can Strategic Participation Be Institutionalized? Union

Representation on American Corporate Boards." *Industrial and Labor Relations Review* 51(4):557–78.

Hutton, Patrick H. 1994. "Review Essays—History and Memory by Jacques Le Goff and Translated by Steven Rendall and Elizabeth Claman / Assassins of Memory: Essays of the Denial of the Holocaust by Pierre Vidal-Naquet and Translated with a Foreword by Jeffrey Mehlman." *History and Theory* 33(1):95–107.

Ichniowski, Casey. 1992. "Human Resource Practices and Productive Labor-Management Relations." In *Research Frontiers in Industrial Relations and Human Resources*, edited by David Lewin, Olivia S. Mitchell, and Peter D. Sherer, 239–72. Madison, Wisc.: Industrial Relations Research Association.

Ichniowski, Casey, Thomas Kochan, David Levine, Craig Olson, and George Strauss. 1996. "What Works at Work: Overview and Assessment." *Industrial Relations* 35(3):299–333.

Ingram, Paul, and Simon Tal. 1995. "Institutional and Resource Dependence Determinants of Responsiveness to Work-Family Issues." *Academy of Management Journal* 38(5):1466–82.

International Labour Office (ILO) of the United Nations. 1998. *World Labour Report*. Geneva, Switzerland: ILO.

IRS Employment Review. 1994. No. 552, January.

———. 1994. No. 556, March.

Jürgens, Ulrich. 1997. "Rolling Back Cycle Times: The Renaissance of the Classic Assembly Line in Final Assembly." In *Transforming Auto Assembly—International Experiences with Automation and Work Organization*, edited by Takahiro Fujimoto, Ulrich Jürgens, and Koichi Shimokawa, 255–73. Frankfurt: Springer Verlag.

Jürgens, Ulrich, Thomas Malsch, and Knuth Dohse. 1993. *Breaking from Taylorism: Changing Forms of Work in the Automobile Industry*. Cambridge: Cambridge University Press.

Katz, Daniel, and Robert L. Kahn. 1965. *Social Psychological of Organizations*. New York: Wiley.

Katz, Harry, and Owen Darbishire. 1999. *Converging Divergences: Worldwide Changes in Employment Systems*. Ithaca: Cornell University Press.

Katz, Harry C., Thomas A. Kochan, and Mark R. Weber. 1985. "Assessing the Effects of Industrial Relations Systems and Efforts to Improve the Quality of Working Life on Organizational Effectiveness." *Academy of Management Journal* 28(3):509–26.

Kaufman, Bruce E., and Morris M. Kleiner, eds. 1995. *Employee Representation: Alternatives and Future Directions*. Madison, Wisc.: Industrial Relations Research Association.

Kelley, Maryellen R. 1996. "Participative Bureaucracy and Productivity in the Machine Products Sector." *Industrial Relations* 35(3):374–99.

Kelman, H.C. 1997. "Negotiating National Identity and Self-Determination in Ethnic Conflicts—The Choice between Pluralism and Ethnic Cleansing." *Negotiation Journal* 13(4):327–40.

Kemske, Floyd. 1998. "HR 2008: A Forecast." *Workforce* 77(1):46–55.

Khanna, Tarun, and Krishna Palepu. 1997. "Why Focused Strategies May Be Wrong for Emerging Markets." *Harvard Business Review* 75(4):41–51.

Kilmann, Ralph H., and Kenneth W. Thomas. 1977. "Developing a Forced-Choice Measure of Conflict-Handling Behavior: The Mode Instrument." *Educational and Psychological Measurement* 37(2):309–25.

Klein, Janice A. 1984. "Why Supervisors Resist Employee Involvement." *Harvard Business Review* 62(5):87–95.

———. 1991. "A Reexamination of Autonomy in Light of New Manufacturing Practices." *Human Relations* 44(1):21–38.

Knowlton, William, and Daniel R. Ilgen. 1980. "Performance Attributional Effects on Feedback from Superiors." *Organizational Behavior and Human Decision Processes* 25(3):441–52.

Kochan, Thomas. 1974. "A Theory of Multi-lateral Bargaining in City Government." *Industrial and Labor Relations Review* 27(4):525–42.

Kochan, Thomas A., Harry C. Katz, and Robert B. McKersie. 1986. *The Transformation of American Industrial Relations.* New York: Basic Books. Reprinted by ILR Press, Ithaca, 1994.

Kochan, Thomas, Brenda Lautsch, and Corinne Bendersky. 2000. "An Evaluation of the Massachusetts Commission against Discrimination's Alternative Dispute Resolution Program." *Harvard Negotiation Law Review* 5 (Spring):233–78.

Kochan, Thomas A., and Saul Rubinstein. 2000. "Toward a Stakeholder Theory of the Firm: The Saturn Partnership." *Organization Science* 11(4):367–86.

Kogut, Bruce, and Udo Zander. 1992. "Knowledge of the Firm, Combinative Capabilities, and the Replication of Technology." *Organization Science* 3(3):383–97.

Kolodny, Harvey, and Moses Kiggundu. 1980. "Towards the Development of a Sociotechnical Systems Model in Woodlands Mechanical Harvesting." *Human Relations* 33(9):623–45.

Komaki, Judith L., Mitzi L. Desselles, and Eric D. Bowman. 1989. "Definitely Not a Breeze: Extending an Operant Model of Effective Supervision to Teams." *Journal of Applied Psychology* 74(3):522–29.

Kraut, Robert. 1994. *Research Recommendations to Facilitate Distributed Work.* Washington, D.C.: National Academy Press.

Kuhlmann, Martin, and Michael Schumann. 1997. "Patterns of Work Organization in the German Automobile Industry." In *Transforming Auto Assembly—International Experiences with Automation and Work Organization,* edited by Takahiro Fujimoto, Ulrich Jürgens, and Koichi Shimokawa, 289–304. Frankfurt: Springer Verlag.

Kuhn, Thomas. 1970. *The Structure of Scientific Revolutions.* Chicago: University of Chicago Press.

Lach, Denise H., and Patricia A. Gwartney-Gibbs. 1993. "Sociological Perspectives on Sexual Harassment and Workplace Dispute Resolution." *Journal of Vocational Behavior* 42(1):102–15.

Lawler, Edward E., III. 1981. *Pay and Organization Development.* Reading, Mass.: Addison-Wesley.

——. 1986. *High-Involvement Management*. San Francisco: Jossey-Bass.

Lax, David A., and James K. Sebenius. 1986. *The Manager as Negotiator: Bargaining for Cooperation and Competitive Gain*. New York: Free Press.

Leana, Carrie R., and Denise M. Rousseau. 2000. *Relational Wealth*. New York: Oxford.

Levesque, Laurie, and Denise M. Rousseau. 1999. "Socialization and Commitment among Adjunct Faculty." Paper presented at the Academy of Management meetings, Chicago, August.

Lewicki, Roy J., Joseph A. Litterer, John W. Minton, and David M. Saunders. 1994. *Negotiation*, 2d ed. Burr Ridge, Ill.: Irwin.

Lewicki, Roy J., Steven E. Weiss, and David Lewin. 1992. "Models of Conflict, Negotiation and Third Party Intervention: A Review and Synthesis." *Journal of Organizational Behavior* 13(3):209–52.

Lewin, David. 1990. "Grievance Procedures in Nonunion Workplaces: An Empirical Analysis of Usage, Dynamics and Outcomes." *Chicago-Kent Law Review* 66(817):823–44.

Lewin, David, and Richard Peterson. 1999. "Behavioral Outcomes of Grievance Activity." *Industrial Relations* 38(4):554–76.

Lewis, Jane, ed. 1993. *Women and Social Policies in Europe*. London: Edward Elgar.

Lies, Elaine. 1998. "Japan Spokesman Adds Fuel to China Apology Flap." Tokyo (Reuters), November 27.

Lipsky, David B., and Ron L. Seeber. 1998. *The Appropriate Resolution of Corporate Disputes: A Report on the Growing Use of ADR by U.S. Corporations*. Ithaca: Cornell/PERC Institute on Conflict Resolution.

Lorde, Audre. 1984. *Sister Outsider: Essays and Speeches*. Trumansburg, N.Y.: Crossing Press.

Lorsch, Jay, and Samantha K. Graff. 1996. "Corporate Governance." In *International Encyclopedia of Business and Management*, 772–82. London: Routledge.

Lynch, Jennifer. 1996. "RCMP: Revitalizing Culture, Motivating People." Report on the Royal Canadian Mounted Police ADR Project. Unpublished paper, PDG Personnel Direction Group, Ottawa, Canada.

Macauley, S., and E. Walster. 1971. "Legal Structures and Restoring Equity." *Journal of Social Issues* 27:17–95.

Maccoby, Michael. 1997. "Learning to Partner and Partnering to Learn." *Research Technology Management* 40(3):55–57.

MacDuffie, John Paul. 1995. "Human Resource Bundles and Manufacturing Performance: Organizational Logic and Flexible Production in the World Auto Industry." *Industrial and Labor Relations Review* 48(2):192–221.

——. 1996. "International Trends in Work Organization in the Auto Industry: National-Level vs. Company-Level Perspectives." In *The Comparative Political Economy of Industry Relations*, edited by Kirsten Wever and Lowell Turner, 71–113. Madison, Wisc.: Industrial Relations Research Association.

——. 1999a. "Global Strategy, Future of the Auto Industry." Presentation at the

UAW Local 595 Conference on Changing Work Rules and New Technology, Linden, N.J., January.

——. 1999b. "The Transfer of Organizing Principles: Cross-Cultural Influences on Replication at Opel Eisenach." In *Organizational and Technological Innovation in the Automotive Industry: Recent Developments*, edited by Anna Comacchio, Giuseppe Volpato, and Arnaldo Camuffo, 119–37. Berlin: Springer Verlag.

MacDuffie, John Paul, and Frits Pil. 1997a. "Changes in Auto Industry Practices: An International Overview." In *After Lean Production: Evolving Employment Practices in the World Auto Industry*, edited by Thomas A. Kochan, Russell D. Lansbury, and John Paul MacDuffie, 9–44. Ithaca: Cornell University/ILR Press.

——. 1997b. "Flexible Technologies, Flexible Workers." In *Transforming Auto Assembly—International Experiences with Automation and Work Organization*, edited by Takahiro Fujimoto, Ulrich Jürgens, and Koichi Shimokawa, 238–54. Frankfurt: Springer Verlag.

MacDuffie, John Paul, Kannan Sethuraman, and Marshall Fisher. 1996. "Product Variety and Manufacturing Performance: Evidence from the International Assembly Plant Study." *Management Science* 42(3):350–69.

Manz, Charles C., and Henry P. Sims Jr. 1993. *Business without Bosses: How Self-Managing Teams Are Building High-Performing Companies*. New York: John Wiley & Sons.

McCabe, Douglas M. 1988. *Corporate Nonunion Complaint Procedures and Systems*. New York: Praeger.

McDermott, Patrick, Ruth Obar, Anita Jose, and Mollie Bowers. 2000. "An Evaluation of the Equal Employment Opportunity Commission Mediation Program." Washington, D.C., U.S. Equal Employment Opportunity Commission.

McGrath, Joseph E. 1984. *Groups: Interaction and Performance*. Englewood Cliffs: Prentice Hall.

Messick, David M., and Keith. P. Sentis. 1985. "Estimating Social and Nonsocial Utility Functions from Ordinal Data." *European Journal of Social Psychology* 15(4):389–99.

Metcalf, David. 1993. "Transformation of British Industrial Relations? Institutions, Conduct and Outcomes, 1980–1990." Discussion paper no. 151, Centre for Economic Performance, London School of Economics.

Meyerson, Debra, Karl E. Weick, and Roderick M. Kramer. 1996. "Swift Trust and Temporary Groups." In *Trust in Organizations: Frontiers of Theory and Research*, edited by R.M. Kramer and T.R. Tyler, 166–95. Thousand Oaks, Calif.: Sage.

Miles, Raymond M., and W.E.D. Creed. 1995. "Organizational Forms and Managerial Philosophies." In *Research in Organizational Behavior*, edited by L.L. Cummings and B.M. Staw, 17. Greenwich, Conn.: JAI Press.

Miller, Jean Baker. 1976. *Toward a New Psychology of Women*. Boston: Beacon Press.

Millon, David. 1993. "New Directions in Corporate Law: Communitarians, Contractarians, and the Crisis in Corporate Law." *Washington and Lee Law Review* 50(4):1373–93.

Millward, Neil, Mark Stevens, David Smart, and William Hawes. 1992. *Workplace Industrial Relations in Transition*. Aldershot, U.K.: Dartmouth.

Milner, Simon. 1994. "Charting the Coverage of Collective Pay Setting Institutions: 1895–1990." Discussion paper no. 215, Centre for Economic Performance, London School of Economics, December.

Milner, Simon, and Edward Richards. 1991. "Determinants of Union Recognition and Employee Involvement: Evidence from London Docklands." *British Journal of Industrial Relations* 29(3):377–90.

Mirvis, Philip H., and Douglas T. Hall. 1996. "Psychological Success and the Boundaryless Career." In *The Boundaryless Career: A New Employment Principle for a New Organizational Era*, edited by Michael B. Arthur and Denise M. Rousseau, 237–55. New York: Oxford.

Mnookin, Robert, and Lawrence Susskind. 1999. *Negotiating on Behalf of Others*. Thousand Oaks, Calif.: Sage.

Monks, John. 1998. Trade Unions, Enterprise and the Future. In *Human Resource Management, The New Agenda*, edited by Paul Sparrow and Mick Marchington, 171–79. London: Financial Times Management.

Moreland, Richard L., and John M. Levine. 2000. "Socialization in Organizations and Work Groups." In *Groups at Work: Advances in Theory and Research*, edited by Marlene Turner, 69–112. Mahwah, N.J.: Lawrence Erlbaum.

Morris, Jonathan. 1996. "Zaibatsu (Keiretsu)." In *International Encyclopedia of Business and Management*, 5109–13. London: Routledge.

Murnighan, J. Keith. 1986. "Organizational Coalitions: Structural Contingencies and the Formation Process." In *Research on Negotiation in Organization*, vol. 1, edited by Roy J. Lewicki, Blair H. Sheppard, and Max H. Bazerman, 155–73. Greenwich, Conn.: JAI Press.

——. 1991. *The Dynamics of Bargaining Games*. Englewood Cliffs, N.J.: Prentice Hall.

Nash, John F. 1950. "The Bargaining Problem." *Econometrica* 18(April):155–62.

Neale, Margaret A., and Max H. Bazerman. 1983. "The Role of Perspective-Taking Ability in Negotiating under Different Forms of Arbitration." *Industrial and Labor Relations Review* 36(3):378–88.

Nonaka, Ikujiro. 1994. "A Dynamic Theory of Organizational Knowledge Creation." *Organization Science* 5(1):14–38.

O'Brien, Dennis. 1997. "The Uncommon Ground of Dialogue." *America* 176(12):12–15.

Olivera, Fernando. 1998. "Memory Systems in Organizations." Doctoral dissertation, Carnegie-Mellon University, Pittsburgh.

Olson, Judith S., and Stephanie Teasley. 1996. "Groupware in the Wild: Lessons Learned from a Year of Virtual Collocation." In *Proceedings of the Conference on Computer Supported Cooperative Work*, edited by M. Ackerman, 419–27. Boston: ACM Press.

Orts, Eric W. 1992. "Beyond Shareholders: Interpreting Corporate Constituency Statutes." *George Washington Law Review* 61(1):14–135.

Ostner, Ilona, and Jane Lewis. 1994. "Gender and the Evolution of European Social Policies." In *European Social Policy: Between Fragmentation and Integration*, edited by Stephan Liebfried and Paul Pierson, 45–57. Washington, D.C.: Brookings Institution.

Ozawa, Connie P. 1991. *Recasting Science: Consensual Procedures in Public Policy Making*. Boulder, Colo.: Westview Press.

Palmer, Karen, Wallace Oates, and Paul Portney. 1995. "Tightening Environmental Standards: The Benefit-Cost or the No-Cost Paradigm?" *Journal of Economic Perspectives* 9(4):119–32.

Pandya, A., F. Rosenfeld, and V. Caffee. 1998. "A Strong Superfund Law Is Crucial To Make Polluters Clean Up Sites." *Asbury Park (New Jersey) Press*, 11 March.

Parus, B. 1998. "Stock Becomes Prevalent as a Compensation Tool." *American Compensation Association News*, September 12–15.

Pasmore, William A., and John J. Sherwood. 1978. *Sociotechnical Systems: A Sourcebook*. San Diego: University Associates.

Pearce, Jone L. 1993. "Toward an Organizational Behavior of Contract Laborers: Their Psychological Involvement and Effects on Employee Coworkers." *Academy of Management Journal* 36(5):1082–96.

Perrow, Charles. 1996. "The Bounded Career and Demise of Civil Society." In *The Boundaryless Career: A New Employment Principle for a New Organizational Era*, edited by Michael B. Arthur and Denise M. Rousseau, 297–313. New York: Oxford.

Peters, Edward. 1955. *Strategies and Tactics in Labor Negotiations*. New London, Conn.: National Foremen's Institute.

Pil, Frits K., and Takahiro Fujimoto. 1999. "Toyoto and Volvo—The Dynamic Nature of Organizational Models." In *Proceedings of Fifty-First Annual Meeting of the Industrial Relations Research Association*, edited by Paula B. Voos, 218–26. Madison, Wisc.: Industrial Relations Research Association.

Pil, Frits K., and John Paul MacDuffie. 1996. "The Adoption of High-Involvement Work Practices." *Industrial Relations* 35(3):423–55.

Porter, Michael E. 1998. "Clusters and Competition: New Agendas for Companies, Governments, and Institutions." Working Papers Collection working paper no. H374 98–080, Division of Research, Harvard Business School, Boston.

Porter, Michael E., and Claas van der Linde. 1995a. "Green and Competitive: Ending the Stalemate." *Harvard Business Review* 73(5):120–34.

———. 1995b. "Toward a New Conception of the Environment-Competitiveness Relationship." *Journal of Economic Perspectives* 9(4):97–118.

Pruitt, Dean G. 1981. *Negotiation Behavior*. New York: Academic Press.

Pruitt, Dean G., and Peter J.D. Carnevale. 1993. *Negotiation in Social Conflict*. Pacific Grove, Calif.: Brooks-Cole.

Rafaeli, Anat. 1998. "Motivation at the Point of Entry: The Implicit Employment Contract in Employment Advertising." In *A Multilevel Approach to Employee Motivation*, edited by Miriam Erez, Hank Thierry, and U. Kleinbeck. New York: Erlbaum.

Rahim, M. Azfulur. 1983. *Rahim Organizational Conflict Inventory—II*. Palo Alto, Calif.: Consulting Psychologists Press.

Raiffa, Howard. 1982. *The Art and Science of Negotiation*. Cambridge, Mass.: Harvard University Press.

——. 1998. Comments at the Robert McKersie Festschrift at MIT, October 30–31.

Rappaport, Anatole. 1960. *Fights, Games and Debates*. Ann Arbor: University of Michigan Press.

Reich, Robert B. 1998. "The New Meaning of Corporate Social Responsibility." *California Management Review* 40(2):8–17.

Reynolds, Lloyd G. 1952–1978. *Labor Economics and Labor Relations*, 1st–7th ed. Englewood Cliff, N.J.: Prentice Hall.

Roe, Mark J. 1998. "German Codetermination and German Securities Markets." In *Corporate Governance Today: Columbia Law School Sloan Project*, 727–38. New York: Columbia Law School.

Ross, Lee, and Connie Stillenger. 1991. "Barriers to Conflict Resolution." *Negotiation Journal* 7(4):389–404.

Roth, Siegfried. 1997. "Germany: Labor's Perspective on Lean Production." In *After Lean Production: Evolving Employment Practices in the World Auto Industry*, edited by Thomas A. Kochan, Russell D. Lansbury, and John Paul MacDuffie, 117–36. Ithaca: Cornell University/ILR Press.

Rousseau, Denise M. 1985. "Issues of Level in Organizational Research: Multilevel and Cross-level Perspectives." In *Research in Organizational Behavior*, vol. 7, edited by L.L. Cummings and B.M. Staw, 1–37. Greenwich, Conn.: JAI Press.

——. 1995. *Psychological Contracts in Organizations: Understanding Written and Unwritten Agreements*. Newbury Park, Calif.: Sage.

——. 2000. "Psychological Contracts in the United States: Diversity, Individualism and Associability." In *Psychological Contracts in Employment: Cross-national Perspectives*, edited by Denise M. Rousseau and Rene Schalk, 250–82. Newbury Park, Calif.: Sage.

Rousseau, Denise M., and M.B. Arthur. 1999. "The Boundaryless Human Resource Function: Building Agency and Community in the New Economic Era." *Organizational Dynamics* 27(4):6–18.

Rowe, Mary. 1984. "The Non-union Complaint System at MIT: An Upward-Feedback Mediation Model." *Alternatives to the High Cost of Litigation* 2(4):10–18. Also reprinted in Leonard L. Riskin and James Westbrook, eds. 1987. *Dispute Resolution and Lawyers*. Saint Paul, Minn.: West Publishing Company, College and School Division, and in Alan Westin and Alfred Feliu. 1988. *Resolving Employment Disputes without Litigation*. Washington, D.C.: Bureau of National Affairs.

——. 1988. "Organizational Response to Assessed Risk." In *Program Record of the 1988 IEEE Electro 1988 Conference, Risk Assessment and Response*. Boston: Institute of Electrical and Electronics Engineers.

——. 1990a. "People Who Feel Harassed Need a Complaint System with Both Formal and Informal Options." *Negotiation Journal* 6(2):161–72.

——. 1990b. "Helping People Help Themselves: An Option for Complaint Handlers." *Negotiation Journal* 6(3):239–48.

———. 1993a. "The Corporate Ombudsman: An Overview and Analysis." In *Negotiation Theory and Practice*, edited by J. William Breslin and Jeffrey Z. Rubin, 433–46. Cambridge: Harvard Program on Negotiation Books.

———. 1993b. "Options and Choice for Conflict Resolution in the Workplace." In *Negotiation: Strategies for Mutual Gain*, edited by Lavinia Hall, 105–19. Thousand Oaks, Calif.: Sage.

———. 1995. "Options, Functions, and Skills: What the Organizational Ombudsperson Might Want to Know." *Negotiation Journal* 11(2):103–14. Also reprinted by the Ombudsman Association.

———. 1997. "Dispute Resolution in the Non-union Environment: An Evolution toward Integrated Systems for Conflict Management?" In *Workplace Dispute Resolution: Directions for the 21st Century*, edited by Sandra Gleason. East Lansing: Michigan State University Press.

Rowe, Mary, and Mary Simon. 2001. "Effectiveness of Organizational Ombudsmen." In *Handbook of the Ombudsman Association*, 1–21. Hillsborough, N.J.: Ombudsman Association.

Royal Commission on Trade Unions and Employers Associations. 1968. "Report," Cmd. 3623. London: HMSO.

Rubery, Jill, and Collette Fagan. 1995. "Comparative Industrial Relations Research: Towards Reversing the Gender Bias." *British Journal of Industrial Relations* 33(2):209–36.

Rubin, Jeffrey Z., and Bert R. Brown. 1975. *The Social Psychology of Bargaining and Negotiations*. New York: Academic Press.

Rubin, Jeffrey, Dean Pruitt, and S. H. Kim. 1994. *Social Conflict: Escalation, Stalemate, and Settlement*, 2d ed. New York: McGraw-Hill.

Rubinstein, Saul A. 1996. "Saturn, The GM/UAW Partnership: The Impact of Co-management and Joint Governance on Firm and Local Union Performance." Doctoral dissertation, MIT.

———. 2000. "The Impact of Co-management on Quality Performance: The Case of the Saturn Corporation." *Industrial and Labor Relations Review* 53(2):197–216.

Rubinstein, Saul A., and Thomas A. Kochan. 2001. *Learning from Saturn: Possibilities for Corporate Governance and Employee Relations*. Ithaca: Cornell University Press.

Rynes, Sara, and Barry Gephart. 2000. *Compensation*. Frontiers in Industrial/Organizational Psychology series. San Francisco: Jossey-Bass.

Sanna, Lawrence J., and Craig D. Parks. 1997. "Group Research Trends in Social and Organizational Psychology: Whatever Happened to Intragroup Research?" *Psychological Science* 8(4):261–67.

Schein, Edgar H. 1992. *Organizational Culture and Leadership*. San Francisco: Jossey-Bass.

Schelling, Thomas. 1960. *The Strategy of Conflict*. Cambridge, Mass.: Harvard University Press.

Schlesinger, Leonard A. 1982. *Quality of Worklife and the Supervisor*. New York: Praeger.

Schlesinger, Leonard A., and Janice A. Klein. 1987. "The First-Line Supervisor:

Past, Present, and Future." In *Handbook of Organizational Behavior*, edited by Jay W. Lorsch, 370–84. Englewood Cliffs, N.J.: Prentice Hall.

Selekman, Sylvia, and Benjamin Selekman. 1956. *Power and Morality in a Business Society*. New York: McGraw-Hill.

Sen, Amartya. 1999. *Development as Freedom*. New York: Knopf.

Siegel, Sidney, and Larry Fouraker. 1960. *Bargaining and Group Decision Making*. New York: McGraw-Hill.

Simon, Howard A., and Yaroslav Sochynsky. 1995. "In-House Mediation of Employment Disputes." *Employee Relations Journal* 21(1):29–51.

Sisson, Keith. 1993. "In Search of HRM." *British Journal of Industrial Relations* 31(2):201–10.

Slaikeu, Karl A., and Ralph H. Hasson. 1998. *Controlling the Costs of Conflict*. San Francisco: Jossey-Bass.

Slichter, Sumner. 1941. *Union Policies and Industrial Management*. Washington, D.C.: Brookings Institution.

Smith, Kenwyn K. 1982. *Groups in Conflict: Prisons in Disguise*. Dubuque: Kendall/Hunt.

Society of Professionals in Dispute Resolution (SPIDR). 2001. *Guidelines for the Design of Integrated Conflict Management Systems within Organizations*. New Orleans: SPIDR.

Sorge, Arndt, and Wolfgang Streeck. 1988. "Industrial Relations and Technical Change: The Case for an Extended Perspective." In *New Technology and Industrial Relations*, edited by Richard Hyman and Wolfgang Streeck, 19–47. Oxford: Basil Blackwell.

Springer, Roland. 1999. "The End of New Production Concepts? Rationalization and Labour Policy in the German Auto Industry." *Economic and Industrial Democracy* 20(1):117–45.

Steele, Shelby. 1998. *A Dream Deferred: The Second Betrayal of Black Freedom in America*. New York: HarperCollins.

Steere, William C., Jr. 1998. *Corporate Governance: When More's at Stake and Meets the Eye*. CEO Series. St. Louis: Center for the Study of American Business.

Stegemeier, Richard J. 1995. *Straight Talk: The Future of Energy in the Global Economy*. Los Angeles: Unocal.

Steiner, Ivan D. 1972. *Group Process and Productivity*. New York: Academic Press.

Storey, John. 1992. *Developments in the Management of Human Resources*. Oxford: Basil Blackwell.

Strauss, George. 2001. "American Experience with Union-Nominated Board Members." In *Competing Model of Employee Participation in the New World of Economic Order*, edited by Ray Markey, 97–118. London: Gower.

Sturdevant Reed, Celeste, Willard R. Young, and Patrick McHugh. 1994. A Comparative Look at Dual Commitment: An International Study. *Human Relations* 47(10):1269–93.

Susskind, Lawrence, and Jeff Cruikshank. 1987. *Breaking the Impasse: Consensual Approaches to Resolving Public Disputes*. New York: Basic Books.

Susskind, Lawrence, Robert Friedman, Charles Heckscher, Larry W. Hunter, Robert McKersie, and Elaine Landry. 1990. "Joint Training in Negotiation as a Strategy for Encouraging More Cooperative Approaches to Collective Bargaining, Final Report to the Bureau of Labor Management Relations and Cooperative Programs, U.S. Department of Labor." Federal grant no. E-9-P-7-0133, August.

Susskind, Lawrence, Paul Levy, and Jennifer Thomas-Larmer. 1999. *Negotiating Environmental Agreements.* San Francisco: Island Press.

Susskind, Lawrence, Sarah McKearnan, and Jennifer Thomas-Larmer. 1999. *The Consensus Building Handbook.* Thousand Oaks, Calif.: Sage.

Sykes, G., and D. Matza. 1957. "Techniques of Neutralization: A Theory of Delinquency." *American Sociological Review* (22):664–70.

Tang, John C., Ellen A. Isaacs, and Monica Rua. 1994. "Supporting Distributed Groups with a Montage of Lightweight Interactions." In *Proceedings of the Conference on Computer Supported Cooperative Work,* edited by R. Furtura and C. Neuwirth, 23–34. Chapel Hill: ACM Press.

Taylor, Charles. 1989. *Sources of the Self: The Making of the Modern Identity.* Cambridge, Mass.: Harvard University Press.

Taylor, Frederick W. 1911. *Shop Management.* New York: Harper & Row.

Tetlock, Phillip E., Randy Peterson, and Josh Lerner. 1996. "Revising the Value Pluralism Model: Incorporating Social Content and Context Postulates." In *Values: Eighth Annual Ontario Symposium on Personality and Social Psychology,* edited by C. Seligman, J. Olson, and M. Zanna, 25–51. Hillsdale, N.J.: Erlbaum.

Thompson, Leigh, and Richard Gonzales. 1997. "Environmental Disputes: Competition for Scarce Resources and Clashing of Values." In *Psychological Perspectives to Environmental and Ethical Issues in Management,* edited by Max H. Bazerman, D. Messick, A. Tenbrunsel, and K. Wade-Benzoni, 75–104. San Francisco: New Lexington Press.

Thompson, Leigh L. 1998. *The Mind and Heart of the Negotiator.* Upper Saddle River, N.J.: Prentice Hall.

Thompson, Leigh L., and George Loewenstein. 1992. "Egocentric Interpretations of Fairness and Interpersonal Conflict." *Organizational Behavior and Human Decision Processes* 51(2):176–97.

Touraine, Alain. 1985. "An Introduction to the Study of Social Movements." *Social Research* 52(4):749–87.

Trades Union Congress (TUC). 1997. *Partners for Progress: New Steps for the New Unionism.* London: TUC.

TUC Partnership Institute. 2001. *Partners for Progress: Winning at Work.* London: TUC.

Turner, Lowell. 1991. *Democracy at Work: Changing World Markets and the Future of Labor Unions.* Ithaca: Cornell University Press.

Tutu, Desmond. 1998. "Between a Nightmare and a Dream: If Reconciliation Can Happen in South Africa, It Can Happen Elsewhere." *Christianity Today* 42(2):25–26.

Ury, William L., Jeanne M. Brett, and Stephen B. Goldberg. 1988. *Getting Disputes Resolved: Designing Systems to Cut the Costs of Conflict.* San Francisco: Jossey-Bass.

Van Buren, Harry. 2000. "The Bindingness of Social and Psychological Contracts: Toward a Theory of Social Responsibility in Downsizing." *Journal of Business Ethics* 25(3):205–19.

Vidal-Naquet, P. 1992. *Assassins of Memory*. New York: Columbia University Press.

Wade-Benzoni, Kimberly, Ann Tenbrunsel, and Max H. Bazerman. 1996. "Egocentric Interpretations of Fairness of Asymmetric, Environmental Social Dilemmas: Explaining Harvesting Behavior and the Role of Communication." *Organizational Behavior and Human Decision Processes* 67(2):111–26.

Walley, Noah, and Bradley Whitehead. 1994. "It's Not Easy Being Green." *Harvard Business Review* 72(3):46–52.

Walster, E., and E. Berscheid. 1967. "When Does a Harm-doer Compensate a Victim?" *Journal of Personality and Social Psychology* 6:35–41.

Walster, E., E. Berscheid, and G. Walster. 1970. "The Exploited: Justice or Justification?" in *Altruism and Helping Behavior*, edited by J. Macauley and L. Berkowitz, 179–294. New York: Academic Press.

——. 1973. "New Directions in Equity Research." *Journal of Personality and Social Psychology* 25:151–76.

Walton, Richard. 1975. "The Diffusion of New Work Structures: Explaining Why Success Didn't Take." *Organizational Dynamics* 3(3):3–22.

——. 1985. "From Control to Commitment in the Workplace." *Harvard Business Review* 63(2):76–84.

Walton, Richard, Joel Cutcher-Gershenfeld, and Robert McKersie. 1994. *Strategic Negotiations: A Theory of Change in Labor-Management Negotiations*. Boston: Harvard Business School Press. Reprinted by ILR Press, Ithaca, 2000.

Walton, Richard E., and Robert B. McKersie. 1965. *A Behavioral Theory of Labor Negotiations: An Analysis of a Social Interaction System*. New York: McGraw-Hill.

——. 1991. *A Behavioral Theory of Labor Negotiations: An Analysis of Social Interaction Systems*. Ithaca: ILR Press.

Weick, Karl E. 1979. *The Social Psychology of Organizing*. Reading, Mass.: Addison-Wesley.

Weick, Karl E., and Karlene H. Roberts. 1993. "Collective Mind in Organizations: Heedful Interrelating on Flight Decks?" *Administrative Science Quarterly* 38(3):357–82.

Weiss, Steven E. 1993. "Analysis of Complex Negotiations in International Business: The RBC Perspective." *Organizational Science* 4(2):269–300.

West, Cornel. 1993. *Race Matters*. Boston: Beacon Press.

Westin, Alan F., and Alfred G. Feliu. 1988. *Resolving Employment Disputes without Litigation*. Washington, D.C.: Bureau of National Affairs.

Wever, Kirsten. 1998. "International Union Revitalization: Enlarging the Playing Field." *Industrial Relations* 37(3):47–54.

Wheeler, David, and Maria Sillanpaa. 1997. *The Stakeholder Corporation*. London: Pitman.

Williamson, Oliver A. 1975. *Markets and Hierarchies: Analyses and Antitrust Implications*. New York: Free Press.

Williamson, Oliver E. 1998. "The Institutions of Governance." *American Economic Review* 88(2):75–79.

Windolf, Paul. 1998. "The Governance Structure of Large French Corporations: A Comparative Perspective." In *Corporate Governance Today: Columbia Law School Sloan Project*, 695–725. New York: Columbia Law School.

Womack, James P., Daniel Jones, and Daniel Roos. 1990. *The Machine That Changed the World*. New York: Macmillan.

Wray, D. E. 1949. "Marginal Men of Industry: The Foremen." *American Journal of Sociology* 54:298–301.

Yukl, Gary A. 1989. *Leadership in Organizations*. Englewood Cliffs, N.J.: Prentice Hall.

Zelizer, Barbie. 1995. "Reading the Past against the Grain: The Shape of Memory Studies." *Critical Studies in Mass Communication* 12(2):213–39.

Ziegenfuss, James T. 1988. *Organizational Troubleshooters: Resolving Problems with Customers and Employees*. San Francisco: Jossey-Bass.

Contributors

Max H. Bazerman is the Jesse Isidor Straus Professor of Business Administration at Harvard Business School. Before joining the Harvard faculty, he was on the faculty of the Kellogg Graduate School of Management of Northwestern University for fifteen years. His research focuses on decision making, negotiation, creating joint gains in society, and the natural environment. He is the author or co-author of over 125 research articles and has published ten books, including *You Can't Enlarge the Pie: The Psychology of Ineffective Government* (Basic Books, 2001, with J. Baron and K. Shonk) and *Judgment in Managerial Decision Making* (Wiley, 2002, now in its fifth edition).

Phillip B. Beaumont is professor of employment relations in the Department of Business and Management at the University of Glasgow. He teaches human resource management and industrial relations and has acted as an adviser to a number of organizations, trade unions, and government bodies. His current research interests include work on down-sizing in the United Kingdom, the diffusion of best-practice human resource management policies in multi-national firms, and the influence of lifelong learning initiatives in individual corporations.

Corinne Bendersky is a Ph.D. candidate in the Institute for Work and Employment Research at the MIT Sloan School of Management. Her research focuses on workplace interventions designed to affect employees' experiences of conflict. Her other research interests include negotiations and conflict management processes, organizational change processes more generally, and organizational culture.

Joel Cutcher-Gershenfeld is executive director of MIT's Engineering Systems Learning Center and is a senior research scientist in MIT's Sloan School of Management. He is co-author of *Lean Enterprise Value* (Palgrave, forthcoming), *Knowledge-Driven Work* (Oxford University Press, 1998), *Strategic Negotiations* (Harvard Business School Press, 1994; reprint, ILR Press, 2000), and five additional co-authored or co-edited books, as well as over sixty articles on large-scale systems change, new work systems, labor-management relations, negotiations, conflict resolution, organizational learning, public policy, and economic development.

Paul S. Goodman holds the Richard M. Cyert Professorship and is professor of organizational psychology at Carnegie Mellon University. His current research examines new forms of work groups, knowledge exchange in weak-tie work environments, organizational errors, and organizational linkages. His most recent books are *Missing Organizational Linkages* (Sage, 2000) and *Technology Enhanced Learning: Opportunities for Change* (Erlbaum, 2001). Goodman is a fellow in both the Society for Industrial and Organizational Psychology and the American Psychological Society.

Leonard Greenhalgh is professor of management at the Amos Tuck School of Business Administration at Dartmouth College. Born and raised in Great Britain, he completed his education in the United States and worked as a manager, entrepreneur, and consultant. He has consulted and provided executive education services for a number of global corporations including General Electric, Ericsson, Goldman Sachs, Rolls Royce, ITT, Boeing, Deutsche Bank, ABB, and Nestlé. His areas of expertise include strategy implementation, leadership, negotiation, and conflict resolution. His book, *Managing Strategic Relationships,* was published by Free Press in 2001.

Lavinia Hall is a consultant on conflict. An attorney, she has worked exclusively as a neutral in complex, multi-party disputes for over two decades. Formerly curriculum director for the Program on Negotiation at Harvard Law School, she is currently senior mediator with Endispute and deputy director of research at Cornell University's Institute on Conflict Resolution. The author of numerous articles on negotiation and conflict management, she edited *Negotiation: Strategies for Mutual Gain* (Sage, 1993).

Charles Heckscher is a professor in the Department of Labor Studies and Employment Relations and director of the Center for Workplace Transformation at Rutgers University. His research focuses on organizational change and its consequences for employees and unions, and on the possibilities for more collaborative and democratic forms of work. He is the author of *The New Unionism: Employee Involvement in the Changing Corporation* (Basic Books, 1988; reprint, ILR Press, 1996) and *White-Collar Blues: Management Loyalties in an Age of Corporate Restructuring* (Basic Books, 1995), and editor of *The Post-Bureaucratic Organization: New Perspectives on Organizational Change* (Sage, 1994, with Anne Donnellon). Before coming to Rutgers he worked for the Communications Workers of America and taught human resource management at Harvard Business School.

Andrew J. Hoffman is assistant professor of organizational behavior at the Boston University School of Management. His research deals with the nature and dynamics of change within institutional and cultural systems. He applies that research toward understanding the cultural and managerial implications of environmental protection for industry. He is the author of *Competitive Environmental Strategy* (Island Press, 2000) and *From Heresy to Dogma: An Institutional History of Corporate Environmentalism* (New Lexington Press, 1997), which was awarded the 2001 Rachel Carson Prize from the Society for Social Studies of Science. He is co-editor of *Organizations, Policy and the Natural Environment* (Stanford University Press, 2002).

Laurence C. Hunter is a professor (now part-time) of applied economics at the University of Glasgow Business School, Scotland. His academic work has been largely in the fields of labor economics, industrial relations, and human resource management. This work has been complemented by his practical involvement in British industrial relations, as a founding member (1974–86) of the Advisory, Conciliation and Arbitration Service (ACAS), as an independent arbitrator, and as chair of the Police Negotiating Board (1986–2000). His current work mostly relates to aspects of the knowledge economy and the management of knowledge workers.

Janice A. Klein is senior lecturer in operations management at MIT's Sloan School of Management. Klein's research focuses on aligning operations and human resource strategies in the areas of job design, team leadership, employee empowerment, and organizational change. She is the author of *Revitalizing Manufacturing: Text and Cases* (Irwin, 1990) and *The American Edge: Leveraging Manufacturing's Hidden Assets* (McGraw-Hill, 1993).

Thomas A. Kochan is the George M. Bunker Professor of Management at MIT's Sloan School of Management. From 1993 to 1995 he served on the Clinton administration's Commission on the Future of Worker-Management Relations, which investigated methods to improve the productivity and global competitiveness of the U.S. workplace. Some of his recent books include *Learning from Saturn: Possibilities for Corporate Governance and Employee Relations* (ILR Press, 2000, with Saul Rubinstein) and *Working in America: A Blueprint for the New Labor Market* (MIT Press, 2001, with Paul Osterman, Richard Locke, and Michael Piore). Kochan is the co-author, with Robert McKersie and Harry Katz, of *The Transformation of American Industrial Relations* (Basic Books, 1986; reprint, ILR Press, 1994), which was recognized by the Academy of Management as the best scholarly book on management published in 1986.

Roy J. Lewicki is the Dean's Distinguished Teaching Professor and professor of management and human resources at the Max M. Fisher College of Business, Ohio State University. Lewicki maintains research and teaching interests in the fields of negotiation and dispute resolution, managerial leadership, organizational justice, and ethical decision making. He is an author or editor of numerous articles and twenty-four books, including *Negotiation* (McGraw-Hill, 1999), *Negotiation: Readings, Exercises and Cases* (McGraw-Hill, 1998), *Essentials of Negotiation* (McGraw-Hill, 2000), and multiple volumes of *Research on Negotiation in Organizations* (JAI Press). He recently completed service as president of the International Association of Conflict Management.

David B. Lipsky is professor of industrial and labor relations and director of the Institute on Conflict Resolution at Cornell University. From 1988 until 1997 he served as dean of the School of Industrial and Labor Relations at Cornell. Lipsky has published extensively on negotiation, conflict resolution, and collective bargaining and has served as a mediator, fact-finder, or arbitrator in numerous public sector labor disputes. Among his publications are *The Appropriate Resolution of Corporate Disputes: A Report on the Growing Use of ADR by U.S. Corporations* (Cornell/PERC Institute on Conflict Resolution, 1998, with Ronald L. Seeber) and *Strikers and Subsidies: The Influence of Government Transfer Programs on Strike Activity* (W.E. Upjohn Institute, 1989, with Robert Hutchens and Robert Stern). He was a member of the inaugural class of the National Academy of Human Resources.

John Paul MacDuffie is associate professor in the Management Department at the Wharton School, University of Pennsylvania. Since 1985,

MacDuffie has carried out research through MIT's International Motor Vehicle Program (IMVP), and he was recently named IMVP's co-director. His research focuses on the rise of lean production as an alternative to mass production, investigating its consequences for economic performance, its diffusion across companies and countries, and its implications for labor-management relations. His work was featured in the best-selling IMVP book, *The Machine That Changed the World* (Macmillan, 1990). He is the author of nearly forty articles and is co-editor of *After Lean Production: Evolving Employment Practices in the World Auto Industry* (Cornell University Press, 1997).

Robert B. McKersie has been on the MIT faculty since 1980 and currently is the Society of Sloan Fellows Professor Emeritus. He served as deputy dean in the Sloan School from 1991 to 1994. From 1971 to 1980 he served as dean of the School of Industrial and Labor Relations at Cornell University. His research interests have been in labor-management relations, with particular focus on bargaining activity. In 1965, he co-authored with Richard Walton *A Behavioral Theory of Labor Negotiations* (McGraw-Hill, 1965; reprint, ILR Press, 1991). Among his other works on bargaining and negotiation is a book entitled *Strategic Negotiations* (Harvard Business School Press, 1994; reprint, ILR Press, 2000, co-authored with Richard Walton and Joel Cutcher-Gershenfeld) and a companion volume entitled *Pathways to Change* (W. E. Upjohn Institute, 1995). He has served on several presidential commissions, is a member of the National Academy of Arbitrators, and was president of the Industrial Relations Research Association.

Lee E. Preston is professor emeritus at the Robert H. Smith School of Business, University of Maryland. He has been a lifetime student of the social and political status of the corporation, and author of more than one hundred academic publications in this area, including *The Rules of the Game in the Global Economy: Policy Regimes for International Business* (2d ed., Kluwer, 1997, with Duane Windsor), and was the editor of the ten-volume series *Research in Corporate Social Performance and Policy* (JAI Press, 1978–88). Most recently, he is co-author of *Redefining the Corporation: Stakeholder Management and Organizational Wealth* (Stanford University Press, 2002).

Denise M. Rousseau is the H. J. Heinz II Professor of Organizational Behavior at Carnegie Mellon University, jointly in the Heinz School of Public Policy and Management and in the Graduate School of Industrial Administration. Her research addresses the influence of work-group processes on performance and the changing psychological contract at work. Her books include *Psychological Contracts in Employment: Cross-National Perspectives* (Sage, 2000, with René Schalk), *Relational Wealth: Advantages of Stability in a Changing Economy* (Oxford, 2000, with Carrie Leana), and *The Boundaryless Career: A New Employment Principle for a New Organizational Era* (Oxford, 1996, with Michael Arthur). Her book *Psychological Contracts in Organizations* (Sage, 1995) won the Academy of Management's best book award in 1996. She is editor-in-chief of the *Journal of Organizational Behavior*.

Mary Rowe is adjunct professor of management at the Sloan School of Management at MIT and serves as one of several ombudspersons for the faculty, staff, and students in the MIT community. In 1982, Rowe was a co-founder of the Corporate Ombudsman Association, now The Ombudsman Association. She has helped to set up ombuds offices in hundreds of corporations, government agencies, and academic institutions and consults widely on conflict management. She has written dozens of articles on complaint handling, design of integrated dispute resolution systems, aspects of workplace diversity, and harassment. She is currently working on the role of peers, "bystanders," and onlookers in organizational conflict management.

Saul Rubinstein is assistant professor in the School of Management and Labor Relations at Rutgers University. His research focuses on the influence of changes in work organization on firms and unions. He has studied new forms of firm governance and co-management that have resulted from joint labor-management efforts to transform industrial relations and work systems. His research has been published in the *Industrial and Labor Relations Review, Industrial Relations, Organization Science,* and the *Journal of Labor Research* and in numerous book chapters. He is the co-author of *Learning from Saturn: Possibilities for Corporate Governance and Employee Relations* (ILR Press, 2001, with Thomas A. Kochan).

Lawrence Susskind is Ford Professor of Urban and Environmental Planning at MIT and director of the MIT-Harvard Public Disputes Program, part of the inter-university Program on Negotiation at Harvard Law School. As president and founder of the not-for-profit Consensus Building Institute, he has mediated more than fifty complex public disputes. He is author of *Breaking the Impasse* (Basic Books, 1987), *Dealing with an Angry Public* (Free Press, 1995), *The Consensus Building Handbook*

(Sage, 1999), and *Negotiating Environmental Agreements* (Island Press, 2001).

Richard E. Walton is the Wallace Brett Donham Professor Emeritus of Business Administration at Harvard Business School. He taught at Harvard from 1968 to 1997, when he retired. He consulted with many leading U.S. corporations and was a director of several companies including most recently Champion Paper International Corporation. He is the author of more than a dozen books and seventy articles on conflict management, organizational change, international diffusion of social innovations, and the implementation of information technology. He is the co-author of *A Behavioral Theory of Labor Negotiations* (McGraw-Hill, 1965; reprint, ILR Press, 1991, with Robert B. McKersie), *Strategic Negotiations* (Harvard Business School Press, 1994; reprint, ILR Press, 2000, with Joel Cutcher-Gershenfeld and Robert B. McKersie), and *Pathways to Change* (W.E. Upjohn Institute, 1995, with Robert B. McKersie and Joel Cutcher-Gershenfeld).

Kirsten S. Wever is executive director of the Institute for Human Sciences at Boston University, developing projects touching on a broad range of international and comparative public policies. She has worked in the areas of international and comparative labor-business-government relations and, more recently, labor market outcomes for women in the advanced capitalist countries. Wever is author of, among other publications, *Negotiating Competitiveness: Employment Relations and Organizational Innovation in Germany and the United States* (Harvard Business School Press, 1995) and is the editor of *Labor, Business, and Change in Germany and the United States* (W.E. Upjohn Institute, 2001).

Jeanne M. Wilson is assistant professor at the School of Business at the College of William and Mary. Her research focuses on new organizational forms, particularly distributed work groups. She has studied the development of trust over time in distributed groups, knowledge transfer in teams that cross organizational boundaries, attributions about performance in international project teams, and the development of shared mental models in software development teams. Her work has been supported by grants from the CitiGroup Behavioral Science Research Council, the Carnegie Bosch Institute, and the National Science Foundation.

Index

343